C++ A Practical Introduction

Brian Hahn

Department of Applied Mathematics
University of Cape Town

BRIAN HAHN

C++
A PRACTICAL
INTRODUCTION

NCC

BLACKWELL
Manchester and Oxford

The right of Brian Hahn to be identified as author of this work has been asserted in accordance with the Copyright, Designs and Patents Act 1988.

First published 1994

First published in USA 1994

NCC Blackwell Ltd.
108 Cowley Road
Oxford OX4 1JF
UK

Blackwell Publishers
238 Main Street
Cambridge, Massachusetts 02142
USA

Editorial office: NCC Blackwell Ltd., Oxford House, Oxford Road, Manchester M1 7ED, UK.

British Library Cataloguing in Publication Data

A CIP catalogue record for this book is available from the British Library.

American Library of Congress Data

A catalog record for this book is available from the Library of Congress.

Typeset in 11 on 13pt Computer Modern by Alden Multimedia Ltd., Northampton.
Printed by Hartnolls Ltd., Bodmin, Cornwall

ISBN 1–85554–325–7

This book is printed on acid-free paper.

Preface

The mythology has built up around the C programming language that it is an extremely difficult language, accessible only to computer systems engineers and such higher beings. Its object-oriented successor C++ is regarded with even greater awe.

This book sets about demystifying this superstition by presenting C++ and the more practical aspects of object-oriented programming as a useful problem solving tool for the rest of us. This is done in two ways. Firstly, the use of the language in solving a wide variety of interesting real world problems is demonstrated. The emphasis is mainly on scientific and engineering applications, although examples from many other areas, such as business and everyday life, are also included. Secondly, applications of object-oriented programming in scientific computing are demonstrated. Object-oriented programming has been taking the computer world by storm in recent years, in spite of the comment by Edsger Dijkstra (winner of virtually every computer science award there is) that "object-oriented programming is an exceptionally bad idea which could only have originated in California". C++ is seen by many professional programmers as the best vehicle for object-oriented programming, and consequently as the software development tool of the future. The use of this exciting new concept in programming is examined in detail in such areas as the arithmetic of complex numbers and matrix manipulation.

The book follows a "teach yourself" approach, and bravely assumes no prior computing experience. This is in spite of the remark which is often made that no-one in their right mind would learn C (or presumably C++) as their first programming language, and which I have taken as a personal challenge! This is perhaps not as ambitious as some might think; C++ brings many improvements to plain old C which render it far less dangerous to beginners.

Although the main features of the language are covered, the book is neither an exhaustive nor systematic reference manual, since this would not be in keeping with its informal approach. Concepts of object-oriented programming, for example, are not therefore introduced *en bloc*, as is common in many texts, but rather in the most natural places as the book develops. For the curious, however, there are helpful syntax and function

v

quick references in the appendices. Turbo C++ users will find the function quick reference particularly helpful, as the Turbo C ++ manual lacks a library function reference.

Emphasis is also placed on programming style throughout the book—writing clear, readable code—in contrast to the dense and often obscure code delighted in by the denizens of the C underworld.

There are many complete programs, being examples and case studies from a wide variety of areas, such as database handling, population modelling, numerical methods, matrix manipulation and general engineering. There are also many examples from business and everyday life.

Each chapter concludes with a summary of the C++ features introduced in the chapter.

There are a large collection of exercises at the end of each chapter, gathered from many years' experience of running hands-on programming courses for beginners and professionals alike, in BASIC, Pascal and C. Complete solutions to many of the exercises appear in an appendix.

There is a comprehensive and instructive index with many subjects appearing under more than one entry.

All programs have been tested with the Turbo C++ 3.0 compiler.

I owe a large debt of gratitude to the student in my first-year class who on an (anonymous) course evaluation form complained, "Why do all the lecturers in this University relish in attacking things such as C?" This rebuke stung me into action, and I immediately made it my business to learn C and C++ (in addition to the Fortran, BASICs and Pascal which I already knew). This book is the result.

I should also like to thank the University of Cape Town for leave in order to write this book, and for financial support for the project; my long-suffering colleages for leaving me alone while I was writing it; and my wife, Cleone, who patiently reminds me when programs won't work that computers are like that, aren't they?

Brian D. Hahn
Department of Applied Mathematics
University of Cape Town
Rondebosch
South Africa
October 1993
email: bdh@maths.uct.ac.za

Contents

1 Getting going   **1**
  1.1   Introduction   1
  1.2   C and C++   2
  1.3   Running C++ programs   3
  Exercises   6

2 Elementary C++   **7**
  2.1   Compound interest again   8
  2.2   Program layout   11
  2.3   Data types   12
  2.4   Literal numeric constants   13
  2.5   Names   14
  2.6   Vertical motion under gravity   17
  2.7   Programming style   18
  2.8   Operators, expressions and assignments   19
  2.9   Basic input and output   25
  2.10 Repeating with `for`   30
  2.11 Deciding with `if`   36
  2.12 Characters and strings   39
  Exercises   45

3 Program preparation   **53**
  3.1   Structure plans   53
  3.2   Structured programming with functions   55
  Exercises   56

4 Introduction to library functions   **59**
  4.1   Projectile motion   59
  4.2   Some useful library functions   61
  Exercises   64

5 Decisions   **67**
  5.1   The `if-else` statements   67

5.2   Logical expressions   72
5.3   Bitwise operators   74
5.4   The `switch` statement   76
5.5   Halting with `exit()`   78
5.6   Statements best avoided   78
Exercises   80

6   Loops   **83**
6.1   Deterministic repetition with `for`   83
6.2   `for` with non-integer increments   86
6.3   Nested `for`s   88
6.4   Non-deterministic loops   89
6.5   Reading an unknown amount of data   98
6.6   Taking stock   99
Exercises   105

7   Errors   **111**
7.1   Compilation errors   111
7.2   Run-time errors   113
7.3   Errors in logic   114
7.4   Rounding error   114
Exercises   116

8   Functions   **119**
8.1   Some basic concepts   120
8.2   Functions that do not return a value   125
8.3   Scope: local and global variables   129
8.4   Macros   133
8.5   Inline functions   134
8.6   References   135
8.7   Pointers   139
8.8   Projects with multiple files   144
8.9   Stubs   147
8.10 Recursion   148
8.11 Function overloading   149
8.12 Default arguments   150
Exercises   153

9   Arrays   **157**
9.1   Introduction   157
9.2   Mean and standard deviation   159
9.3   Some more basic information   161

9.4   Frequency distribution: a bar chart 163
9.5   On arrays, pointers and function parameters 164
9.6   Dynamic arrays 166
9.7   Sorting a list: the Bubble Sort 169
9.8   Sorting a list: Quick Sort 171
Exercises 175

10 Strings   **179**
10.1 Some basics 179
10.2 Arrays of strings: top of the class 183
10.3 On strings and pointers 184
10.4 Counting words 189
10.5 Basic text file I/O with stream objects 191
10.6 Some string functions 192
Exercises 193

11 Structures and unions   **197**
11.1 Structures 197
11.2 Unions 200
11.3 Bit fields 200
11.4 Passing structures to functions 201
11.5 Linked lists 203
Exercises 208

12 C streams and files   **209**
12.1 Standard streams 209
12.2 Text files 210
12.3 Binary files 218
12.4 Towards a student record database 220
12.5 A binary search 225
12.6 Sorting student records 227
Exercises 230

13 Graphics   **231**
13.1 Some basics 231
13.2 **myworld**: a world coordinate graphics module 241
13.3 Examples 247
13.4 The Julia set 252
13.5 The Mandelbrot set 254
13.6 Other graphics goodies 255
Exercises 256

14 Objects: a touch of class   **259**
14.1 Encapsulation   260
14.2 Constructors and destructors   268
14.3 Inheritance   277
14.4 Polymorphism   283
Exercises   287

15 Operator overloading for a complex class   **289**
15.1 Constructors for our complex class   290
15.2 Basics of operator overloading   290
15.3 Overloading the + operator   294
15.4 Overloading the assignment operator   295
15.5 Friends   298
15.6 Overloading complex multiplication and division   299
15.7 TComplex class declaration and implementation   300
15.8 Complex roots by Newton's method   302
15.9 A complex transfer function   304
15.10 Overloading the [ ] (subscript) operator   305
Exercises   307

16 The C++ iostream library   **309**
16.1 The ios class   309
16.2 Output   310
16.3 Input   312
16.4 Stream I/O with files   314
16.5 Overloading the stream operators   316
Exercises   307

17 Matrices with class   **319**
17.1 Developing a matrix class   319
17.2 Reachability of spies   327
17.3 Leslie matrices: population growth   330
17.4 Markov chains   334
17.5 Solution of linear equations   338
17.6 Binary file matrix I/O   344
17.7 The finite element method   345
17.8 TMatrix class declaration and implementation   345
Exercises   349

18 Numerical methods   **351**
18.1 Equations   351
18.2 Integration   356

18.3 First-order differential equations 359
18.4 Runge-Kutta methods 365
18.5 A differential equation modelling package 366
18.6 Partial differential equations: a tridiagonal system 373
Exercises 378

Epilogue Programming style   **381**

A Keywords   **383**

B Operators   **385**

C Syntax quick reference   **387**
C.1 Pre-processor directives 387
C.2 Fundamental type declarations 387
C.3 Functions 388
C.4 Class declarations 389
C.5 Pointers *et al.* 389
C.6 General 390

D Function quick reference   **393**

E ASCII character codes   **435**

F Solutions to selected exercises   **437**

Index   **453**

Chapter 1

Getting going

1.1 Introduction
1.2 C and C++
1.3 Running C++ programs
  • Greetings • AIDS cases • Compound interest
Summary
Exercises

1.1   Introduction

The first computer I programmed, 25 years ago, was called an ICT 1301, and occupied a large room. Only one person could use it at a time, and programs had to be punched on cards. It could remember about 240 different numbers in its "fast" memory and a few thousand in its "slow" memory, which was on a rotating drum that you could hear ticking as it spun. It was very slow!

The computer you will use for the programs in this book most likely sits on a desk (or maybe on your lap or in your hand), displays information on a colour monitor, can access many thousands of numbers almost instantaneously, and is much faster and easier to use. Computer technology has advanced so much during this period that the personal computer is now firmly entrenched in almost every walk of life in the Western world, and affects most careers, particularly those in scientific and engineering fields.

You may not have used a computer before (except possibly to play games), but you are probably familiar with using a calculator. The simplest sort can only do basic arithmetic and display the answer. Smarter ones have

1

memory locations where intermediate results may be stored, and function keys such as sin, log, etc. The most sophisticated calculators allow you to store sequence of operations (instructions) needed to find the solution of the problem. This sequence of instructions is called a *program*. To carry out the entire set of calculations you need only load the program into the calculator, press the run key, supply the necessary data, and sit back while the machine churns out the answer. A computer, whether it is a small personal one like the IBM PC, or a large impersonal mainframe is in principle only an advanced programmable calculator, capable of storing and executing sets of instructions, called programs, in order to solve specific problems.

You may have used a computer before, but only to run software packages written by someone else. Spreadsheets, databases and word processors fall into this category. If you have taken the trouble to start reading this book, you probably have an interest in science or engineering, and are curious enough about programming to want to write your *own* programs to solve your particular problems, instead of relying on someone else's more general package.

1.2   C and C++

The particular set of rules or conventions for coding instructions to a computer is called a *programming language*. In the same way that there are many spoken languages there are also many computer languages, e.g. C++, Pascal, Fortran, True BASIC, etc. Some operations look almost the same in most languages (e.g. assigning the value 1 to the variable x) whereas others (e.g. printing a message) look a little different, as you can see in Table 1.1.

The generally accepted version of the language C (the precursor of C++) was spelt out by Brian Kernighan and Dennis Ritchie in 1978. C has developed a reputation for being difficult to learn and unreliable to use. This is because it was originally designed for people who wanted to program at a fairly "low" level and who knew exactly what they were doing. It therefore lacks many of the checks and balances provided by stricter languages

C++	*Pascal*	*Fortran*
`x = 1;`	`x:= 1;`	`x = 1`
`cout << "Hi there\n";`	`writeln( 'Hi there' );`	`PRINT*, 'Hi there'`

Table 1.1: Three ways of saying the same thing.

like Pascal. C++ is an extension to C which removes many of the earlier pitfalls, and which is based on the modern concept of *object-oriented programming*. It was invented by Bjarne Stroustrup (*The C++ Programming Language*, Addison-Wesley, 1987). The current version of C++ is 2.1, and this is the version implemented by the Turbo C++ 3.0 compiler, which is used in this book. Since C is rapidly being eclipsed by C++ (Jeff Duntemann describes it as a "quaint button-hook language" in *PC Techniques*) you do not need a C background for this book. However, since you may indeed have such a background, there will be occasional references to C, particularly where C++ offers an improvement. Most authors treat C++ as an extension of C, as if it were not a language in its own right. I prefer to use the name C++ to cover the acceptable parts of C, as well as the extensions.

1.3 Running C++ programs

The sample programs in this section are meant to get you going in C++ as soon as possible, and to give you some practice with the Turbo C++ system. It is assumed that you have access to the Turbo C++ manuals; details of the Editor and the Integrated Development Environment (IDE) will not therefore be discussed here.

Don't worry too much at this stage about how the programs work; plenty of explanations will follow in due course.

Greetings

The following program is a variation on the traditional first program in C or C++. It is almost the shortest program possible.

```
// My first C++ program
#include <iostream.h>
main()
{
  cout << "Hi there";
  return 0;
}
```

You should get the message

```
Hi there
```

(If you run this from the Turbo C++ IDE you will need to press **Alt-F5** to see the output.) To make this a little more personal, change the program to

```
// My first C++ program
#include <iostream.h>
main()
{
    char name[128];
    cout << "What is your name? ";
    cin >> name;
    cout << "Hail, " << name;
    return 0;
}
```

Now the output looks as follows (your response is in italics):

```
What is your name? Caesar
Hail, Caesar
```

AIDS cases

The following program computes the number of accumulated AIDS (HIV) cases $A(t)$ in the United States in year t according to the formula

$$A(t) = 174.6(t - 1981.2)^3.$$

```
#include <iostream.h>
main() // AIDS cases in US
{
    float a;
    int t;

    cout << "Enter year: ";
    cin >> t;
    a = 174.6 * (t - 1981.2) * (t - 1981.2) * (t - 1981.2);
    cout << "Accumulated AIDS cases in US by year " << t << ": " << a;
    return 0;
}
```

If you supply the value 2000 for the year you should get the output

```
Accumulated AIDS cases in US by year 2000: 1160159.75
```

Using trial and error try to find out when there will be about 10 million accumulated cases.

Also try typing a mistake in the value of t (2,000 for example) to see how Turbo C++ responds.

You will have noticed that Turbo C++ has the irritating habit of flashing back to the Edit window after the program has run, so that you need to press **Alt-F5** to see the output. A neat way to avoid this is to put the statement

```
getch();
```

immediately before **return 0;**, and to add the line

```
#include <conio.h>
```

anywhere before **main()**. This instructs the program to "get" a character from the keyboard. It will therefore wait for you to press any key, giving you an opportunity to examine the output.

Compound interest

Suppose you have $1000 saved in the bank, which compounds interest at the rate of 9% per year. What will your bank balance be after one year? You must obviously be able to do the problem in principle yourself, if you want to program the computer to do it. The logical breakdown, or *structure plan*, of the problem is as follows:

1. Get the data (initial balance and interest rate) into the computer
2. Calculate the interest (9% of $1000, i.e. $90)
3. Add the interest to the balance ($90 + $1000, i.e. $1090)
4. Print (display) the new balance.

This is how the program looks:

```
// calculates balance after interest compounded
#include <iostream.h>
#include <conio.h>
main()
{
  float balance, interest, rate;
  balance = 1000;
  rate = 0.09;
  interest = rate * balance;
  balance = balance + interest;
  cout << "New balance: " << balance << "\n";
  getch();
  return 0;
}
```

Run the program and note that no input (from the keyboard) is required now (why not?). The output should be **1090**.

Note that the effect of "\n" in the `cout` statement is to give a line feed (new line).

Summary

- A computer program is a set of coded instructions for solving a particular problem.
- `cin >> ...` is for getting input from the keyboard.
- `cout << ...` is for sending output to the screen.

Exercises

1.1 Write a program to compute and print the sum, difference, product and quotient of two numbers A and B (supplied from the keyboard). The symbols for subtraction and division are - and / respectively. Use the program to discover how Turbo C++ reacts to an attempted division by zero.

1.2 The energy stored on a condenser is $CV^2/2$, where C is the capacitance and V is the potential difference. Write a program to compute the energy for some sample values of C and V.

Solutions to most exercises are in Appendix F.

Chapter 2

Elementary C++

2.1 Compound interest again
2.2 Program layout
   • Comments
2.3 Data types
2.4 Literal numeric constants
   • Integer constants • Floating point constants
2.5 Names
   • Identifiers • Case sensitivity • Variables • Symbolic constants
   • Enumerated types • `typedef`
2.6 Vertical motion under gravity
2.7 Programming style
2.8 Operators, expressions and assignments
   • Arithmetic operators - Precedence • Increment and decrement operators
   - Precedence
   • Assignments and assignment operators - Simple assignments - More examples
   - Multiple assignments - Assignment operators • Expressions
   • The comma operator • Typecasting
   • Operator precedence
2.9 Basic input and output
   • Output with `cout` - Formatting iostream output • `printf()` • Output on a printer
   • Input with `cin` - Reading data from a text file
2.10 Repeating with `for`
   • The `for` loop • Danger! • Square rooting with Newton • Money again
   • Differential interest rates
2.11 Deciding with `if`
   • The `if` statement
2.12 Characters and strings
   • Characters • Strings • Character string variables
Summary
Exercises

7

By now you will probably be wanting to write your own programs. In this chapter we will look in detail at how to write C++ programs to solve simple problems. There are two essential requirements for successfully mastering this art:

- The exact rules for coding instructions must be learnt;
- A logical plan for solving the problem must be developed.

This chapter is devoted mainly to the first requirement: learning some basic coding rules. Once you have mastered these, we can go on to more substantial problems.

All C++ constructs introduced in this and subsequent chapters (and some which are not) are summarized in Appendix C. Appendix D has a quick reference to library functions.

2.1   Compound interest again

In Chapter 1 you ran a program to compute compound interest:

```
// calculates balance after interest compounded
#include <iostream.h>
#include <conio.h>
main()
{
 float balance, interest, rate;
 balance = 1000;
 rate = 0.09;
 interest = rate * balance;
 balance = balance + interest;
 cout << "New balance: " << balance << "\n";
 getch();
 return 0;
}
```

We will now discuss in detail how the program works. When you run a Turbo C++ program, for example with **Alt-R/R**un or with the *hot key* **Ctrl-F9**, a number of important processes take place. Suppose your program (the *source code*) has the name **money**, with the extension **.cpp** (the default).

- When you run the program, a *pre-processor* first inserts the contents of any *header* files into the source code. The header files have the extension **.h**, and contain special declarations or *prototypes* for the library procedures you will use, such as **cout** and **getch()**. The instruction to include a header file is `#include < `*filename*`.h>`, and is an example of a *pre-processor directive*.

- The source code is then *compiled* into binary code, producing a file with the **.obj** extension.
- Your **.obj** file is then *linked* with some special pre-compiled library files to produce the final **.exe** version.
- The **.exe** version is executed, and the program runs.

Note that the **.exe** version can also be run as a stand-alone program from DOS once you have left the Turbo C++ IDE.

Also note that Turbo C++ automatically invokes its C++ compiler if your file has the extension **.cpp**. If however you use the extension **.c**, the C compiler is invoked. This may compile faster if you are not using any official C ++ extensions (which will generate compiler errors).

The process that concerns us most at the moment is *compilation*. During compilation, space in the computer's *random access memory* (RAM) is allocated for any numbers (data) which will be generated by the program. This part of the memory may be thought of as a bank of boxes, or *memory locations*, each of which can hold only one number at a time. These memory locations are referred to by symbolic names in the program. So the statement

```
balance = 1000
```

allocates the number 1000 to the memory location named `balance`. Since the contents of `balance` may be changed during the program it is called a *variable*.

The statements in our program between the *block markers* `{ ... }` are interpreted as follows:

1. Put the number 1000 into memory location `balance`
2. Put the number 0.09 into memory location `rate`
3. Multiply the contents of `rate` by the contents of `balance` and put the answer in `interest`
4. Add the contents of `balance` to the contents of `interest` and put the answer in `balance`
5. Output a message followed by the contents of `balance`
6. Stop.

During execution, these translated statements are carried out in order from the top down. After execution, the memory locations used will have the following values:

```
balance  : 1090
interest : 90
```

```
rate     : 0.09
```

Note that the original contents of `balance` is lost.

The remaining lines of the program are also very important. `main()` defines the *main function* as everything inside the following block markers. The basic unit in a C++ program is a function. Every program must have one and only main function. Functions in C++ return values, indicated by the `return` statement. The main function does not have to return a value. However, you may want to run your program from a batch file in DOS, in which case the return value can be checked to see if it ran. A return value of 0 usually means success.

All the variables in the program must be declared. This is done here by `float`, which means they are all floating point numbers with or without fractional parts.

The statements after `float` are *executable*, i.e. they do the actual computing.

Try the following exercises:

1. Run the program as it stands.
2. Change the first executable statement to read

   ```
   balance = 2000;
   ```

   and make sure that you understand what happens when you run the program again.
3. Leave out the line

   ```
   balance = balance + interest;
   ```

   and re-run. Can you explain what happens?
4. Try to rewrite the program so that the original contents of `balance` is *not* lost.

A number of questions have probably occurred to you by now, such as

- What names may be used for memory locations?
- How can numbers be represented?
- What happens if a statement won't fit on one line?
- How can we organize the output more neatly?

These questions, and hopefully many more, will be answered in the following sections. However, before we write any more complete programs there are some basic concepts which need to be introduced.

2.2 Program layout

The basic structure of a simple C++ program is:

```
pre-processor directives
main()
{
    variable declarations
    executable statements
    return 0;
}
```

Note the following:

- A C++ program consists of *tokens*, separated by *whitespace*.
  A token is a significant sequence of characters, e.g. `float`, `rate`. There are six classes of tokens: keywords (`float`), identifiers (`rate`), constants (`0.09`), string literals (`"New balance: "`), operators (`+`), and punctuators (`;`) — also known as separators. We will come across all of these in due course.
  Whitespace is the collective name for blanks (spaces), horizontal and vertical tabs, newline characters, and comments (see below).
- A C++ *statement* is a sequence of tokens, separated by whitespace, and terminated by a semi-colon. A statement may therefore be split over several lines, as long as it ends with a semi-colon. A pre-processor directive is not technically part of the C++ language, and is therefore *not* terminated by a semi-colon.
- Blanks between tokens are not significant (except in string literals) and should therefore be used freely to improve the readability of a program. Blank lines may be used to separate logical sections.

Comments

There are two ways to indicate comments:

- Comments may be enclosed between the symbol pairs `/*` and `*/` (as in C).
  In general, comments may not be nested, although Turbo C++ lets you override this with the **Options/ Compiler/Source** command. Nested comments are useful when you are developing a program and want to "comment out" a section of code which may itself contain comments.
- Anything after a double slash (`//`) up to the next new line is interpreted as comment.

2.3   Data types

C++ has a number of *fundamental data types*, of which int and float are two examples. The different data types and their properties are summarized in Table 2.1. We will come across all of them in due course.

Note that int and **short int** mean the same. You can also use **signed** or **signed int** for int, and **unsigned** for **unsigned int**. These rather confusing synonyms are baggage inherited from C.

Properties of the fundamental data types are defined the header files **limits.h** and **float.h**.

Before we go any further we need to look briefly at how information is represented in a computer.

A *bit* is the basic unit of information in a computer. It is something which has only two possible states, usually described as "on" and "off". The *binary digits* 0 and 1 can therefore be used to represent these two states mathematically (hence the term *digital* computer). The word "bit" in a contraction of " *bi*nary digi*t* ".

Numbers in a computer's memory must therefore be represented in *binary code*, where each bit in a sequence stands for a successively higher power of 2. The binary codes for the decimal numbers 0 to 15, for example, are shown in Table 2.2.

Type	Size (bytes)	Range
char	1	−127 to 127
unsigned char	1	0 to 255
int, short int	2	−32 768 to 32 767
unsigned int	2	0 to 65 535
long	4	−2 147 483 648 to 2 147 483 647
unsigned long	4	0 to 4 294 967 295
float	4	3.4×10^{-38} to 3.4×10^{38} (7-digit precision)
double	8	1.7×10^{-308} to 1.7×10^{308} (15-digit precision)
long double	10	3.4×10^{-4932} to 3.4×10^{4932} (19-digit precision)

Table 2.1: Numeric data types, sizes and ranges

Decimal	Binary	Hexadecimal	Decimal	Binary	Hexadecimal
0	0000	0	8	1000	8
1	0001	1	9	1001	9
2	0010	2	10	1010	A
3	0011	3	11	1011	B
4	0100	4	12	1100	C
5	0101	5	13	1101	D
6	0110	6	14	1110	E
7	0111	7	15	1111	F

Table 2.2: Binary and hexadecimal codes

A *byte* is the amount of computer memory required for one character, and is eight bits long. Since each bit in a byte can be in two possible states, this gives 2^8, i.e. 256, different combinations. The sizes of the data types in Table 2.1 are given in bytes.

Hexadecimal code (see Table 2.2) is often used because it is more economical than binary. Each hexadecimal digit stands for an integer power of 16. E.g.

$$2A = 2 \times 16^1 + 10 \times 16^0 = 32 + 10 = 42$$

One byte can be represented by two hex digits.

Octal code is less common than hexadecimal: each digit represents a power of 8.

Microcomputer memory size (and disk capacity) is measured in bytes, so 64K for example means slightly more than 64 000 bytes (since 1K actually means 1024). Microcomputers are sometimes referred to as 8-, 16- or 32-bit machines. This describes the length of the units of information handled by their microprocessors (chips). The longer these units, the faster the computer.

2.4 Literal numeric constants

A *literal numeric constant* is a token representing a fixed numeric value, like 123 or 1e-3.

Integer constants

Integer constants may be decimal (i.e. base 10), octal or hexadecimal.

Decimal constants from 0 to $4\,294\,967\,295$ $(2^{32} - 1)$ are allowed. If a constant starts with a zero, it is interpreted as octal.

Octal constants start with zero and may contain only the digits 0–7.

Hexadecimal constants start with 0x or 0X, and may contain only hexadecimal digits.

E.g.

```
int i = 010;  //  8 (octal)
int j = 10;   // 10 (decimal)
int k = 0x10; // 16 (hex)
```

The suffix L or l attached to any constant forces it to be represented as long, while the suffix U or u forces it to be unsigned. Both suffixes may be used on the same constant, in any order.

Floating point constants

A *floating point constant* may be written in two ways. It may be written as a signed or unsigned string of digits with a decimal point, e.g.

```
0.09    37.    37.0    .0    0.    -.123456
```

It may also be written in *scientific notation* with an integer exponent. In this form a decimal point is not necessary. E.g.

```
2.0E2         (200.0)
2E2           (200.0)
4.12E+2       (412.0)
-7.321E-4     (-0.0007321)
```

A floating point constant is of type **double** by default. It can be *coerced* into type **float** or **long double** with the suffix f (F) or l (L) respectively.

2.5   Names

Identifiers

An *identifier* is the symbolic name used to represent objects in a C++ program (object here is not being used in the object-oriented sense; it simply means a thing). An identifier must

- consist only of alphanumeric characters (letters and digits) and under-scores (_);
- start with a letter or an underscore.

An identifier may be as long you like, but only the first 32 characters are significant. E.g.

```
r2d2       // valid
pay_day    // valid
pay-day    // invalid
2a         // invalid
_2a        // valid, but not recommended (see below)
name$      // invalid
```

Certain identifiers are reserved as keywords. They are listed in Appendix A. Some of them start with underscores, and the Turbo C++ libraries have many built-in identifiers that start with underscores. So it is best to avoid starting your own identifiers with underscores. In fact you might like to avoid them altogether; they are difficult to read in some styles of print, and it's easy to type a hyphen instead of one.

Case sensitivity

It may come as a surprise to you, if you are not familiar with C, that identifiers are *case sensitive*, e.g. `rate` and `Rate` represent different objects.

Many C++ programmers write identifiers representing variables (see below) in lowercase except for the first letter of the second and subsequent words, if the identifier consists of more than one word run together. This style is known as *camel caps*, the uppercase letters representing a camel's humps. E.g. `camelCaps`, `payDay`, `placeInClass`.

Variables

A *variable* is a region of memory whose value can be changed by a program. All C++ variables must be declared to be of a certain type: fundamental, or *derived*. Derived types are made up from the fundamental types; we shall see a lot of them later.

Variables in Turbo C++ are not automatically initialized to zero, as in some other languages. Upon declaration they take whatever garbage value happens to be in the memory addresses assigned by the compiler.

If a variable of an integer type (`int`, `long` etc.) is increased above its maximum value in a calculation its value wraps around through the minimum and starts again, e.g.

```
int c = 32767;
c++;       // shorthand for c = c + 1: c = -32768 now
```

Note that a variable may be initialized in its declaration. This is an example of a feature of C++ which allows a number of distinct operations to be combined in a single statement — in this case declaration and assignment.

To promote good programming style, every variable declared should be described with a comment.

Symbolic constants

A *symbolic constant* (often simply called a constant, as opposed to a *literal* constant) is a value which is fixed and cannot be changed in a program.

There are two ways of defining a symbolic constant .

The **const** modifier in a declaration defines a *typed* constant, e.g.

```
const double c = 2.997928e8;
```

Any attempt to change the value of **c** (the speed of light) will cause an error, as well it should!

Simple expressions involving other constants may also be used in a **const** declaration:

```
const float g = 9.8;
const float ten_g = 10 * g;
```

Technically, **const** is a *modifier* because it modifies how a variable may be accessed. It is used when it is important for the constant to have a data type.

The second way to define a constant is with the **#define** pre-processor directive, e.g.

```
#define RATE 0.09
```

Note that there is no semi-colon since it is not a C++ statement. If you do include a semi-colon (a common error) it will be construed as part of the constant. This directive is equivalent to using your word processor to replace occurrences of RATE in the source code with 0.09.

It has become conventional for C++ programmers to write such defined identifiers in uppercase.

Turbo C++ has many defined constants in various header files. For example, the **math.h** header file has several useful symbols, such as M_E (*e*), M_PI (π), M_PI_2 ($\pi/2$) and M_SQRT2 ($\sqrt{2}$). You can see them all by loading **math.h** into your Turbo C++ editor.

Defined constants are examples of *macros*.

Enumerated types

A set of constants representing consecutive int values can be created with the keyword **enum**:

```
enum {CLUB, HEART, DIAMOND, SPADE};
int suit = HEART;
```

Values start at zero by default, so this is identical to the directives

```
#define CLUB 0
#define HEART 1
. . .
```

suit therefore has the value 1.

```
typedef
```

An *alias* for any data type can be created with **typedef**. This is often done in conjunction with **enum**:

```
typedef enum
{
   JAN = 1, FEB, MAR, APR, MAY, JUN, JUL, AUG, SEP, OCT, NOV, DEC
} Months;
Months birthmonth = NOV;
```

The alias Months is associated with the enumerated list of month names. The variable birthmonth is of type Months. Note that JAN is set to 1. The other values are adjusted accordingly, so birthmonth has the value 11. Values may be assigned to any of the constants; they do not have to be consecutive.

2.6 Vertical motion under gravity

If a stone is thrown vertically upward with an initial speed *u*, its vertical displacement *s* after a time *t* has elapsed is given by the formula

$s = ut - gt^2/2$, where g is the acceleration due to gravity. Air resistance has been ignored. We would like to compute the value of s, given u and t. Note that we are not concerned here with how to derive the formula, but how to compute its value. The logical preparation of this program is as follows:

1. Get (input) values of g, u and t into the program
2. Compute the value of s according to the formula
3. Print (output) the value of s
4. Stop.

This plan may seem trivial to you, and a waste of time writing down. Yet you would be surprised how many beginners, preferring to rush straight to the computer, try to program step 2 before step 1. It is well worth developing the mental discipline of planning your program first — if pen and paper turns you off why not use the Turbo C++ editor? You can even enter the plan as comment lines in the program.

The program is as follows:

```
// Vertical motion under gravity
#include <iostream.h>
#include <conio.h>
main()
{
   const float g = 9.8;    // acceleration due to gravity (constant)
   float s ;               // vertical displacement
   float t;                // time
   float u;                // launch velocity

   cout << "Enter u and t: ";
   cin >> u >> t;
   s = u * t - g / 2 * t * t;
   cout << "s: " << s << endl;
   getch();
   return 0;
}
```

endl generates a new line on the screen.

2.7   Programming style

Programs that are written any old how, while they may do what is required, can be difficult to follow when read a few months later, in order to correct or update them (and programs that are worth writing will need to be maintained in this way).

Some C programmers have delighted in writing terse and obscure code; there is at least one annual competition for the most incomprehensible C program. This must have contributed in part to C's reputation as a difficult language.

A large body of responsible programmers, however, believe it is extremely important to develop the art of writing programs which are well laid out, with all the logic clearly described. This is known as *programming style*, and should be manifest in most of the programs in this book (occasional lapses are in order to save space . . .). Guidelines for good style are laid out in the Epilogue.

The program in Section 2.6 has been written with this in mind:

- There is a comment at the beginning describing what the program does.
- All the variables have been declared *and described* on separate lines, in alphabetical order. You may like to include initialization with the declaration and description, e.g.

```
float t = 6;        // time
```

- Blanks have been used on either side of the equal signs and the operators (e.g. *).
- Blank lines have been used to separate distinct parts of the program.

You may like to develop your own style; the point is that you **must** pay attention to readability.

2.8   Operators, expressions and assignments

Any program worthy of the name actually does something. What it basically does is to evaluate expressions, such as

```
u * t - g / 2 * t * t
```

in the program of Section 2.6, and to execute statements, such as

```
s = u * t - g / 2 * t * t;
cout << "s: " ...
```

(Remember, a *statement* in C++ is an expression followed by a semi-colon.)

The evaluation of expressions is achieved by means of *operators*. C++ has no less than seven kinds of operators for evaluating expressions: arithmetic, increment, decrement, bitwise, relational, logical, and negation. We are going to look at the first three kinds in this section.

Arithmetic operators

There are five arithmetic operators: + (addition), – (subtraction), * (multiplication), / (division), and % (modulus). An operator with two *operands* is called *binary*. When it has only one operand it is called *unary*. Addition and subtraction can be unary or binary. Here are some examples of expressions involving these operators:

```
z = a + b / c;
x = -a;        // unary minus
b / (2 * a);
```

When both operands in a division are of an integer type, the fractional part is truncated (chopped off). The modulus operation returns the integer remainder after division of its integer operands. The sign of the remainder is the product of the signs of the operands. E.g.

```
10 / 3      // returns 3
10 % 3      // returns 1
-10 % 3     // returns -1
```

There is no exponentiation (raise to the power) operator. This is because C was invented by computer scientists who never imagined anyone would want such an operator. There is however a function pow(a, b) which returns a^b as a float value. It requires the header file **math.h** to be included.

Precedence

The usual *precedence* rules of arithmetic are followed: * and / have a higher precedence than + and –. If you are in doubt you can always use parentheses, which have a higher precedence. Thus a + b * c is evaluated by default as a + (b * c).

Where arithmetic operators in an expression have the same precedence the operations are carried out from left to right. So a / b * c is evaluated as (a / b) * c, and *not* as a / (b * c).

Increment and decrement operators

If you are not familiar with C you will find the increment (++) and decrement (--) operators intriguing. They provide a shorthand way of increasing or decreasing their operands by 1, and are one of the trademarks of C. E.g.

```
x++;              // increase x by 1
++x;              // increase x by 1
```

```
x--;                   // decrease x by 1
--x;                   // decrease x by 1
```

x++ is the same as the slightly more long-winded x = x + 1.

Note that the semi-colons make statements of all these expressions.

Did you realise that this is where C++ gets its name: one better than C?

When these operators appear in assignments (i.e. *variable* = *expression* — defined more fully below) their position is crucial, since the expression on the right may be incremented or decremented before or after its value is assigned to the variable on the left. And so we have *post-*incrementing/decrementing, e.g.

```
a = x++;    // set a to x, then increment x
b = x--;    // set b to x, then decrement x
```

and *pre-*incrementing/decrementing, e.g.

```
a = ++x;    // increment x, then set a to new value of x
b = --x;    // decrement x, then set b to new value of x
```

The *pre* means the increment or decrement occurs *before* the assignment is made.

Note that it does not make sense to have x++ on the left-hand side of an assignment; therefore it is not allowed.

Precedence

The pre-increment and pre-decrement operators both have higher precedence than the arithmetic operators. So the code

```
int x = 1;
int y;
y = x + ++x;
```

sets x to 2 and y to 4. x is first incremented to 2, and then added to its new value to give 4.

Old time C programmers delight in writing concise yet obscure code like this. The practice stems from the days when computer memory was limited, and when execution time was critical; sometimes the obscure code runs a little faster.

However, with the multi-megabytes of RAM and 486 or more power available today you simply can't use those excuses any more. Why not say what you mean, and use an extra statement:

```
++x;
y = x + x;       // no ambiguity now!
```

Post-incrementing or decrementing is a little more subtle. The code

```
int x = 1;
int y;
y = x + x++;
```

sets y to 3. You can think of the post-incrementing being done in a temporary register, and only being applied to its operand after the expression is evaluated. Once again, it is better to write clearly what you mean.

Assignments and assignment operators

If you are a non-C programmer you will be puzzled by this heading. Languages like BASIC and Fortran (and even Pascal) use expressions, like A + B, to construct assignments, such as

```
C = A + B
```

and there the story ends.

In C (and C++), however, *expressions* are the all-important animals, and assignments are simply one type of expression. Therefore assignments need operators, just like addition and multiplication do.

Simple assignments

The simple assignment operator is the equal sign =. We have already seen a few examples of its use. The most common form of a simple assignment is

```
lvalue = rvalue;
```

The right-hand side could be a conventional expression evaluating to *rvalue* (for "right" value). *lvalue* (pronounced "el-value") must be an object (i.e. a region of memory) able to receive a value, e.g. a variable as in

```
x = a + sqrt( b ) + cos( c );
n = n + 1;          // increase the value of n by 1 (or n++)
```

More examples

The formulae

$$F = GME/r^2,$$

$$c = \sqrt{a^2 + b^2}/(2a),$$

$$A = P(1 + r/100)^n$$

may be translated into the following simple assignments:

```
f = G * m * e / r / r;
c = sqrt( a * a + b * b ) / (2 * a);   // sqrt header in math.h
a = p * pow( 1 + r/100, n );           // pow header in math.h
```

Multiple assignments

Since a C++ assignment is an expression, it must have a value. The rule is that an assignment takes on the value of its lvalue. So the value of the assignment

```
c = 1;
```

is actually 1, which is the lvalue received by c. This provides a means of making *multiple assignments*:

```
a = b = c = 1;
```

C++ starts at the right and evaluates the assignment c = 1. Its lvalue is 1, so this value is assigned to b. Since the value of the assignment b = 1 is also 1, this value is finally assigned to a as well.

Things can get a little more complicated, as in

```
a = b + (c = 4);
```

which has the same effect as the code

```
c = 4;
a = b + c;
```

This is much clearer, and therefore preferable. Multiple assignments should be restricted to multiple initialization of variables.

Assignment operators

A statement like

```
sum = sum + x;
```

occurs so frequently in C++ that it may be written more concisely as

```
sum += x;
```

The double symbol += is called an *assignment operator*. There are altogether 10 assignment operators. The remaining ones are: -=, *=, \=, %=, <<=, >>=, &=, ^=, and |= (see later). Each assignment operator reduces the expression

var = var op expr ;

to the shorter form

var op= expr;

Their precedence level in the general scheme of things is shown in Appendix B.

Expressions

We have seen that expressions do the real work in a C++ program, and that a statement is simply an expression terminated by a semi-colon. The *order* in which Turbo C++ evaluates operands in an expression is not specified, except where the precedence rules make this clear. In other words, in the expression

```
1/b++ + b++
```

it is not clear at which stage b will be incremented. The compiler attempts to rearrange the expression to generate the best code. It is therefore best to avoid writing expressions in which a value is modified more than once, as in the example above. In general, you should avoid writing expressions that both modify and use the value of the same object.

The comma operator

The *comma operator* is another one of those C odditites inherited by C++.
Expressions in a statement may be separated by commas. The comma in this case is an operator (with the lowest possible precedence level). Evaluation

is from left to right. However, the data type and value of the final right-most evaluation are returned as the type and value of the whole comma expression. So

```
int i;
int j = 1;
int k = 10;
i = (j++, k++);
```

returns the value 10 for i (remember, k is incremented after the assignment). However, omitting the parentheses returns the value 1, since the assignment has a higher precedence than the comma, although the comma expression as such will still have the value 10.

It is best to avoid making use of the value of a comma expression. Its main use is in multiple expressions in a **for** loop, where its value is not needed.

Typecasting

Sometimes we need a variable in a calculation to be treated as if it were of a different type. For example, we might want to retain the fractional part of the quotient when an integer is divided by another integer. We can make use of *typecasting*:

```
int i, j;
float x;
...
x = i / float(j);
```

The expression **float(j)** is called a *typecast*, or an *explicit type conversion*, meaning that j is treated as a **float** variable in the expression.

All the fundamental types (and your own derived types) may be used like this in typecasting.

The older alternative C form of typecast is **(float) j**.

Operator precedence

The precedence levels of all the operators discussed in this section are shown in Appendix B.

2.9 Basic input and output

We have been using **cin** and **cout** for input and output (I/O). These are actually *objects* (in the object-oriented programming sense) defined in the **C++ iostream** library. They have been designed to make basic I/O fairly straightforward, so that you don't need to worry too much about it while you are trying to learn C++.

A *stream* is a concept which is is fundamental to C++, and may be thought of a stream of data connecting a program to some device, such as the keyboard, or the monitor, or a disk file.

Output with cout

cout stands for "character out", because it is a stream of output characters, i.e. characters that can be displayed on a screen. The operator <<, which is actually the left-shift operator, has been overloaded (a piece of C++ jargon meaning the operator has a different meaning in this context) to enable you to insert characters into this stream. So

```
cout << i;
```

inserts the characters representing the value of i into the output stream (<< is pronounced "put to").

You can output any type of variable like this, and also character strings:

```
cout << "The answer is: " << x;
```

Remember that each variable or string sent to cout is an operand of the << operator.

Formatting iostream output

To control the format of the output, you can use *manipulators*, e.g.

```
#include <iostream.h>
#include <iomanip.h>
main()
{
  float x = 123.4567;
  cout << setprecision(2);
  cout << "x:";
  cout << setw(10) << x << endl;
  cout << "x:";
  cout << setw(15) << x << endl;
}
```

Output:

```
x:      123.46
x:           123.46
```

setprecision() sets the number of digits after the decimal point. setw() sets the total field width. Most of the format states remain set until you reset them. However the field is set only for the current output, and must be reset each time if you want to specify it.

If you use manipulators that take parameters, as these do, you must include the **iomanip.h** header file. In that case you don't need to include **iostream.h** as well.

The **hex**, **oct** and **dec** manipulators output integer values in hexadecimal, octal and decimal. They remain in force until the base is reset. The following code displays the numbers 11–20 in decimal, octal and hexadecimal:

```
int i;
for (i = 11; i <= 20; i++)
{
  cout << setw(4) << i << "  ";
  cout << setw(2) << oct << i << "  ";
  cout << setw(3) << setfill( '0') << hex << i << endl;
  cout << dec << setfill(' ');    // reset the defaults
}
```

Output:

```
...
  14  16  00e
  15  17  00f
  16  20  010
...
```

The **setfill()** manipulator left-fills the field with the specified character (which must be given between *single* quotes).

endl is a manipulator which inserts a line feed (new line) into the output stream.

printf()

In C output to the standard output device (usually the monitor) is usually handled by the **print()** function; its prototype is declared in **stdio.h**. Although **cout** is very handy, there are some things that **printf()** can do more concisely, once you have got the hang of it, e.g. formatted output. The following code produces the same output as above:

```
#include <stdio.h>
main()
```

```
      {
          int i;
          for (i = 11; i <= 20; i++)
            printf( "%4d   %2o   %03x\n", i, i, i );
          ...
```

The general form of `printf()` is

    printf(*"control string"*, *argument list*)

The *control string* contains characters that will be displayed literally on the
screen, and/or format commands that control how the values of arguments
are displayed. The control string may also contain an *escape sequence*. This is
a sequence starting with the special escape character (\), which instructs the
compiler to treat the sequence in an unusual way (i.e. to escape from the
normal interpretation). E.g. the sequence \n in a string sends a line feed.
Possible escape codes are listed in Table 2.4 (see Section 2.12).

The *format codes* used above display integers in decimal (%d), octal (%o)
and hexadecimal (%x) forms. The field width may be specified for integers
(%wd); a zero preceding the width specifier will pad with zeros from the
left.

The details of `printf()` are quite complicated; there are more examples
under its entry in Appendix D.

Output on a printer

You can send program output to a PC printer (or any disk file) quite easily, as
follows:

```
      #include <fstream.h>
      main()
      {
        fstream myout( "prn", ios::out );       // a sort of declaration
        myout << "This output is on the printer" << endl;
        return 0;
      }
```

`myout` is an object of the **fstream** class, which is simply a generalization of
the **cout** object of the **iostream** class. Replacing **cout** with **myout** now
sends all corresponding output to the printer. The header file is **fstream.h**.
It's not necessary to include **iostream.h** as well because **fstream** "inherits"
all the **iostream** facilities (which is why **endl** still works). The **fstream**
myout statement is the object-oriented equivalent of a declaration. More of
this later.

You can send output to any disk file in the same way. Just change the **fstream** statement:

```
fstream diskout( "junk.dat", ios::out );
```

Of course, you can always run the **.exe** version of your program from the DOS command line and redirect the output to the printer or a disk file:

```
myprog > prn
```

Input with cin

The compound interest program in Section 2.1 supplies the data by assigning it:

```
balance = 1000;
rate = 0.09;
```

This is fine if you never want to change the data. But if you want to change it, the program must be recompiled every time. This could be extremely inefficient if the program is large with many such data assignments.

The **cin** object, however, allows you to supply the data *while the program is running*. **cin** stands for "character in". Its operator **>>** ("get from") gets data from the standard input stream. It works rather like **cout** in reverse:

```
cout << "Enter the balance and interest rate: ";
cin >> balance >> rate;
```

The direction of the **>>** operator makes it clear that data moves from the input stream to the variable.

Numeric data for **cin** should be separated by at least one blank, and may be on more than one line.

Reading data from a text file

It often happens that you need to test a program by reading a lot of data. Suppose you were writing a program to find the average of 10 numbers. It becomes a great nuisance to type in all the data each time you run the program (since programs seldom work correctly the first time). The following trick is very useful.

Store the data in a text (ASCII) file on disk (you can set it up with your C++ editor). E.g. create a text file **junk.dat** to contain two numbers on one line, say, separated by a blank. Then run this program:

```
#include <fstream.h>
main()
{
 int i, j;
 fstream myin( "junk.dat", ios::in );

 if (!myin)          // check whether the file was found
   { cout << "File not found - try again!" << endl;
     return 1;
   }

 myin >> i >> j;
 printf( "Data read: %4d%4d\n", i, j );
 return 0;
}
```

The object `myin` is the input equivalent of `myout` above. This way your data only needs to be entered once.

The section of code starting with `if` checks whether the file you specified is found (in the current directory). The details of this statement will be discussed later. A check like this is imperative when you use disk files, because C++ (like C) has the disconcerting habit of reading from (and writing to) files that aren't there — sometimes with disastrous consequences. Note that the `return` value is 1 as opposed to 0, so that this error condition can be detected from a DOS batch file.

2.10   Repeating with `for`

So far we have seen how to get numbers into a C++ program, how to do some arithmetic with them, and how to output answers. In this section we look at a new feature: repetition.

Run the following program:

```
#include <iomanip.h>
main()
{
 int i;
 for (i = 1; i <= 20; i++)
    cout << setw(3) << i;
 return 0;
}
```

Just for fun, replace `<< i` with `<< '*'`.

You might be a little surprised at this one:

```
char ch;
for (ch = 'a'; ch <= 'z'; ch++)
   cout << ch;
cout << endl;
```

Try changing the program to print the alphabet backwards. (We will discuss `char` type later in the chapter.)

The `for` loop

The `for` loop is one of the most powerful constructs in any programming language. One of its simplest forms is

```
for (i = j; i <= k; i++) statement;
```

In this case i is an integer variable, and j and k may be constants, variables or expressions. The *statement* is executed repeatedly. The values of j and k determine how many repeats are made. i starts with the value j, and is incremented at the end of each loop. Looping stops once i exceeds the value of k, and execution proceeds in the normal way with the next statement. i will have the value $k + 1$ after completion of the loop.

More generally, `for` has the syntax

```
for (initialization; condition; increment) statement;
```

initialization initializes the loop counter, looping continues while *condition* is true, and *increment* defines how the loop counter is incremented.

The double symbol `<=` is a *relational operator*, which has the obvious meaning: less than or equal to. We will discuss relational operators in more detail below.

Now let's try something slightly more adventurous. Whatever happens, don't leave out `nosound()`!

```
#include <dos.h>
#include <stdlib.h>
main()
{
 int i;
 randomize();                 // include stdlib.h
 for (i = 1; i <= 10; i++) {
   sound( random(1000) );     // include dos.h and stdlib.h
```

```
        delay( 500 );                // include dos.h
        nosound();                   // include dos.h
    }
    return 0;
}
```

The important thing to note here is that if a *group* of statements is to be repeated by a **for** loop they must be enclosed in *block markers* {...}. Statements thus enclosed are treated syntactically as a single statement, called a *compound statement*. Pascal programmers will note that the block markers correspond to the **begin-end** of that language, except that the last statement in the group *must* be terminated by a semi-colon.

A common error is to end the **for** clause with a semi-colon:

```
    for (i = 1; i <= 10; i++) ;
```

Can you explain what happens if you do this in the above program? The semi-colon terminates the statement to be executed: in this case nothing except incrementing i. So nothing is basically repeated 10 times, after which C++ executes the statements in the block markers *once*.

By the way, **random**(n) returns a random integer between 0 and $(n-1)$, and **randomize**() "seeds" the random number generator with the time of day. **sound**(n) turns on the PC speaker at n hertz, **nosound**() switches off the speaker, and **delay**(n) suspends program execution for n milliseconds (to enable you to hear the sound before it is switched off). Library functions such as these are summarized in Appendix D.

Danger!

The following example illustrates the dangers lurking in integer arithmetic that we mentioned in Section 2.5. It is well known that the sum of the reciprocals of the squares of the whole numbers converges to a limit, i.e. the sum

$$1/1^2 + 1/2^2 + 1/3^2 + \ldots + 1/n^2$$

gets closer to a fixed number, called the limit, as n gets bigger. Run the following code for some values of n, say between 10 and 250:

```
    int i, n;
    float x = 0;
    cin >> n;
    for (i = 1; i <= n; i++)
    x = x + 1.0 / (i * i);
    cout << setw(10) << setprecision(6) << x;
```

The sum is obtained by repeatedly updating the value of x, which must be initialized to zero, to avoid garbage.

For n greater than about 180 something strange happens: the sum starts to get *smaller*. Eventually a division overflow occurs. This is because the value of i * i moves past the maximum size allowed for **int** and starts again at the minimum value. See if you can correct the code to give the right answer for $n = 256$, which is 1.641035.

Square rooting with Newton

The square root x of any positive number a may be found using only the arithmetic operations of addition, subtraction and division, with *Newton's method*. This is an iterative (repetitive) procedure that refines an initial guess; there is a more general discussion in Chapter 15.

The structure plan of the algorithm to find the square root, and the program with sample output for $a = 2$ is as follows:

1. Input a
2. Initialize x to 1
3. Repeat 6 times (say)
    Replace x by $(x + a/x)/2$
    Print x
4. Stop.

```
// Square rooting with Newton
#include <conio.h>
#include <iostream.h>
#include <math.h>
#include <stdio.h>
main()
{
  int i;          // iteration counter
  double a;       // number to be square rooted
  double x = 1;   // guess at square root of a

  cout << "Enter number to square rooted: ";
  cin >> a;

  for (i = 1; i <= 6; i++) {
  x = (x + a / x) / 2;
   printf( "%20.14f\n", x );
  }

  cout << endl;
  printf( "Turbo C++'s value: %20.14f\n", sqrt(a) );
```

```
    getch();
    return 0;
}
```

Output:

```
Enter number to square rooted:
    1.50000000000000
    1.41666666666667
    1.41421568627451
    1.41421356237469
    1.41421356237310
    1.41421356237310
Turbo C++'s value:     1.41421356237310
```

The value of x converges to a limit, which is $\sqrt{a}$. Note that it is identical to the value returned by Turbo C++'s library function **sqrt**. Most computers and calculators use a similar method internally to compute square roots and other standard mathematical functions.

Note the use of **double** type to get greater precision. Note also the use of the **f** format code in **printf** to display a floating point value. In this case it is used with a *precision specifier* p as in (%*w.p*f) to display the number of w columns correct to p decimal places.

Money again

The next program computes compound interest on an initial balance over a number of years. Run it for a period of about 10 years and see if you can follow how it works. Save it for use in Exercise 2.25 at the end of the chapter.

```
// Compound growth of an investment
#include <conio.h>
#include <iostream.h>
#include <iomanip.h>
#include <stdio.h>
main()
{
    int period;    // period of investment
    int year;      // year counter
    float bal;     // balance
    float rate;    // interest rate

    clrscr();      // clears the screen; include <conio.h>
    cout << "Initial balance: ";
    cin >> bal;
    cout << "Period of investment (years): ";
    cin >> period;
```

```
        cout << "Annual interest rate: ";
        cin >> rate;
        cout << endl;
        cout << "Year" << setw(15) << "Balance" << endl << endl;

        for (year = 1; year <= period; year++) {
          bal = bal + rate * bal;
          printf( "%4d%15.2f\n", year, bal );
        }
        getch();
        return 0;
    }
```

Note that a string (sequence of characters) is right-justified by `cout`. Note also that a combination of `cin`, `cout` and `printf()` often provides the neatest way of handling I/O.

The next program is a variation on the last one. Suppose we have to service four different savings accounts, with balances of $1 000, $500, $750 amd $12 050. We want to compute the new balance for each of them after 9% interest has been compounded. Try it out.

```
        // customers' savings accounts
        #include <iostream.h>
        #include <stdio.h>
        #include <conio.h>
        main()
        {
          int acct;          // counter
          int line;          // cursor position (row)
          float newbal;      // new balance after interest
          float oldbal;      // old balance
          float rate = 0.09; // interest rate

          clrscr();
          for (acct = 1; acct <= 4; acct++) {
            line = acct;
            gotoxy( 1, line );              // include <conio.h>
            cout << "Old balance: ";
            cin >> oldbal;
            newbal = oldbal + rate * oldbal;
            gotoxy( 30, line );             // same line as previous input
            cout << "New balance:";
            printf( "%9.2f", newbal );
          }
          getch();
          return 0;
        }
```

Note the effects of indenting the statements inside the block markers of the `for` loop. It makes it easier for you to spot the block when you read the program.

`line` represents the row on the screen where the output must go. `gotoxy()` ensures that **newbal** appears on the same line as **oldbal** for each account.

Differential interest rates

Most banks offer differential interest rates — more for the rich, less for the poor. Suppose in the above example that the rate is 9% for balances less than $5 000, but 12% otherwise. We can easily amend the program to allow for this by removing the initialization for **rate**, and inserting after **cin >> oldbal** the lines

```
if (oldbal < 5000)
   rate = 0.09;
else
   rate = 0.12;
```

Try this out with sensibly chosen data to verify that it works. For example, $4 000 will grow to $4 360, whereas $5 000 will grow to $5 600.

2.11   Deciding with `if`

We will discuss the `if` statement just introduced more fully in this section.

As an example, suppose that the final course mark of students attending a university course is calculated as follows. Two examination papers are written at the end of the course. The final mark is either the average of the two papers, or the average of the two papers and the class record mark (all weighted equally), whichever is the higher. The following program computes and prints the mark of each student in a class of three, with the comment PASS or FAIL (50% being the pass mark).

```
//final mark for course based on class record and exams
#include <conio.h>
#include <fstream.h>
#include <stdio.h>
main()
{
   int stu;       // student counter
   float crm;     // class record mark
   float exmavg;  // average of two exam papers
```

```
float final;  // final mark
float p1, p2; // marks for two exam papers

fstream myin( "marks", ios::in );
clrscr();
printf( "%15s%15s%15s\n\n", "Class record", "Exam average",
        "Final mark" );

for (stu = 1; stu <= 3; stu++) {
  myin >> crm >> p1 >> p2;
  exmavg = (p1 + p2) / 2;
  if (exmavg > crm)
    final = exmavg;
  else
    final = (p1 + p2 + crm) / 3;
  printf( "%15.2f%15.2f%15.2f  ", crm, exmavg, final );
  if (final >= 50)
    cout << "PASS";
  else
    cout << "FAIL";
  cout << endl;
}
getch();
...
```

The data are stored in a disk file **marks** to make input more efficient. For example, for a sample class of three students, the data could be

```
40 60 43
60 45 43
13 98 47
```

i.e. the first student has a class record of 40 with exam marks of 60 and 43. Her final mark should be 51.5 (class record not used), whereas the second student's final mark should be 49.3 (class record used).

Note that the format code **%15s** in the first **printf()** statement right-justifies a string over 15 columns.

The `if` statement

In the last example we saw a situation where the program must in a sense make decisions: whether or not to include the class record, and whether to pass or fail the student. As the programmer you cannot anticipate which of these possibilities will occur when writing the program, so it must be designed to allow for all of them. We need a *conditional branch* statement, which is another of the most powerful facilities in any programming language. Its

Relational Operator	Meaning	Example
<	less than	if (ch < 'z') { ... }
<=	less than or equal	while (i <= imax) { ... }
==	equal	if (x == 1) { ... }
!=	not equal	while (ch != EOF) { ... }
>	greater than	if (j>k) { ... }
>=	greater than or equal	if (b * b >= 4 * a * c) { ... }

Table 2.3: Relational operators

simplest form in C++ is

```
if (condition)
    statement1;
else
    statement2;
```

The **else** clause is optional. If *condition* is true *statement1* is executed; otherwise if the **else** part is present *statement2* is executed. Both statements may be compound statements enclosed in block markers. Execution then continues in the normal way with the next statement.

If you are a non-C programmer you may be surprised to learn that "true" in C and C++ means *any value other than zero*. C++ has no Boolean (true/false) type like Pascal. If an expression evaluates to zero it is false — any other value is true. E.g. the expression (1 + 2) is true. More conventional looking expressions may be constructed with the six *relational operators* shown in Table 2.3. Their place in the general operator scene is depicted in Appendix B. A common mistake is to use the assignment operator = instead of the equals relational operator ==.

Expressions formed with these relational operators are sometimes called *Boolean*. They can be combined with each other using the *logical operators* ! (negation), && (AND) (think of the & as "and"), and || (OR) (from highest to lowest precedence). As usual, parentheses may be used to changed the order of precedence. These are discussed more fully in Chapter 5.

For example, suppose we wanted to write the class (grade) of each student's final mark in the above program. We could replace the statements

```
if (final >= 50)
    cout << "PASS";
```

```
        else
           cout << "FAIL";
```

by the following:

```
        if (final >= 75)
           cout << "1";
        if (final >= 70 && final < 75)
           cout << "2+";
        if (final >= 60 && final < 70)
           cout << "2-";
        if (final >= 50 && final < 60)
           cout << "3";
        if (final < 50)
           cout << "FAIL";
```

The `cout` in each statement is executed only if all the conditions in the associated `if` are true.

2.12   Characters and strings

An obvious shortcoming of the final mark program in Section 2.11 is that the students' *names* don't feature at all. To remedy this, we need to look briefly at characters and strings. However, let's first make some changes to the program. First, insert the declaration

```
        char name[21];
```

which allows for names of up to 20 letters (including initials, blanks, etc.). The purpose of the 21st character will be explained in a moment. Then alter the first `printf()` statement to include the heading `Name`:

```
        printf( "%-20s%-15s%-15s%-15s\n\n", "Name", "Class record",
                                 "Exam average", "Final mark" );
```

Just to be different, there are minus signs in the string format codes, to *left-justify* the headings.

Assuming that the names will occupy the first 20 columns of each line in the data file, input from the file will now be handled like this:

```
        myin.get( name, 20 );
        myin >> crm >> p1 >> p2 >> ws;
```

get() is a special *member* function of the class from which the object `myin` is descended, and is invoked as shown. It gets the next 20 characters from the text file and reads them into `name`. Details of how this works will be discussed when we get into object-oriented programming later. The intention here is to show you fairly easy ways of doing basic file I/O which you need to take on trust at the moment.

The line starting `myin >> crm ...` is the same as before, except for the `ws` manipulator, which extracts and discards whitespace (blanks, tabs, new-lines) from the input stream. This is necessary to extract the blanks and the line feed after the last number (p2), before the next name is read by `get()`. Otherwise any blanks and the line feed after the value of p2 will be read as part of the next name. The `ws` manipulator was not needed before, because when a fundamental data type is being read all leading whitespace is automatically extracted.

Each name and mark is displayed with the statement

```
printf( "%-20s%5.2f%15.2f%15.2f  ", name, crm, exmavg, final );
```

It has been adjusted slightly to left-justify the marks.

Finally you should change the data file **marks** by inserting some names. Remember to allow *at least* 20 columns for the names — it doesn't matter if you leave more, because `myin` discards whitespace when looking for numeric data:

```
Ahmed AB             40 60 43
Baker CD             60 45 43
Ntuli MX             13 98 47
```

If you run the amended program you should get output like this:

Name	Class record	Exam average	Final mark
Ahmed AB	40.00	51.50	51.50 PASS
Baker CD	60.00	44.00	49.33 FAIL
Ntuli MX	13.00	72.50	72.50 PASS

Characters

A *character constant* is a character enclosed in *single* quotes, e.g. 'C'. Turbo C++ has a fundamental type **char** which needs one byte of storage. A **char** variable can hold an ASCII character (see Appendix E) or an integer in the range -128 to 127. Because **char** variables are synomous with integers this allows for very easy manipulation of characters. E.g. the statements

```
char ch;
ch = 'A';
ch++;
```

leaves the value `'B'` in `ch` since the ASCII codes of letters of the alphabet are contiguous. Furthermore, `ch` can be used in an arithmetic expression, and will have the value 66 — the ASCII code for the character B.

Turbo C++ also has an `unsigned char` type with a range from 0 to 255 which can be used to store integers in this range.

Turbo C++ also supports a *wide character constant* which holds two characters, prefixed by an L, e.g. `L'ae'`. This is in order to support character sets with more than 256 characters, so that more than one byte is needed to represent a character.

Characters are displayed with `printf()` using the `%c` format specifier. E.g. if `ch` has the value `'B'` the statement

```
printf( "%c %d\n", ch, ch );
```

produces the output

```
B 66
```

Strings

A string constant, or *string literal* is a sequence of characters enclosed in *double* quotes. String literals may be concatenated (joined) simply by writing them next to each other; any intervening whitespace is discarded:

```
cout << "You will know the truth " "and the truth will set you free";
```

A backslash may also be used, but then the backslash must be the last character on the line, and the next line must start immediately with the continued string.

String constants may also contain *escape* codes. These are special symbols representing non-printable control codes and other ASCII values. The Turbo C++ escape codes are listed in Table 2.4. For example, you can ring the bell with

```
cout << "\a";
```

or include double quotes in a string for direct speech:

```
cout << "Pilate said, \"What is truth?\"";
```

Escape code	*Meaning*	*Escape code*	*Meaning*
\a	alarm bell	\\	backslash
\b	backspace	\'	apostrophe (single quote)
\f	form feed	\"	double quote
\n	new line	\?	question mark
\r	carriage return	\0...	string of octal digits
\t	horizontal tab	\x...	string of hex digits
\v	vertical tab		

Table 2.4: Turbo C++ escape codes

The octal and hex codes allow you to enter any ASCII code directly into a string, character or integer constant:

```
char ch = '\x27';    // single quote
```

Note that to enter a backslash in a string you must type two of them. This is important when entering a DOS path as a string, e.g.

```
"c:\\tc\\test.cpp"
```

If you enter single backslashes here \t gets compiled as a horizontal tab, so there's no way your path will be found! However, pathnames in #include directives should have only one backslash.

Character string variables

C++ does not have a "string" type to represent words, as Turbo Pascal and most versions of BASIC do. Instead a string must be declared as an *array* of single characters. E.g.

```
char name[80];
```

declares **name** to be a string of 80 single characters. A particular character in the string is referenced with square brackets after the array name, e.g. name[28]. In C++ all arrays are indexed from zero. So the first character is in name[0], while the last one is in name[79]. Arrays are discussed in more detail in Chapter 9.

An important feature of strings is that the compiler inserts a special character at the end of a string, called the *null terminator*. It is the null character, with ASCII code zero, so it can be represented with an octal escape code as '\0'. This is to enable the compiler to find the end of the string. This must be taken into account when declaring a string. E.g. for a string to hold the word TURBO it must be at least six characters long, i.e. declared as **char name[6]**. The character **name[5]** will hold the null terminator. The null character is represented in Turbo C++ by the **NULL** macro, defined in **stdio.h** and other header files.

There is therefore a world of difference between the character '**A**' and the string "**A**". The latter occupies two bytes — the second one for the null terminator.

A string (e.g. **name**) may be read from the keyboard with **gets(name)** (include **stdio.h**). The newline is read, but replaced by the null terminator. A danger inherent in reading strings like this is that C++ will not check whether the string is too long to fit into the declared array. If it is too long, it will still store the excess characters somewhere in memory, with disastrous consequences, if part of your program code or data happens to be there also. To prevent such an error you could always declare strings with 128 characters, e.g.

```
char name[128];
```

because that is the length of the DOS internal input buffer. You cannot therefore enter more than 128 characters into **name**. (This only holds for typical PCs). The same problem can arise if you use **cin**:

```
cin >> name;
```

Safer ways of reading strings will be discussed when we look at strings in more detail in Chapter 10.

A string may be initialized at declaration:

```
char string[ ] = "To be or not to be";
```

Note that Turbo C++ will count the number of characters for you.

The easiest way to assign a string is with **strcpy** (include **string.h**):

```
char name[80];
strcpy( name, "Turbo" );
```

Summary

- Pre-processor directives are instructions to be carried out before the program is compiled. They are not terminated by semi-colons.

- Header files with the **.h** extension contain prototypes of library functions needed in a program. They are included with the **#include** directive.
- Every program must have a **main()** function.
- C++ statements are expressions terminated by semi-colons.
- Everything after **//** in a statement is a comment. Comments may also be enclosed between **/*** and ***/**.
- Identifiers are the symbolic names given to objects in a C++ program. They are case sensitive. They must start with a letter or an underscore.
- A variable is a region of memory whose value may be changed.
- All variables must be declared with a type.
- Types are fundamental, derived or user-defined.
- Typed constants, declared with **const**, may not be changed in a program.
- The **#define** pre-processor directive may be used to define a symbolic constant (macro).
- An expression is a means of evaluating a formula using constants, operators, variables and functions.
- There are seven kinds of operators for evaluating expressions, which operate according to rules of precedence.
- The arithmetic operators are **+**, **-**, *****, **/** and **%** (modulus). When an integer is divided by another integer the fractional part of the the quotient is truncated. The relational operators **<**, **<=**, **>**, **>=**, **==** (equals), and **!=** (not equal) compare two operands. The logical operators **&&** (AND), **||** (OR), and **!** (negation) operate on true-false operands.
- The increment **++** and decrement **--** operators increase and decrease their operands by 1. The operators may come before (pre) or after (post) their operands.
- The value zero is interpreted as false in **if** statements. Any other value is true.
- In C++ an assignment is an expression and therefore has a value.
- Assignments may be single or multiple.
- There are ten assignment operators: **+=**, **-=**, ***=**, **/=**, **%=**, **>>=**, **<<=**, **&=**, **|=**, and **^=**.
- You should avoid writing expressions that both modify and use the value of the same object.
- Parentheses may always be used to override the precedence rules.
- The comma is an operator in C++.

- Variables may be coerced into a different type by typecasting.
- Input and output is handled most easily with the predefined `cin` and `cout` stream objects, and may be formatted.
- Output may also be done with the C function `printf()`.
- Data may be input from a disk file by creating your own object of the `fstream` class which behaves like `cin`.
- A `for` loop repeats a block of statements.
- A compound statement is a group of statements enclosed in {block markers}. It is treated as a single statement.
- `if-else` enables a program to decide between alternatives.
- Single character constants are enclosed in single quotes.
- A string constant is a sequence of characters enclosed in double quotes.
- String constants may contain special escape codes.
- A string variable is an array of single characters.
- The last character in a string is always the null character (terminator).

Exercises

2.1 Evaluate the following expressions, given that `float a = 2, float b = 3, float c = 5`, and `int i = 2, int j = 3`. Answers are given in parentheses.

```
a * b + c            (11.0)
a * (b + c)          (16.0)
b / c * a            (1.2)
b / (c * a)          (0.3)
a / i / j            (0.333333)
i / j / a            (0.0)
17 / 5               (3)
4 / 3 / 4            (0)
4 / (3 / 4)          (division by zero)
17 % (4 % 3)         (0)
```

2.2 Decide which of the following constants are not acceptable in C++, and state why not:

   (a) 9,87   (b) .0   (c) 25.82   (d) −356231
   (e) 3.57*E2 (f) 3.57E2.1 (g) 3.57E+2 (h) 3,57E−2

2.3 State, giving reasons, which of the following are not valid C++ identifiers:

   (a) a2   (b) a.2   (c) 2a   (d) 'a'one
   (e) aone   (f) _x_1   (g) miXedUp (h) pay day
   (i) U.S.S.R. (j) Pay_Day (k) min*2 (l) const

2.4 Find the values of the following expressions by writing short programs to evaluate them (answers in parentheses):
  (a) the sum of 5 and 3 divided by their product   (0.53333)
  (b) the cube root of the product of 2.3 and 4.5   (2.17928 — use `pow()`)
  (c) $\sqrt{2}$ (1.41421 — use `sqrt()`)
  (d) the square of 2π (39.4784 — use M_PI in **math.h** for π)
  (e) $2\pi^2$ (19.7392)
  (f) $1\,000(1 + 0.15/12)^{60}$ (2 107.18 — the balance when $1000 is deposited for 5 years at 15% p.a. compounded monthly)

2.5 Translate the following expressions into C++:
  (a) $p + \frac{w}{u}$ (b) $p + \frac{w}{u+v}$ (c) $\frac{p+\frac{w}{u+v}}{p+\frac{w}{u-v}}$ (d) $x^{1/2}$
  (e) y^{y+z} (f) x^{y^z} (g) $(x^y)^z$ (h) $x - x^3/3! + x^5/5!$

2.6 Translate the following into C++ assignments:
  (a) Add 1 to the value of i and store the result in i.
  (b) Cube i, add j to this, and store the result in i.
  (c) Set g equal to the larger of the two variables e and f.
  (d) If d is greater than zero, set x equal to minus b.
  (e) Divide the sum of a and b by the product of c and d, and store the result in x.

2.7 Write a program to calculate x, where

$$x = \frac{-b + \sqrt{b^2 - 4ac}}{2a}$$

and $a = 2$, $b = -10$, $c = 12$ (use `cin` to input the data). (Answer 3.0)

2.8 There are eight pints in a gallon, and 1.76 pints in a litre. The volume of a tank is given as 2 gallons and 4 pints. Write a program which reads this volume in gallons and pints and converts it to litres. (Answer: 11.36 litres)

2.9 Write a program to calculate petrol (gas) consumption. It should assign the distance travelled (in kilometres) and the amount of petrol used (in litres) and compute the consumption in km/litre as well as in the more usual form of litres per 100 km. Write some helpful headings, so that your output looks something like this:

Distance	Litres used	Km/L	L/100Km
528	46.23	11.42	8.76

2.10 Write some lines of C++ which will exchange the contents of two variables a and b, using only one additional variable t.

2.11 Try the previous problem *without* using any additional variables!

2.12 If C and F are Celsius and Fahrenheit temperatures respectively, the formula for conversion from Celsius to Fahrenheit is $F = 9C/5 + 32$.

  (a) Write a program which will ask you for the Celsius temperature and display the equivalent Fahrenheit one with some sort of comment, e.g.

  ```
  The Fahrenheit temperature is: ...
  ```

  Try it out on the following Celsius temperatures (answers in parentheses): 0 (32), 100 (212), −40 (−40!), 37 (normal human temperature: 98.6).

  (b) Change the program to use a **for** loop to compute and write the Fahrenheit equivalent of Celsius temperatures ranging from $20°$ to $30°$ in steps of $1°$.

2.13 Write a program that displays a list of integers from 10 to 20 inclusive, each with its square root next to it.

2.14 Write a program to find and display the sum of the successive integers 1, 2, ..., 100. (Answer: 5050)

2.15 Write a program to find and display the sum of the successive *even* integers 2, 4, ..., 200. (Answer: 10100)

2.16 Ten students in a class write a test. The marks are out of 10. All the marks are entered in a disk file **marks**. Write a program which will read all ten marks from the file and find and display the average mark. Try it on the following marks:

  ```
  5  8  0  10  3  8  5  7  9  4   (Answer: 5.9)
  ```

2.17 The pass mark for the test in the previous problem is 5 out of 10. Change your program so it uses an **if-else** to find out how many students passed the test.

2.18 Write a program which generates some random integers **r** with **rand()** (include **stdlib.h**) and counts how many of them are greater than and less than RAND_MAX/2, where RAND_MAX (also in **stdlib.h**) is the largest random number returned by **rand()**.
   Try increasing the number of random numbers generated. What do you expect?

2.19 What are the values of **x** and **a** (both **float**) after the following program section has been executed?

  ```
  a = 0;
  i = 1;
  x = 0;
  ```

```
a = a + i;
x = x + i / a;
a = a + i;
x = x + i / a;
a = a + i;
x = x + i / a;
a = a + i;
x = x + i / a;
```

2.20 Rewrite the program in Exercise 2.19 more economically by using a `for` loop.

2.21 Work out by hand the output of the following program for n = 4:

```
// mystery
#include <iostream.h>
#include <math.h>
main()
{
  float s, x;
  int n, k;
  cout << "Enter n: ";
  cin >> n;
  s = 0;

  for (k = 1; k <= n; k++)
    s += 1 / (float(k) * float(k));

  cout << sqrt( 6 * s ) << endl;
  return 0;
}
```

If you run this program for larger and larger values of n you will find that the output approaches a well-known limit.

2.22 The steady-state current I flowing in a circuit that contains a resistance $R = 5$, capacitance $C = 10$, and inductance $L = 4$ in series is given by

$$I = \frac{E}{\sqrt{R^2 + (2\pi\omega L - \frac{1}{2\pi\omega C})^2}}$$

where $E = 2$ and $\omega = 2$ are the input voltage and angular frequency respectively. Compute the value of I. (Answer: 0.0396)

2.23 The electricity accounts of residents in a very small town are calculated as follows:

- if 500 units or less are used the cost is 2 cents (100 cents = $1) per unit;

- if more than 500, but not more than 1 000 units are used, the cost is $10 for the first 500 units, and then 5 cents for every unit in excess of 500;
- if more than 1 000 units are used, the cost is $35 for the first 1 000 units plus 10 cents for every unit in excess of 1 000;
- in addition, a basic service fee of $5 is charged, no matter how much electricity is used.

Write a program which reads the names and consumptions of the following users from a disk file and displays the name, consumption and total charge for each user:

```
Ahmed, A B          200
Baker, C D          500
Essop, S A          700
Jansen, G M        1000
Smith, Q G         1500
```

(Answers: $9, $15, $25, $40, $90)

2.24 Suppose you deposit $50 per month in a bank account every month for a year. Every month, after the deposit has been made, interest at the rate of 1% is added to the balance. E.g. after one month, the balance is $50.50, and after two months it is $101.51.

Write a program to compute and print the balance each month for a year. Arrange the output to look something like this:

```
MONTH        MONTH-END BALANCE

  1               .50.50
  2               101.51
  3               153.02
 ...
 12               640.47
```

2.25 If you invest $1 000 for one year at an interest rate of 12%, the return is $1 120 at the end of the year. But if interest is compounded at the rate of 1% *monthly* (i.e. 1/12 of the annual rate), you get slightly more interest in the long run. Adapt the compound growth program in Section 2.10 to compute the balance after a year of compounding interest in this way. The answer should be $1 126.83. Evaluate the formula for this result separately as a check: $1\,000 \times 1.01^{12}$.

2.26 A plumber opens a savings account with $100 000 at the beginning of January. He then makes a deposit of $1 000 at the end of each month for the next 12 months (starting at the end of January). Interest is calculated and added to his account at the end of each month (before the $1 000 deposit is made). The monthly interest rate depends on the amount A in his account at the time when interest is calculated, in the following way:

$$A \leq 110\,000 : \quad 1\%$$

$$110\,000 < A \leq 125\,000 : \quad 1.5\%$$

$$A > 125\,000 : \quad 2\%$$

Write a program which displays, for each of the 12 months, under suitable headings, the situation at the end of the month as follows: the number of the month, the interest rate, the amount of interest and the new balance. (Answer: values in the last row of output should be 12, 0.02, 2 534.58, 130 263.78).

2.27 It has been suggested that the population of the United States may be modelled by the formula

$$P(t) = \frac{197\,273\,000}{1 + e^{-0.03134(t - 1913.25)}}$$

where t is the date in years. Write a program to compute and display the population every *ten* years from 1790 to 2000. Use the library function **exp(x)** (**math.h**) to compute the exponential e^x.

Use your program to find out if the population ever reaches a "steady state", i.e. whether it stops changing.

2.28 A mortgage bond (loan) of amount L is obtained to buy a house. The interest rate r is 15% (0.15) p.a. The fixed monthly payment P which will pay off the bond exactly over N years is given by the formula

$$P = \frac{rL(1 + r/12)^{12N}}{12[(1 + r/12)^{12N} - 1]}.$$

(a) Write a program to compute and print P if $N = 20$ years, and the bond is for $50\,000$. You should get $658.39.

(b) It's interesting to see how the payment P changes with the period N over which you pay the loan. Run the program for different values of N (use **cin**). See if you can find a value of N for which the payment is less than $625.

(c) Now go back to having N fixed at 20 years, and examine the effect of different interest rates. You should see that raising the interest rate by 1% (0.01) increases the monthly payment by about $37.

2.29 It's useful to be able to work out how the period of a bond repayment changes if you increase or decrease your monthly payment P. The formula for the number of years N to repay the loan is given by

$$N = \frac{\log(\frac{P}{P-rL/12})}{12\log(1+r/12)}.$$

(a) Write a new program to compute this formula. Use the library function **log()** (**math.h**) for the logarithm. How long will it take to pay off the loan of $50 000 at $800 a month if the interest remains at 15%? (Answer: 10.2 years — nearly twice as fast as when paying $658 a month!)

(b) Use your program to find out by trial-and-error the smallest monthly payment that can be made to pay the loan off — this side of eternity. **Hint:** recall that it is not possible to find the logarithm of a negative number, so P must not be less than $rL/12$.

Chapter 3

Program preparation

3.1 Structure plans
  • Quadratic equation
3.2 Structured programming with functions
Summary
Exercises

The examples in this book so far have been very simple logically, since we have been concentrating on the technical aspects of writing Turbo C++ statements correctly. However, real problems are far more complex, and to program successfully we need to understand a problem thoroughly, and to break it down into its most fundamental logical stages. In other words, we have to develop a systematic procedure or *algorithm*, for solving the problem. There are a number of methods which assist in this process of algorithm development. In this chapter we look at one such approach. This is to use structure plans, which we have already seen briefly.

3.1   Structure plans

A structure plan is an example of what is called *pseudo-code*. The plan may be written at a number of levels, each of increasing complexity, as the logical structure of the program is developed.

Suppose we want to write a program to convert a temperature on the Fahrenheit scale (where water freezes and boils at 32° and 212° respectively) to the more familar Celsius centigrade scale. A first level structure plan might be a simple statement of the problem:

1. Read Fahrenheit temperature
2. Calculate and write Celsius temperature
3. Stop.

Step 1 is pretty straightforward, but step 2 needs elaborating, so the second level plan could be something like this:

1. Input Fahrenheit temperature (F)
2. Calculate Celsius temperature (C):
    2.1. Subtract 32 from F and multiply by 5/9
3. Output the value of C
4. Stop.

There are no hard and fast rules about how to write structure plans. The essential point is to cultivate the mental discipline of getting the logic of a

1. Start
2. Input data (a, b, c)
3. If $a = 0$ then
    If $b = 0$ then
        If $c = 0$ then
            Print 'Solution indeterminate'
        else
            Print 'There is no solution'
    else
        $x = -c/b$
        Print x (only one root: equation is linear)
    else if $b^2 < 4ac$ then
        Print 'Complex roots'
    else if $b^2 = 4ac$ then
        $x = -b/(2a)$
        Print x (equal roots)
    else
        $x_1 = (-b + \sqrt{b^2 - 4ac})/(2a)$
        $x_2 = (-b - \sqrt{b^2 - 4ac})/(2a)$
        Print x_1, x_2
4. Stop.

Figure 3.1: Quadratic equation structure plan

program clear before attempting to write the program. The "top down" approach of structure plans means that the overall structure of a program is clearly thought out before you have to worry about the details of syntax (coding), and this reduces the number of errors enormously.

Quadratic equation

When you were at school you probably solved hundreds of quadratic equations of the form

$$ax^2 + bx + c = 0.$$

A structure plan of the complete algorithm for finding the solution(s) x, given any values of a, b and c, is shown in Figure 3.1.

3.2   Structured programming with functions

Many examples later in this book will get rather involved. More advanced programs like these should be structured by means of your own functions. These are are dealt with in detail in Chapter 8. A function is a self-contained section of code which can communicate with the `main()` function in specific ways, and which may be invoked or "called" by `main()`. The `main()` function itself will then look very much like a first level structure plan of the problem. C++ in fact lends itself to structured programming, because of the pivotal role played by functions.

   For example, the quadratic equation problem may be structure planned at the first level as follows:

1. Read the data
2. Find and print the solution(s)
3. Stop.

Using a function to do the dirty work, this may be translated directly into a C++ `main()` function (excluding declarations):

```
cin >> a >> b >> c;
solveQuadratic( a, b, c );
return 0;
```

(The details of how to code this particular problem are left as an exercise in Chapter 8.)

Summary

- An algorithm is a systematic logical procedure for solving a problem.
- An algorithm must be developed for a problem before it can be coded.
- A structure plan is a representation of an algorithm in pseudo-code.
- A function is a separate collection of C++ statements designed to handle a particular task, and which may be activated (invoked) whenever needed.

Exercises

The problems in these exercises should all be structure planned, before being coded into C++ (where appropriate).

3.1 This structure plan defines a geometric construction. Carry out the plan by sketching the construction:

> 1. Draw two perpendicular x- and y-axes
> 2. Draw the points A (10, 0) and B (0, 1)
> 3. While A does not coicide with the origin repeat:
>> Draw a straight line joining A and B
>> Move A one unit to the left along the x-axis
>> Move B one unit up on the y-axis
> 4. Stop.

3.2 Consider the following structure plan, where M and N represent **int** variables:

> 1. Set $M = 44$ and $N = 28$
> 2. While M not equal to N repeat:
>> While $M > N$ repeat:
>>> Replace M by $M - N$
>> While $N > M$ repeat:
>>> Replace N by $N - M$
> 3. Write M
> 4. Stop.

(a) Work through the structure plan, sketching the contents of M and N during execution. Give the output.

(b) Repeat (a) for $M = 14$ and $N = 24$.

(c) What general arithmetic procedure does the algorithm carry out (try more values of M and N if necessary)?

3.3 Write a program to convert a Fahrenheit temperature to a Celsius one. Test it on the data in Exercise 2.12.

3.4 A builder is given the measurements of five planks in feet (') and inches ("). He wants to convert the lengths to metres. One foot is 0.3048 metres, and one inch is 0.0254 metres. The measurements of the planks are: 4'6", 8'9", 9'11", 6'3" and 12'0" (i.e. the first plank is 4 feet 6 inches long). Store the data in a file.

Write a program to display (under suitable headings) the length of each plank in feet and inches, and in metres, and to find and display the total length of planking in metres. (Answer: the total length is 12.624 metres)

3.5 Write a program to read any two real numbers (which you may assume are not equal), and write out the larger of the two with a suitable message.

3.6 Write a program to read a set of 10 numbers (from a file) and write out the *largest* number in the set.

Now adjust the program to write out the *position* of the largest number in the set as well, e.g. if the data is

       4 7 2 9 3 -1 0 6 8 -2

the output should be 9 (largest number) and 4 (fourth number in the set).

3.7 Write a program to compute the sum of the series

$$1 + 1/2 + 1/3 + \ldots + 1/100.$$

The program should write the current sum after every 10 terms (i.e. the sum after 10 terms, after 20 terms, ..., after 100 terms).

Hint: the expression N % 10 will be zero only when N is a multiple of 10. Use this in an **if** statement to write the sum after every 10th term. (Answer: 5.18738 after 100 terms)

3.8 To convert the **int** variable **mins** minutes into hours and minutes you would first use integer division (**mins / 60** gives the whole number of hours) and then the modulus operator (**mins % 60** gives the number of minutes). Write a program which reads a number of minutes and converts it to hours and minutes.

Now write a program to convert seconds into hours, minutes and seconds. Use integer type again. Try out your program on 10 000 seconds, which should convert to 2 hours 46 minutes and 40 seconds.

3.9 Try to write the structure plans for Exercises 5.2 and 5.5 (don't try to write the programs until you've worked that far).

Chapter 4

Introduction to library functions

4.1 Projectile motion
4.2 Some useful library functions
Summary
Exercises

So far you should be able to write a C++ program which gets data into the computer, performs simple arithmetic operations on the data, maybe involving loops and decisions, and outputs the results of the computation in a comprehensible form. However, more interesting problems are likely to involve special mathematical functions like sines, cosines, logarithms, etc. Just as most calculators have keys for these functions, C++ allows you to compute many functions directly. We have already seen a few examples of these *library functions*.

4.1 Projectile motion

We want to write a program to compute the position (x- and y-coordinates) and the velocity (magnitude and direction) of a projectile, given t, the time since launch, u, the launch velocity, a, the initial angle of launch (in degrees), and g, the acceleration due to gravity.

The horizontal and vertical displacements are given by the formulae

$$x = ut\cos a, \quad y = ut\sin a - gt^2/2.$$

59

The velocity has magnitude V such that $V^2 = \sqrt{V_x^2 + V_y^2}$, where its horizontal and vertical components, V_x and V_y, are given by

$$V_x = u\cos a, \quad V_y = u\sin a - gt,$$

and V makes an angle θ with the ground such that $\tan\theta = V_x/V_y$. The program is:

```
#include <iostream.h>
#include <math.h>
#include <stdio.h>
#include <conio.h>
// projectile position and velocity
main()
{
    const float g = 9.8;
    float a;     // angle of launch in degrees
    float t;     // time in flight
    float th;    // direction at time t
    float u;     // launch velocity
    float v;     // resultant velocity
    float vx;    // horizontal velocity
    float vy;    // vertical velocity
    float x;     // horizontal displacement
    float y;     // vertical displacement

    cin >> a >> t >> u;
    a = a * M_PI / 180;                  // convert angle to radians
    x = u * cos( a ) * t;
    y = u * sin( a ) * t - 0.5 * g * t * t;
    vx = u * cos( a );
    vy = u * sin( a ) - g * t;
    v = sqrt( vx * vx + vy * vy );
    th = atan( vy / vx ) * 180 / M_PI;
    printf( "x: %8.2f\ty: %8.2f\n", x, y );
    printf( "V: %8.2f\t\xe9: %8.2f\n", v, th );
    getch();
    return 0;
}
```

If you run this program with the data

```
45  6  60
```

you will get the following output:

```
x:    254.56     y:    78.16
V:     45.48     θ:   -21.10
```

Note the use of the \t escape code in printf() to tabulate the output, and also the \x escape code to display the character θ (the ASCII code for θ is 233, or e9 in hex).

You can see from the negative value of θ that the projectile is coming down.

The argument of a function may be a C++ expression of appropriate type, including another function. So V could have been computed directly as follows:

```
v = sqrt( pow(u * cos(a), 2) + pow(u * sin( a ) - g * t, 2) );
```

Angles for the trigonometric functions must be expressed in radians, and are returned in radians where appropriate. To convert degrees to radians, multiply the angle in degrees by $\pi/180$, where π is the well-known transcendental number 3.1415926..., represented by the constant M_PI in **math.h**.

4.2   Some useful library functions

Brief descriptions of many of the enormous collection of library functions supported by Turbo C++ appear in Appendix D. A short list of some of the more common ones follows. x stands for a **double** expression unless otherwise stated. Header files are indicated.

abs(x): absolute value of int x (**math.h**).

acos(x): arc cosine (inverse cosine) of x (**math.h**).

asin(x): arc sine (inverse sine) of x (**math.h**).

atan(x): arc tangent of x in the range $-\pi$ to π (**math.h**).

atan2(y, x): arc tangent of y/x in the range $-\pi$ to π (**math.h**).

atof(s): (read as "a to f") converts the string s to its floating point value. E.g. atof("1.23") returns the number 1.23 (**math.h**). This provides an alternative means of input, e.g.

```
char str[128];
double val;
gets( str );        // enter value as string
val = atof( str );  // convert it to double
```

atoi(s): ("a to i") converts the string s to its integer value. E.g. atoi("123") returns the number 123 (**stdlib.h**).

`ceil(x):` smallest integer which exceeds **x**, i.e. rounds up to nearest integer (**math.h**). E.g. `ceil(-3.9)` returns -3, `ceil(3.9)` returns 4.

`clock():` number of "ticks" of the system clock since the program started running. To find the time in seconds divide by the macro `CLK_TCK` (**time.h**).

`clrscr():` clears the current text window (**conio.h**).

`complex(x, y):` creates a complex number with real part **x**, imaginary part **y** (**complex.h**). Technically, `complex` is a class from which complex objects (in the object-oriented programming sense) can be created. It can be used as a type declaration also. E.g.

```
#include <iostream.h>
#include <complex.h>
main()
{
  complex z (1, 1);          // constructor
  complex i (0, 1);          // sqrt(-1)
  cout << conj(z) << endl;   // complex conjugate of z
  z = complex(2, 2);         // assign a different value
  cout << i * z << endl;
}
```

Many of the mathematical functions take and return complex values if you include **complex.h** instead of **math.h**.

`conj(z):` complex conjugate of complex **z** (**complex.h**).

`cos(x):` cosine of **x**.

`cosh(x):` hyperbolic cosine of **x** (**math.h**).

`ctime():` converts the system date and time to a string (**time.h**). This requires some features we haven't seen yet, but you can try it out if you like. The example gives a continuous display of the time second (note how the cursor is switched off and on again):

```
#include <time.h>
#include <conio.h>
#include <stdio.h>
main()
{
  time_t theTime;
  clrscr();
  _setcursortype( _NOCURSOR );

  do {
    time( &theTime );                    // get the time
    gotoxy( 30, 12 );
```

```
        puts( ctime( &theTime ) );        // convert it to a string
    } while (!kbhit());

    _setcursortype( _NORMALCURSOR );
    return 0;
}
```

delay(x): suspends execution for unsigned (int) x milliseconds (**dos.h**).

exp(x): value of the exponential function e^x (**math.h**).

fabs(x): absolute value of float x (**math.h**).

floor(x): largest integer not exceeding x, i.e. rounds down to nearest integer (**math.h**). E.g. floor(-3.9) returns -4, floor(3.9) returns 3.

getch(): returns the next character entered at the keyboard without echoing it to the screen (**conio.h**).

getche(): returns the next character entered at the keyboard, echoing it to the screen (**conio.h**).

gets(str): reads a string of characters including whitespace from the standard input (usually the keyboard) until receiving a newline, which is replaced by a null terminator (**stdio.h**).

gotoxy(x, y): moves the cursor to column int x and row int y of the text window (**conio.h**).

imag(z): imaginary part of complex z (**complex.h**).

itoa(n, str, b): converts int n to its string equivalent in str (**stdlib.h**). int b is the number base used in the conversion.

kbhit(): returns true (non-zero) if a character is waiting in the keyboard buffer, i.e. detects when the keyboard has been hit (**conio.h**).

log(x): natural logarithm of x (**math.h**).

log10(x): base 10 logarithm of x (**math.h**).

norm(z): square of the absolute value of complex z (**complex.h**).

nosound(): stops the noise started by sound() (**dos.h**).

pow(x, y): returns x^y (**math.h**).

pow10(n): returns 10^n where n is int (**math.h**).

`puts(str)`: writes the string `str` to standard output (usually the screen), plus a newline (**stdio.h**).

`rand()`: random integer in the range zero to `RAND_MAX` (**stdlib.h**).

`random(n)`: random integer in the range zero to $n - 1$ (**stdlib.h**).

`randomize()`: seeds the random number generator from the system time, so include **time.h** as well as **stdlib.h**.

`real(z)`: real part of complex `z` (**complex.h**).

`sin(x)`: sine of `x` (**math.h**).

`sinh(x)`: hyperbolic sine of `x` (**math.h**).

`sound(f)`: turns on the PC speaker at the frequency `int f` hertz (cycles per second) (**dos.h**).

`sqrt(x)`: square root of `x` (**math.h**).

`strcpy(str1, str2)`: copies string `str2` into `str1` (**string.h**).

`tan(x)`: tangent of `x` (**math.h**).

`tanh(x)`: hyperbolic tangent of `x` (**math.h**).

`time()`: current date and time as number of seconds elapsed since GMT midnight on 1 January 1970 (**time.h**). See `ctime()` for an example.

`tolower(c)`: converts `char c` to lowercase (**ctype.h**).

`toupper(c)`: converts `char c` to uppercase (**ctype.h**).

Summary

- Library functions may be used to perform a variety of mathematical, trigonometric and other operations.

Exercises

4.1 There are 39.37 inches in a metre, 12 inches in a foot, and three feet in a yard. Write a program to read a length in metres (which may have a decimal part) and convert it to yards, feet and inches. (Check: 3.51 metres converts to 3 yds 2 ft 6.19 in.)

4.2 Write some C++ statements which will:
  (a) find the length C of the hypotenuse of a right-angle triangle in terms of the lengths A and B of the other two sides;
  (b) find the length C of a side of a triangle given the lengths A and B of the other two sides and the size in degrees of the included angle θ, using the cosine rule:

$$C^2 = A^2 + B^2 - 2AB\cos\theta.$$

4.3 Translate the following formulae into C++ expressions:
  (a) $\log(x + x^2 + a^2)$
  (b) $(e^{3t} + t^2 \sin 4t) \cos^2 3t$
  (c) $4 \arctan 1$
  (d) $\sec^2 x + \cot y$ (there is no sec or cot library function)
  (e) $\cot^{-1}|x/a|$ (inverse cotangent)

4.4 A sphere of mass m_1 impinges obliquely on a stationary sphere of mass m_2, the direction of the blow making an angle α with the line of motion of the impinging sphere. If the coefficient of restitution is e it can be shown that the impinging sphere is deflected through an angle β such that

$$\tan\beta = \frac{m_2(1+e)\tan\alpha}{m_1 - em_2 + (m_1 + m_2)\tan^2\alpha}$$

Write a program to read values of m_1, m_2, e, and α (in degrees) and to compute the angle β in degrees.

Chapter 5

Decisions

5.1 The `if-else` statements
- Bending moment in a beam • Top of the class • The `if-else-if` ladder • Nested `if`s

5.2 Logical expressions
- Simulation of a switching circuit

5.3 Bitwise operators
- Binary output

5.4 The `switch` statement

5.5 Halting with `exit()`

5.6 Statements best avoided
- The conditional expression • The `goto` statement

Summary

Exercises

Apart from its ability to add numbers extremely quickly, a computer's other major attribute is to be able to make decisions, as we saw briefly in Chapter 2. It is this facility, together with its ability to repeat statements endlessly without getting bored, which gives the computer its great problem-solving power. The fundamental decision-making construct in C++ is the `if` construct, of which the `CASE` construct is another form.

5.1 The `if-else` statements

We have seen some simple examples of the `if-else` statements already. Further examples, which become more involved, are given in this section.

Bending moment in a beam

A light uniform beam $0 < x < L$ is clamped with its ends at the same level, and carries a concentrated load W at $x = a$. The bending moment M at any

67

point x along the beam is given by two different formulae, depending on the value of x relative to a, viz.

$$M = W(L - a)^2[aL - x(L + 2a)]/L^3 \quad (0 \le x \le a),$$
$$M = Wa^2[aL - 2L^2 + x(3L - 2a)]/L^3 \quad (a \le x \le L).$$

The following program extract computes the bending moment every metre along a 10 metre beam, with a load of 100 Newtons at a point 8 metres from the end $x = 0$:

```
float a, a2, l, l2, l3, l_a2, m, w, x;
l = 10;
w = 100;
a = 8;
a2 = a * a;
l_a2 = (l - a) * (l - a);
l2 = l * l;
l3 = l * l2;
for (x = 0; x <= l; x++) {
  if (x <= a)
    m = w * l_a2 * (a * l - x * (l + 2 * a)) / l3;
  else
    m = w * a2 * (a * l - 2 * l2 + x * (3 * l - 2 * a)) / l3;
  cout << x << "    " << m << endl;
}
```

Note that the **for** loop has a **float** counter. While this is technically allowed, you may find that rounding error causes one too few or too many loops. We will address this problem in Chapter 6.

Top of the class

A class of students write a test, and each student's name (maximum of 15 characters) and mark is entered in a data file. Assume there are no negative marks. We want to write a program which prints out the name of the student with the highest mark, together with his/her mark. We are assuming that there is only *one* highest mark. The problem of what to do when two or more students share the top mark is discussed in Chapter 9.

A first level structure plan for this problem could be:

1. Start
2. Find top student and top mark
3. Print top student and top mark.

Step 2 needs elaborating, so a more detailed plan might be:

>   1. Start
>   2. Initialize topMark (to get process going)
>   3. Repeat for all students
>>   Read name and mark
>>   If mark > topMark then
>>>   Replace topMark with mark
>>>   Replace topName with name
>   4. Print topName and topMark
>   5. Stop.

The program (for a sample class of 3 students) is:

```
int i;              // student counter
float mark;         // general mark
float topMark = 0;  // top mark: can't be less than zero
char name[16];      // general name
char topName[16];   // top student

fstream myin( "marks", ios::in );
if (!myin) {                          // check for file existence
  cout << "Data file not found - program aborted" << endl;
  return 1;
}

for (i= 1; i <= 3; i++) {
  myin.get(name, 15);
  myin >> mark >> ws;
  if (mark > topMark) {
    strcpy(topName, name);
    topMark = mark;
  }
}

cout << "Top student: " << topName << endl;
cout << "   Top mark: " << topMark << endl;
```

Work through the program by hand for a few turns to convince yourself that it works. Try it out on the following sample data:

```
Ahmed AB              40
Baker CD              60
Ntuli MX              13
```

The if-else-if ladder

Recall the final mark program of Chapter 2. To write the grade (1, 2+, 2−, 3 or F) of each student's final mark we suggested the following code:

```
if (final >= 75)
   cout << "1";
if (final >= 70 && final < 75)
   cout << "2+";
if (final >= 60 && final < 70)
   cout << "2-";
if (final >= 50 && final < 60)
   cout << "3";
if (final < 50)
   cout << "FAIL";
```

This is inefficient and may waste precious computing time. There are actually five separate **if** statements. The (logical) expressions in *all five* (e.g. **final >= 75**) have to be evaluated for each student, although we know that only one can be true; a student cannot get a first class pass and also fail! The following is a more efficient way of coding the problem. For good measure, we will also count how many passed in the first class, how many in the second class, and so on. The **int** variables **firsts**, **upSeconds**, **lowSeconds**, **thirds** and **fails** represent the number of students in each of these respective classes.

```
if (final >= 75) {
   cout << "1";
   firsts++;
}
else if (final >= 70 && final < 75) {
   cout << "2+";
   upSeconds++;
}
else if (final >= 60 && final < 70) {
   cout << "2-";
   lowSeconds++;
}
else if (final >= 50 && final < 60) {
   cout << "3";
   thirds++;
}
else {
   cout << "F";
   fails++;
}
```

This saves time because C++ stops checking as soon as it finds a true expression. So if **final >= 75** is true, it won't bother to check further. The onus rests on you therefore to code the construct correctly, so that *only one* of the expressions is true.

Note how indentation makes the structure easier to follow.

The following layout is recommended for the general `if-else-if` construction:

```
if (expression1)
    statement1;
else if (expression2)
    statement2;
else if (expression3)
    statement3;
...

...

else
    statementE;
```

This is called the `if-else-if` *ladder*. C++ evaluates the expressions from the top down. When it finds a true expression (recall that zero is false, while any other value is true), it executes the associated statement, and bypasses the rest of the ladder. If none of the expressions is true, it executes the final statement (if there is a final `else` clause).

Note that an `else` clause is not a statement in its own right: it must be tacked on to an `if` statement. However, each `if` must nonetheless be terminated with a semi-colon.

Nested `if`s

In general, `else` belongs to the closest `if` that does not already have an `else` associated with it. You can always use block markers to overrule this, but be careful. The next example illustrates the importance of correctly placed block markers.

Consider once again programming the solution of the ubiquitous quadratic equation, $ax^2 + bx + c = 0$. It is necessary to check if $a = 0$, to prevent a division by zero:

```
disc = b * b - 4 * a * c;
if (a != 0)
  if (disc < 0)
    cout << "Complex roots";
  else {
    x1 = (-b + sqrt( disc )) / (2 * a);
    x2 = (-b - sqrt( disc )) / (2 * a);
  }
```

Inserting an extra pair of block markers as shown below, however, makes a division by zero certain if $a = 0$, because the `else` is now forced to belong to the first `if`, instead of the second one by default:

```
disc = b * b - 4 * a * c;
if (a != 0) {      // inserted
  if (disc < 0)
    cout << "Complex roots";
}                  //  inserted
  else {
    x1 = (-b + sqrt( disc )) / (2 * a);
    x2 = (-b - sqrt( disc )) / (2 * a);
  }
```

5.2   Logical expressions

As mentioned in Chapter 2, C++ has no logical or Boolean type, like Pascal and Fortran do. Expressions which evaluate to zero are interpreted as true in the appropriate context; any other value is false.

We introduced the six relational operators in Chapter 2: <, <=, == (equals), != (not equals), >, and >=.

Possibly one of the most common errors in C is to use the assignment instead of == when testing for equality:

```
if (a = 0) ...
```

This is syntactically correct, since the assignment has a value, which may be true or false. Fortunately, Turbo C++ will spot this and give you a

```
possible incorrect assignment
```

warning (however, the code will still compile).

Many C programmers like to shorten their code to the extreme, so you will often see the statement

```
if (expression != 0)
  statement;
```

abbreviated to

```
if (expression)
  statement;
```

which saves typing no less than three characters. Can you see why this shorthand works? If **expression** evaluates to a non-zero value, it will be true, and therefore the (logical) expression

```
expression != 0
```

will of necessity also be true. Since the wear and tear saved on fingers and keyboard is minimal, I would go for the slightly longer but definitely much clearer form!

Although for the purposes of carrying out **if-else** statements any non-zero value is true, Turbo C++ assigns the value 1 to a true expression. E.g. in

```
k = i < j;
```

k will have the value 1 if the expression i < j is true.

We also introduced the two logical operators **&&** (AND) and **||** (OR), and the negation operator **!** (NOT) briefly in Chapter 2. Table 5.1 shows the effects of these operators on the expressions *expr1* and *expr2*. Remember that true (T) is any non-zero value, while false (F) is zero. The precedence levels of these operators are shown in Appendix B. As usual, precedences may be overridden with parentheses. Examples:

```
(b * b == 4 * a * c) && (a != 0)
(final >= 60) && (final < 70)
(a != 0) || (b != 0) || (c != 0)
!((a == 0) && (b == 0) && (c == 0))
```

It is never wrong to use parentheses to make the logic clearer, even if they are syntactically unnecessary.

Incidentally, the last two expressions above are logically equivalent, and are false only when $a = b = c = 0$. It makes you think, doesn't it?

expr1	*expr2*	! *expr1*	*expr1* && *expr2*	*expr1* || *expr2*
F	F	T	F	F
F	T	T	F	T
T	F	F	F	T
T	T	F	T	T

Table 5.1: Truth table

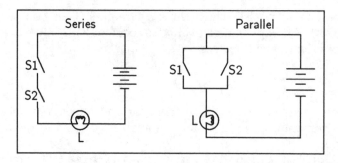

Figure 5.1: Switching circuits

Simulation of a switching circuit

In the following program segment the variables s1 and s2 represent the state
of two switches (ON = true; OFF = false) and 1 represents the state of a light.
The program simulates the circuits in Figure 5.1, where the switches are
arranged either in series or parallel.

```
int 1, s1, s2;
cin >> s1 >> s2;
1 = s1 && s2;      // series
//1 = s1 || s2;    // parallel
cout << 1;
```

When the switches are in series, the light will be on only if both switches
are on. This situation is represented by s1 && s2. When the switches are in
parallel, the light will be on if one or both of the switches is on. This is
represented by s1 || s2.

5.3   Bitwise operators

C++ has six *bitwise* operators which can operate directly on the internal
binary code representation of a number.

The operators & (bitwise AND), | (bitwise inclusive OR) and ^ (bitwise
exclusive OR) perform their operations on the corresponding bits of their
operands, e.g.

```
a = b & c;     // logical AND on bits of b and c
```

The inclusive OR is logically the same as ||. The exclusive OR differs from the
inclusive OR in that it returns true only if its operands have opposite truth
values.

The operators << and >> shift the bits of their left operands left and right respectively, according to the value of their right operands, e.g.

```
x = x << 4;    // times 16
```

Shifting all the bits left (right) by one position is equivalent to multiplying (dividing) by 2. This provides a very fast way of multiplying and dividing by powers of 2.

After a left (right) shift, zeros are filled in on the right (left). If a 1 is shifted out it disappears.

The operator ~ (one's complement) flips all the bits of its operand, e.g.

```
a = ~b
```

Precedence of the bitwise operators is shown in Appendix B.

Binary output

C++ allows you to display a number directly in octal or hex, but not in binary. The next program shows a neat way of printing an integer in binary, using << and &:

```cpp
//binary output of an int
#include <iostream.h>
#include <conio.h>
main()
{
  int i, n;
  cout << "Number in decimal: ";
  cin >> n;
  cout << "Number in binary: ";

  for (i = 1; i <= 8 * sizeof( n ); i++) {
    if (n & 0x8000)
      cout << "1";
    else
      cout << "0";
    n = n << 1;
  }
  cout << endl;
  getch();
  return 0;
}
```

Sample output:

```
Number in decimal: 32767
Number in binary: 0111111111111111
```

The hex constant 0x8000 is 2^{16}, i.e. 1 followed by 15 zeros in binary. The expression n & 0x8000 will be true only if n has a 1 in the same bit position, in which case "1" is output. The statement n = n << 1 shifts all the bits in n one position to the left, so that the next most significant bit of n may be tested against the leading 1 in 0x800. This process is repeated for each bit in n. Neat isn't it?

sizeof() is technically an *operator*, not a function. It returns the length of its argument in bytes.

Incidentally, if you display the binary for -32768 (the smallest integer) you will see why integer values wrap around between this value and 32767.

With a bit of ingenuity you can use & and | to "poke" individual bits.

5.4   The switch statement

The switch statement is also conditional, and enables a program to decide between a number of situations, based on a selector which takes certain (preferably integer or char) values. It is very useful, for example, in menu selection programs:

```
// menu selection
#include <stdio.h>
#include <conio.h>
#include <ctype.h>
main()
{
  char answer;
  do {
    clrscr();
    printf( "MENU OF THE DAY\n\n" );
    printf( "A: Do this\n" );
    printf( "B: Do that\n" );
    printf( "C: Do the other\n" );
    printf( "Q: Quit\n\n" );
    printf( "What is your choice? " );
    answer = toupper( getche() );   // convert answer to uppercase
    printf( "\n" );

    switch (answer) {
      case 'A':
        printf( "Doing this" );
        break;
      case 'B':
        printf( "Doing that" );
        break;
```

```
      case 'C':
        printf( "Doing the other" );
        break;
      case 'Q':
        break;
      default:
        printf( "Sorry, try again!" );
    }
    if (answer != 'Q') {
      printf( "\nPress any key to continue ... " );
      getch();
    }
  } while (answer != 'Q');
  return 0;
}
```

This can be recoded with nested **if-elses**, but the structure is much neater (and consequently clearer) with a **switch**.

The general form of the **switch** statement is

```
  switch (expression){
      case value1:
            statement1;
            break;
      case value2:
            statement2;
            break;

      ...

      default:
            statementD;

  }
```

C++ checks each *value* (selector) until one is found which is equal to *expression*. The corresponding *statement* is executed, and control is transferred to the next statement after the **switch** statement. The optional **default:** selector specifies what to do if none of the values matches the expression.

A **break** statement is necessary to exit from each **case.** if you omit all the **breaks**, as soon as a value is found to match the expression, *all the subsequent statements are executed unconditionally*—which is probably not what you intended. And if it is what you intended, please avoid it; the code will be difficult to follow, and even more difficult to modify.

5.5   Halting with `exit()`

The **main()** function should end with a **return n** statement to avoid a compiler warning. The value of **n** is returned to DOS or the executing program. Different values may be returned from different points in the program.

Another way of halting a program is with **exit(n)**, which does a general shutdown. The argument **n** is returned to DOS or the executing program, and may be used to determine why the program halted.

5.6   Statements best avoided

The two statements introduced in this section are best avoided, for stylistic reasons. They are mentioned in case you encounter them in someone else's code.

The conditional expression

The *conditional expression* is a shorthand version of **if-else**, and takes the form

> *expression1* ? *expression2* : *expression3* ;

expression1 is evaluated. If it is true, the result of the entire expression is *expression2*; otherwise the result is *expression3*. The conditional expression is identical to the **if-else** statement

> if (*expression1*)
>   *expression2*;
> else
>   *expression3*;

Since this is much clearer it is to be preferred.

The goto statement

The statement

> goto LABEL

transfers control unconditionally to the statement labelled **LABEL** (a label is an unused identifier followed by a colon). E.g.

```
        goto THERE;
        x = 67.8;
THERE: y = -1;
```

The statement x = 67.8 is never executed, perhaps causing a ship to sink, an aeroplane to crash, or a shuttle launch to abort.

goto is *never* needed in C or C++. It's hard to see why it has been retained, except perhaps as a way of helping old BASIC and Fortran addicts to kick the habit!

Novices may ask why goto was ever needed. Its use goes back to the bad old days of unstructured versions of BASIC and Fortran, which lacked compound statements and else statements. Consider the following (clear) segment of code:

```
if (exp1)
    { i = 1; j = 2; }
else if (exp2)
    { i = 2; j = 3; }
else
    { i = 3; j = 4; }
```

It says it all. In the absence of block markers and else it must be coded as the following tangle of "spaghetti":

```
        if (!exp1) goto L1;
            i = 1;
            j = 2;
            goto L3;
    L1: if (!exp2) goto L2;
            i = 2;
            j = 3;
            goto L3;
    L2: i = 3;
            j = 4;
    L3: ...
```

Need we say more? except that goto should never be used—it will not be found in any examples in this book. It is mentioned here purely for historical and pedagogical reasons.

Summary

- The if-else statements allow for the conditional execution of blocks of statements.

- `if-else`s may be nested.
- An expression is false if it has the value zero, and true if it has any other value.
- C++ returns a value of 1 for a relational expression if it is true, and 0 if it is false.
- The logical operators `&&` (AND) and `||` (OR) operate on true/false operands.
- The negation operator `!` reverses the truth value of its operand.
- The bitwise operators `&` (AND), `|` (inclusive OR), `^` (exclusive OR), `<<` (left shift), `>>` (right shift), and `~` (bit flip) perform logical operations on the bits in their operands.
- The `switch` statement may be used to select a particular action based on the value of a selector.
- `break` statements should be used in a `switch` statement to exit from each `case`.
- The conditional expression is a shorthand version of `if-else`, which is not so easy to follow.
- The `goto` statement branches unconditionally, and should be avoided at all costs.
- A label is an unused identifier followed by a colon.

Exercises

5.1 Write a program which reads two numbers (which may be equal) and writes out the larger one with a suitable message, or if they are equal, writes out a message to that effect.

5.2 Write a structure plan and program for the following problem: read 10 integers and write out how many of them are positive, negative or zero.

5.3 Design an algorithm (i.e. write the structure plan) for a machine which must give the correct amount of change from a $10 note for any purchase costing less than $10. The plan must specify the number and type of all notes and coins in the change, and should in all cases give as few notes and coins as possible. (Define your own denominations if necessary.)

5.4 Write a program for the general solution of the quadratic equation $ax^2 + bx + c = 0$. Use the structure plan developed in Chapter 3. Your program should be able to handle all possible values of the data *a*, *b*, and *c*. Try it out on the following values of *a*, *b* and *c*:

(a) 1, 1, 1 (complex roots);
(b) 2, 4, 2 (equal roots of -1.0);
(c) 2, 2, -12 (roots of 2.0 and -3.0).

Rewrite your program with complex type (**complex.h**) so that it can handle complex roots, as well as all the other special cases.

5.5 Develop a structure plan for the solution of two simultaneous linear equations (i.e. the equations of two straight lines). Your algorithm must be able to handle all possible situations, viz. lines which are intersecting, parallel, or co-incident. Write a program to implement your algorithm, and test it on some equations for which you know the solutions, e.g.

$$x + y = 3$$
$$2x - y = 3$$

($x = 2$, $y = 1$). **Hint**: begin by deriving an algebraic formula for the solution of the system

$$ax + by = c$$
$$dx + ey = f.$$

The program should read the coefficients *a*, *b*, *c*, *d*, *e* and *f*.

5.6 The largest **int** value supported by Turbo C++ is defined as **INT_MAX** in **limits.h**. Use a bitwise shift operator to compute this value directly as $2^{15} - 1$, bearing in mind that an attempt to compute 2^{15} will cause wraparound.

Chapter 6

Loops

6.1 Deterministic repetition with `for`
  • Factorials! • Binomial coefficient • Limit of a sequence
6.2 `for` with non-integer increments
6.3 Nested `for`s
  • The telephone • Loan repayments
6.4 Non-deterministic loops
  • A guessing game • The `do-while` statement • Doubling time of an investment
  • The `while` statement • `while` versus `do-while` • `while` and `for` • Prime numbers
  • Taylor series for sine • The `break` and `continue` statements
6.5 Reading an unknown amount of data
6.6 Taking stock
  • Modelling a population of gnus • Chaos
Summary
Exercises

We have already seen some examples of the powerful `for` statement, which is used to execute a block of statements repeatedly. This type of structure where the number of repetitions must be determined in advance, is sometimes called *deterministic repetition*. However, it often happens that the condition to end a loop is only satisfied during the execution of the loop itself. This type of structure is called *non-deterministic*. This chapter is mainly about non-deterministic loops, but to make the transition we will first look at some more examples of `for` loops.

6.1   Deterministic repetition with `for`

As we have seen, the general form of `for` is

> `for` (*initialization*; *condition*; *increment*)
>   *statement*;

initialization initializes the loop counter, looping continues while *condition* is true, and *increment* defines how the loop counter is incremented. All three are expressions.

Sometimes it is convenient for *initialization* and *increment* to be comma expressions, e.g.

```
for (x = 0, y = 0; x + y < 100; x++, y++) ...
```

Factorials!

The following program prints a list of n and $n!$ where

$$n! = 1 \times 2 \times 3 \times \ldots \times (n-1) \times n.$$

```
#include <stdio.h>
main()
{
    long double fact = 1;
    unsigned long lfact = 1;
    int n;

    for (n = 1; n <= 20; n++) {
        lfact = n * lfact;
        fact =  n * fact;
        printf( "%3d  %20lu  %20.0Lf\n", n, lfact, fact );
    }
    return 0;
}
```

Do you trust `lfact` or `fact`, and why?

Note the format codes for `unsigned long (lu)` and `long double (Lf)`.

Binomial coefficient

This is widely used in statistics. The number of ways of choosing r objects out of n without regard to order is given by

$$\binom{n}{r} = \frac{n!}{r!(n-r)!} = \frac{n(n-1)(n-2)\cdots(n-r+1)}{r!}, \tag{6.1}$$

$$\text{e.g.} \binom{10}{3} = \frac{10!}{3! \times 7!} = \frac{10 \times 9 \times 8}{1 \times 2 \times 3}.$$

If the form involving factorials is used, the numbers can get very big, causing the wrap-around illustrate in the factorial example. But using the right-most expression in Equation (6.1) is much more efficient:

```
#include <iostream.h>
main()
{
  unsigned int bin = 1;
  unsigned int k, n, r;
  cout << "n and r? ";
  cin >> n >> r;

  for (k = 1; k <= r; k++)
    bin = bin * (n - k + 1) / k;
  cout << "NcR: " << bin << endl;
  return 0;
}
```

Limit of a sequence

for loops are ideal for computing successive members of a sequence. This example also highlights a problem that sometimes occurs when computing a limit. Consider the sequence

$$x_n = a^n/n!, \quad n = 1, 2, 3, \ldots$$

where a is any constant, and $n!$ is the factorial function defined above. The question is: what is the limit of this sequence as n gets indefinitely large? Let's take the case $a = 10$. If we try to compute x_n directly we could get into trouble, because $n!$ gets large very rapidly as n increases, and wrap-around or overflow could occur. However, the situation is neatly transformed if we spot that x_n is related to x_{n-1} as follows:

$$x_n = ax_{n-1}/n.$$

There are no numerical problems now. The following program computes x_n for $a = 10$, and increasing values of n, and prints it for every tenth value of n:

```
#include <stdio.h>
main()
{
  int n;
  float a = 10;
  float x = 1;

  for (n = 1; n <= 100; n++) {
    x = a * x / n;
```

```
        if (n % 10 == 0)
            printf( "%3d    %12.4e\n", n, x );
    }
    return 0;
}
```

Output:

```
    10      2.7557e+03
    20      4.1103e+01
    30      3.7700e-03
    40      1.2256e-08
    50      3.2880e-15
    60      1.2018e-22
    70      8.3482e-31
    80      1.3972e-39
    90      0.0000e+00
   100      0.0000e+00
```

From these results it appears that the limit is zero; this may be proved mathematically.

6.2   `for` with non-integer increments

There are many situations in scientific and engineering computing when one wants to make non-integer increments in a loop. Consider again the stone thrown vertically upwards in Chapter 2. Suppose it is launched at time $t = 0$ seconds, and we want to compute its position $s(t)$ between times $t = t_0$ and $t = t_1$ every dt seconds. These times are most unlikely to be integers.
    The obvious thing to do is to set up a `for` loop:

```
#include <iostream.h>
#include <stdio.h>
main()
{
    const double g = 9.8;
    double dt, s, t, t0, t1;
    double u = 60;

    cout << "Enter t0, t1, dt: ";
    cin >> t0 >> t1 >> dt;

    for (t = t0; t <= t1; t += dt) {
        s = u * t - g / 2 * t * t;
        printf( "%18.8e   %8.2f\n", t, s );
    }
    return 0;
}
```

The problem here is to stop looping at the right place. If you run the program with $t_0 = 0$, $t_1 = 1$, and $dt = 0.1$ you will find that the final value of t used in the loop is 0.99, and not 1 as expected. This is because of rounding error. At the end of the last executed loop the value of t is actually $0.99 + \epsilon$, where ϵ is a very small number, as a result of the repeated increments `t += dt`. If there were to be another loop, its final value would be $t_1 + \epsilon$, which would violate the condition `t <= t1`.

The solution is to add a small quantity to `t1` in the condition, big enough to guarantee the final loop, but not so big as to generate an extra loop. One way to achieve this is to add a multiple of `DBL_EPSILON` (**float.h**—not to be confused with ϵ above) to `t1`. This constant is the smallest **double** value obtainable with your C++ compiler. The `for` statement would then read

```
for (t = t0; t <= t1 + 10 * DBL_EPSILON; t += dt)
```

where the factor 10 is obtained by trial-and-error. Another (probably better) way is to add a fraction of `dt` to `t1` in the condition, e.g. `0.1 * dt`.

A further interesting problem arises. Suppose we still want to compute $s(t)$ every dt seconds, but only want to print it every h seconds—this is a common problem in numerical analysis, where the step-length dt might be very small. It helps now to introduce an **int** variable, say `i`, as an iteration counter. Suppose `i` is initialized to 1, and we always want output on the first iteration. We therefore have to skip the next h/dt iterations before printing again. This means that we want output whenever $(i-1)$ is an exact multiple of h/dt. This can be achieved by prefacing the `printf()` above with an **if**,

```
if ((i-1) % (int( h/dt + 10 * DBL_EPSILON )) == 0)
    printf ...
```

where the same allowance has been made for rounding error, and the value of h must be input.

Again, we could use `0.1 * dt` instead of `10 * DBL_EPSILON`.

The complete program to calculate $s(t)$ from $t = t_0$ to t_1 in steps of dt, with output every h seconds is then

```
#include <iostream.h>
#include <float.h>
#include <stdio.h>
main()
{
   const double g = 9.8;
   double dt, h, s, t, t0, t1;
   double u = 60;
   int i = 1;
```

```
    cout << "Enter t0, t1, dt, h: ";
    cin >> t0 >> t1 >> dt >> h;

    for (t = t0; t <= t1 + 10 * DBL_EPSILON; t += dt) {
      s = u * t - g / 2 * t * t;
      if ((i-1) % (int( h/dt + 10 * DBL_EPSILON )) == 0)
        printf( "%18.8e  %8.2f\n", t, s );
      i++;
    }
    return 0;
}
```

int is used to typecast its argument to int type.

6.3   Nested fors

for loops can be nested inside each other. The loop counter of the inner for moves faster.

The telephone

This example imitates the ringing of a certain type of telephone (don't leave out the nosound() statements!):

```
    #include <dos.h>
    main()
    {
      int i, tring;

      for (tring = 1; tring <= 2; tring ++) {
        for (i = 1; i <= 30; i++) {
          sound( 600 );
          delay( 30 );
          nosound();
          sound( 1500 );
          delay( 30 );
          nosound();
        }
        delay( 2000 );
      }
    }
```

Loan repayments

If a regular fixed payment P is made n times a year to repay a loan of amount A over a period of k years, where the nominal annual interest rate is

r, P is given by

$$P = \frac{rA(1 + r/n)^{nk}}{n[(1 + r/n)^{nk} - 1]}. \tag{6.2}$$

The next program uses nested **fors** to print a table of the repayments on a loan of $1 000 over 15, 20 or 25 years, at interest rates that vary from 10% to 20% per annum. P is directly proportional to A in Equation (6.2). Therefore the repayments on a loan of any amount may be found from the table generated by the program, by simple proportion.

```
float a = 1000;  // principal
int n = 12;      // number of payments per year
float k, p, rate, x;

clrscr();
printf( "rate    15 yrs   20 yrs   25 yrs   30 yrs\n" );
printf( "\n" );

for (rate = 0.1; rate <= 0.2501; rate += 0.01) { // loop on interest rate
  printf( "%3.0f%%", 100 * rate );               // ... allow for rounding

  for (k = 15; k <= 30; k += 5) {         // loop on period of repayment
    x = pow( 1 + rate / n, n * k );
    p = rate / n * a * x / (x - 1);
    printf( "%9.2f", p );
  }
  printf( "\n" );
}
```

Some sample output:

rate	15 yrs	20 yrs	25 yrs	30 yrs
10%	10.75	9.65	9.09	8.78
11%	11.37	10.32	9.80	9.52
...				
24%	20.58	20.17	20.05	20.02
25%	21.36	20.98	20.88	20.85

Note that to print the % symbol it must be repeated in the **printf()** control string.

6.4 Non-deterministic loops

Deterministic loops all have in common the fact that you can work out in principle exactly how many repetitions are required before the loop starts. But in the next example, there is no way *in principle* of working out the number of repeats, so a different construct is needed.

A guessing game

The problem is easy to state. The program "thinks" of an integer between 1 and 10 (i.e. generates one at random). You have to guess it. If your guess is too high or too low, the program must say so. If your guess is correct, a message of congratulations must be displayed.

A little more thought is required here, so a structure plan might be helpful:

1. Generate random integer
2. Repeat:
           Ask user (assumed male) for guess
           If guess is too low
                   Tell him it is too low
           Otherwise if guess is too high
                   Tell him it is too high
           Otherwise
                   Polite congratulations
      Until guess is correct
3. Stop.

Here is the program:

```c
#include <stdio.h>
#include <stdlib.h>
#include <time.h>
main()
{
    int i, number, myguess;
    char s[80];

    randomize();                    // seed the random number generator
    number = random( 10 ) + 1;      // in the range 1 to 10

    do {
      puts( "What is your guess? " );
      gets( s );
      myguess = atoi( s );
      if (myguess < number)
        printf( "Too low\n" );
      else if (myguess > number)
        printf( "Too high\n" );
```

```
      else {
        printf( "Well done!\n" );
        for (i = 1; i <= 10; i++) printf( "\7" );
      }
    }
    while (number != myguess);
  }
```

Try it out a few times. Note that the **do-while** loop repeats as long as `number` is not equal `myguess`. There is no way of knowing in principle how many loops will be needed before they are equal. The problem is truly non-deterministic.

Note also the alternative form of input by means of `gets()` and `atoi()`. This avoids a time consuming include of **iostream.h**.

The do-while statement

The general form of the **do-while** statement is

```
    do {
      statement;
    } while (condition);
```

The block markers are not strictly necessary when there is only one statement; however, they improve readability.

The **do-while** repeats *statement* while the expression *condition* remains true (or until it becomes false). The condition is tested after each repeat before making another repeat. Since the condition is at the end of the loop, *statement* will always be executed *at least once*. We saw in Chapter 5 that **do-while** is useful for programming menu selection, since the menu must be presented at least once.

Doubling time of an investment

Suppose we have invested some money which draws 10% interest per year, compounded. We would like to know how long it takes for the investment to double. More specifically, we want a statement of the account each year, *until* the balance has doubled. The English statement of the problem hints heavily that we should use a non-deterministic loop. The structure plan and program for the problem are:

1. Start
2. Initialize balance, year, rate, interest
3. Write headings

4. Repeat

      Update balance according to interest rate

      Write year, interest, balance

   until balance exceeds twice original balance

5. Stop.

```
int year = 0;
double interest, newbal, oldbal, rate;
char str[80];

cout << "Original balance:";
cin >> oldbal;
rate = 0.1;
newbal = oldbal;
printf( "%4s   %10s   %10s\n", "Year", "Interest", "Balance" );

do {
  interest = rate * newbal;
  newbal += interest;
  year++;
  printf( "%4d   %10.2f   %10.2f\n", year, interest, newbal );
} while (newbal <= 2 * oldbal);
```

Note that the more natural phrase in the structure plan "until balance exceeds twice original balance" must be coded as

```
while (newbal <= 2 * oldbal);
```

This condition is checked each time before another iteration. Repetition occurs only if the condition is true. The **do-while** must be executed at least once, since you must invest your money for at least a year for anything to happen. The output looks like this (for an opening balance of $1 000):

```
Year      Interest      Balance
 1        100.00        1100.00
 2        110.00        1210.00
...
 7        177.16        1948.72
 8        194.87        2143.59
```

Note that when the last repeat has been completed, the condition to repeat is false for the first time, since the new balance ($2 143.59) is more than $2 000. Note also that a deterministic **for** *cannot* be used here because we don't know how many iterations are going to be needed until after the program has run (although in this example perhaps you *could* work out in advance how many repeats are needed?).

If you want to write the new balance only while it is *less* than $2 000, all that has to be done is to move

```
printf( "%4d    %10.2f    %10.2f\n", year, interest, newbal );
```

until it is the first statement in the do-while loop (interest will have to be initialized to zero). Note that the starting balance of zero is written now.

The original do-while can be replaced by a slightly different while statement, as follows:

```
while (newbal < 2 * oldbal) {
  interest = rate * newbal;
  newbal += interest;
  year++;
  printf( "%4d    %10.2f    %10.2f\n", year, interest, newbal );
}
```

Either form is acceptable, although the purists might prefer the while version since this states the condition for repeating clearly at the beginning of the loop. This condition is immediately apparent to anyone reading the program; you do not have to search for the end of the loop to find the condition to repeating.

The while statement

In general the while statement looks like this:

```
while (condition)
   statement;
```

The while construct repeats the *statement* (which may be a number of statements in block markers) *while* its *condition* remains true. The condition therefore is the condition to repeat once again. The condition is tested each time *before* *statement* is repeated. Since the condition is evaluated before *statement* is executed, it is possible to arrange for *statement* not to be executed at all under certain circumstances.

while versus do-while

A problem coded with while can logically always be rewritten with do-while, and vice versa (try it if you are skeptical!). The question then arises: when should we use do-while and when should we use while?

This is a matter of taste. There is, however, a large body of opinion among programmers which maintains that it is good programming style for conditions under which loops are repeated to be stated at the *beginning* of the loop. This favours the `while` construct, since its condition is stated at the beginning. However, in situations where at least one repeat must be made, it often seems more natural to use the `do-while` construct.

`while` and `for`

Note that the `for` statement as presented in Section 6.1 is identical to the following:

```
initialization;
while (condition) {
    statement;
    increment;
}
```

In fact the compiler often generates identical code.

Prime numbers

Many people are obsessed with prime numbers, and most books on programming have to include a program to test if a given number is prime. So here's mine.

A number is prime if it is not an exact multiple of any other number except itself and 1, i.e. if it has no factors except itself and 1. The easiest plan of attack then is as follows. Suppose P is the number to be tested. See if any numbers N can be found that divide into P without remainder. If there are none, P is prime. Which numbers N should we try? Well, we can speed things up by restricting P to odd numbers, so we only have to try odd divisors N. When do we stop testing? When $N = P$? No, we can stop a lot sooner. In fact, we can stop once N reaches $\sqrt{P}$, since if there is a factor greater than $\sqrt{P}$ there must be a corresponding one less than $\sqrt{P}$, which we would have found. And where do we start? Well, since $N = 1$ will be a factor of any P, we should start at $N = 3$. The structure plan is as follows:

1. Read P
2. Initialize N to 3
3. Find remainder R when P is divided by N
4. While $R \neq 0$ and $N < \sqrt{P}$ repeat:
   Increase N by 2
   Find R when P is divided by N

    5. If $R \neq 0$ then

         P is prime

    Else

         P is not prime

    6. Stop.

Note that a `while` loop is going to be used because there may be no repeats—
R might be zero the first time. Note also that there are *two* conditions
under which the loop will stop. Consequently, an `if` is required after
completion of the loop to determine which condition stopped it. Here's the
program:

```
main()
{
    int n = 3;
    unsigned long p, r;
    double sqrtp;
    char str[20];
    cout << "Gimme an odd integer: ";
    cin >> p;
    sqrtp = sqrt( p );
    r = p % n;

    while (r != 0 && n < sqrtp) {
      n += 2;
      r = p % n;
    }

    if (r != 0)
      cout << p << " is prime" << endl;
    else
      cout << p << " is NOT prime" << endl;
    return 0;
}
```

Try it out on the following: 4 058 879 (not prime), 193 707 721 (prime) and
2 147 483 647 (prime). If such things interest you, the largest prime number
at the time of writing is $2^{756\,839} - 1$. It has 227 832 digits and takes up
about seven pages of newsprint. Obviously this program cannot test such a
large number, since it's unimaginably greater than the largest integer
which can be represented by a C++ fundamental type. Ways of testing
such huge numbers for primality are described in D.E. Knuth, *The Art of
Computer Programming. Volume 2: Seminumerical Algorithms* (Addison-
Wesley, 1981).

Taylor series for sine

You may have wondered how a computer calculates functions such as sine and cosine. Really ancient computers actually used to look up tables entered in memory, but young and upwardly mobile ones are more cunning. Mathematically, it can be shown that $\sin x$, for example, is the sum of an infinite series (called a Taylor series), as follows:

$$\sin x = x - \frac{x^3}{3!} + \frac{x^5}{5!} - \frac{x^7}{7!} + \cdots$$

We obviously can't compute the sum of an infinite series, but we can at least arrange to stop after the terms in the series are all less than some prescribed value, say 10^{-6}. It can be shown that we can always get a term less than some arbitrarily small number by going far enough in the Taylor series. As an exercise you should try to write a structure plan before studying the program below. The main idea is to construct each term in the series from the previous one, as described in the limit problem in Section 6.1. In constructing the denominator each time, use has been made of the fact that if k is any integer, $2k$ is even and $2k+1$ is odd. So if $k=0$ labels the first term (x), the second term (labelled by $k=1$) can be obtained from the first term by multiplying it by

$$\frac{-x^2}{2k(2k+1)}.$$

Work out the first few terms by hand as a check. The program is as follows:

```
main()
{
   int k = 1;             // term counter
   int maxTerms = 10;    // max number of terms
   double error = 1e-6;  // max error allowed
   double sine;          // sum of series
   double term;          // general term in series
   double x;             // angle in radians

   cout << "Angle in degrees: ";
   cin >> x;
   x = x * M_PI / 180;    // convert to radians
   term = x;              // first term in series
   sine = term;           // get started

   while (fabs( term ) > error && k <= maxTerms) {
      term = -term * x * x / (2 * k * (2 * k + 1));
```

```
      k++;
      sine = sine + term;
   }

   if (fabs( term ) > error)
      cout << "Series did not converge" << endl;
   else {
      cout << "After " << k << " terms Taylor series gives "
                       << sine << endl;
      cout << "Turbo C++ library function: " << sin(x) << endl;
   }
   return 0;
}
```

Note that **fabs()** is needed to return the absolute value of a **double** value. If you use **abs()** (a fairly natural mistake), the program compiles but gives the wrong answer, since **abs()** returns a integer, rounded down. As soon as **term** is less than 1, **abs(term)** will be zero, and the **while** loop will stop.

while is appropriate here since the initial term might be small enough.

Note also that there are two conditions for terminating the loop. Consequently, an **if** is required after the **while** to establish which condition was satisfied.

If you know some C already, you may be tempted to use a **for** loop with a **break** to escape from the loop when **term** gets small enough:

```
for (k = 1; k <= maxTerms; k++) {
   if (fabs( term ) <= error)
      break;
   term = -term * x * x / (2 * k * (2 * k + 1));
   sine = sine + term;
}
```

Although this works perfectly well, it is definitely *not recommended* (some programmers will definitely disagree!). The reasons are as follows. My objection is that all the conditions to stop repeating are not clear at the very top of the loop—after a cursory glance you might think it is a deterministic loop. But, you may argue, I am splitting hairs; after all, the second condition to stop repeating is in the very next line. However, after a few months you might introduce further **breaks** later in the block. The trouble is that this innocent looking structure allows for ad-hoc modifications later—at which stage you might easily loose track of what all the conditions for repeating are.

The principle is: *all conditions for repeating should be stated clearly in one place—at the top or the end of the loop*.

The break and continue statements

The **break** statement may be used to jump out of a loop structure as we have just seen, although this is not recommended, e.g.

```
do {
  if (condition1)
    break;
  ...
} while (condition2);
```

It has a legitimate use, however, in the **switch** statement, as we saw in Chapter 5.

The **continue** is a variation of **break**. It forces a loop to start its next iteration prematurely, e.g.

```
for (i = 1; i <= 10; i++) {
  ...
  if (condition)
    continue;
  ...
}
```

When **condition** is true the rest of the loop is ignored, i is incremented, and a new loop starts immediately. The use of **continue** is not recommended for the same reasons that **break** is not.

6.5   Reading an unknown amount of data

A **while** statement may be used to read an unknown amount of data from a disk file. Suppose we have some numbers in the disk file **data**. The following program reads the data, prints them, and finds their mean:

```
#include <fstream.h>
main()
{
  fstream myin( "data", ios::in);
  int n = 0;
  double mean, sum, x;
  sum = 0;

  while (myin >> x) {            // read x and test for EOF
    sum += x;                    // add x
    cout << x << "   ";          // print it
    n++;                         // count it
  }
```

```
if (n != 0) {
  mean = sum / n;
  cout << "Sum: " << sum << "   mean: " << mean << endl;
}
else
  cout << "Sorry, no data" << endl;
return 0;
}
```

The program creats an object `myin` of the class `fstream`, and initializes it to
the disk file **data**. All text files have a special *end-of-file* character to mark the
end of the file. If `myin` attempts to read this character it returns a value of
false. Hence the condition in the `while` statement serves a double purpose: to
read data, and to detect an attempt to read past the end of the file. See
Chapter 16 for more details.

Note that the program also works when there is no data in the file, because
the end-of-file is detected immediately. In that case, since `n` will be zero, a
division by zero must be prevented.

6.6   Taking stock

Once you have mastered loops a great vista of interesting and solvable
problems begins to unfold. Two such problems are presented in this section.

Modelling a population of gnus

The wildebeest (gnu) population in the Kruger National Park, South Africa,
declined from about 14 000 in 1969 to 6 700 in 1975, giving rise to considerable
concern (see Table 6.1). Mathematical modelling techniques were applied to
this problem, as described in A.M. Starfield and A.L. Bleloch, *Building Models
for Conservation and Wildlife Management* (MacMillan, 1986).

The population in year k may be divided into four biologically distinct age
groups: c_k, the number of new-born calves; y_k, the number of yearlings; t_k, the
number of two-year-olds; w_k, the number of adults (older than two years).

We can think of the population as a vector with four components, each
measured annually (in January, when the females calve). The essence of the
problem is to predict the next year's vector, given an initial population at
some time. At this stage we turn to the game rangers, who tell us that
yearlings do not produce young—this is the prerogative of the two-year-olds
and adults. We thus have the equation modelling the dynamics of calves:

$$c_{k+1} = aw_{k+1} + a't_{k+1}, \tag{6.3}$$

where a and a' are the birth-rates (number of expected offspring per individual per year) for adults and two-year-olds respectively. It turns out that the best way to model yearling population dynamics is simply

$$y_{k+1} = bc_k, \tag{6.4}$$

where b is the overall survival-rate for calves. Obviously this year's yearlings can only come from last year's calves, so $b < 1$.

For the other two age groups life is fairly uncomplicated. Their members die of practically only one cause—lion attack. This is modelled as follows. It seems that lion are indiscriminate in their attacks on all groups except the calves. Therefore the number of yearlings taken by lion is in direct proportion to the fraction of yearlings in the total non-calf population, and so on. Of course the number taken in year k is also in proportion to the number of hunting lion in year k—call this number l_k. So we can model the number of two-year-olds and adults with

$$t_{k+1} = y_k - \frac{gl_k y_k}{y_k + t_k + w_k} \tag{6.5}$$

and

$$w_{k+1} = w_k + t_k - \frac{gl_k(t_k + w_k)}{y_k + t_k + w_k}, \tag{6.6}$$

where g is the lion kill-rate (number of gnu taken per lion per year).

The order in which these equations are computed is important. w_{k+1} and t_{k+1} must be computed *before* c_{k+1}.

After consultation with game rangers, a is estimated as 0.45, and a' as 0.15 (Starfied and Bleloch). The lion kill-rate is between 2.5 and 4 (lion have other choices on their menu), and calf survival b is between 0.5 and 0.7.

More precise values of g and b for each year were found "experimentally" by seeing which values gave a total population that agreed more or less with the annual census figures. Fitting the model to the census data was further complicated by the culling (killing by rangers) of wildebees between 1969 and 1972, to relieve pressure on the vegetation. However, since culling is indiscriminate among the non-calf population it is easy to argue that the term gl_k in Equations (6.5) and (6.6) must be replaced by $(gl_k + d_k)$, where d_k is the total number culled in year k. This number is accurately known.

The model run starts in 1969 ($k = 1$), with $c_1 = 3660$, $y_1 = 2240$, $t_1 = 1680$ and $w_1 = 6440$. These figures are from the census. Table 6.1 shows the total population predicted by the model compared with the census data. The

Year	l_k	d_k	b	g	Census	Model 1	Model 2
1969	500	572	0.5	4	14 020		
1970	520	550	0.5	4	11 800	12 617	13 140
1971	530	302	0.5	4	10 600	11 233	12 932
1972	540	78	0.5	4	8 000	9 847	12 248
1973	550	0	0.7	3.5	7 700	8 457	11 369
1974	540	0	0.7	3.5	–	7 679	11 239
1975					6 700	6 779	11 120

Table 6.1: Wildebeest model data and output

column headed *Model 1* shows projections taking the annual culling into account, whereas *Model 2* assumes *no* culling (by setting $d_k = 0$ when running the model). Note also that a particular projection is based on the input in the previous row, e.g. if $l_1 = 500$, $d_1 = 572$, $b = 0.5$ and $g = 4$, the model predicts

$$c_2 + y_2 + t_2 + w_2 = 12617.$$

The parameters g and b are realistic. 1970–1972 were dry years in the Park, when lion killed regularly at waterholes. This justifies the higher g and lower b values. In subsequent years the lion did not kill so freely, since the improved vegetation and declining wildebeest population made the prey more difficult to find. The same factors lead to a higher calf survival.

The program below implements this model. Note that two sets of variables are used to represent the age groups. c, y, t and w represent values in year k, while nc, ny, nt and nw represent values in year $k + 1$. One might have been tempted to code the update equations as follows:

```
y = b * c;
t = y - (g * l + d) * y / (y + t + w);
...
```

This, however, would mean that we would be using *next year's* y, obtained from Equation (6.4), on the righthand side of Equation (6.5), instead of *this* year's. Using two sets of variables means that the set representing the current year's values must be updated at the end of each year in readiness for next year's update. Try the program out with different parameter values, to see what happens. Also try running it for longer.

```
main()
{
```

```
int line = 5;              // line on output screen
int yr;                    // year
double a = 0.45;           // adult birth-rate
double ad = 0.15;          // a': two-year-old birth-rate
double c = 3660;           // calves
double y = 2240;           // yearlings
double t = 1680;           // two-year-olds
double w = 6440;           // adults
double nc, ny, nt, nw;     // next year's population
double l, d, b, g;         // model parameters
double tot;                // total population

clrscr();
highvideo();
cputs( "Starfield's Wildebees Model (Ctrl-break twice to end)" );
normvideo();
gotoxy(1, 3);              // line 3
cputs( "Year    l    d    b    g     Model" );
gotoxy(1, 5);

for (yr = 1969; yr <= 1974; yr++) {
  if (yr == 1969)
    cprintf( "%4d    ", yr );
  cin >> l >> d >> b >> g;
  ny = b * c;
  nt = y - (g * l + d) * y / (y + t + w);
  nw = w + t - (g * l + d) * (t + w) / (y + t + w);
  nc = a * nw + ad * nt;
  c = nc;
  y = ny;
  t = nt;
  w = nw;
  tot = c + y + t + w;
  line++;
  gotoxy(1, line);
  cprintf( "%4d", yr+1 );
  gotoxy( 27, line);
  cprintf( "%7.0f", tot );
  gotoxy( 6, line);
}

return 0;
}
```

Some new library functions have been introduced here. They all handle direct-video output (as opposed to output to the standard output device, which may be redirected to a DOS file). Their prototypes are declared in **conio.h**.

cprintf() (c for console) is similar to printf(), except that it does not translate \n into a carriage-return (\r) as well, as printf() does.

`highvideo()` selects high intensity characters (only for **conio.h** functions). `normvideo()` selects normal intensity. You can guess how to select low intensity.

`cputs()` is the **conio.h** equivalent of `puts()`.

Chaos

It has been said that a picture is worth a thousand words. If you have a scientific or engineering interest in programming, you will be keen to draw graphs. Turbo C++ graphics is discussed in detail in Chapter 13 — a preview is given here without much explanation.

A very interesting iterative relationship that has been studied a lot recently is defined by

$$y_{k+1} = ry_k(1 - y_k).$$

Given y_0 and r, successive y_k's may be computed very easily, e.g. if $y_0 = 0.2$ and $r = 1$, then $y_1 = 0.16$, $y_2 = 0.1334$, and so on. This formula is often used to model population growth in cases where the growth is not unlimited, but is restricted by shortage of food, living area, etc.

y_k exhibits fascinating behaviour, known as *mathematical chaos*, for values of r between 3 and 4 (independent of y_0). The following program plots y_k against k. Values of r that give particularly interesting graphs are 3.3, 3.5, 3.5668, 3.575, 3.5766, 3.738, 3.8287, and many more that can be found by patient exploration.

A two-dimensional form of this problem is related to the *Mandelbrot set*.

```
#include <stdio.h>
#include <graphics.h>
#include <conio.h>
main()
{
  int k;
  float r, y;
  char ch;
  int graphdriver, graphmode;
  graphdriver = DETECT;
  initgraph( &graphdriver, &graphmode, "o:\\ama\\borlandc\\bgi" );
  y = 0.2;

  do {
    restorecrtmode();
    printf( "r: " );
    scanf( " %f", &r );
    setgraphmode( graphmode );
```

```
        putpixel(0, y, WHITE);

        for (k = 1; k <= getmaxx(); k ++) {
          y = r * y * (1 - y);
          putpixel( k, 0.5 * getmaxy() * (1 - y), WHITE );
        }                                        // ... blow up y and invert

        getch();
      } while (r);              // stop when r = 0

      closegraph();
      return 0;
    }
```

Turbo C++ graphics programs require access to special **.bgi** (Borland Graphics Interface) files, which should be supplied with the software. The third argument of **initgraph()** must be a string giving the path to the subdirectory where the **.bgi** files may be found. Remember that the backslash must be repeated, otherwise the character following it is interpreted as an escape character.

Don't forget the ampersands (**&**) in front of the non-string arguments of **initgraph()** and **scanf()**. Their significance will emerge later.

scanf() is the input equivalent of **printf()** (include **stdio.h**). It also needs a control string with format codes describing the values to be input. **cin** is much easier to use, but including **iostream.h** takes a good deal longer than **stdio.h**!

The smallest area which can be lit up on a graphics screen with a particular graphics card is called a *pixel* (picture element). The VGA graphics card, for example, supports 640 pixels horizontally and 480 vertically in high resolution mode. Just to be perverse, the coordinates of the top left corner of the screen are $(0, 0)$, while those of the bottom right corner are $(639, 479)$.

getmaxy() returns the vertical dimensions of the screen in pixels. The argument

```
    0.5 * getmaxy() * (1 - y)
```

of **putpixel()** serves to (a) enlarge the value of y_k to fill half the screen, and (b) invert it so that it appears the right way up.

Summary

- A **for** statement should be used to program a deterministic loop, where the number of repeats is known to the program (i.e. in principle to the programmer) *before* the loop is encountered. This situation is characterized by the general structure plan:

> Repeat N times:
> > Block of statements to be repeated

where N is known or computed *before* the loop is encountered for the first time, and is not changed by the block.

- A `while` or a `do-while` statement should be used to program a non-deterministic repeat structure, where the exact number of repeats is *not* known in advance. Another way of saying this is that these statements should be used whenever the truth value of the condition for repeating is changed in the body of the loop. This situation is characterized by the following two structure plans:

> > While *condition* is true repeat:
> > > statements to be repeated (reset truth value of *condition*).

or

> > Repeat:
> > > statements to be repeated (reset truth value of *condition*)
> > while *condition* is true.

Note that *condition* is the condition to repeat.

- The statements in a `while` construct may sometimes never be executed.
- The statements in a `do-while` construct are always executed at least once.
- If the loop counter in a loop is not an integer, there could be problems with rounding error.
- Loops may be nested to any depth.
- Good programming style requires that the condition for repeating a loop should be stated at the top or at the end of the loop.

Exercises

6.1 Write a program to find the sum of the successive even integers 2, 4, ..., 200. (Answer: 10100)

6.2 Write a program which produces a table of $\sin x$ and $\cos x$ for angles x from $0°$ to $90°$ in steps of $15°$.

6.3 A person deposits \$1 000 in a bank. Interest is compounded monthly at the rate of 1% per month. Write a program which will compute the monthly balance, but write it only *annually* for 10 years (use nested `for` loops, with the outer loop for 10 years, and the inner loop for 12 months). Note that after 10 years, the balance is \$3 300.39, whereas if interest had been compounded annually at the rate of 12% per year the balance would only have been \$3 105.85.

6.4 There are many formulae for computing π (the ratio of a circle's circumference to its diameter). The simplest is

$$\frac{\pi}{4} = 1 - 1/3 + 1/5 - 1/7 + 1/9 - \ldots \qquad (6.7)$$

which comes from putting $x = 1$ in the series

$$\arctan x = x - \frac{x^3}{3} + \frac{x^5}{5} - \frac{x^7}{7} + \frac{x^9}{9} - \ldots \qquad (6.8)$$

(a) Write a program to compute π using Equation (6.7). Use as many terms in the series as your computer will reasonably allow (start modestly, with 100 terms, say, and re-run your program with more and more each time). You should find that the series converges very slowly, i.e. it takes a lot of terms to get fairly close to π.

(b) Rearranging the series speeds up the convergence:

$$\frac{\pi}{8} = \frac{1}{1 \times 3} + \frac{1}{5 \times 7} + \frac{1}{9 \times 11} \ldots$$

Write a program to compute π using this series instead. You should find that you need fewer terms to reach the same level of accuracy that you got in (a).

(c) One of the fastest series for π is

$$\frac{\pi}{4} = 6 \arctan \frac{1}{8} + 2 \arctan \frac{1}{57} + \arctan \frac{1}{239}.$$

Use this formula to compute π. Don't use the library function `atan()` to compute the arctangents, since that would be cheating. Rather use Equation (6.8).

6.5 The following method of computing π is due to Archimedes:

1. Let $A = 1$ and $N = 6$
2. Repeat 10 times, say:
    Replace N by $2N$
    Replace A by $\sqrt{2 - \sqrt{(4 - A^2)}}$
    Let $L = NA/2$
    Let $U = L/\sqrt{1 - A^2/2}$
    Let $P = (U + L)/2$ (estimate of π)
    Let $E = (U - L)/2$ (estimate of error)
    Print N, P, E
3. Stop.

Write a program to implement the algorithm.

6.6 Write a program to compute a table of the function

$$f(x) = x \sin\left[\frac{\pi(1 + 20x)}{2}\right]$$

over the (closed) interval $[-1, 1]$ using increments in x of (a) 0.2 (b) 0.1 and (c) 0.01. Watch out for rounding error.

Use your tables to plot a graph of $f(x)$ for the three cases, and observe that the tables for (a) and (b) give totally the wrong picture of $f(x)$. When you have learnt some graphics get your program to draw the graph of $f(x)$ for the three cases superimposed.

6.7 The transcendental number e (2.718281828 ...) can be shown to be the limit of

$$\frac{1}{(1 - x)^{1/x}}$$

as x tends to zero (from above). Write a program which shows how this expression converges to e as x gets closer and closer to zero.

6.8 A square wave of period T may be defined by the function

$$f(t) = \begin{cases} 1 & (0 < t < T) \\ -1 & (-T < t < 0). \end{cases}$$

The Fourier series for $f(t)$ is given by

$$\frac{4}{\pi} \sum_{k=0}^{\infty} \frac{1}{2k+1} \sin\left[\frac{(2k+1)\pi t}{T}\right].$$

It is of interest to know how many terms are needed for a good approximation to this infinite sum. Taking $T = 1$, write a program to compute and display the sum to n terms of the series for t from 0 to 1 in steps of 0.1, say. Run the program for different values of n, e.g. 1, 3, 6, etc.

A graphical version of the solution is given in Chapter 13.

6.9 If an amount of money A is invested for k years at a nominal annual interest rate r (expressed as a decimal fraction), the value V of the investment after k years is given by

$$V = A(1 + r/n)^{nk}$$

where n is the number of compounding periods per year. Write a program to compute V as n gets larger and larger, i.e. as the compounding periods become more and more frequent, like monthly, daily, hourly, etc. Take $A = 1000$, $r = 4\%$ and $k = 10$ years. You should observe that your output gradually approaches a limit. **Hint**: use a `for` loop which doubles n each time, starting with $n = 1$.

Also compute the value of the formula Ae^{rk} for the same values of A, r and k (use the library function `exp()`), and compare this value with the values of V computed above. What do you conclude?

6.10 Write a program to compute the sum of the series $1 + 2 + 3\ldots$ such that the sum is as large as possible without exceeding 100. The program should write out how many terms are used in the sum.

6.11 One of the programs in Section 6.4 shows that an amount of $\$1\,000$ will double in about seven years with an interest rate of 10%. Using the same interest rate, run the program with initial balances of $\$500$, $\$2\,000$ and $\$10\,000$ (say) to see how long they all take to double. The results may surprise you.

6.12 Write a program to implement the structure plan of Exercise 3.2.

6.13 Use the Taylor series

$$\cos x = 1 - \frac{x^2}{2!} + \frac{x^4}{4!} - \frac{x^6}{6!} + \ldots$$

to write a program to compute $\cos x$ correct to four decimal places (x is in radians). See how many terms are needed to get 4-figure agreement with the library function `cos()`.

6.14 A man borrows $10 000 to buy a used car. Interest on his loan is compounded at the rate of 2% per month while the outstanding balance of the loan is more than $5 000, and at 1% per month otherwise. He pays back $300 every month, except for the last month, when the repayment must be less than $300. He pays at the end of the month, *after* the interest on the balance has been compounded. The first repayment is made one month after the loan is paid out to him. Write a program which writes out a monthly statement of the balance (after the monthly payment has been made), the final payment, and the month of the final payment.

6.15 A projectile, the equations of motion of which are given in Chapter 4, is launched from the point O with an initial velocity of 60 m/s at an angle of 50° to the horizontal. Write a program which computes and writes out the time in the air, and horizontal and vertical displacement from the point O every 0.5 seconds, as long as the projectile remains above a horizontal plane through O.

6.16 When a resistor (R), capacitor (C) and battery (V) are connected in series, a charge Q builds up on the capacitor according to the formula

$$Q(t) = CV(1 - e^{-t/RC}).$$

if there is no charge on the capacitor at time $t = 0$. The problem is to monitor the charge on the capacitor every 0.1 seconds in order to detect when it reaches a level of 8 units of charge, given that $V = 9$, $R = 4$ and $C = 1$. Write a program which writes the time and charge every 0.1 seconds until the charge first exceeds 8 units (i.e. the last charge written must exceed 8). Once you have done this, rewrite the program to output the charge only while it is strictly less than 8 units.

6.17 If a population grows according to the *logistic* model, its size $X(t)$ at time t is given by the formula

$$X(t) = \frac{KX_0}{(K - X_0)e^{-rt} + X_0},$$

where X_0 is the initial size at time $t = 0$, r is the growth-rate, and K is the *carrying capacity* of the environment. Write a program which will compute and print values of $X(t)$ over a period of 200 years. Take $X_0 = 2$, $r = 0.1$ and $K = 1000$. Experiment with different values of K, and see if you can interpret K biologically.

6.18 Adapt the prime number program in Section 6.4 to find all the prime factors of a given number (even or odd).

6.19 You can write a program to sound like a siren as follows (see the telephone example in Section 6.3 for the library functions to use). Use a `for` loop to generate a sound of duration 10 milliseconds which rises in frequency from 400 to 500 hertz. Then use another `for` loop to make the sound drop back from 500 to 400 hertz. Finally, enclose both loops in an outer `for` which repeats the whole process a number of times. (Make sure to use a different counter in the outer loop.)

Chapter 7

Errors

7.1 Compilation errors
  • Warning messages • Linkage errors • Semantic errors
7.2 Run-time errors
  • The interactive debugger • Error interception
7.3 Errors in logic
7.4 Rounding error
Summary
Exercises

Even experienced programmers seldom get programs to run correctly the first time. In computer jargon, an error in a program is called a *bug*. The story is that a moth short-circuited two thermionic valves in one of the earliest computers. This primeval (charcoaled) "bug" took days to find. The process of detecting and correcting such errors is called *debugging*. There are four main classes types of errors:

- *compilation* errors
- *run-time* errors
- errors of *logic*
- *rounding* error.

In this chapter we deal with the sort of errors that can arise with the programming we have done so far.

7.1   Compilation errors

Compilation errors are errors in syntax and construction, like spelling mistakes, that are picked up by the compiler during compilation, the process

111

whereby your program is translated into machine code. They are the most frequent type of error. The compiler displays a message, which may or may not be helpful, when it encounters such an error.

There are a large number of compiler error messages, which will be listed in the user's manual that comes with your particular compiler. Since the compiler is not as intelligent as you are, the error messages can sometimes be rather unhelpful—even misleading. A few common examples from the Turbo C++ compiler are given below.

, expected

This one can be misleading. It usually means you left a comma out of a list of declarations, but it could also mean that you left a *semi-colon* out of the *previous* statement!

{ expected

A left brace was left out, maybe immediately after the `main()` statement. Incidentally, you can check for *matching pairs* of { }, < >, [ ], /* */, " " and ' '. Place the cursor under one member of the pair. Search forward for its match with **Ctrl-Q[**, and backward with **Ctrl-Q]**.

Declaration was expected

This is usually caused by a missing delimiter, but also occurs, for example, if you *insert* a semi-colon after `main()`, or after any function header in its implementation (see Chapter 8).

Expression syntax

This is a general cry for help when something's wrong. Again, it could simply be that you forgot to terminate the previous statement with a semi-colon.

Function *function* should have a prototype

This one at least is fairly obvious. To find the prototype in Turbo C++ use context sensitive help by pressing **Ctrl-F1** with the cursor anywhere under the function name. Help then gives you the function prototype and description.

There are many, many more compiler errors—you will probably have discovered a good number on your own by now. With experience you will gradually become more adept at spotting your mistakes.

Warning messages

There are also times when the code compiles correctly, but the compiler thinks you have made a programming error. In such cases, *warning* messages are displayed, such as

> *Identifier* `is assigned a value that is never used`

Another helpful warning is given if you use = instead of == in an `if` condition:

> `Possibly incorrect assignment`

Linkage errors

Linkage errors also come under the general heading of compilation errors. These may occur when you are attempting to link one or more **.obj** files with precompilied **.lib** files. E.g. the graphics library may not be linked automatically (check this with **Options/Linker/Libraries**), in which case you will get a message like

> `Undefined symbol _initgraph in module` *NAME*

Semantic errors

There are a related group of error, which we might call *semantic* errors. The program compiles, runs, and gives results. The algorithm is correct, but the answers are wrong! These are obviously the most difficult of all errors to unravel.

I made such an error in coding the Taylor series program in Chapter 6. I incorrectly used `abs()`, instead of `fabs()`, to find the absolute value of `double term` (less than 1). Since `abs(term)` returned zero, the `while` loop never executed at all, giving answers which were fortunately way out (so I knew they were wrong). Even with the help of the debugger, it took quite a few minutes to spot the error.

You may also get these sort of errors with `scanf()`. E.g. if you use the `f` format code to read a `double` value, instead of `lf`, your program runs, but the value read is garbage.

7.2 Run-time errors

If a program compiles successfully, it will run. Errors occurring at this stage are called run-time errors, and are invariably *fatal*, i.e. the program "crashes". E.g.

> `Floating point error: Divide by 0.`
> `Floating point error: Domain.`
> `Floating point error: Overflow.`

The first one is obvious. The second one occurs when the result is NAN (not a number), e.g. after attempting to evaluate 0.0/0.0. The third means the result is +INF (infinity), or −INF.

The interactive debugger

Turbo C++ has an interactive debugger, which is one of its outstanding features. Its usefulness cannot be emphasised enough.

You can, for example, run through a program line by line with **F7**, keeping an eye on the values of variables in the Watch window. You can step into functions (**F7**), or over them (**F8**). You can mark a breakpoint at a line, and run to that point, or run to the cursor position with **F4**. You can use **D**ebug/ **E**valuate/modify to change the value of a variable while a program is running. You can step into code in a different file.

If you are serious about programming you should spend some time mastering the debugger.

Error interception

C++ has facilities for intercepting certain run-time errors, such as attempting to read from a non-existent file. These are discussed at the appropriate place.

7.3   Errors in logic

These are errors in the actual algorithm you are using to solve a problem, and are the most difficult to find; the program runs, but gives the wrong answers! It's even worse if you don't realize the answers are wrong. The following tips might help you to check out the logic.

- Try to run the program for some special cases where you know the answers.
- If you don't know any exact answers, try to use your insight into the problem to check whether the answers seem to be of the right order of magnitude.
- Try working through the program by hand (or use the debugger) to see if you can spot where things start going wrong.

7.4   Rounding error

At times, as we have seen, a program will give numerical answers to a problem which appear inexplicably different from what we know to be the correct mathematical solution. This can also be due to *rounding error*, which results from the finite precision available on the computer, e.g. two or four bytes per variable, instead of an infinite number.

Run the following program extract:

```
double x = 0.1;
do {
  x = x + 0.001;
  printf( "%f  %12.4e\n", x, x - 0.2 );
} while (x != 0.2);
```

You will find that you need to crash the program to stop, e.g. with **Ctrl-break** on a PC. x never has the value 0.2 *exactly*, because of rounding error. In fact, x misses 0.2 by about 8.3×10^{-17}, as can be seen from x - 0.2. It would be better to replace the while clause with

```
while (x <= 0.2);
```

or

```
while (fabs(x - 0.2) > 1e-6);
```

In general, it is always better to test for "equality" of two non-integer expressions in this way, e.g.

```
if (fabs(a - b) < 1e-6) puts( "a practically equals b" );
```

Rounding error may be reduced somewhat (although never completely eliminated) by using **long double**. Generally, however, in scientific computing **double** should be sufficient.

Rounding error may also be reduced by a mathematical re-arrangement of the problem. If the well-known quadratic equation is written in the less familiar form

$$x^2 - 2ax + e = 0,$$

the two solutions may be expressed as

$$x_1 = a + \sqrt{a^2 - e},$$
$$x_2 = a - \sqrt{a^2 - e}.$$

If e is very small compared with a, the second root is expressed as the difference between two nearly equal numbers, and considerable significance is lost. E.g. taking $a = 5 \times 10^6$ and $e = 0.001$ gives $x_2 = 0$, if the variables are **double**. However, the second root may also be expressed mathematically as

$$x_2 = \frac{e}{a + \sqrt{a^2 - e}} \approx \frac{e}{2a}.$$

Using this form gives $x_2 = 10^{-10}$, which is much more accurate.

Summary

- Compilation errors are mistakes in the syntax (coding).
- Execution (run-time) errors occur while the program is running
- Input/output errors may be intercepted at run-time.
- The debugger may be used to work through a program, statement by statement.
- Logical errors are errors in the algorithm used to solve the problem.
- Rounding error occurs because the computer can store numbers only to a finite accuracy. It is reduced but never completely eliminated by a type with higher precision.

Exercises

7.1   The Newton quotient

$$\frac{f(x+h) - f(x)}{h}$$

may be used to estimate the first derivative $f'(x)$ of a function $f(x)$, if h is "small". Write a program to compute the Newton quotient for the function

$$f(x) = x^2$$

at the point $x = 2$ (the exact answer is 4) for values of h starting at 1, and decreasing by a factor of 10 each time. The effect of rounding error becomes apparent when h gets "too small", i.e. less than about 10^{-6}.

7.2   The solution of the set of simultaneous equations

$$ax + by = c$$
$$dx + ey = f$$

(Exercise 5.5) is given by

$$x = (ce - bf)/(ae - bd),$$
$$y = (af - cd)/(ae - bd).$$

If $(ae - bd)$ is small, rounding error may cause quite large inaccuracies in the solution. Consider the system

$$0.2038x + 0.1218y = 0.2014,$$
$$0.4071x + 0.2436y = 0.4038.$$

Show that with four-figure floating point arithmetic the solution obtained is $x = -1$, $y = 3$. This level of accuracy may be simulated in the solution of Ex. 5.5 with some statements like

```
ae=int(a*e*1e4)/1e4
```

and appropriate changes in the coding. The exact solution, however, which can be obtained with `double` variables, is $x = -2$, $y = 5$. If the coefficients in the equations are themselves subject to experimental error, the "solution" of this system using limited accuracy is totally meaningless.

7.3 This problem, suggested by R.V. Andree, demonstrates another numerical problem called *ill-conditioning*, where a small change in the coefficients causes a large change in the solution. Show that the solution of the system

$$x + 5.000y = 17.0$$
$$1.5x + 7.501y = 25.503$$

is $x = 2$, $y = 3$, using the program for Ex. 5.5 with full accuracy. Now change the term on the right-hand side of the second equation to 25.501, a change of about one part in 12 000, and observe that a totally different solution results. Also try changing this term to 25.502, 25.504, etc. If the coefficients are subject to experimental errors, the solution is again meaningless. One way to anticipate this sort of error is to perform a *sensitivity analysis* on the coefficients: change them all in turn by the same percentage, and observe what effect this has on the solution.

Chapter 8

Functions

8.1 Some basic concepts
- Newton's method again • Rotation of co-ordinate axes • Declarations: prototypes
- Function definitions (implementations) • Returning a value with **return** • Header files
- Parameters and arguments • Arguments passed by value

8.2 Functions that do not return a value
- A menu system with windows • Pop-up windows

8.3 Scope: local and global variables
- Scope • Local variables • Global variables • The scope resolution operator
- Function parameters • Register and volatile variables • External variables
- Function modifiers

8.4 Macros
- Conditional compilation

8.5 Inline functions

8.6 References
- Reference parameters: pass by reference • Reference variables • Returning a reference
- Illegal references

8.7 Pointers
- Passing by reference with pointers • Pointers and type checking • Null pointers
- Danger: the uninitialized pointer • Void pointers • Near and far pointers

8.8 Projects with multiple files
- Libraries • Preventing multiple includes

8.9 Stubs

8.10 Recursion

8.11 Function overloading

8.12 Default arguments

Summary

Exercises

If expressions are the lifeblood of a C++ program, *functions* are its backbone. We saw in Chapter 3 that the logic of a non-trivial problem should be broken down into separate chunks, each carrying out a particular well-defined task.

Each of these tasks can be coded as a function, to be invoked by the `main()` function. Since `main()` is itself a function, the body of any function is coded in the same way as `main()`, as we shall see now.

8.1   Some basic concepts

We first look at some examples of functions before discussing details.

Newton's method again

Newton's method (see also Chapter 15) may be used to solve a general equation $f(x) = 0$ by repeating the assignment

$$x \text{ becomes } x - \frac{f(x)}{f'(x)},$$

where $f'(x)$ is the first derivative of $f(x)$, until $f(x)$ is close enough to zero.

Suppose that $f(x) = x^3 + x - 3$. Then $f'(x) = 3x^2 + 1$. The program below uses Newton's method to solve this equation starting with $x = 2$, and stopping either when the absolute value of $f(x)$ is less than 10^{-6}, or after 20 iterations, say. It uses two functions: `F(x)` for $f(x)$ and `Df(x)` for $f'(x)$.

```
#include <stdio.h>
#include <math.h>
#define FALSE 0
double F(double x);        // function f(x)
double Df(double x);       // derivative f'(x)
main()
{
    int converged = FALSE;     // convergence flag
    int its = 0;               // iteration counter
    int maxIts = 20;           // maximum iterations
    double eps = 1e-6;         // maximum error
    double x;                  // the unknown

    printf( "Enter your guess for x: " );
    scanf( "%lf", &x );        // format code lf for double

    while (!converged && its < maxIts) {
        x = x - F(x) / Df(x);
        printf( "%7.4f  %10.4e\n", x, F(x) );
        its++;
        converged = fabs( F(x) ) <= eps;
    }
```

```
    if (converged)
      printf( "Newton CONverged\n" );
    else
      printf( "Newton DIverged\n" );
    return 0;
}
double F(double x)
{
   return x * x * x + x - 3;
}
double Df(double x)
{
   return 3 * x * x + 1;
}
```

Note that there are two conditions that will stop the **while** loop: either convergence, or the completion of 20 iterations. Otherwise the program could run indefinitely.

Note also that the format code **%lf** must be used with **scanf()** when reading a **double** value

Rotation of co-ordinate axes

Functions are particularly useful when arithmetic expressions, which can become long and cumbersome, need to be evaluated repeatedly. A good example is the rotation of a Cartesian co-ordinate system. If such a system is rotated counter-clockwise through an angle of a radians, the new co-ordinates (x', y') of a point referred to the rotated axes are given by

$$x' = x \cos a + y \sin a$$
$$y' = -x \sin a + y \cos a$$

where (x, y) are its co-ordinates before rotation of the axes. The following program uses two functions to determine the new co-ordinates:

```
#include <math.h>
#include <iostream.h>
double Xnew( double x, double y, double a );
double Ynew( double x, double y, double a );
main()
{
   double a, x, y;
   cout << "Enter a, x, y: ";
   cin >> a >> x >> y;
   cout << "Xnew: " << Xnew( x, y, a );
```

```
   cout << "  Ynew: " << Ynew( x, y, a ) << endl;
   return 0;
}
double Xnew( double x, double y, double a )
{
   return x * cos(a) + y * sin(a);
}
double Ynew( double x, double y, double a )
{
   return - x * sin(a) + y * cos(a);
}
```

Note that the header file **math.h** is included in the preamble to `main()`.

Declarations: prototypes

We need to look at some details now. The code for a function comes in two parts: the prototype (declaration), and the definition.

A function like any other object in C++ must be declared before it is referenced. If it returns a value, the general form is

   type name (*parameter declarations*);

where *type* is the type of the value returned. A function may return any of the data types, e.g.

```
   float Junk( float a, int b );
```

If the type is omitted, it is `int` by default. That explains why `main()` returns an integer, incidentally.

If a function does not return a type it should be declared `void`. Also if it has no parameters, the keyword `void` should be supplied as the parameter list. This is to avoid accidentally calling the function with an argument (possible in C, but not C++). E.g.

```
   void Plonk( int &a, float &b );    // see later for explanation of &
   void DisplayMenu( void );
```

There are different forms of declarations. The ones shown here are the more modern professional form called function *prototypes*. They come at the top of the main program before `main()`. Note that the prototypes are terminated by semi-colons. They may also be lumped together in a header file, and included with the `#include` directive. In C++ a function must have a prototype. In C a function without a prototype returns an integer value by default.

Strictly, you can use *nameless* parameters in the prototype, declaring only their types, e.g.

```
float Junk( float, int );
```

However, it is much better to put in the parameter names, for the sake of clarity.

Some programmers use the convention of writing the first letter of function names in uppercase. This serves to distinguish them from library functions, where all letters are lowercase.

Function definitions (implementations)

After being declared, the function must still be defined, or implemented. This may be done immediately, but usually after the closing block marker of the **main()** function. Functions may be defined in any order. The general form of the definition is

```
type name ( parameter declarations )
{
    body of the function
}
```

Note that there is **no semi-colon** after the header in the definition.

The parameters must be named in the function definition.

In old-fashioned C code you might find the parameters in the definition declared between the function name and the opening block marker of its body.

Returning a value with return

If a function returns a value, this value must be specified as an expression in a **return** statement. E.g.

```
float half( float x )
{
    return x / 2;
}
```

The returned value is accessed by referencing the function name.

Do not attempt to return the function's name, or to use it in the definition, unless you are defining it recursively (see below).

return may also be used to force a return at some point other than the end of the function. This should be avoided except in the case of functions defined recursively.

Header files

These are files consisting of function prototypes and other declarations. They are included, as we have seen, in your source code before compilation by the pre-processor as follows:

```
#include <stdio.h>
#include "myheads.h"
```

If the filename is enclosed in double quotes, the compiler first searches the current working directory, and then any include directories specified in the configuration file, e.g. with **O**ptions/**D**irectories. If the filename is enclosed in angle brackets, it searches the include directories only—never the current working directory.

Parameters and arguments

A *parameter* in a function declaration is a *dummy* name, i.e. it exists only for the purpose of defining the function, and represents a general variable of the same type. It therefore has no connection with a variable of the same name outside the function declaration. Obviously, the same name does not have to be used when referencing (calling, invoking) the function. E.g. Ynew() in the co-ordinate rotation program above may be referenced as

```
Ynew( u, v, M_PI/2 );
```

When a function is referenced, the identifiers in its parameter list are called *arguments*. E.g. in the above reference to Ynew(), u, v, and M_PI/2 are arguments, whereas in the prototype, x, y, and a are parameters.

Arguments passed by value

When a function is referenced, the arguments are evaluated, and these *values* are passed (copied if you like) to the corresponding parameters in the function definition. For best results, the arguments should match the function's declared parameter types, i.e. int arguments should be passed to int parameters, etc. However, values of *compatible* types (e.g. int and double) may be *promoted* or demoted. So, for example, an int argument passed to a double parameter is promoted, whereas a double argument passed to an int parameter is demoted, by having its fractional part truncated.

Technically, C++ passes arguments *by value*. This means that if a parameter is changed inside a function definition, the corresponding argument is *unchanged* on return. E.g.

```
#include <stdio.h>
double Half( double x );
main()
{
  double y = 13;
  printf( "%f  %f\n", Half(y), y );
}
double Half( double x )
{
  x = 0;              // accident!!
  return x / 2.0;
}
```

The argument y still has the value 13 on return (although the function incorrectly returns 0 instead of 6.5 as expected).

The advantage of call by value is that it avoids a possibly disastrous *side effect*, where a function might accidentally change one of its arguments. It does, however, make it a little more difficult if you do actually *want* to change an argument. We'll see how to do this shortly.

8.2 Functions that do not return a value

A void function is the equivalent of a Pascal procedure or a Fortran subroutine. It performs an operation, rather than calculating and returning a value. E.g. the function

```
void PrettyLine( int n );    // prototype
```

prints a line of n asterisks:

```
void PrettyLine( int n )
{
  int i;
  for (i = 1; i <= n; i++)
    printf( "%c", '*' );
  printf( "\n" );
}
```

Note that since it is void, it has no **return** statement.

Note also that a *local* variable (i) may be declared in a function definition. Such a variable cannot be seen by **main()** or any other function.

A menu system with windows

Menu-driven programs provide good examples of the use of void functions. Each option, and any special effects (like text windows), can be handled by a separate function. The following program gives a very basic template of such a system. You can adapt it to your own needs.

```c
#include <conio.h>
#include <ctype.h>
void DisplayAll( void );
void DisplayMenu( void );
void EnterMarks( void );
void MenuWindow( void );
void OutputWindow( void );
void Pause( void );
char ans;                            // global variable
main()
{
  clrscr();
  do {
    DisplayMenu();
    if (ans == 'A')
      DisplayAll();
    else if (ans == 'E')
      EnterMarks();
  }
  while (ans != 'Q');
  normvideo();                       // shutdown nicely
  clrscr();
  _setcursortype( _NORMALCURSOR );   // make sure cursor is on
}                                    // end of main()

void DisplayAll( void )
/* displays names and marks */
{
  OutputWindow();
  cprintf( "DisplayAll here ... not operative yet" );
  Pause();
  clrscr();
} /* DisplayAll */

void DisplayMenu( void )
/* displays menu and gets option */
{
  MenuWindow();
  cprintf( "STUDENT RECORD SYSTEM: MAIN MENU\n\r" );
  cprintf( "A: Display all names and marks\n\r" );
  cprintf( "E: Enter new set of marks\n\r" );
  cprintf( "N: Display names only\n\r" );
```

```
      cprintf( "I: Insert student name\n\r" );
      cprintf( "S: Statistics\n\r" );
      cprintf( "Q: Quit\n\r" );
      cprintf( "Type your option (do NOT press Enter): " );
      ans = getch();
      ans = toupper( ans );
      putch( ans );
   } /* DisplayMenu */

   void EnterMarks( void )
   /* Enter new set of marks */
   {
      int i;
      OutputWindow();
      cprintf( "EnterMarks here ... not operative yet" );
      Pause();
      clrscr();
   } /* Entermarks */

   void MenuWindow( void )
   {
      window( 1, 1, 80, 12 );
      highvideo();
      clrscr();                          // sets all output to highvideo
      _setcursortype( _NOCURSOR );       // switch off the cursor
   } /* MenuWindow */

   void OutputWindow( void )
   {
      window( 1, 13, 80, 25 );
      normvideo();
      clrscr();                            // sets all output to normvideo
      _setcursortype( _NORMALCURSOR );   // switch cursor on
   } /* OutputWindow */

   void Pause( void )
   {
      cprintf( "\n\r" );
      cputs( "Press any key to continue ... " );
      getch();
   } /* Pause */
```

ans is a *global* variable, meaning that it is known to all functions in the file and to main(). Global variables should be used carefully and sparingly, since accidentally changing one in a function can cause a bug which is very difficult to spot. It is convenient here, since more than one function needs to reference ans. The alternative is to pass it as an argument to functions that need it.

All the new functions introduced here are prototyped in **conio.h**. These *direct-video* I/O functions provide much faster screen I/O than the standard

I/O routines. However, **conio.h** functions are only available with Borland products (like Turbo C++). If you go in for screen I/O in a big way, you should define your own direct-video functions in a separate file (module), using the **conio.h** routines for the moment. Then if you want to port (move) your program to another environment, all you have to do is change the **conio.h** calls. These will be easier to find gathered in one place, rather than scattered all over the program. Compiling multiple files of this nature is discussed below in Section 8.8.

A *window* may be opened on the text screen with the function

```
window( x1, y1, x2, y2 );
```

(**conio.h**) where x1 and y1 are the column and row of the top left corner of the window, and x2 and y2 are the column and row of the bottom right corner. E.g.

```
window( 1, 1, 80, 25 );
```

defines the default window covering the whole screen. All text output from **conio.h** functions is restricted to this window, until the next call to window(). Output from **stdio.h** functions is not restricted.

cprintf() does not translate the newline character (\n) into a newline/carriage-return pair (\n\r) as printf() does. It therefore needs \r to move the cursor to the beginning of a line, as well as \n to generate a new line.

putch() and cputs() put a character and a string onto the screen respectively.

_setcursortype() switches the cursor off and on with arguments _NOCURSOR and _NORMCURSOR respectively.

If you have Turbo C++ it is a good exercise to use **F7** to trace into each function as the program runs. This will give you a good feel for how it works.

Pop-up windows

Pop-up windows are all the rage; you can create them very easily in C++. The basic idea is that an area of the screen can be "saved", to be displayed again later. The following program shows two overlapping windows, retrieving the one at the back. The **new** operator, which is used to create dynamic memory, is discussed later in Chapter 9.

```
#include <conio.h>
main()
{
    char *win1;
    int left, top, right, bottom;
```

```
left = 1; top = 1; right = 15, bottom = 15;
win1 = new char[ 2 * (right - left + 1) * (bottom - top + 1) ];
clrscr();
window( left, top, right, bottom );              // window 1
textbackground( GREEN );
clrscr();
gettext( left, top, right, bottom, win1 );       // save it
getch();
window( 4, 4, 18, 18 );                          // window 2
textbackground( MAGENTA );
clrscr();
getch();
textbackground( BLACK );
clrscr();                                        // rub out window 2
puttext( left, top, right, bottom, win1 );       // window 1 again
getch();
window( 1, 1, 80, 25 );                          // whole screen
textbackground( BLACK );
clrscr();
return 0;
}
```

gettext() copies the specified part of the screen into the buffer win1. Since each character needs two bytes of storage, the minimum required buffer size is $2hw$, where h is the height and w is the width in characters of the screen area to be copied. In this example, new is used to create a dynamic array of characters as the buffer.

putttext() copies the text saved in win1 to the specified area of the screen.

A related function, movetext() (see Appendix D), moves a rectangular area of the display to a different part of the screen without saving it.

Note that clrscr() clears a window to its background colour.

8.3   Scope: local and global variables

Run the following program, which uses a function Fact() to compute factorials:

```
#include <stdio.h>
unsigned long Fact( int n );
int i;
main()
{
  for (i = 1; i <= 12; i++)
    printf( "%3d %12lu\n", i, Fact(i) );
  return 0;
}
```

```
unsigned long Fact( int n )
{
    unsigned long temp = 1;
    for (i = 2; i <= n; i++)
        temp = temp * i;
    return temp;
}
```

Output:

2	1
4	6
6	120
8	5040
10	362880
12	39916800

There are two problems with the output. `Fact(i)` is displayed next to i+1, and `Fact(i)` is only displayed for odd i. Can you find the bug and correct it?

The best way to see what is happening is get into the Turbo C++ debugger and use **F7** to trace into `Fact()`.

This program illustrates the dangers of using global variables. Remove the `int i` declaration before `main()`, and declare i inside `main()`, and inside `Fact()`. All your troubles will disappear.

Scope

The *scope* of an identifier (usually a variable) is the range of program lines over which that identifier is accessible. You can think of scope as an identifier's range of view. Statements within the identifier's scope can see it and use it. Statements outside its scope cannot use it. A variable might not even exist outside its scope.

C++ scoping allows for three types of variables: local, global, and function parameters.

Local variables

Variables declared inside a function (including `main()`) are *local* to that function, i.e. their scope extends only throughout the function. Thus `int x` declared in a function has no relation to `int x` declared in `main()` or any other function. This is actually a special case of the more general rule, which states that the scope of a variable extends throughout the *block* in which it is declared, a block being delimited by block markers. You can therefore declare variables inside blocks nested in a function, although this is not recommended. You might find this in some old C programs.

A function's local variables are stored in an area of memory call the *stack*, along with the function's return address. They are also called *automatic variables*, which means they are automatically created and destroyed by the code.

When a function is executed, it allocates space on the stack for its local variables. After it returns, the stack space is deleted, and values stored there are lost. Local variables therefore do *not* normally retain their values between function calls.

A local variable which is not initialized has an *unpredictable* (garbage) value when the function is entered.

If a local variable is declared and initialized with the **static** *storage class specifier* it is allocated permanent space by the compiler, and does retain its final value between function calls, e.g.

```
void CountMe( void )
{
  static int counter = 0;
  ...
  counter++;
  printf( "This function has been called %d times\n", counter );
}
```

When the program is compiled, the static variable **counter** is declared and initialized to zero. This is its value on the first call of **CountMe**. On return after the first call, its value is 1, and this value is retained for the next call. If you do not explicitly initialize a static variable it is automatically initialized to zero on compilation.

A static variable is also local to the function declaring it.

Global variables

Global variables are declared anywhere outside a function; the best place to do this is before **main()**. They are known throughout the whole program, and may be used in any function.

Global variables are stored in a memory area called the *data segment*, and are automatically initialized to zero by the compiler.

The scope resolution operator

In C a global variable is "hidden" by a local variable of the same name. In C++ the *scope resolution operator* :: may be used to "unhide" the global variable, e.g.

```
int counter;       // global
main()
{
  int counter = 1;  // local
  ::counter++;      // update global counter
  ...
```

Function parameters

The scope of function parameters in a declaration is limited to that declaration; the same identifiers may be used elsewhere without ambiguity.

Register and volatile variables

The storage class specifier **register** is used to declare a *register* variable, e.g.

```
register int quickCount;
```

Such variables are stored directly in a processor register, and are consequently processed faster. They can be used to good effect as loop counters.

Since a register might not be available, you can only *request* space in a register, not insist on it.

Use the **volatile** modifier to explicitly demand that a local variable *not* be considered for register storage. Volatile variables are needed, for example, for values that might be altered by an interrupt routine operating independently of the program.

External variables

An *external* variable is a global variable declared in another module (file). Suppose a file **this.cpp** has a global variable

```
int thisGlobal;
```

If a different file, **that.cpp**, wants to access **thisGlobal**, it must be declared in **that.cpp** with the **extern** storage class specifier:

```
extern int thisGlobal;
```

Note that the compiler doesn't need to know where to find **thisGlobal**, but only that it is external.

Function modifiers

Functions themselves are external by default, i.e. a function defined in one file may call a function defined in another file (multi-file programs are discussed in Section 8.8).

The storage class specifier `static` in a function header restricts a function to the file in which it is defined.

8.4 Macros

We have seen how to define symbolic constants with the `#define` preprocessor directive:

```
#define YEAR 1993
```

`YEAR` is an example of a *macro*: a symbol which when compiled expands into something else, in this case the text `1993`.

Macros can be quite complex. Some of the C++ library functions are in fact written as macros, e.g. `getchar()` and `getc()` (you can see the macros in the **stdio.h** header file).

Conditional compilation

Suppose you are developing (and therefore debugging) a large program. To see what's going on it is very helpful to have `printf()` statements all over the place, to indicate where a program is executing, what values certain variables have, etc. However, you would most likely want to remove all these extraneous `printf()`s, once the program is fully debugged. Consider the following code:

```
#define DEBUGGING
main()
{
   ...
 #ifdef DEBUGGING
    statements;
 #endif
```

The `#define` directive defines the symbol `DEBUGGING` with no associated text. However, the symbol is nonetheless defined; this fact is determined by the `#ifdef` directive, which will cause `statements` to *compiled*. When you have finished debugging, all you need to do is leave out the directive

```
#define DEBUGGING
```

Since DEBUGGING is now not defined, it is not detected by #ifdef, and so statements are not compiled: hence the term *conditional* compilation.

You can extend this into the equivalent of an if-else ladder:

```
#ifdef DEBUGGING
   statement1;
#elif BETATESTING
   statement2;
#else
   statement3;
#endif
```

Don't forget the #endif (and it's #elif, not #elseif).

The use of conditional compilation in preventing multiple includes is discussed in Section 8.8.

8.5   Inline functions

Functions are vital in writing even a medium-sized program. Although function calls are very quick, a large number of function calls can degrade a program's performance. C++ provides a partial remedy to this problem in the form of *inline* functions. Consider the following example:

```
#include <stdio.h>
#include <string.h>
inline void Backwards( char *str )
{
   int i;
   for (i = strlen( str )-1; i >= 0; i--)
     printf( "%c", str[i] );
   printf( "\n" );
}
main()
{
   Backwards( "palindrome" );
   return 0;
}
```

The function Backwards() prints its string argument backwards. This could be helpful in searching for palindromes: phrases that read the same backwards as forwards. Don't worry at this stage about the weirdo way of declaring Backwards()' parameter: we'll look at that later in the chapter. What is significant is that the function is declared with the keyword inline. The effect of this is that during compilation all calls to Backwards() are replaced by the actual code in the function definition. Although this leads to slightly longer code, it can be significantly faster.

An inline function must be defined in full before it is used. That is why its definition appears before `main()`. Note that because it is defined in full it doesn't require a separate prototype (this holds for any function, by the way). Apart from this, inline functions are written in the same was as ordinary functions.

8.6 References

Earlier in the chapter we mentioned that since an argument is passed to a function by value, it cannot be changed on return. But what happens when we *want* to change an argument? A function normally only returns a single value. We might want to return more than one value, e.g. mean, standard deviation, etc., and the most convenient way is through the arguments.

Suppose we want to write a function `Swop()` to exchange the values of its two arguments. We might try to do it as follows:

```
void Swop( double a, double b )
{
  double temp;
  temp = a;
  a = b;
  b = temp;
}
```

(with a prototype, obviously). However, although this compiles quite happily, it has no effect on the values of the arguments corresponding to the parameters **a** and **b** (try it if you are not convinced).

To get the arguments to change in C is a little messy, as we shall see in a moment. C++, however, has a neater way of doing it. All you have to do is to insert an **&** in front of each parameter in the prototype and the header. Here is the working version of the function with a test program:

```
#include <stdio.h>
void Swop( double &a, double &b );
main()
{
  double x = 13;
  double y = 99;
  Swop( x, y );
  printf( "%f %f\n", x, y );
  return 0;
}
```

```
void Swop( double &a, double &b )
{
    double temp;
    temp = a;
    a = b;
    b = temp;
}
```

Check that it works. We will now look at how it works.

Reference parameters: pass by reference

The objects &a and &b in the above program are called *reference parameters*. What actually happens is that the declaration &a forces C++ to pass the *address* of the argument x to the function. So any operations performed on the parameter a inside the function are actually performed on the argument x. The argument is said to be *passed by reference*, instead of by value.

Here's another example: a function Double() which doubles its argument:

```
void Double( double &a );
main()
{
    double x = 2;
    Double( x );
    return 0;
}
void Double( double &a )
{
    a = 2 * a;
}
```

Use the Turbo C++ Watch window to watch the value of x doubling. Incidentally the Watch window is a handy of checking small programs— you don't need to waste time including **stdio.h** or **iostream.h**.

Note that you could not write the function's name as **double**; this would clash with the keyword.

C++ allows a *constant* reference to be passed. This has advantages when passing structures, for example (see Chapter 11).

Reference variables

C++ also allows you to declare a *reference variable*, which is best thought of as an *alias* (nickname) for another variable. Consider the following:

```
int i;
int &ir = i;
i = 13;
ir++;
```

It's quite instructive to use the Turbo C++ Watch window to see the values of both i and ir as the program executes. You will see that at all times they both have the same values. Whatever happens to i also happens to ir, and vice versa. The declaration

```
int &ir = i;
```

makes ir a *reference* to i. In other words, any reference in the program to ir is also a reference to i. ir is simply another name for i. What actually happens is that the compiler assigns the address of i to ir.

We can now see how passing a function parameter by reference, as illustrated above, works. You can think of passing the argument x to the reference parameter &a as the reference declaration

```
double &a = x;
```

Now whatever happens to the parameter a inside the function is also happening to the argument x, because in fact they are the same thing. Reference variables are seldom used in their own right; their main use is as reference parameters.

An important rule to remember when using reference variables is that once a reference variable is initialized *it may not be reassigned*. It is always tied to the variable in its declaration.

There are four situations in which references do not have to be initialized: when declared extern, when used as function parameters, in class declarations (see Chapter 14), or when used as function return types.

C programmers may think that the & is the address-of operator of yore; it is similar, but not identical (see below).

Returning a reference

You may wonder why a function should be able to return a reference. One reason is that this allows a function call to appear on the *lefthand* side of an assignment. If you are familiar with C you will know that an enormous amount of grief is caused by its refusal to check whether array subscripts are out of bounds. The following program uses a function SafeAssign() which returns a reference to check this (if you are not familiar with C arrays you will have to wait for Chapter 9 to appreciate the importance of such checking):

```
#include <stdlib.h>
#include <stdio.h>
int &SafeAssign( int x[ ], int n );
#define SIZE 10
main()
{
  int x[SIZE] = {1, 2, 3, 4, 5, 6, 7, 8, 9, 10};

  SafeAssign(x, 0) = 13;
  return 0;
}
int &SafeAssign( int x[ ], int n )
{
  if (n <= 0 || n >= SIZE) {
    puts( "Array subscript out of range" );
    exit( n );
  }
  else
    return x[n];
}
```

A statement like

```
SafeAssign(x, n) = ...;
```

is able to assign a value to element x[n] of the array because the function
returns the address of that array element. If the subscript is out of range, a
message is displayed, and the program terminates, preventing possible
memory corruption.

Once we have discussed operator overloading we will see how to replace
this function call by more natural notation:

```
x[n] = ...;
```

Illegal references

If a function is to appear on the lefthand side of an assignment (as above) it
should never return a reference to a local variable which resides on the
stack (e.g. to a parameter passed by *value*). The reason is that after the
function return, but before the assignment, the stack is re-used for other
things. Whatever the stack was re-used for then gets overwritten by the
assignment. This causes a mangled stack which will most likely crash the
program.

8.7 Pointers

If you are not throroughly familiar with C you may have quaked at the standard horror stories about pointers: how they can accidentally destroy your program data, overwrite the operating system, hang up the machine, etc. Now they can do all these things if used incorrectly. However, they also make for extremely powerful and versatile programming when you know how to use them. Like PCs themselves, you will wonder how you ever did without them.

Because they are a large subject, and need some getting used to, we are going to discuss pointers in small doses as the need arises from time to time. The motivation at this particular point is that they provide the classic C means of passing arguments to functions by reference. We have seen that you can do this with reference parameters in C++, but you need to know how it used to be done in C for two reasons: you may have to read some old C code that does this, and C library functions that pass by reference do it in this way.

Enter the following program:

```
main()
{
    int i, *p;
    i = 13;
    p = &i;
    return 0;
}
```

If you are using Turbo or Borland C++ enter i, *p, &i and p in the Watch window, and step through the program with **F8**. If you don't have Watch facilities, insert the following **printf()**:

```
printf( "%d %d %p %p\n", i, *p, &i, p );
```

(note the format code **%p**). You will notice that i and *p have the same values (13), while & and p hold hexadecimal values, e.g. FF44. In the Watch window, these hex codes are prefaced with DS: (for data segment).

The declaration

```
int *p;
```

declares p to be a *pointer* to any variable of type int. A pointer is simply a special type of variable that holds a memory address instead of a conventional number. At this stage the pointer is *undefined*, in the same way that an ordinary variable is on declaration. It holds any old garbage address. If i is declared int, the statement

        p = &i;

stores in p the *address* of i. & is the address-of operator: it returns the address in memory of its operand. It should not be confused with the & in a reference declaration. So the above statement should be read as:

>   *Let the value of* p *become the address of* i

In our example this address is FF44. p is therefore said to "point to" x, since it holds the address of x.

You can think of the address as a post office box number. Now it's one thing to know the P.O. box number, but it's another thing to get the mail out of the box. To get the mail, we must go to the post office, produce the key, unlock the box, and take out the mail. The equivalent of doing this in C++ is using the *indirection* operator *. The expression

        *p

returns the *value of the variable* pointed to by p. Read it as

>   *The value at address* p

You can call it the *value-at operator* if you like. This indirection operator is the reverse of the address-of operator, so *&i returns 13: the value at the address of i.

The indirection operator is so called because it accesses a variable indirectly, through its address. Thus (*p)++ in the above code will increment the value of i indirectly—its name is not mentioned. Note that parentheses are used here. The precedence table in Appendix B indicates that indirection has the same precedence as the increment operator, and that evaluation is from right to left. So what will *p++ return? Well, p++ means increment the value in p, which is an address. If you print or watch p++ in our example you will see its value is FF46, i.e. an increase of *two*. That is because p points to an integer, and integers occupy two bytes. The next integer address is therefore two bytes along from FF44. So when applied to a pointer, the increment operator returns the next address. Logical, really.

Indirection is also called *dereferencing*: using a pointer to get to its addressed data. The operation *p is therefore said to dereference p. The relationships between i, p and *p are shown in Figure 8.1.

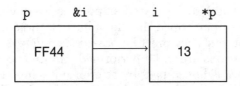

Figure 8.1: Relationships between i and its pointer p, where int *p = &i

This value-at terminology also makes sense of the pointer's declaration:

```
int *p;
```

Read this as

The value at p must be an integer

Note that *p is an alias of i in exactly the same sense that the reference variable ir in Section 8.6 is an alias. *p can be written wherever it is appropriate to write i.

Passing by reference with pointers

As we have seen a parameter can only be passed by value to a function, i.e. if a function changes a parameter value, the change is not reflected in the corresponding argument on return. C++ allows you to pass a reference parameter if you want the function to change the parameter. You can't do this, however, in plain C; you have to do it indirectly, by passing a pointer to the parameter. The function Swop() in Section 8.6 used reference parameters to exchange the values of its two parameters. This is how it must be written in C:

```
void Swop( double *a, double *b );
main()
{
    double x = 1, y = 2;
    Swop( &x, &y );
    return 0;
}
void Swop( double *a, double *b )
{
    double temp;
    temp = *a;
    *a = *b;
    *b = temp;
}
```

The parameters **a** and **b** are declared as pointers to `double`. The operations inside `Swop()` are all performed on the values at these addresses. Since the parameters are pointers, they must be passed the *addresses* of the arguments on which the operations are to be performed. Hence the arguments must be preceded by **&**s. This is how a pass by reference is simulated in C.

Please appreciate the potential disaster that could arise if you omit an **&** when passing an address. The function will still interpret the value of the argument as an address, because it's being passed to a pointer parameter. The operations inside the function will then be carried out on the contents of that unsuspecting address, wherever it may be!

This explains why `scanf()` must be passed the address of a variable to be read; it expects a pointer because it has to change the value of the variable.

Pointers and type checking

A pointer is bound to a particular type by its declaration, so an attempt to assign the address of a different type will generate a compiler error (in C++). E.g. the code

```
float *p;
int x = 1;
p = &x;
```

generates the error message

```
Cannot convert 'int *' to 'float *'
```

Null pointers

Uninitialized pointers can be dangerous, since they hold random addresses, as can be seen in the Watch window. A pointer can be made to point "nowhere": an address that can be tested for. Nowhere is in fact zero—it's the only address a pointer cannot reach. Such a pointer is called a *null* pointer. A number of header files, such as **stddef.h**, **stdio.h**, **stdlib.h**, **string.h**, etc., define a symbol NULL which may be used to define a null pointer (among other things):

```
int *p;
p = NULL;
```

It's a good idea to initialize all pointers to NULL. You can then easily check later in a program whether a pointer contains a meaningful address:

```
if (fp != NULL)
    ...                 // statements using pointer fp
else
    cout >> "Invalid pointer address";
```

If **fp** has been initialized to NULL, but has not been assigned an address **statement** will not execute. However, if **fp** has not been initialized to NULL, it will contain a random address; this neat test will then not work.

Because NULL is zero (false), this test can be shortened to

```
if (fp)
    statement;
```

In fact it compiles to the same code as the longer form. Read it is

If **fp** *is valid*

Danger: the uninitialized pointer

The trick of initializing pointers to NULL avoids the classic C error: the uninitialized pointer. Consider the following:

```
int *p;
int x = 13;
*p = x;
```

The address **p** is undefined (random), so the value of **x** (13) is written in some unknown memory location: maybe where part of your program code is stored, maybe somewhere in the operating system! A pointer *must* first be given a valid address:

```
int *p, y;
int x = 13;
p = &y;      // p holds the address of y
*p = x;
```

Note incidentally that the declaration of an ordinary variable, e.g. **int y**, gives it a fixed address.

Void pointers

A pointer may be declared to point to an unspecified type of data:

```
void *buffer;
```

Such a pointer is called a *void* pointer. It is not bound to a specific data type. A void pointer should not be confused with a null pointer, which does not address any valid data.

Void pointers are most commonly used to address buffers that hold raw data in transit. Such buffers are usually created out of dynamic memory with C functions like `malloc()`, which have been largely superseded by `new` (see the discussion on dynamic memory in Chapter 10).

Near and far pointers

An address in a typical PC memory consists of two 16-bit parts: the *segment* and the *offset*. A *near* pointer can hold a 16-bit address, i.e. it can only reach memory addresses within 64K from any segment. A *far* pointer can hold a 32-bit address, i.e. it can include the segment address value, and can therefore reach any memory location.

Pointers may be declared near or far as follows:

```
double near *p1;
double far *p2;
```

It's usually best to declare pointers without the `near` or `far` qualifiers. The compiler will select the size of a pointer according to the memory model in use at the time.

8.8   Projects with multiple files

Once you start writing your own functions, you can save a great deal of time by placing them in separate files and compiling them separately. You can then link the precompiled file to a main program using a *project*: a special configuration file that specifies the different parts of a multi-file program. This process is illustrated with the following very simple example:

1. Create a file **fungs.cpp** with two simple function definitions, e.g.

```
#include <stdio.h>
void fung1( void )
{
  puts( "inside fung1" );
}
void fung2( void )
{
  puts( "inside fung2" );
}
```

Note that **stdio.h** must be included since the prototype for `puts()` will be needed when the file is compiled.

2. Create a header file **fungs.h** for their prototypes:

```
void fung1( void );
void fung2( void );
```

3. Now create a main program in the file **fungstst.cpp**:

```
#include "fungs.h"
main()
{
    fung1();
    fung2();
    return 0;
}
```

Note that the filename **fungs.h** must be in quotes, since it is (presumably) in the current directory.

4. Finally use the Turbo C++ Project Manager to create a project as follows:

- Select **P**roject/**O**pen project...
- Type the project name (say **fungstst.prj**) in the Load Project File dialogue box (**.prj** is the default extension for project files), and choose the **Ok** button. A Project window will then open.
- To select the files to be linked by the project, press **Ins**. The Add Item to Project List dialogue box appears. Use this box in the normal way to select the files **fungstst.cpp** and **fungs.cpp** for the project. Click the **Done** button when you have finished.

  Now use **C**ompile/**M**ake (**F9**) to produce **fungstst.exe**. Run it in the usual way. From a directory listing you will see that the object files **fungs.obj** and **fungstst.obj** have been created in the process. Alternatively, **Ctrl-F9** compiles, makes and runs the current project.

  Whenever you want to work on this project again, use the Project Manager to open the project file. The functions in **fungs.cpp** will only be recompiled if **fungs.obj** has got out of date. However, you can force a complete recompilation if you want to with **B**uild all.

  Before you attempt to compile another program, you should close the project. Otherwise **C**ompile/**M**ake automatically remakes the project.

- Suppose now you want to use a global variable int x which must be accessible to the functions in **fungs.cpp**. Insert at the top of **fungs.cpp** the declaration

```
extern int x;
```

Edit fung1() and fung2() to print the value of x. Then declare x and assign some value to it in the main program in **fungstst.cpp**. Remake the project and run it.

- If there is a project in the current directory when you start up Turbo C++ it is automatically opened. You may find it convenient to save projects in special subdirectories.

The Turbo C++ *User's Guide* has more useful information on the Project Manager.

Libraries

You may eventually develop a large number of functions, scattered over a large number of files. You may find yourself spending a great deal of time trying to figure out which functions are in which files, so you can decide which files to use in your project. What you need at this stage is a *library*, i.e. a *collection* of **.obj** (compiled) files with the extension **.lib**.

To create a library, use a *librarian* such as **tlib.exe** (supplied with Turbo C++). Suppose you want to build the single file **fungs.obj** into a library. At the DOS command line type

```
tlib fungs.lib + fungs.obj
```

The result is the library file **fungs.lib** which you can now insert into the project file instead of **fungs.cpp** or **fungs.obj**. Try it.

More generally you can collect a number of files:

```
tlib mylib + fung1 + fung2
```

The default extension for the first argument is **.lib**, and for the subsequent ones is **.obj**. Once embedded in a library, the **.obj** files are called *modules*. Modules may be removed from a library with the subtraction operator –.

A major advantage of libraries is that the linker will only pull in those **.obj** modules needed for a particular compilation. Also the size of the collected **.obj** files is nearly always smaller than the combined sized of the individual files.

If you are not using graphics you can save time during linkage by switching off automatic graphics library linkage (with **Options/Linker/ Libraries**).

See the Turbo C++ *User's Guide* for more useful information on the librarian.

Preventing multiple includes

When developing large programs you often run the risk of including the same header file more than once. The following trick is useful. Suppose the header file is **junk.h**. Start it with the lines

```
#ifndef __JUNK_H
#define __JUNK_H 1
```

and end it with the line

```
#endif
```

The effect of this is that if the symbol `__JUNK_H` is not already defined it will be defined (with the true value of 1), and all the text up to `#endif` is included as usual. However, if the file has already been included, the symbol `__JUNK_H` will be defined, so the text after it will *not* be included.

8.9 Stubs

A large program will have many functions. To plan and code them all before compiling anything is asking for trouble. But because functions should be declared before being used, how can we avoid this? The answer is to use *stubs*, which declare the functions, but do nothing. So declare all the functions you think you will be using, as stubs, and fill them in one at a time, compiling after each fill-in. That way it's much easier to catch the compilation errors:

```
// the Big One
void first( void );
void last ( void );
main()
{
  first();
  last();
  return 0;
}
```

```
void first( void )
{ }
void last ( void )
{ }
```

It may not do much at this stage, but at least it compiles!

8.10   Recursion

Many mathematical functions (and procedures in general) may be defined *recursively*, i.e. in terms of simpler cases of themselves. For example, the factorial function may be defined recursively as

$$n! = n \times (n-1)!$$

given that 1! is defined as 1. C++ allows functions to call themselves. This process is called *recursion*. Our factorial function of Section 8.3 may be written as a recursive function as follows:

```
#include <iostream.h>
double Factorial( int number );
main()
{
  cout << Factorial(10) << endl;
  return 0;
}
double Factorial( int number )
{
  if (number > 1)
    return number * Factorial( number - 1 );
  else
    return 1;
}
```

This is the way functions which return a value are generally computed recursively. An `if` statement handles the general recursive definition; the `else` part handles the special case for which the function is defined.

Recursion is an advanced topic, although it appears deceptively simple. You may wonder how `Factorial()` really works. It is important to distinguish between the function being *called* and *executed*. When the initial call takes place **number** has the value 10, so the `if` statement in `Factorial()` is invoked. However, the value of `Factorial(9)` is not known at this stage, so a *copy* is made of all the statements in the function which will need to be executed once the value of `Factorial(9)` is known. The reference to `Factorial(9)` makes `Factorial()` call itself, this time with a value of 9 for `number`. Again the `if` statement is invoked, and again C++ discovers that it doesn't know the value of `Factorial(8)`. So another (different) copy is made of all the statements that will need to be executed once the value of `Factorial(8)` is known. And so each time `Factorial()` is called, separate copies are made of all the statements *yet to be executed*. Finally, the compiler finds a value of `number` (1) for which it knows the value of `Factorial()`, so at last it can begin to execute (in reverse order) the pile of statements which have been dammed up inside the memory.

This discussion illustrates the point that recursion should be used carefully. While it is perfectly in order to use it in a case like this, it can chew up huge amounts of computer memory and time.

A recursive function which does not return a value is used to implement the Quick Sort algorithm in Chapter 9.

8.11 Function overloading

You may have wondered how many of the library functions can return values of different types, although they have the same name, e.g. `pow()` can return a `double` or a `complex` result. This is achieved through *function overloading*. C++ allows multiple declarations of the same function, as long as at least one of the parameters differ in each case.

As an example, consider the library function `pow(a, b)`. It returns a^b by evaluating the expression

```
exp(b * log(a))
```

However, if `b` is an integer, the evaluation of this expression (if repeated sufficiently often in a long program) could take significantly longer than simply multiplying `a` by itself `b` times. So we will write two overloaded functions `Power(a, b)` to handle the situation:

```
#include <iostream.h>
#include <math.h>
double Power( double a, double b );
double Power( double a, int b );
main()
{
  double x, y;
  int b;
  cin >> x >> y;
```

```
      cout << Power( x, y ) << endl;
      cin >> x >> b;
      cout << Power( x, b ) << endl;
      return 0;
}
double Power( double a, double b )
{
      cout << "double double arguments: ";
      return pow( a, b );
}
double Power( double a, int b )
{
      int i;
      double product = a;
      cout << "double int arguments: ";
      for (i = 2; i <= b; i++)
        product = product * a;
      return product;
}
```

The `cout` statement inside each version of `Power()` is to convince you that C++ does indeed choose a different one each time.

8.12   Default arguments

C++ allows you to supply default argument values. This can be useful when a function has a lot of arguments, most of which can conveniently be set to some default. However, there might be occasions when you want to specify non-default values. Run the following example:

```
#include <iostream.h>
#include <iomanip.h>
void MyOut( double x, int w = 10, int p = 1 );
main()
{
      double x;
      cin >> x;
      MyOut( x );
      MyOut( x, 5 );
      MyOut( x, 9, 3 );
      return 0;
}
void MyOut( double x, int w, int p )
{
      cout << setfill( 'b' ) << setprecision(p) << setw(w) << x << endl;
}
```

If the input value of x is 1.23456, the output is

```
bbbbbbb1.2
bb1.2
bbbb1.235
```

The second and third parameters of MyOut have default values. If w (width) is not supplied, it takes the value 10, and if p (precision) is not supplied, it takes the value 1.

Default values must come last in the parameter list, and must appear only in the function prototype.

Summary

- Good structured programming requires real problem-solving programs to be broken down into functions.
- A function has a prototype (declaration) and a definition.
- A function may return a value (of the type with which it is declared) or it may be void.
- If a function returns a value, this value must be specified in a return statement.
- If a function has no parameters the keyword void should be supplied as the parameter list.
- Header files consist of prototypes and other declarations.
- When a function is referenced the identifiers in its parameter list are called arguments.
- Arguments are passed to a function by value. This means that if a parameter is changed inside a function the corresponding argument is unchanged on return.
- The scope of an identifier is the range of program lines over which that identifier is accessible.
- A local variable is one which is declared inside a function (including main()). Its scope is limited to the function.
- A local variable is called an automatic variable, because it is automatically created and destroyed by the code. It is stored on the stack.
- A local variable does not normally retain its value between function calls.
- A local variable which is not initialized has an unpredictable value when the function is entered.

- A local variable declared with the **static** storage class modifier retains its final value between function calls. A static variable is automatically initialized to zero, but may be explicitly initialized to any value.

- A global variable is one declared anywhere outside a function (usually at the beginning of a program). Its scope extends throughout the whole program.

- A global variable is automatically initialized to zero.

- The scope resolution operator : : is used in a function to unhide a global variable with the same name as a local variable.

- The scope of a function parameter in a declaration is limited to that declaration (i.e. a function parameter is a dummy variable).

- The **register** storage class specifier is used to request that a variable be stored directly in a register for faster processing. The request may not be granted.

- The **volatile** modifier is used to insist that a variable not be considered for register storage.

- An external variable is a global variable declared in another module (file). To access it from a different module it must be declared with the **extern** storage class specifier in the accessing module.

- A function is external by default (it may be called from another file). However, the **static** keyword in a function declaration restricts the function to the file in which it is defined.

- The **#define** directive defines a macro: a symbol which expands into something else when compiled.

- Definition of a macro may be tested for with the **#ifdef** and **#ifndef** directives.

- The **#ifdef**, **#ifndef**, **#elif** and **#endif** directives are used for conditional compilation.

- All references to an inline function are replaced by the actual function code during compilation. This makes for faster but longer code. An inline function must be defined in full before it is used.

- A reference variable is an alias for another variable. Whatever is done to one is also done to the other.

- A parameter is passed by reference simply by prefacing it with the **&**. This effectively passes the address of the corresponding argument to the function. The parameter is then an alias for the argument, so any changes to it inside the function also happen to the corresponding argument.

- A pointer is a special variable which holds the memory address of another variable. It is declared with the indirection or value-at operator *.
- The address-of operator & returns the memory address of a variable.
- The value-at operator * returns the value addressed by a pointer. This is called dereferencing a pointer. It is the reverse of the address-of operation.
- Undefined pointers are dangerous because they hold random addresses. A pointer may be assigned the address NULL (defined in header files such as **stddef.h**, **stdio.h**, **stdlib.h**, etc.). NULL may be tested for in an if statement before a pointer is used.
- A void pointer is one which is not bound to a specific type.
- A near pointer can only hold the 16-bit offset part of an address within a segment of memory. A far pointer can hold the full 32-bit address of any memory location.
- A project is a configuration file that specifies the different parts of a multi-file program.
- The Turbo C++ Project Manager is used for all aspects of project handling.
- Precompiled **.obj** files may be collected together into libraries (**.lib** files) by a librarian, such as `tlib.exe`.
- A **.obj** file embedded in a library is called a module.
- Stubs are empty functions which are useful when developing large programs.
- C++ functions may be defined recursively.
- Functions of the same name (and the same or different type) may be overloaded if they differ in at least one parameter.
- Default values of parameters may be specified in a function prototype.

Exercises

8.1 Change the function `PrettyLine()` of Section 8.2 so that it will draw a line of any specified character. The character to be used must be passed as an additional parameter. E.g. `PrettyLine(6, '$')` should draw six dollar symbols. Use the following prototype:

```
void PrettyLine( int n, char sym );
```

8.2 Write your own function

```
double MyPow( double a, double b );
```

to return the value of a^b, calculated as

```
exp( b * log(a) )
```

Try it out in a test program (remember to include **math.h**).

8.3 Write a program which uses the Newton quotient $[f(x+h) - f(x)]/h$ to estimate the first derivative of $f(x) = x^3$ at $x = 1$, using successively smaller values of h: 1, 10^{-1}, 10^{-2}, etc. Use a function for $f(x)$.

8.4 Write a function

```
void Half( double &a );
```

(using a reference parameter) to halve its argument, i.e. the value stored in the argument must be halved.

8.5 Rewrite the function **Half()** in Exercise 8.4 in the old C way using a pointer parameter:

```
void Half( double *p );
```

8.6 Rewrite the function **Swop()** in Section 8.6 using pointer parameters:

```
void Swop( double *a, double *b );
```

8.7 Write your own C++ function to compute the exponential function directly from the Taylor series:

$$e^x = 1 + x + \frac{x^2}{2!} + \frac{x^3}{3!} + \ldots$$

The series should end when the last term is less than 10^{-6}. Test your function against the library function **exp()**.

8.8 Write a function **Bin(int n, int r)** which returns the binomial coefficient $n!/r!(n-r)!$ as defined in Chapter 6.

8.9 Write a function

```
int Round( double x );
```

which returns the value of x rounded to the *nearest* integer. E.g. **Round(4.5)** should return 5, while **Round(4.49)** should return 4. See the Trapezoidal Rule example in Chapter 18 for the code.

8.10 If a random variable X is distributed normally with zero mean and unit standard deviation, the probability that $0 \le X \le x$ is given by the standard normal function $\Phi(x)$. This is usually looked up in tables, but it may be approximated as follows:

$$\Phi(x) = 0.5 - r(at + bt^2 + ct^3),$$

where $a = 0.4361836$, $b = -0.1201676$, $c = 0.937298$, $r = \exp(-0.5x^2)/\sqrt{2\pi}$, and $t = 1/(1 + 0.3326x)$.
Write a function to compute $\Phi(x)$, and use it in a program to write out its values for $0 \le x \le 4$ in steps of 0.1. Check: $\Phi(1) = 0.3413$.

8.11 Write a function

```
int Quad( complex &x1, complex &x2, double a, double b, double c );
```

which computes the roots of the quadratic equation $ax^2 + bx + c = 0$. The parameters a, b and c (which may take any values) are the coefficients of the quadratic, and x1, x2 are the two roots (if they exist), which may be equal. See Figure 3.1 for the structure plan. The function itself must return the following values, according to the number and type of roots:

  −1: complex roots (discriminant < 0);
   0: no solution ($a = b = 0$, $c \ne 0$);
   1: one real root ($a = 0$, $b \ne 0$, so the root is $-c/b$);
   2: two real roots (which could be equal);
  99: any x is a solution ($a = b = c = 0$).

Use the **complex** class in **complex.h** to find the complex roots (see Chapter 4).

8.12 The Fibonacci numbers are generated by the sequence

$$1, 1, 2, 3, 5, 8, 13, \ldots$$

Can you work out what the next term is? Write a recursive function

```
unsigned long F( int n );
```

to compute the Fibonacci numbers F_0 to F_{20}, using the relationship

$$F_n = F_{n-1} + F_{n-2},$$

given that $F_0 = F_1 = 1$.

8.13 The first three Legendre polynomials are $P_0(x) = 1$, $P_1(x) = x$, and $P_2(x) = (3x^2 - 1)/2$. There is a general *recurrence* formula for Legendre polynomials, by which they are defined recursively:

$$(n+1)P_{n+1}(x) - (2n+1)xP_n(x) + NP_{n-1}(x) = 0.$$

Define a recursive function

```
double P( int n, double x );
```

to generate Legendre polynomials, given the form of P_0 and P_1. Use your function to compute P(2, X) for a few values of X, and compare your results with those using the analytic form of $P_2(x)$ given above.

Chapter 9

Arrays

9.1 Introduction
- Array declaration • No bounds checking!

9.2 Mean and standard deviation
- Reading an unknown amount of data

9.3 Some more basic information
- Initializing arrays • Using sizeof() with arrays • Multi-dimensional arrays

9.4 Frequency distribution: a bar chart

9.5 On arrays, pointers and function parameters
- Arrays and pointers • Arrays as function parameters

9.6 Dynamic arrays
- Simple dynamic variables

9.7 Sorting a list: the Bubble Sort

9.8 Sorting a list: Quick Sort

Summary

Exercises

Situations often arise in real problem solving where we need to handle a large amount of data in the same way, e.g. to find the mean of a set of numbers, to sort a list of numbers or names, to analyse a set of students' test results, or to solve a system of linear equations. To avoid an enormously clumsy program, where perhaps hundreds of identifiers are needed, we can use *arrays*. These may be regarded as variables with components (*elements*), rather like vectors or matrices. They are written in the normal way, except that a subscript is enclosed in square brackets after the variable name, e.g. x[3], y[i + 2 * n].

9.1 Introduction

To see the basic idea enter the following program, which generates an array of 10 random integers in the range 1–10:

```
#include <stdlib.h>
main()
{
  int ranInts[10], i;
  randomize();

  for (i = 0; i <= 9; i++)
    ranInts[i] = 1 + random( 10 );
  return 0;
}
```

Add `ranInts[0],10` (i.e. 10 elements of the array, starting at number 0) to the Watch window, and step through the program a few times with **F8**. Note that `randomize()` ensures that you get a different sequence each time.

You can restrict the Watch to only part of the array. Activate the Watch window (**Alt** plus the window number). You can edit the highlighted expression. E.g. change it to `ranInts[2]`, and only the *third* element of the array is displayed. Try changing this further to `ranInts[2],3`. Note that you can go beyond the end of the array, but you will get garbage.

Array declaration

An array is a contiguous region of storage, declared as

> *type identifier* [*size*] ;

where *type* is the *base type* of the array, and *size* is the number of elements. E.g.

> `double x[10];`

declares x an array of 10 `double` elements, `x[0]`, `x[1]`, ..., `x[9]`. *In C++ the first element of an array is always numbered 0.* This simple fact has caused untold misery to countless programmers, for the following reason.

No bounds checking!

C++ does not check array bounds! If you have declared `double x[10]`, this means 10 elements, *starting at 0*. The last element of the array is therefore `x[9]`. If you therefore make the rather natural mistake of referencing `x[10]`, you will get garbage (look at `ranInts[10]` in the Watch window). Worse still, if you assign a value to `x[10]` at best it will be inaccessible, and at worst it will overwrite some vital part of your program (or you operating system!).

This may seem incredibly irresponsible behaviour on the part of the authors of C++ (and C). The reason, however, is historical. C was originally designed to replace assembly language coding. In order to do this most efficiently it performs very little checking, which would slow execution down dramatically. *You* are expected to do the checking.

9.2 Mean and standard deviation

As another (more useful) example, let's compute the sample mean and standard deviation of a set of N observations. The mean is defined as

$$\overline{X} = \frac{1}{N} \sum_{i=1}^{N} X_i,$$

where X_i is the ith observation. The standard deviation s is defined as

$$s^2 = \frac{1}{N-1} \sum_{i=1}^{N} (X_i - \overline{X})^2.$$

The next program computes these two quantities from data read from the disk file **data**. The first item of data in the file is the value of N. This is followed by exactly N observations.

```
#include <fstream.h>
#include <math.h>
main()
{
   const int maxElts = 100;    // max number of observations
   int i;                      // loop counter
   int n;                      // actual number of observations

   double mean = 0;            // mean
   double stdDev = 0;          // standard deviation
   double x[maxElts];          // array for all observations

   fstream myin( "data", ios::in);
   if (!myin) {                // check if file is there
      cout << "File not found - try again!" << endl;
      return 1;
   }

   myin >> n;                  // first read number of obs
   if (n > maxElts) {
      cout << "Too much data - increase maxElts to " << n <<
              " and try again!" << endl;
      return 2;
   }
```

```
for (i = 0; i <= n-1; i++) {  // remember that first elt is 0!
    myin >> x[i];
    mean += x[i];                // sum of x[i]s
}
mean = mean / n;                 // calculate mean

for (i = 0; i <= n-1; i++)
    stdDev = stdDev  + (x[i] - mean) * (x[i] - mean);
stdDev = sqrt( stdDev / (n - 1) );  // calculate std dev

cout << "Mean:     " << mean << endl;
cout << "Std dev:  " << stdDev << endl;
return 0;
}
```

Try this with some sample data, e.g.

```
10   5.1   6.2   5.7   3.5   9.9   1.2   7.6   5.3   8.7   4.4
```

You should get a mean of 5.76 and a standard deviation of 2.53 (to two decimal places).

The declaration `double x[maxElts]` sets up an array with 100 elements, `x[0]`, `x[1]`, ..., `x[99]`. However, the sample data above consists of only 10 numbers, so only the first 10 elements are used. Note that the value of N must be read first (and must be correct), before the N values may be read. Clearly, N must not exceed `maxElts` (the program checks this).

After the first `for` loop is complete, the first ten elements of the array look like this:

x[0]	x[1]	x[2]	...	x[9]
5.1	6.2	5.7	...	4.4

Now that the data are safely stored in the array, they may be used again, simply by referencing the array name x with an element number. This facility is necessary for computing the standard deviation s according to the formula above—the data must all be read to compute the mean, and the mean must be computed before all the data is re-used to compute s. (To be fair, there is another way of calculating the standard deviation, which doesn't require the use of an array:

$$s^2 = \frac{1}{N-1} \sum_{i=1}^{N} X_i^2 - N\overline{X}^2.$$

As an exercise, rewrite the program without an array, reading all the data into a single variable x.)

Reading an unknown amount of data

It is quite possible that you don't know exactly how much data there is; it might have been entered by a PhD student, or collected by some data logging device. We can adapt the technique introduced in Chapter 6 to input an unknown amount of data, by replacing the section

```
myin >> n;                      // first read number of obs
...
mean = mean / n;                // calculate mean
```

in the last program with the following:

```
n = 0;
while (myin >> a) {             // read and test for EOF
   n++;                         // counter
   if (n > maxElts) {
      cout << "Too much data - increase maxElts to " << n <<
             " and try again!" << endl;
      return 2;
   }
   x[n-1] = a;
   mean += x[n-1];
}
mean = mean / n;               // calculate mean
```

a must also be declared `double`. If you use the same data file as before remember to remove the number of observations from it.

Note that the nth element must be assigned to x[n-1]. Assigning it to x[n] could cause an overwrite at the end of the array if there are exactly maxElts elements.

If the need to specify `maxElts` is a serious restriction the data can be stored in a binary (random access) file instead of an array (see Chapter 12). You could also use a dynamic array (see below).

9.3   Some more basic information

Initializing arrays

An array may be initialized on declaration as follows:

```
int digits[10] = {0, 1, 2, 3, 4, 5, 6, 7, 8, 9};
```

Some values may be left out:

```
int digits[10] = {0, 1, 2, 3};
```

In this case the first four elements are initialized. The remaining elements are set to zero if the array is global, or to garbage if it is local.

If you can't be bothered to count the elements on initialization you can leave out the size:

```
int digits[ ] = {0, 1, 2, 3, 4, 5, 6, 7, 8, 9};
```

This is particularly useful when initializing strings, when it would be a nuisance to count all the characters (and remember to add one for the null terminator):

```
char message[ ] = "Cannot open file\n";
```

The reason why this particular syntax works will become clear later when we look at the relationship between arrays and pointers.

An array declaration may be prefaced with the **const** modifier if you don't want any of its elements changed.

Using `sizeof()` with arrays

Since the **sizeof()** operator returns the number of bytes occupied in memory by its argument it may be used to find the size (i.e. number of elements) of an array, e.g.

```
int array[ ] = {0, 1, 2, 3, 4};
#define MAX_ELTS sizeof( array ) / sizeof( array[0] )
```

`sizeof( array[0] )` returns the number of bytes used by an individual element. Note that `sizeof( array )` returns the number of bytes used by the array, not its size.

If the array is very long, the compiler is better at finding its size this way than you may be!

Multi-dimensional arrays

Arrays can be multi-dimensional. E.g. the matrix

$$\begin{bmatrix} 1 & 2 & 3 \\ 4 & 5 & 6 \end{bmatrix}$$

may be represented by the two-dimensional array

```
int mat[2][3] = { {1, 2, 3}, {4, 5, 6} };
```

`mat` is basically an array of two three-integer arrays. Note how it is initialized, and that it is stored in row-column order.

Of course each subscript starts at zero. So the value of `mat[1][2]` is 6. Matrices are rather difficult to manipulate in C, especially when it comes to passing them as arguments of functions. C++ classes provide a much more elegant and safer representation (Chapter 17).

9.4 Frequency distribution: a bar chart

It is possible to compute a mean and standard deviation without an array. Our next example however could be done without an array only with great difficulty.

Suppose we want to analyse the results of a test written by a class of students. We would like to know how many students obtained percentage marks in the range 0–9, 10–19, ..., 90–99. Each of these ranges is called a *decile*, numbered from zero for convenience. We also need to cater for the bright sparks who get 100 or more (the eleventh "decile"). Suppose the numbers of students who get marks in these ranges are as follows:

```
1   0   12   9   31   26   49   26   24   6   1
```

e.g. 12 obtained marks in the range 20–29. We need an array `int f[11]`, say, with 11 eleven elements, where each element stores the number of students with marks in that particular range, e.g. `f[2]` should have the value 12. The following program prints a bar chart of the *frequency distribution* `f`, where each asterisk represents one student in that range:

```
// Bar chart of frequency distributions
#include <fstream.h>
#include <stdio.h>
main()
{
    int f[11];          // frequencies
    int i, k;           // counters

    fstream myin( "freq", ios::in );
    if (!myin) {
        cout << "File does not exist - try again";
        return 1;
    }
```

```
         for (i = 0; i <= 10; i++) {
           myin >> f[i];
           printf( "%3d", 10*i );
           if (i < 10)
             printf( " - %2d", 10*i+9 );
           else
             printf( " +    " );
           printf( " %3d: ", f[i] );

           for (k = 1; k <= f[i]; k++)
             printf( "*" );

           printf( "\n" );
         }
         return 0;
       }
```

Output:

```
         0 -  9     1: *
        10 - 19     0:
        20 - 29    12: ************
        30 - 39     9: *********
        40 - 49    31: *******************************
        50 - 59    26: **************************
        60 - 69    49: *************************************************
        70 - 79    26: **************************
        80 - 89    24: ************************
        90 - 99     6: ******
       100 +        1: *
```

Note the absence of asterisks for the 10–19 decile. This is because f[1] has the value zero, so that the for loop on k does not execute when i has the value 1.

Of course, in a real situation, the frequencies will not be presented to you neatly on a plate. You are more likely to have a list of the actual marks. You should adapt the program to read a sample set of marks, in the range 0–100, and to convert them into frequencies. The basic mechanism is

```
         myin >> mark;
         d = floor( mark / 10 );      ! int d is the decile
         f(d)++;                      ! another mark in the dth decile
```

9.5   On arrays, pointers and function parameters

Arrays and pointers

It may come as a surprise to you that in C++ (and C) an *array name* is actually a pointer. To see this, recall the program in Section 9.1 to generate an array `int ranInts[10]` of 10 random integers. Declare a pointer

```
int *p;
```

and make the assigment

```
p = ranInts;
```

Now after the code to generate `ranInts` insert the lines

```
for (i = 0; i <= 9; i++) {
   printf( "%3d", *p );
   *p++;
}
```

The array name `ranInts` is in fact the address of the first element `ranInts[0]`. You may have wondered if you could output an entire array by `printf()`ing it; you cannot, because the name is a pointer.

Incidentally, since p above is also the address of `ranInts[0]`, the value stored in `ranInts[i]` can be extracted indirectly by the expression `*(p+i)`. Use this notation to output the array in the **for** loop.

Just to confuse you even more, C (and C++) allows you to abbreviate the indirection operation `*(p+i)` to simply `p[i]`. This makes sense in a C sort of way: if an array name is a pointer, why can't we also treat a pointer as an array? Why not, indeed. You should try this notation out also.

Arrays as function parameters

There are a number of ways of passing an array as an argument to a function. The generally accepted and most efficient way of doing this is to pass the array name to a pointer to the same base type. The following code illustrates a function `SumArray()` which returns the sum of an array passed as an argument:

```
int SumArray( int *list, int size );
main()
{
   int nums[ ] = {0, 1, 2, 3, 4, 5};
   int sizeNums = sizeof( nums ) / sizeof( nums[0] );
   int sum;
   sum = SumArray( nums, sizeNums );
   return 0;
}
int SumArray( int *list, int size )
```

```
{
    int i, sum;
    sum = 0;

    for (i = 0; i <= size-1; i++)
        sum += list[i];
    return sum;
}
```

The declaration int *list in the prototype declares the first parameter list a pointer to an integer. The function is invoked with the array nums—the address of the first element of the array. This address is passed to the pointer list inside the function. Individual elements of the array are referenced with list[i] (the shorthand form mentioned above). You could instead have *(list+i), which is a little cumbersome, although maybe fractionally less confusing.

Note that the array is actually passed by reference (since you are passing its starting address). This means you can also use the function to change any of its elements.

An alternative way of passing an array, which seems more obvious and natural, is to change the prototype (and definition) to

```
int SumArray( int list[ ], int size );
```

No other change is needed in the program. Try it out. This form explains why the shorthand form list[i] was developed, but it does not on the other hand emphasize the fact that the array is still being passed by reference (which it is, as you can easily verify).

9.6   Dynamic arrays

Arrays declared for example as

```
int ranInts[1000];
```

are stored on the stack. This means that the maximum number of elements must be allowed for, even though all the space may never be used. If you have many such arrays, you could run into memory problems. A neat way round this problem is to declare *dynamic* arrays. Such an array is created at runtime, with only as much space as you require, and not more. It can then be deleted after you have finished with it, and its space freed up for other use.

The next program will set up a dynamic array of any size consisting of random integers in the range 1–100:

```
#include <iomanip.h>
#include <stdlib.h>
main()
{
    int *ranInts, i, numElts;
    randomize();

    cout << "How many elements shall we have? ";
    cin >> numElts;
    ranInts = new int[ numElts ];

    if (!ranInts) {
        cout << "Sorry no free memory";
        return 1;
    }

    for (i = 1; i <= numElts; i++)
        ranInts[i-1] = 1 + random( 100 );

    cout << numElts << " random numbers coming up ..." << endl;

    for (i = 1; i <= numElts; i++) {
        cout << setw(5) << ranInts[i-1];
    }

    cout << endl;
    delete[ ] ranInts;
    return 0;
}
```

Note the following:

- **ranInts** is now declared as a *pointer* to **int**.
- The **new** operator in

    ```
    ranInts = new int[ numElts ];
    ```

    sets up (allocates) a block of dynamic memory (on the *heap* as opposed to the stack) large enough to store **numElts int** elements (plus an few extra bytes for overheads). The assignment gives **ranInts** the starting address of this block.
- **new** is technically an operator, not a function, although you can enclose its operand in parentheses if you must.
- If enough space is not available **new** returns **NULL**. You should always test for this before using the dynamic object, as above.

- `ranInts` may now be treated as an array in the normal way.
- When you have finished with `ranInts` you can delete the space allocated to it with the `delete` operator. The syntax for `delete` has a chequered history. Earlier versions of C++ (e.g. Borland C++ Version 2.0) required you to specify the number of elements when deleting an array, e.g.

```
delete[ numElts ] ranInts;
```

Borland and Turbo C++ Version 3.0 however do not require even empty brackets, although they may be optionally used as in the code above. You should do likewise; it helps to remind you that you are in fact deleting an array, and furthermore, we will see later that brackets must be used when deleting dynamic arrays of class objects.

- The operators **new** and **delete** are not part of C; they completely replace the C functions which handle dynamic memory, such as `malloc()`, `calloc()`, `free()`, etc. These functions are mentioned briefly in Appendix D.

Simple dynamic variables

Simple dynamic variables may also be created and deleted:

```
double *p;
p = new double;
*p = 1.2345;
...

delete p;
```

A dynamic variable may be allocated in its declaration:

```
double *p = new double;
```

Dynamic variables (not arrays) may also be initialized with **new**:

```
double *p = new double (1.2345);
```

As a general principle you should always delete a dynamic variable in the block in which it is allocated. For example, if a dynamic variable is allocated in a function and its address is assigned to a *local* pointer, the pointer ceases to exist on return, although the block of memory still exists. If the dynamic variable is not deleted before this, it becomes inaccessible, because its address (the pointer) is lost, and so this block of memory can never be freed.

9.7 Sorting a list: the Bubble Sort

One of the standard applications of arrays is sorting a list of numbers into, say, ascending order. The basic idea is that the unsorted list is read into an array. The numbers are then ordered by a process which essentially passes through the list many times, swopping consecutive elements that are in the wrong order, until all the elements are in the right order. Such a process is called a Bubble Sort, because the smaller numbers rise to the top of the list, like bubbles of air in water. (In fact, in the version shown below, the largest number will "sink" to the bottom of the list after the first pass, which really makes it a "Lead Ball" sort.) There are many other methods of sorting, which may be found in most textbooks on computer science (one of them, the Quick Sort, is given in the next section). These are generally more efficient than the Bubble Sort, but its advantage is that it is by far the easiest method to program. A structure plan for the bubble sort is as follows:

1. Initialize N (length of list)
2. Read the list X
3. Repeat $N - 1$ times with counter K:
   Repeat $N - K$ times with counter J:
       If $X_j > X_{j+1}$ then
           Swop the contents of X_j and X_{j+1}
4. Print the list X, which is now sorted.

As an example, consider a list of five numbers: 27, 13, 9, 5 and 3. They are initially read into the array **X**. Part of the computer memory for this problem is sketched in Table 9.1. Each column shows the list during each *pass*. A

	1st pass	*2nd pass*	*3rd pass*	*4th pass*
x[1]:	27/13	13/9	9/5	5/3
x[2]:	13/27/9	9/13/5	5/9/3	3/5
x[3]:	9/27/5	5/13/3	3/9	9
x[4]:	5/27/3	3/13	13	13
x[5]:	3/27	27	27	27
	4 tests	3 tests	2 tests	1 test

Table 9.1: Memory during a Bubble Sort

stroke in a row indicates a change in that variable during the pass as the program works down the list. The number of tests ($X_j > X_{j+1}$?) made on each pass is also shown in the table. Work through the table by hand with the structure plan until you understand how the algorithm works.

Sorting algorithms are compared by calculating the number of tests they carry out, since this takes up most of the execution time during the sort. On the Kth pass of the Bubble Sort there are exactly $N - K$ tests, so the total number of tests is

$$1 + 2 + 3 + \ldots + (N - 1) = N(N - 1)/2$$

(approximately $N^2/2$ for large N). For a list of five numbers there are therefore 10 tests, but for 10 numbers there are 45 tests. The computer time needed goes up as the square of the length of the list.

The program below uses the function **BubbleSort()** to sort 100 random numbers. It departs slightly from the structure plan above, which will make $N - 1$ passes, *even if the list is sorted before the last pass*. Since most real lists are partially sorted, it makes sense to check after each pass if any swops were made. If none were, the list must be sorted, so unnecessary (and therefore time-wasting) tests can be eliminated. In the function, the variable **sorted** is used to detect when the list is sorted, and the outer loop is coded instead as a non-deterministic **do-while** loop. **BubbleSort()** is tested here on a list of random integers in the range 1–N, which is implemented as a dynamic array:

```
#include <stdio.h>
#include <stdlib.h>
void BubbleSort( double *x, int n );
main()
{
  double *list;
  int i, num;
  char str[10];

  randomize();
  puts( "How many random integers do you want to sort?" );
  gets( str );
  num = atoi( str );

  list = new double[ num ];
  for (i = 1; i <= num; i++)
    list[i-1] = 1 + random( num );

  printf( "Sort starting now ...\n" );
  BubbleSort( list, num );
  printf( "\nSorting done ...\n" );
```

```
      for (i = 1; i <= num; i++)
        printf( "%5.0f", list[i-1] );

      printf( "\n" );
      delete[ ] list;
      return 0;
    }
    void BubbleSort( double *x, int n )
    {
      int j, k, sorted;
      double temp;

      k = 0;

      do {                              // outer loop of bubble sort
        k++;                            // count the passes
        sorted = 1;                     // they might be sorted

          for (j = 1; j <= n - k; j++)  // count the tests
            if (x[j-1] > x[j]) {        // are they in order?
              temp = x[j-1];            // No ...
              x[j-1] = x[j];
              x[j] = temp;
              sorted = 0;               // a swop was made
            }
      } while (!sorted);                  // must be sorted now
    }
```

9.8 Sorting a list: Quick Sort

Try sorting 1000 numbers with the Bubble Sort. It takes quite a while (about 10 seconds on my 386 machine). Sorting 10 000 numbers (a not inconceivable problem) would take about 100 times longer.

The famous Quick Sort algorithm, invented by C.A.R. Hoare in 1960, is much faster. It is based on the "divide and conquer" approach: to solve a big problem, break it down into smaller subproblems, and break each subproblem down in the same way, until they are small enough to solve. As someone has remarked,

> Every problem has a smaller problem inside, waiting to get out.

How do we break our sorting problem down into manageable subproblems? Well, have a look at the following list:

Number :	19	30	14	28	8	32	72	41	87	33
Position :	1	2	3	4	5	6	7	8	9	10

The value 32 in position 6 has a special property. All the values to the left of it are less than 32, while all the value to the right of it are greater than 32. The value 32 is said to *partition* the sorting problem into two subproblems: a left subproblem, and a right subproblem. These may each be sorted separately, because no value in the left subproblem can ever get into the right subproblem, and vice versa. Furthermore, the value 32 is in the correct position in the right subproblem—it is the smallest value there.

You might think it was a lucky shot that 32 neatly partitioned the list to start with. The brilliance of the algorithm is that given any list, we can always create a partition with the left-most value, without too much difficulty.

Have a look now at a rearrangement of the list:

32	19	41	14	28	8	72	30	87	33
L	L_1							R_1	R

The extreme ends are labelled L and R. We are going to partition the list with the value 32, currently at position L. We define counters L_1 and R_1 with initial values as shown.

The idea now is to move L_1 to the right, while making sure that

every value to the left of position $L_1 \leq$ *partition value*

and then to move R_1 to the left, while making sure that

every value to the right of position $R_1 >$ *partition value*.

Doing this gets us to this situation:

32	19	41	14	28	8	72	30	87	33
L		L_1					R_1		R

What now? There seems to be a deadlock. But no, just swop the value in position L_1 (41) with the value in position R_1 (30):

32	19	**30**	14	28	8	72	**41**	87	33
L		L_1					R_1		R

We can now carry on moving L_1 and R_1, subject to the rules stated above, until we get to this scene:

32	19	30	14	28	8	72	41	87	33
L					R_1	L_1			R

However, the situation now is different. L_1 and R_1 have *crossed*, so we must have found the partition point: it is at position R_1. All that remains to be done now is to swop the values at L (32) and R_1 (8), giving us a partitioned array, with 32 as the partition:

8	19	30	14	28	**32**	72	41	87	33
L					R_1	L_1			R

We can now partition any problem with its left-most value. So the resulting subproblems can be partitioned in the same way. We simply continue partitioning subproblems, until the subproblems have only one member, which must be sorted!

This type of "divide and conquer" algorithm is what recursion was made for. Here is the a recursive implementation. It can be used with the main program which runs BubbleSort() in Section 9.7 (after some minor alterations to it):

```
/*------QuickSort--------------------------------------------------*/
/*                                                                 */
/* This function sorts an array x of r numbers into ascending      */
/* order using C A R Hoare's QuickSort.  The sorted list is        */
/* returned in the array x.  The parameter l must be set to 1 on   */
/* entry.                                                          */
/*                                                                 */
/* Calls void swop( double &a, double &b )                        */
/*                                                                 */
/*------QuickSort--------------------------------------------------*/

void QuickSort( double *x, int l, int r )
{
   int l1, r1;

   if (l < r) {
      l1 = l;
      r1 = r;

      do {
         while (l1 < r && x[l1-1] <= x[l-1])
            l1++;
         while (l < r1 && x[r1-1] >= x[l-1])
            r1--;
         if (l1 < r1)
            Swop( x[l1-1], x[r1-1] );
      } while (l1 < r1);

      Swop( x[l-1], x[r1-1] );
```

```
      QuickSort( x, l, r1-1 );
      QuickSort( x, r1+1, r );
   }
} /* QuickSort */

void Swop ( double &a, double &b )
/* swops the values of a and a */
{
   double t;
   t = a;
   a = b;
   b = t;
} /* Swop */
```

Note that the swopping is implemented as a function `Swop()` using C++ reference parameters. You should try working through the program by hand with the sample array in the figures.

Try the Quick Sort out on 1000 numbers also. You should be impressed! It has been proved that Quick Sort needs approximately $N \log_2 N$ comparisons as opposed to the Bubble Sort's $N^2/2$.

You may be interested to learn that Quick Sort slows down tremendously if the list is already nearly sorted (try it on a sorted list). However, it will work just as fast in this case if you choose a value near the middle of the subproblem for the partition value, instead of the left-most value. Happy sorting!

PS: once we have dealt with structures (Chapter 11) you will be able to write a function to time operations such as a sort (see Exercise 11.1).

Summary

- Arrays are useful for representing and processing large amounts of data.
- An array consists of a contiguous block of elements of the same type (the base type).
- The first element of an array in C++ is always numbered 0. E.g. the declaration

```
   int x[10];
```

  sets up an array of ten `int` elements `x[0]`, `x[1]`, ..., `x[9]`.
- The size of an array is the number of elements it has.
- The `sizeof` operator returns the total number of bytes occupied by an array, *not* its size.
- C++ does not perform bounds checking on arrays. If you assign a value to a non-existent array element you may overwrite something vital.

- Arrays may be initialized and may be declared with the `const` modifier.
- An array name is a pointer, i.e. it contains the address of the first element of the array.
- An array may be passed to a function parameter declared as a pointer to the same base type as the array.
- The shorthand notation `p[i]` dereferences the `i`th address from `p`, i.e. it is equivalent to `*(p+i)`.
- The `new` operator is used to allocate dynamic memory. `delete` destroys it. These operators are not part of C, and replace the old `malloc()` and `free()` functions.
- If dynamic memory is attached to a local pointer in a function it must be deleted before returning from the function. Otherwise the address of the block of memory is lost and it becomes inaccessible.

Exercises

9.1 If `num` is an `int` array with 100 elements write the lines of coding which will

(a) put the first 100 positive integers (1, 2, ..., 100) into the elements `num[0]`, ..., `num[99]`;

(b) put the first 50 positive even integers (2, ..., 100) into the elements `num[0]`, ..., `num[49]`;

(c) assign the integers in *reverse* order, i.e. assign 100 to `num[0]`, 99 to `num[1]`, etc.

9.2 Write some statements to put some Fibonacci numbers (1, 1, 2, 3, 5, 8, ...) into an array `f[0]`, ... What is the largest one which can be represented exactly?

9.3 Salary levels at an educational institution are (in thousands of dollars): 9, 10, 12, 15, 20, 35 and 50. The number of employees at each level are, respectively, 3000, 2500, 1500, 1000, 400, 100, 25. Write a program which finds and writes:

(a) the average salary level;

(b) the number of employees above and below the average level;

(c) the average salary earned by an individual in the institution.

9.4 This exercise illustrates the use of arrays in counting frequencies.

A wumpus (which can be displayed by writing the integer 2 as a character) starts at the top of a cleared screen. He moves down the screen one line at a time, but at the same time moves *one* column to the left or right at random—50% to the left, 50% to the right (i.e. he never stays in the same column). He does this indefinitely, until you press any key to stop (do { ... } while (!kbhit())).

(a) Write a program which displays the wumpus moving in this way. Hints: Let x record his position each time. Start with x = 40. Write x blanks followed by his face, followed by a line feed. Repeat until any key is pressed.

Your program may crash if the wumpus falls off the edge of the screen. Adjust it to put him back at column 40 if he reaches column 1 or 80.

(b) Now record *how many times* he lands in each column. Use an array f[x] to keep count of how many times he lands in column x. Display an informal bar chart on the text screen depicting the frequencies f[x]. Your output should look something like this:

```
...
39: *******************
40: *****************************
41: **************
42: *****************
...
```

(i.e. each asterisk represents landing once in that column). Display the bar chart for a range of frequencies, say 29 to 51. You may have to scale the frequencies.

9.5 Write a program which finds the mean of the elements of an array, and the element of the array furthest in absolute value from the mean. E.g. if the array elements are

```
-4, 0, 5, -1, 10, 3, 4, 1, 2, 4
```

the element 10 is furthest from the mean.

9.6 Develop a structure plan for the problem of writing all the primes less than 1 000 (1 and 2 are generally regarded as primes, and will probably have to be dealt with separately). Write the program. **Hint**: use an array to store the primes as they are found.

9.7 In an experiment N pairs of observations (X_i, Y_i) are made. The *best straight line* that may be drawn through these points (using the method of *Least Squares*) has intercept A on the x-axis and slope B, where

$$B = (S_1 - S_2 S_3/N)/(S_4 - S_2^2/N),$$
$$A = S_3/N - S_2 B/N,$$

and $S_1 = \sum X_i Y_i, S_2 = \sum X_i, S_3 = \sum Y_i, S_4 = \sum X_i^2$. The *correlation coefficient* R is given by

$$R = \frac{NS_1 - S_2 S_3}{\sqrt{NS_4 - S_2^2}\,\sqrt{NS_5 - S_3^2}},$$

where $S_5 = \sum Y_i^2$. ($R = 1$ implies a perfect linear relationship between X_i and Y_i. This fact can be used to test your program.) All the summations are over the range 1 to N. The observations are stored in a text file. It is not known how many observations there are. Write a program to read the data and compute A, B and R. **Hint**: you don't need arrays!

9.8 If a set of points (X_i, Y_i) are joined by straight lines, the value of Y corresponding to a value X which lies on a straight line between X_i and X_{i+1} is given by

$$Y = Y_i + (X - X_i)\frac{(Y_{i+1} - Y_i)}{(X_{i+1} - X_i)}.$$

This process is called *linear interpolation*. Suppose no more than 100 sets of data pairs are stored, in ascending order of X_i, in a text file. Write a program which will compute an interpolated value of Y given an arbitrary value of X keyed in at the keyboard. It is assumed that X is in the range covered by the data. Note that the data must be sorted into ascending order with respect to the X_i values. If this were not so, it would be necessary to sort them first.

Chapter 10

Strings

10.1 Some basics
    • String pointers • String assignments • Reading a string
10.2 Arrays of strings: top of the class
    • Initializing an array of strings
10.3 On strings and pointers
    • Sorting words • Dynamic strings • Arrays of pointers • Pointers to pointers
    • Initializing arrays of pointers • `main()` parameters
10.4 Counting words
10.5 Basic text file I/O with stream objects
10.6 Some string functions
Summary
Exercises

In this chapter we look at some of the interesting things that can be done with strings.

10.1   Some basics

We saw in Chapter 2 that a string of characters may be represented by an array of single characters, e.g.

```
char line[80];
```

declares an array of 80 characters. A string must always have a null terminator. In this example you should therefore only use 79 of the elements, i.e. up to and including `line[78]`. Such an array is called a *string variable*.

179

Because an array name is a pointer, strings may be initialized in the following useful way:

```
char strArray[ ] = "Some bug here";
```

This saves you having to count the characters. Strictly you should only use this form for a string if you want to change it later in the program (so that you can access indiviual characters). Some overheads are involved: on compilation the literal characters from **"Some bug here"** are copied to another location reserved for the array **strArray**.

String pointers

An alternative form of initialization, which should be used if the string is not meant to be changed is:

```
char *strPtr = "Can't open file";
```

(to prevent it from being changed you can use the **const** modifier). The compiler treats this form differently. The characters are stored at a fixed address, and the compiler initializes the pointer **strPtr** to the address of the first character in the string.

Remember that a string pointer like **strPtr** is not a *string*; it is a *pointer* to the first character of a string stored elsewhere. String pointers are used more generally in function prototypes: you will often see such **char** * declarations there.

A long literal string may be split over a number of lines with single backslash characters. Any spaces on either side of such backslashes are inserted into the string, but not the backslashes themselves:

```
char *p = "Rose are red,\
Violets are blue. \
I'm schizophrenic,\
And so am I.";
```

String assignments

You should take care when using the assignment operator with strings.

If you are using a string pointer as declared in

```
char *strPtr = "This is a string";
```

you may later reassign **strPtr** to address a different literal string:

```
strPtr = "A different string";
```

However, this is *not* possible with string variables (arrays of **char**), in spite of the equivalence of arrays and pointers. If you declare the string array

```
char strArray[ ] = "A string array";
```

you may *not* assign a different string with the assignment

```
strArray = "A new string array";   // wrong wrong wrong
```

(which Turbo Pascal programmers might be tempted to do). This is because of the way the respective declarations are compiled.

The correct way to reassign a string variable is with the **strcpy()** function:

```
#include <string.h>
#include <stdio.h>
main()
{
  char strArray[ ] = "This is a longish string";
  strcpy( strArray, "A shorter one" );
  puts( strArray );
  return 0;
}
```

strcpy() copies its second string argument *with its null terminator* into its first argument, overwriting anything which is already there. However, if the new string is shorter, the longer string will still have its original characters stored beyond the new null terminator, as you can easily see in the Watch window if you put a Watch on the individual characters of **strArray**. You must ensure that the target string is long enough to hold the new string. If it isn't memory will be overwritten.

Reading a string

The simplest way to read a string from the keyboard is with **gets()**. To avoid possibly overwriting data if the entered string is too long you can declare a string of length 128:

```
char string[128];
puts( "Enter string:" );
gets( string );
puts( string );  // just to check
```

This works on PCs because the DOS input buffer will not accept more than 127 characters.

gets() reads the newline character but does not insert it into the string. Instread the null terminator is inserted.

Note that using the C++ input stream object

```
cin >> string;
```

does not provide this protection as **cin** can overwrite the end of the buffer.

Of course it may be convenient to have shorter strings. The **iostream** class member function **get()** allows you to specify the maximum number of characters to be read. Suppose you want to input no more than 5 characters from the keyboard:

```
char string[6];
char ch;
cin.get( string, 5, '\n' );
cin.get( ch );
if (ch != '\n')
   cout << "max length exceeded!" << endl;
```

Check this in the Watch window. The first form of the member function with three arguments,

```
cin.get( string, 5, '\n' );
```

extracts up to 5 characters into **string**, stopping when the specified *termination* character is found (the newline character in our case). The termination character is *neither extracted, nor stored* in **string**. The null terminator is inserted into **string**.

The next form of the member function **get()**,

```
cin.get( ch );
```

reads the next character, which may be the newline character, or not, depending on whether or not the string is within the specified length.

If **cin.get(ch)** does not read a newline character, the input has been truncated; this will have implications for any subsequent input.

If a possible leftover newline character could be a problem use the **getline()** member function:

```
cin.getline( string, 5, '\n' );
```

This extracts the termination character (which incidentally defaults in these member functions to the newline character) from the input stream but does not store it in **string**.

10.2 Arrays of strings: top of the class

There are a number of ways of handling arrays of strings. Since a string is an array of characters, one way is as a two-dimensional array of characters.

The program in Chapter 6 to find the student with the highest mark in a class assumes that there is only one such student. We need to use an array if there is a possibility of more than one name at the top:

```
// Top of the class again
#include <fstream.h>
#include <string.h>
#define MAX 100            // size of class
main()
{
   int i = 0;              // student counter
   int numTop = 1;         // there must be at least one
   double mark;            // general mark
   double topMark = 0;     // top mark: can't be less than zero
   char name[16];          // general name
   char topName[MAX][16];  // list of top students' names

   fstream myin( "marks", ios::in );
   if (!myin) {                          // check for file existence
     cout << "Data file not found - program aborted" << endl;
     return 1;
   }

   while (myin) {
     myin.get( name, 15 );
     myin >> mark >> ws;                 // extract whitespace
     if (mark > topMark) {
       topMark = mark;                   // reset the top mark
       numTop = 1;                       // only one at the top now
       strcpy(topName[0], name);         // remember? starts at 0!
     }
     else if (mark == topMark) {
       numTop++;                                  // advance counter
       strcpy( topName[numTop-1], name );  // add her name to the list
     }
   }

   cout << "Top students:" << endl << endl;
   for (i = 1; i <= numTop; i++)                  // print their names
     cout << topName[i-1] << topMark << endl;
}
```

The declaration

```
char topName[MAX][16];
```

sets up `topName` as an array of `MAX` strings, each of which is a character array of 16 characters. The `i`th such string is referenced as `topName[i-1]`. Since each student in the class could theoretically have the top name, we have to allow for `MAX` names.

The stream object `myin` returns `NULL` once the end of the file has been reached.

As an exercise run through the program by hand with the following data:

```
Botha               58
De Klerk            72
Jones               72
Murray              72
Rogers              90
Smith               90
```

Then run it as a check (the first 15 columns of each line in **marks** must be reserved for the names. Note that at the end the name `Murray` will still be in the array `topName` (in element number 2), but his name will not be output because `numTop` has been reset to 2, and will prevent this. (You can examine the array `topName` in the Watch window.)

Initializing an array of strings

An array of strings may be initialized as follows:

```
char days[7][4] =
{
   "Sun", "Mon", "Tue", "Wed", "Thu", "Fri", "Sat"
};
```

The number of rows (7) may be omitted. This way the strings must all have the same length. We will see in Section 10.3 how to use pointers to handle arrays of strings with different lengths.

10.3   On strings and pointers

Sorting words

In C++ single characters may be compared directly (alphabetically) in an `if` statement, e.g.

```
char ch;
ch = getch();
```

```
if (ch >= 'a' && ch <= 'z')
  puts( "lowercase" );
else if (ch >= 'A' && ch <= 'Z')
  puts( "UPPERCASE" );
else
  puts( "not a letter" );
```

The stream objects **cin** and **cin** could just as easily have been used; however, **stdio.h** and **conio.h** are quicker to include than **iostream.h**.

As we have seen, a **char** variable may be treated just like an **int** variable. A **char** variable is represented by its (integer) ASCII code. The comparison works because the ASCII codes of the alphabetic letters are contiguous and constitute what is called a *lexical collating sequence*.

In languages like BASIC and Turbo Pascal strings may be compared alphabetically in an **if** statement. This cannot be done in C++ because strings are arrays of characters, and arrays are pointers. To compare strings alphabetically, we use the **strcmp()** function in **string.h**. The following code reads two strings of 5 letters or less, and prints them in alphabetical order:

```
char str1[6], str2[6];
gets( str1 );
gets( str2 );
if (strcmp( str1, str2 ) < 0) {
  puts( str1 ); puts( str2 );
}
else {
  puts( str2 ); puts( str1 );
}
```

strcmp(str1, str2) returns a negative value if **str1** is ahead of **str2** alphabetically (i.e. if **str1** < **str2**), zero if the strings are the same, and a positive value if **str1** > **str2**. The comparision is made up to the null terminators; any garbage in the array beyond them is ignored.

As a result of the ASCII collating sequence, the strings **str1** in Table 10.1 are all "less than" the strings **str2**. Note that the blank is significant in strings.

strcmp() takes into account differences betweeen upper- and lowercase. A similar function, **strcmpi()** ignores such differences (**i** for ignore).

The following program uses an amended form of the **BubbleSort()** function of Chapter 9 to sort up to 100 strings (with up to 127 characters) entered from the keyboard. Only the header and two other lines of **BubbleSort()** need to be changed (only the changed lines are shown below). Try the program out. It has some subtle new features, which are

str1	str2
"a"	"b"
" a"	"a"
"a "	"aa"
"MCBEAN"	"McBEAN"
"MC BEAN"	"MCBEAN"

Table 10.1: In each case **str1** is "less than" **str2**.

explained below.

```
#include <stdio.h>
#include <string.h>
#include <stdlib.h>
#define MAX_STRINGS 100
char *ReadStr( void );
void BubbleSort( char *x[ ], int n ); // pass an array of pointers now
main()
{
   char ch[10];                  // buffer
   char *strings[MAX_STRINGS];   // array of MAX_STRINGS pointers
   int i;
   int numStrings;              // number of strings to sort

   puts( "How many strings to be sorted?" );
   gets( ch );
   numStrings = atoi( ch );
   puts( "Enter your strings:" );

   for (i = 0; i < numStrings; i++)
      strings[i] = ReadStr();

   BubbleSort( strings, numStrings );
   puts( "Your sorted strings are:" );

   for (i = 0; i < numStrings; i++)
      puts( strings[i] );
   return 0;
}
char *ReadStr( void )                  // create a dynamic string
{
   char *p;
   char buffer[128];
   gets( buffer );
   p = new char[1 + strlen(buffer)];   // dynamic memory for string
```

```
    strcpy( p, buffer );
    return p;                        // return its address
}
void BubbleSort( char *x[ ], int n )  // pass an array of pointers now
    ...
    char *temp;                      // must be a pointer now
    ...
        if (strcmpi( x[j-1], x[j] ) > 0)    // comparing strings now
}
```

Explanations will now follow.

Dynamic strings

One way to represent the list of strings to be sorted is by an array of MAX_STRINGS strings, each of fixed length MAX_LENGTH:

```
char strArray[MAX_STRINGS][MAX_LENGTH];
```

However, the problem with this is that the strings might be of vastly differing lengths, so a lot of valuable memory space could be wasted. We get around this difficulty with two neat and powerful devices: *dynamic strings*, and *arrays of pointers*.

The function ReadStr() reads a string from the keyboard into the char array buffer. It then uses new to create a dynamic character array to store the string:

```
p = new char[1 + strlen(buffer)];
```

strlen() returns the number of characters read into buffer *excluding* the null terminator. The dynamic string therefore needs an extra element for the null terminator. strcpy() then copies the string buffer to p. Note that ReadStr() can return p because it has been declared a pointer to char.

Having read a string, ReadStr() assigns its address to strings[i], which we must now look at.

Arrays of pointers

An array of pointers is the second of the two devices needed in order to represent an array of strings of differing lengths.

The declaration char *strings declares a pointer to char, so the declaration

```
char *strings[MAX_STRINGS];
```

declares an *array* of MAX_STRINGS pointers (to char). A particular element of the array, e.g. strings[i], will be a string pointer, i.e. the starting address of a string. The address assigned to it by ReadStr() is the address of the dynamic string read by ReadStr(). So at the end of the day, we have an array of the starting addresses of the strings (all of different lengths) to be sorted.

The array of pointers is then passed to BubbleSort(). Note the parameter declaration char *x[ ] (one of the three changes to BubbleSort(). Now we come to the most important feature of the string sort. BubbleSort() has been passed an array of pointers x. It sorts this array according to the string pointed to by each x[j]. So when two strings x[j-1] and x[j] are not in alphabetical order, as determined by strcmpi(), *the addresses of the two strings must be swopped*. This is achieved by the three lines (which have remained unchanged from the original version of BubbleSort()):

```
temp = x[j-1];                  // exchange pointers now!
x[j-1] = x[j];
x[j] = temp;
```

temp must therefore be declared a pointer to char (the third change to BubbleSort(). This method of representing any sort of list with an array of pointers is extremely powerful. The individual items are not touched. All the manipulation is done on the pointers addressing them, and this is much faster.

To stress the fact that the sort actually moves the addresses of the strings around, insert the code

```
for (i = 0; i < numStrings; i++)
  printf( "%p ", strings[i] );
printf( "\n" );
```

into main() before and after the call to BubbleSort(). The %p format code enables the addresses to be displayed.

Pointers to pointers

Because pointers and arrays are equivalent, the declaration

```
char *x[ ]
```

in BubbleSort()'s header actually declares x as a pointer to a pointer. x is the name of the array, so it is a pointer (to the first element of the array). However, each element is a string (a pointer to char), so x is in fact a pointer to a pointer. The declaration is therefore exactly equivalent to

```
char **x
```

which you may see in older C code, and some library function prototypes. However, the form `char *x[ ]` is much clearer, and is therefore to be preferred.

Initializing arrays of pointers

The following code initializes an array of string pointers with a set of messages, of any lengths:

```
char *message[ ] =
{ "Can't open file", "Press any key to continue",
  "What a stupid thing to do", "Enter the number again" };
int numMessages = sizeof( message ) / sizeof( char* );
int i;

for (i = 0; i < numMessages; i++)     // display all messages
  puts( message[i] );
```

`sizeof(message)` returns the number of bytes occupied by the pointers (addresses). `sizeof(char*)` is the number of bytes used by a single pointer to `char`.

`main()` parameters

Arrays of pointers provide the means for passing arguments from the DOS command line to a C++ program. The `main()` function can take parameters, e.g.

```
main( int argc, char *argv[ ] )
```

`argc` is the number of parameters entered after the program's name plus one for the program's path. `argv` is an array of string pointers. The first element `argv[0]` is the program's path (represented as a string). `argv[1]` addresses the first command-line parameter, and so on (see Chapter 12 for an example).

10.4   Counting words

When the authorship of a piece of prose is uncertain it sometimes helps to calculate the average number of words per sentence, and the standard deviation of this statistic. A first-year class of mine once found that with samples of about 700 lines, G.K. Chesterton is easily distinguishable from

Lord Macaulay, the former having a significantly shorter mean sentence length, with a larger standard deviation. One of the exercises at the end of the chapter invites you to write a program to compute the average sentence length of a sample of text. An important part of the problem is to detect, extract and count whole words in the text. The next program reads a text file of any length and counts the number of words in it.

It is assumed that words are separated by at least one blank—a word is defined as a string of one or more non-blank characters. So punctuation marks, like commas and full stops will not be counted as separate words, as long as they are not preceded by blanks.

The problem now is, how do we detect complete words? This takes time to think out. It often helps to think how you would explain the problem (not even the answer) to someone who didn't know the first thing about it. Imagine a stream of characters coming past you. How would you know when a complete word had passed? Surely, when a letter changes to a blank—it's the *change* from letter to blank that signals the end of a word. Realizing this will give you the Aha! experience that problem solvers rave about. So the essence of the problem is to read the text one character at a time, keeping a record of the *previous* character (`oldCh`) in order to compare it with the *current* character (`ch`). Basically if the previous character is a letter when the current one is blank, we've found another word. This needs to be tightened up a little, because words can also be separated by a newline character, assuming that words are not split between lines. If we also assume that words consist only of the 52 lower- and uppercase letters of the alphabet (this can easily be extended to included punctuation marks, etc.) then our test for another word is that the previous character is alphabetic while the current is not.

Finally, `oldCh` must be initialized to a blank, to start the ball rolling.

```
#include <fstream.h>
#include <string.h>
main()
{
  fstream myin ("text", ios::in);
  char alphabet[ ] = "abcdefghijklmnopqrstuvwxyz"
    "ABCDEFGHIJKLMNOPQRSTUVWXYZ";  // concatenated
  char ch, oldCh;
  int words = 0;

  oldCh = ' ';
  while (myin.get(ch)) {
    if (strchr(alphabet, oldCh) && !strchr(alphabet, ch))
      words++;
    oldCh = ch;
  }
```

```
    if (strchr(alphabet, oldCh))
       words++;                      // very last ch could be end of word
    return 0;
    }
```

`strchr(alphabet, ch)` searches `alphabet` for an occurrence of `ch`. It returns `NULL` if it is not found (or its address if it is found, but we are not concerned about that here).

The member function `get()` of the `myin` stream object extracts the next character from the input stream, returning `NULL` only if the end-of-file character is extracted. The last character in the file before the end-of-file marker will be in `oldCh`. If this is a letter the last word will not be counted unless we test for it specially after the `while` loop has finished executing.

10.5   Basic text file I/O with stream objects

We have already seen how to use stream objects to get input from text files. The C++ I/O stream library makes it very easy to reverse this process, i.e. to send output to text files. The following program sends a string to a text file **out** (erasing any previous contents if it already exists):

```
    #include <fstream.h>
    main()
    {
      fstream myOut( "out", ios::out );
      char *s = "This is a test";
      myOut << s;
      return 0;
    }
```

You can in fact use `myOut` to send output to the file exactly as you use `cout` to send output to the screen.

`myOut` inherits a member function `put(ch)` which inserts a single character into the output stream. It is the output equivalent of `get(ch)`. The following example shows how `get()` and `put()` may be used to copy a text file **in** a character at a time to another file **out**:

```
    #include <fstream.h>
    main()
    {
      char ch;
      fstream myin("in", ios::in);
      fstream myout("out", ios::out);
```

```
while (myin.get(ch))
  myout.put(ch);

return 0;
}
```

10.6   Some string functions

Some other useful string functions that we have not seen yet are described here.

strcat(dest, src) concatenates (joins) string src to the end of string dest (which is also returned).

strcspn(str1, str2) returns the number of characters of string str1 that are *not* also in string str2. It can be used to find the number of characters in a string preceding a certain punctuation mark.

strlwr(str) converts the uppercase letters in string str to lowercase.

strrev(str) reverses the order of characters in str except for the null terminator.

strset(str, ch) assigns character ch to all characters in string str up to but not including the null terminator.

strupr(str) converts the lowercase letters in str to uppercase.

Other string functions are described in Appendix D.

Summary

- A string is represented in C++ as a **char** array terminated by a null byte.
- A string pointer is a pointer to **char** and holds the address of the first character of the string.
- An array of strings may be declared as a fixed size array of character arrays, all of the same length.
- An array of strings of varying lengths may be declared as an array of pointers. Each pointer addresses a string which may created on the heap with **new**.
- Arguments may be passed from the DOS command line to a program through the **main()** function parameters.
- An **fstream** object may be created to send output to a text file in the same way that **cout** sends output to the screen.
- The **iostream** member functions **get()** and **put()** may be used to handle single character I/O to and from text files.
- C++ has a rich library of functions for handling strings.

Exercises

10.1 Write a program which reads some text from a file and counts the number of blanks in it. Extend it to remove the blanks.

10.2 Write a program which reads a sentence (ending in a full stop—the only one) from the keyboard and prints it backwards, without the full stop. Assume that the sentence is less than 80 characters. You might like to extend your program to check whether a sentence is a palindrome, i.e. one which reads the same backwards as forwards, such as

> *Reward a Toyota drawer*

(someone who draws Toyotas, presumably), or Napoleon's classic lament,

> *Able was I ere I saw Elba*

Assume there is no punctuation, and remove all the blanks first.

10.3 A formula, called Zeller's Congruence, may be used to compute the day of the week, given the date (within a certain range of dates). The formula is

$$f = ([2.6m - 0.2] + k + y + [y/4] + [c/4] - 2c) \text{ modulo } 7,$$

where the square brackets denote the integer part and

- m is the month number, with January and February taken as months 11 and 12 of the preceding year, so March is then month 1, and December month 10;
- k is the day of the month;
- c is the century number;
- y is the year in the century;
- $f = 0$ means Sunday, 1 means Monday, etc.

E.g. 23rd August 1963 is represented by $m = 6$, $k = 23$, $c = 19$, $y = 63$; 1st January 1800 is represented by $m = 11$, $k = 1$, $c = 17$, $y = 99$.

Write a program to read the date in the usual form (e.g. 27 3 1993 for 27th March 1993) and write the given date and the day of the week (in words) on which it falls. **Hint:** use an array of pointers for the days of the week. Test your program on some known dates, like today's date, or your birthday, or 7th December 1941 (Sunday).

The formula will not work if you go too far back. Shakespeare and Cervantes both died on 23rd April 1616. Shakespeare died on a Tuesday, but Cervantes died on a Saturday! This is because England had not yet adopted the Gregorian calendar and was consequently ten days behind the rest of the world. The formula will also not work if you go too far forward.

10.4 Write a program which will read a number in binary code (e.g. 1100— no blanks between the digits) and write its decimal value (12 in this case). **Hint:** read the number as a string, and make use of the fact that the string is an array of characters.

10.5 Write a program to make a copy of a text file, converting the contents to uppercase. Try it out on the following text:

> *Now is the time*
> *for all good men*
> *to come to the aid of the party.*

10.6 Write a program which reads some text from a file, removes all the blanks, and prints it out in five-letter groups, separated by blanks. E.g. the text

> *Twas brillig and the slithy toves*
> *did gyre and gimble in the wabe*

should be printed as

```
Twasb rilli gandt hesli thyto vesdi dgyre andgi mblei nthew abe
```

10.7 Student numbers at the University of Cape Town are constructed from the first letter and next two *consonants* of the student's surname, the first three letters of her first name (padded from the right with Xs if necessary, in both cases), followed by a three-digit number, left-filled by zeros if necessary, to distinguish students for whom these six characters are the same. E.g. Napoleon Onaparte could get the student number ONPNAP001, while Charles Wu could get WXXCHA001.

Write a program which reads a student's surname and first name, in some convenient way, and prints out her student number (you can assume the suffix 001 for everyone).

10.8 Sometimes it is convenient to "pack" text and numeric data into strings. Such strings need to be "unpacked" again. Write a program to read a line of text containing a student's surname and initials, terminated by a comma, and followed by two marks, separated by at least one blank, e.g.

```
Smith JR,   34.6    78.9
```

The program should unpack the string into a string for the name and initials, and two **double** variables for the marks. You may need to consult Appendix D for string functions not mentioned in this chapter.

10.9 Write a program to read text from a file and compute the average number of words per sentence, and its standard deviation. Assume that sentences end with full stops, which occur nowhere else.

10.10 Languages exhibit a characteristic frequency distribution of single letters if a large enough sample of text is analysed. For example, in Act III of *Hamlet* the blank has a frequency of 19.7%, "e" 9.3%, "o" 7.3%, while "z" occurs only 14 times out of 35224 characters. (The blank is important because it gives an indication of word length.) Write a program to determine the letter frequency of a sample of text in a text file. Assume that blanks only occur singly (otherwise you must first reduce all multiple blanks to single blanks).

10.11 Write a program which will read a person's name and address from a disk file and use the data to write a "form letter" with a special offer to paint his house. The data in the file should be in the form

```
Jones
31
Campground Rd
```

If this data is used, the program output should be as follows:

```
Dear Mr Jones
We will paint your house with Sloshon at half price!
You can have the smartest house in Campground Rd.
The Jones family will be able to walk tall again.
Your neighbours at number 33 will be amazed!
```

The items in italics are read (or derived) from the data in the file.

Chapter 11

Structures and unions

11.1 Structures
- typedef and structures

11.2 Unions

11.3 Bit fields

11.4 Passing structures to functions
- Passing the time of day

11.5 Linked lists
- Forward declarations of incomplete structures

Summary

Exercises

The basic types in C++ are called fundamental types, e.g. `int`, `char`, `double`, etc. From these basic types any number of *derived types* can be built, such as arrays and pointers, as we have already seen.

A further very useful derived type is the structure, which we look at briefly in this chapter. We will not spend a great deal of time on structures, since they are superseded by C++ classes. However, they do provide a helpful introduction to classes.

11.1 Structures

An array is a collection of elements, all of the same type. A *structure*, however, enables you to collect variables of different types under one name. This facility enables you to handle a complicated collection of data as a single unit. Enter the following program. Step through it with `first` and `second` in the Watch window:

197

```
#include <string.h>
main()
{
  struct studentType {
    char name[20];
    double mark;
  };
  studentType first, second;

  strcpy( first.name, "Jones, PR" );
  first.mark = 98;
  second = first;
  return 0;
}
```

A structure is declared with the keyword **struct**, with a list of variable declarations, called *members*, enclosed in braces. Each member declaration and the structure declaration must end with a semi-colon.

struct declares a derived type: in this case **studentType**. You then declare variables of this type in the normal way:

```
studentType first, second;
```

(In C, declaration of structure variables must be preceded by the keyword **struct**. This is not necessary in C++.)

Structure members are referenced with a dot:

```
first.mark = 98;
```

The dot is technically an operator called the *structure-member operator*. It has the highest precedence level (Appendix B). The process is also called *dot notation*.

The scope of a member name is the **struct** declaration, i.e. member names must be unique within the same stucture, but do not conflict with names used in other contexts. You could, for example, have a separate variable **int mark**, or another structure with the same member names.

Note that one structure variable may be assigned to another of the same type:

```
second = first;
```

Values of all **first**'s members are copied into the corresponding members of **second**.

A structure variable may be initialized on declaration:

```
studentType third = { "Major, J", 13 };
```

Arrays of structures may be declared:

```
studentType juniors[100];
```

A member of a particular element of the array is then referenced as

```
juniors[i].mark
```

(the dot comes *after* the array index). Arrays of structures are initialized as follows:

```
studentType juniors[2] = {{"Major, J", 12}, {"Clinton, B", 13}};
```

Structures may be nested, i.e. a member of one structure may be a structure itself. Multiple dot notation is used to reference members of the nested structures.

A function may return a structure type.

A structure variable may also be declared immediately after the closing brace of a structure declaration:

```
struct studentType {
    char name[20];
    double mark;
} first, second;
```

The example we have been using is very simple. In a real situation, more information would be needed, e.g.

```
struct studentType {
    char name[20];          // surname and initials
    char address[4][20];    // 4 lines for address
    char telephone[10];
    char id[9];             // registration number
    int gender;             // 0 for male, 1 for female
    int birthDate;          // e.g. 461121
};
```

typedef and structures

In old C code you might come across the following neat use of **typedef** to avoid having to use the keyword **struct** every time a structure variable is declared:

```
typedef struct studentType {
    char name[20];
    double mark;
} StudentType;
```

This does not create a new type; it associates a type (`struct studentType`) with a simpler alias (`StudentType`). The alias usually has its first letter in uppercase to distinguish it from the original type. The structure *tag* (name) can also be omitted:

```
typedef struct {
    char name[20];
    double mark;
} StudentType;
```

Variables may now be declared with type `StudentType`:

```
StudentType first = { "Thatcher M", 101 };
```

11.2   Unions

A *union* is similar to a structure, with the striking and very important difference that all the members have the same starting address, and hence overlap. A structure's members, on the other hand, follow on from each other in contiguous blocks of memory. Together they enable you to do weird and esoteric things, such as separating the two bytes of an integer:

```
union word {
    unsigned w;
    struct {
        char lobyte;
        char hibyte;
    } bytes;
};
word x;
```

`x.bytes.hibyte` follows immediately after `x.bytes.lobyte` in memory, but `x.w` has the same starting address as `x.bytes.lobyte`. So `x.bytes.hibyte` overlaps with the most significant byte of `x.w`. The precise arrangement depends on your computer architecture; this sort of hacking should be done with great care!

11.3   Bit fields

You can specify the number of *bits* occupied by members of a structure (or union). This can save a lot of space. E.g.

```
struct person {
    unsigned age : 7;          // 0 .. 127
```

```
    unsigned gender : 1;      // 0 = male, 1 = female
    unsigned children : 4;    // 0 .. 15
    unsigned : 4;             // unused
};
```

This is called a *bit-field* structure. The **age** member is stored in 7 bits, which allows enough room to hold values from 0 to 127. The **gender** member, however, needs only 1 bit to represent male or female. The last (unnamed) bit field is a *placeholder*. It is used to bring the total number of bits to 16, which is advisable. Placeholders, which may be anywhere in the structure, are optional but recommended.

11.4 Passing structures to functions

Structures may be passed as arguments to functions in a number of ways.

If you want to update a member, the structure should be passed by reference. In C++ this is possible using a reference parameter. In this example, a variable of our structure **studentType** is passed to a function **Fung()** which updates the **mark** member. Check this using the Watch window.

```
struct studentType {
   char name[20];
   double mark;
};
void Fung( studentType &joe );      // reference parameter
main()
{
   studentType student;
   Fung( student );
   return 0;
}
void Fung( studentType &joe )
{
   joe.mark = 99;
}
```

Suppose you want to write a function to output the structure members. Since you don't want to risk accidentally changing any members, you decide to pass it by value:

```
#include <stdio.h>
void Fung( studentType joe )
{
   printf( "%s  %4.0f\n", joe.name, joe.mark );
}
```

This will certainly do the job, but passing large structures by value is very time consuming, since each member is copied to the corresponding member of a local variable. C++, however, allows you to pass a *constant* reference:

```
void Fung( studentType const &joe );
```

This gives you the best of both worlds: the structure is passed by reference (only the address is passed), yet it cannot be modified accidentally.

To pass a structure by reference in C a pointer to the structure must be passed:

```
void Fung( struct studentType *joe )
{
   (*joe).mark = 17;
}
```

The argument must then be passed with the address-of operator:

```
Fung( &student );
```

Parentheses are need in the expression (*joe).mark because the dot operator has a higher precedence than indirection. This is rather cumbersome, so modern C uses the *arrow operator*:

```
joe->age = 17;
```

Incidentally, the arrow operator can be used anywhere as a convenient alias, by declaring a pointer to a structure which has an awkward name. Just remember to initialize the pointer correctly!

Many library functions require structures to be passed by reference in this way, as the next example shows.

Passing the time of day

dos.h declares a structure **time** as follows (*sic*):

```
struct  time   {
    unsigned char   ti_min;     /* Minutes */
    unsigned char   ti_hour;    /* Hours */
    unsigned char   ti_hund;    /* Hundredths of seconds */
    unsigned char   ti_sec;     /* Seconds */
};
```

To get the system time declare a variable, say t, of this type and pass its address to the library function **gettime()**:

```
#include <dos.h>
#include <stdio.h>
main()
{
   time t;
   gettime( &t );
   printf( "%02d:%02d:%02d.%02d\n",
             t.ti_hour, t.ti_min, t.ti_sec, t.ti_hund );
   return 0;
}
```

gettime() fills in your structure variable t with the required information.

11.5 Linked lists

One of the classical and most powerful applications of pointers is in setting up and manipulating *linked lists*. It is also one of the most difficult to understand—I usually have to resort to drawing a lot of diagrams before I can follow what is going on. A thorough study of linked lists and related topics such as binary trees is beyond the scope of this book, and not in keeping with its ethos, so only relatively simple examples will be given here.

The basic idea is to represent a list of items with a chain of dynamic variables, all linked together (as an alternative, say, to an array of the items). The beauty of such a dynamic list is that it can be made to grow and shrink to accommodate whatever you need to store in it. An "item" could be a very complicated structure representing, for example, all relevant information about a particular customer, so that the linked list becomes a customer database.

Each of these dynamic variables in the list should hold a value, and also *point to the next variable* in the chain. Such an object is sometimes a *node*. It can be represented by a structure with two members: a single value (to keep things simple), and a pointer to another node. C++ allows the following rather curious structure declaration:

```
struct node {
  int data;
  node *next;                   // pointer to next node
};
```

A variable of this type is usually represented as follows, the top box being for the value, and the bottom one for the pointer to the next node:

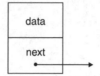

We then declare two pointers to this type:

```
node *end = NULL;          // ends at the head initially
node *p;                   // pointer to a general node
```

p is the address of a general node, while **end** marks the end of the list. The two most important things about a linked list are where it starts (its head) and where it ends. We could have a separate pointer to mark the beginning of the list, but this can also be done with a NULL pointer (since this can be tested for). Initially, the list will be empty, so **end** should point to both the beginning and the end. This is effected by initializing it to NULL. A NULL pointer is often represented by the symbol for earthing an electrical conductor:

Let's now set up a list with only one node, containing the integer value **num**. Firstly, dynamic storage must be allocated for the node:

```
p = new node;
```

This assigns to **p** the address of a block of dynamic memory able to hold one node of type **node**. Next, give it a value (that's easy):

```
p->data = num;
```

We are using the more convenient arrow operator: this is the same as the clumsier

```
(*p).data = num;
```

Finally, and this is the only really tricky part, we must arrange for **end** to point to the end of the list. Where is that? Well, the last (and only node) added is pointed to by **p**, so **end** must hold this address:

```
end = p;
```

If the value of **num** is 1, the situation now looks like this:

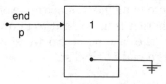

To insert a new node at the end of the chain, however long, the only other requirement is to give the new node the address of the end of the chain:

```
p->next = end;
```

This must be done *before* updating **end** to point to the new node now forming the end of the chain.

This process can be repeated as often as you like. The following piece of code will set up a linked list of three nodes holding the integers 1, 2, 3, providing of course that **end** still has the value NULL when the loop starts:

```
for (i = 1; i <= 3; i++) {      // set up a linked list of 3 nodes
    p = new node;               // create a new node
    p->data = i;                // give it some data
    p->next = end;              // point it to the previous node
    end = p;                    // update the end of the list
}
```

The list is shown in Figure 11.1.

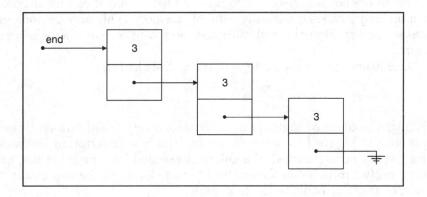

Figure 11.1: A linked list

Having set up the list, the next thing is to *traverse* it and print all the values. This is psychologically satisfying, because it's sometimes hard to believe the list is really there in memory, since none of the nodes have names in the usual sense. This is where it is important to know where the end of the list is—end is the address of the last node. So we start by giving our general pointer p the address of the end of the list:

```
p = end;
```

Then we print the value in that node, and give p the address of the *next* node, which is pointed to by p->next:

```
printf( "%d ", p->data );     // print the data
p = p->next;                  // p now addresses the next node
```

How do we detect the beginning of the list? Remember that the pointer in the first node (at the head of the list) is NULL—this can be tested for, so the above two statements can be enclosed in a **while** loop:

```
p = end;
while (p != NULL) {
   printf( "%d ", p->data );     // print the data
   p = p->next;                  // p now addresses the next node
}
```

p is only NULL after the last execution of the loop, when it is given the address pointed to by the first node. This process demonstrates how important it is to have the pointer **end** pointing to the end of the list—otherwise you could never find it.

One of the advantages of using a linked list is that it can be disposed of when no longer needed, releasing valuable memory. This may be done as we traverse the list from the end, although now a little more housekeeping is required.

Once again, give p the address of the end of the list:

```
p = end;
```

You might be tempted to delete p (i.e. the last node) straight away. However, if you look at Figure 11.1 you will see that this is a prescription for disaster. With the last node removed, the link to the second last one is broken, and it consequently can never be found. So *before* deleting p, the end marker **end** should be made to point to the next node:

```
end = p->next;
```

Now p may be safely deleted, and the general pointer p given the address of the new end of the list:

```
p = end;
```

This process must be carried out as long as the end marker **end** is not NULL:

```
p = end;                   // start at the end
while (p != NULL) {
  printf( "deleting %d\n", p->data );
  end = p->next;           // disconnect end from last node ..
                           // ... and point to next one instead
  delete p;                // delete the disconnected node
  p = end;                 // p now addresses last remaining node
}
```

If you don't understand this completely, perhaps you should also resort to drawing some diagrams.

Before you go any further, you should put these pieces together in a working program to create a linked list, print it, and delete it.

Forward declarations of incomplete structures

If you go in for dynamic data structures (i.e. linked lists, etc.) in a big way you may some day find yourself trying to create two or more structures which refer to each other with pointer members. You must declare structures before you can use them; but you can't declare them all ahead of each other!

To solve this problem you are allowed to make *incomplete* **struct** declarations.

Suppose you want to declare two structures **tweeldleDum** and **tweedleDee**, each with a pointer member to an object of the other's **struct** type. You can do it like this:

```
struct tweedleDum;          // incomplete struct declaration

struct tweedleDee {
   tweedleDum *ptrDum;      // pointer to tweedleDum object
};

struct tweedleDum {
   tweedleDee *ptrDee;      // pointer to tweedleDee object
};
```

The first declaration of **tweedleDum** is incomplete, and must be finished at some point for the code to compile. This is similar to Pascal's forward declaration, which allows procedures to call each other.

Summary

- A structure is a collection of one or more members of the same or different types, declared with the **struct** keyword.
- Members of a structure are referenced with the dot operator, which has the highest precedence.
- Structures may be assigned to each other.
- A structure should be passed to a reference parameter in a function to avoid copying each member to a member of a local structure in the function.
- A structure may be passed to a **const** reference parameter in a function to avoid its members being updated in the function.
- A function may return a structure.
- Arrays of structures may be declared, and arrays may be declared as structure members.
- Structures may be nested.
- The arrow operator with a pointer may be used to reference a structure member.
- Unions are similar to structures, except that all their members overlay each other by starting at the same memory address.
- A bit-field structure specifies how many bits each member occupies.
- A member of a structure may be a pointer to an object of the structure type. Linked lists may be created in this way.

Exercises

11.1 Use **gettime()** (Section 11.4) to write a function **double Tis()** to return the system time in seconds and hundredths of a second since midnight. Use **Tis()** to compare sorting times for a Bubble Sort and a Quick Sort of about 10 000 numbers (depending on what sort of computer you are using!).

11.2 Write a program which uses **Tis()** (Exercise 11.1) to behave like a primitive stop-watch. It should prompt the user to hit any key to start, and any key to finish (using **getch()** and **kbhit()**.

11.3 Use the ideas of Exercise 11.2 to write a program which measures your reaction time. This can be done by making the program sound a short note a random period of time after starting, and then measuring the time that elapses before you hit a key.

Chapter 12

C streams and files

12.1 Standard streams
12.2 Text files
  • Reading text files • `fgets()` and standard input • Writing text files
  • Updating text files • Testing for file existence • File access modes
  • The `printf()` and `scanf()` families
12.3 Binary files
12.3 A binary search
12.4 Sorting student records
Summary
Exercises

C++ does a lot of background I/O housekeeping for you. We have seen that `cin`, `cout`, and related `iostream` objects can handle text I/O involving keyboard, monitor and disk files very easily. When we have looked in more detail at classes we will be able to see how these features work.

However, it is necessary to look behind the scenes somewhat at the more primitive C input/output, in order to get a better understanding of the innovations introduced by C++. In this chapter we look briefly at how C handles I/O.

It's important to understand the difference between files and streams in C. A *file* is the actual physical device involved, e.g. a disk file, a printer, the console. A *stream* is an abstract link between a program and a file, and may be thought of as a stream of data flowing between program and file.

12.1 Standard streams

C has five special *standard* streams which are automatically "opened" and "closed" for you (you've been using them all the time without knowing).

They are **stdin**, **stdout**, **stdprn**, **stderr** and **stdaux**, and are declared in **stdio.h**.

stdin is associated with the *standard input device* (the keyboard), and **stdout** and **stderr** are both associated with the *standard output device* (the screen).

stdin and **stdout** are both redirectable with the DOS input (<) and output (>) redirection symbols from the command line. Standard error output **stderr** is however not normally redirectable, so to guarantee that important error messages are displayed on the screen use a statement like

```
fputs( "Something is definitely wrong!", stderr );
```

fputs() works like **puts()** but requires you to specify the stream to which you want to write text.

stdprn is associated with the printer, so you can print text with

```
fputs( "This is on the printer", stdprn );
```

(you might need to flush the output buffer with **fflush(stdprn)**.

A standard stream may be used as a file pointer in any function that takes a file pointer as an argument (see below).

12.2   Text files

Text files are ASCII files consisting of lines of readable text, like your **.cpp** program files.

Reading text files

The following program reads a text file from disk one character at a time and writes it to standard output. It must be run from the DOS command line, giving the file you want to display as a command line argument. E.g. if the program is compiled as **readch.exe**, to display the file **text** enter a command line like

```
c:\turboc>readch text
```

The program is:

```
// readch.cpp
#include <stdio.h>
#include <stdlib.h>
```

```
main( int argc, char *argv[ ] )
{
  FILE *fp;
  char ch;

  if (argc <= 1)
  { puts( "You must enter a file name" );
    return 1; }

  fp = fopen( argv[1], "r" );

  if (fp == NULL)
  { puts( "Can't find file" );
    return 2; }

  while ((ch = fgetc(fp)) != EOF)
    putchar(ch);

  fclose(fp);
  return 0;
}
```

Note that the program checks whether there is a command line argument, and takes appropriate action if there is not.

The all-important statement in this program is the one that opens the stream and connects it to the disk file:

```
fp = fopen( argv[1], "r" );
```

fp is declared as a *file pointer* to FILE, which is an alias for a structure declared in **stdio.h**. This structure contains various details about the stream represented by **fp**. **fp** is also sometimes called a *stream variable*.

The **fopen()** statement associates the file named in **argv[1]** with the file pointer **fp**. If you were not using a command line argument you could have said

```
fp = fopen( "text", "r" );
```

to open the disk file **text**. **fopen()** doesn't need to appear in an assignment to operate, but this is recommended for the following reason. **fopen()** returns a NULL value only if for some reason the file could not be opened. C will happily read from and write to non-existent files; you can imagine the consequences! This disaster may be prevented by testing whether **fopen()** returns a NULL pointer.

The second argument **"r"** of **fopen()** opens the file for reading only, and protects it from being overwritten. The different values allowed for this argument appear in Table 12.1.

fgetc(fp) reads and returns a single character ch from the stream associated with its argument fp. It returns the value of the predefined symbolic constant EOF when the end of the file is detected, or if any errors are detected.

putchar(ch) sends the character ch to stdout. Since standard output may be redirected, you can use this program to make a copy of a file, e.g.

```
c:\turboc>readch text > text.cpy
```

For that matter you can print it with

```
c:\turboc>readch text > prn
```

Finally, fclose(fp) closes the stream, disconnecting it from the file. This is not strictly necessary, since the program closes any open files before ending. However, it's considered good housekeeping to close files yourself: it shows that you knew they were open!

To read a text file a line at time, you need to know the maximum length of a line. Suppose it is 120. Then declare a string

```
char buffer[121];
```

and use something like

```
while (fgets( buffer, 120, fp )) != NULL)
    fputs( buffer, stdout );
```

fgets() reads up to and including the next newline character, or at most 120 characters. It returns NULL when it fails, i.e. when it reaches the end of the file.

fputs() should be used for output in this case instead of puts(), because puts() writes an additional newline character of its own at the end of the string.

fgets() and standard input

You cannot specify the number of characters to be input from the keyboard with gets(). However, there is nothing to stop you from doing this with fgets() if you supply stdin as the file pointer. E.g. the following code reads no more than 20 characters from the keyboard:

```
char name[21];
fgets( name, 20, stdin );
```

Remember that any of the standard streams may be used as a file pointer with any function that takes a file pointer argument.

Writing text files

Writing to a text file, for example on a disk, is just as easy. The following program reads one character at a time from the keyboard, and writes it to the file **junk**. This continues until you press the DOS end-of-file key, **Ctrl-z** (followed by **Enter**):

```
#include <stdio.h>
main()
{
  FILE *fp;
  char ch = '';
  fp = fopen( "junk", "w" );

  while ((ch = getchar()) != EOF)
    fputc( ch, fp );

  flushall();
}
```

The second argument of **fopen()** (the file *access mode*) is now "w". This means a new file is created for writing (and an existing file of the same name is overwritten—be warned!).

fputc() writes a character to the file.

Because output is buffered, it may not all go the disk file at once. To force data to be written to the disk, a file may be *flushed* with

```
fflush( fp );
```

Alternatively, all open files can be flushed with

```
flushall();
```

Note that **flush()** has two **f**s, while **flushall()** has only one, just to keep you on your toes!

Closing a file with **fclose()** automatically flushes the buffer. If the file was opened for writing, closing it automatically updates its DOS directory date stamp.

To write a string to a text file, use **fputs()**:

```
fputs( "This is on a disk", fp );
```

Unlike **puts()**, **fputs()** does not automatically send a new line character to the output stream. To force a new line use **fputc()** after writing the string:

```
fputc( '\n', fp );
```

Updating text files

Text can be appended (added on) at the end of a text file if it is opened with the "a+" access mode. If the file does not exist, a new file with the specified name is created. Sometimes it is useful, especially on a network system, to keep a log of when a particular program is run. The follow code appends the date and time to the text file **mylog** every time the program containing it is run:

```
\\update.cpp
#include <stdio.h>
#include <time.h>
main( int argc, char *argv[] )
{
    time_t theTime;
    FILE *fp;
    time( &theTime );
    fp = fopen( "mylog", argv[1] );
    fputs( ctime( &theTime ), fp );
    puts( ctime( &theTime ) );
    fclose( fp );
}
```

The file access mode must be supplied from the command line, e.g.

```
c:\turboc>update a+
```

(if the program is compiled as **update.exe**). This example also enables you to experiment with different access modes. E.g. if you use **w** the file is over-written, and the previous information in it is lost.

time() returns the date and time in its argument, which must be of the predefined **time_t** type. Passing this argument in turn to **ctime()** renders the date and time as a string. Note the arguments of **time()** and **ctime()** must be pointers (addresses).

You can only append to a text file, or rewrite it from the beginning; you cannot read a line somewhere in the middle and replace it. If you need to do this a lot you should rather use binary files, which we will look at shortly. However, if you do want to update part of a text file, you have to read it line by line, copying each line to a scratch file, making an alterations on the way. At the end you can rename the scratch file with the original file's name using **rename()**. Suppose the original file is called **text**. Then

```
rename( "scratch", "text" );
```

will do the trick. You can then delete **scratch** with **remove()**:

```
remove( "scratch" );
```

However, remember to close **scratch** first. Removing an open file is asking for trouble.

If you do this with valuable files it would be wise to make a backup first. It is not too difficult to write some code to do this. Suppose you want to have the extension **.bak** for the backup. The following program illustrates the basic idea. It accepts a filename from the command line, replaces the extension with **.bak** and outputs the backup name for you to check:

```
#include <alloc.h>
#include <stdio.h>
#include <string.h>
main( int argc, char *argv[ ] )
{
  int filelen;                          // filename length minus extension
  char *filename;
  char *backname;
  filename = strdup( argv[1] );
  filelen = strcspn( filename, "." );   // find the "."
  backname = new char[filelen + 4];     // create a dynamic string
  strncpy( backname, filename, filelen ); // copy filename minus ext
  backname[filelen] = ' ';              // insert a null terminator
  strcat( backname, ".bak" );           // concatenate extension
  puts( backname );
  delete backname;
  free( filename );
  return 0;
}
```

strdup() makes a duplicate of the command line argument, returning the address of the duplicate. It automatically allocates the required heap space with the old-fashioned C function **malloc()** (see Appendix D), which must be deleted with **free()** (not **delete**).

strcspn() is used to return the length of the filename before the extension dot (if any).

The C++ operator **new** allocates dynamic memory for the backup name (the extra 4 bytes being for the dot and the extension).

strncpy() copies the filename without its extension (if any) to the backup name. However, it leaves **backname** *without a null terminator*, which must be inserted. This little problem can be avoided if the old C function **calloc()** is used to allocate memory:

```
(char *) calloc( 1, filelen + 4 );
```

(char *) is a typecast which returns a pointer to **char**. This is needed since **calloc()** returns a void pointer by default. The call to **calloc()** allocates 1 item of size `filelen` + 4 bytes, but unlike `malloc()`, sets every byte to zero. Thus every byte is a null terminator, so it is not necessary to insert one explicitly. The memory must be deallocated with `free()`.

Finally the extension is stuck on the end of `backname` with `strcat()`.

Coming back to the question of updating a text file, before you write to a scratch file you need to check whether a file of that name already exists. It might be that you should avoid overwriting it!

Testing for file existence

File existence can be checked easily by testing the pointer returned by `fopen()`. Suppose you want to find out whether or not a file with name `filename` exists. Try to open the file for reading, with the `"r"` access mode. A `NULL` pointer will be returned only if the file does not exist, and you can code your response accordingly, e.g.

```
main( int argc, char *argv[ ] )
{
  FILE *fp;
  char *filename;
  filename = strdup( argv[1] );
  fp = fopen( filename, "r" );
  if (fp == NULL) {
    puts( "File does not exist" );
    ...
  }
  else {
    puts( "File already exists" );
    ...
  }
```

File access modes

File access modes are summarized in Table 12.1. In addition a t or b may be appended to the string to specify a text or binary file (the default is governed by the global variable _fmode set in **stdio.h**). The t or b may also be inserted between the initial letter and the +. E.g. `"rt+"` is the same as `"r+t"`.

The `printf()` and `scanf()` families

Output to a text file may be formatted with `fprintf()`, which works just like `printf()`. The following little program reads one line at a time from the file **text**, numbers the line, and writes the numbered line to another file **text.num**. This could be very useful in producing a numbered printout of a

Mode string	Description
"r"	Read only.
"w"	Write only. Creates a new file or overwrites an existing one.
"a"	Append. Writes (only) at the end of an existing files, or creates a new file.
"r+"	Update. Reads/writes on an existing file.
"w+"	Update. Creates a new file for read/write or overwrites an existing one.
"a+"	Update. Appends (read or write) at the end of the file, or creates a new file.

Table 12.1: File access modes

program for easier reference. You can pretty it up a bit to accept command line arguments, replace extensions, check before overwriting, etc.

```
#include <stdio.h>
main()
{
    char buffer[256];
    int line = 0;
    FILE *in, *out;

    in = fopen( "text", "r" );              // input file
    out = fopen( "text.num", "w" );         // output file

    while (fgets( buffer, 255, in ) != NULL) {
        line++;                             // line number
        fprintf( out, "%3d: %s", line, buffer );
        putchar( '.' );                     // feedback on screen
    }
    puts( "done" );
    fclose(in);
    fclose(out);
    return 0;
}
```

Note the file pointer is the *first* argument of `fprintf()`.

The point about `putchar('.')` is that it gives the user some feedback on the screen while the file I/O is taking place. It's always a good idea to let the user know something is happening. Otherwise he may get worried and reboot unnecessarily.

sprintf() is a string version of printf(). It enables you to write formatted output to a string:

```
char buffer[256];
double d = 12.345;
sprintf( buffer, "The answer is %8.2f", d );
```

buffer could then be written to a file. This device is also useful for displaying numeric values on a graphics screen.

In the earlier chapters of this book we have used C++ fstream objects related to cin to handle numeric input from text files. This is because it is easier to use (and less error-prone) than its C counterpart fscanf().

fscanf() operates rather like fprintf() in reverse. The following code reads two double values, separated by at least one blank, from the first line of a text file **data**:

```
double a, b;
FILE *fp;
fp = fopen( "data", "r" );
fscanf( fp, "%lf %lf", &a, &b );   // remember the &s!
```

If the data values are separated by some other symbol, e.g. one comma, the format code "%lf,%lf" should be used. The general rule is that non-white-space characters in the format code cause fscanf() to extract and discard matching characters from the input stream (whitespace being blanks, tabs and newlines).

Don't forget the ampersands (&) for the input variables. scanf() must modify their values; therefore their addresses must be passed to it.

12.3   Binary files

A *binary file* is regarded by C++ as a chunk of bytes. Data in a binary file is represented directly in binary code. This gives binary files a number of advantages over text files: faster access speed, smaller storage space, and also the ability to transfer any type of item, from an integer to a gargantuan array of structures, with a single statement. Binary files may also be accessed *randomly*, whereas text files must be accessed *sequentially* like songs on a cassette tape. Why then do we ever use text files? Well, for text processing, when you want to able to read the file with the naked eye.

As a simple introduction, the following program creates a new binary file **data**, writes ten integers to it and reads them back again, to prove that they went there:

```
#include <stdio.h>
main()
{
  FILE *fp;
  int i;
  int a;

  fp = fopen( "data", "w+b" );
  if (!fp) {
    puts( "Can't open file" );
    return 1;
  }

  for (i = 1; i <= 10; i++)
    fwrite( &i, sizeof( int ), 1, fp );

  fseek( fp, 0, SEEK_SET );

  for (i = 1; i <= 10; i++) {
    fread( &a, sizeof( int ), 1, fp );
    printf( "%d ", a );
  }

  fclose( fp );
  return 0;
}
```

The b in fopen()'s access mode string means open a binary file. w+ means create a new file for update (read and write). Remember always to test for a successful fopen(). There is nothing that upsets a system quite like writing to a non-existent file, especially if you try to read back from it!

fwrite() has four parameters:

- the address of the item from which bytes are copied to the file;
- the number of bytes in one item;
- the number of such items to be written;
- a file pointer.

Associated with the file is its *current file pointer* (not to be confused with fp, the pointer to FILE). It is one of the members of the FILE structure. It records the position in the file, in terms of bytes from the beginning, at which reading or writing is taking place. So after the first for loop has finished the current file pointer will be at 20 bytes, since the file holds 10 integers each of 2 bytes. (The function ftell(fp) may be used to return the current file pointer as an long int.) Each time fwrite() is executed the current file pointer advances by the number of bytes specified by the second argument of `fwrite()`.

In order to read the data back, we must first set the current file pointer back to the beginning of the file. This is done with `fseek()`. The form used here is

```
fseek( fp, 0, SEEK_SET );
```

which moves the current file pointer forward 0 bytes from the beginning of the file, i.e. positions it at the beginning. `SEEK_SET` means move forward from the beginning according to the number of bytes specified by the second argument.

`fread()` is the reverse of `fwrite()`. Its first argument is the destination address to which the specified number of bytes must be copied from disk. If the variable is not big enough, the excess bytes are sprayed all over the place!

An object of a derived type may be read as a single item. If `a` is declared as `int a[10]` the statement

```
fread( &a, sizeof( a ), 1, fp );
```

reads the entire array of 10 elements, i.e. it reads one item of `sizeof( a )` bytes. Alternatively, the individual elements could be read with

```
fread( &a, sizeof( int ), 10, fp );
```

i.e. read 10 items of `sizeof( int )` bytes.

The binary file itself can't tell if it's storing single integers or an array. All it knows is that it has a stream of bytes. You can read them as something else if you wish, e.g. five `float` variables. Of course they will look quite different then!

12.4   Towards a student record database

Binary files are ideal for representing databases. The basics are illustrated in this section with some very simple operations on a student record database.

First of all we must design the database. To keep the details simple, suppose we want to record only two items of information for each student: the name and one mark. We can define a structure `studentType` for this:

```
#define NAME_LEN 20
struct studentType {
  char name[NAME_LEN+1];
  float mark;
} student;
```

```
// student.h: include file for student record system
// must be included after stdio.h
#define NAME_LEN 20
struct studentType {
  char name[NAME_LEN+1];
  float mark;
} student;
char buffer[128];
FILE *fp;
```

Figure 12.1: Header file **student.h**

We are allowing up to 20 characters for the name (plus one for the null terminator). **student** is a general variable of this type which we will write to the file. Since we will have a number of small programs which need this declaration we will create a header file **student.h** for it, with two other general declarations, as shown in Figure 12.1. Note that it must be included *after* **stdio.h**, since the latter header defines FILE.

Entering new records

The next program, **benter.cpp**, reads names and marks from the keyboard (until **Ctrl-Z** is entered) and writes them to the binary file **student.rec**. The file is opened for appending, so that the program may be used to append more data at any stage. If the specified file does not exist, one is created. Use **benter.cpp** to enter a few names and marks.

```
// benter.cpp
// Enter student records to new or existing binary file
#include <stdio.h>
#include <string.h>
#include <stdlib.h>
#include "student.h"
#define NAME_LEN 20
main()
{

  fp = fopen( "student.rec", "a+b" );   // open binary file for append
  puts( "Enter name (ctrl-z + ENTER to end):" );

  while (gets(buffer) != NULL) {        // input until ctrl-z
    strncpy( student.name, buffer, NAME_LEN );
    if (strlen( buffer ) >= NAME_LEN)
      student.name[NAME_LEN] = '';       // insert null terminator
    puts( "Enter mark:" );
    gets( buffer );
```

```
        student.mark = atof( buffer );
        fwrite( &student, sizeof( studentType ), 1, fp );
        puts( "Enter name (ctrl-z + ENTER to end):" );
    }

    fclose( fp );                              // tidy up
}
```

`gets()` returns NULL on end-of-file.

`strncpy()` copies the first NAME_LEN characters from **buffer** to **student.name**. If the string in **buffer** is too long, the null terminator must be inserted explicitly. The important statement here is

```
    fwrite( &student, sizeof( studentType ), 1, fp );
```

It writes one item of **sizeof(studentType)** bytes from **student** to the file.

Displaying records

The easiest way to display the contents of the database is to read it sequentially:

```
    // bshow.cpp
    // display all student records
    #include <stdio.h>
    #include "student.h"
    main()
    {
        fp = fopen( "student.rec", "rb" );   // for binary read only
        if (!fp) {
            puts( "File not found" );
            return 1; }

        puts( "Student records:" );

        while (fread( &student, sizeof( studentType ), 1, fp )) {
            printf( "%-*s %5.0f\n", NAME_LEN, student.name, student.mark );
        }

        fclose( fp );
    }
```

`fread()` returns zero if the read is unsuccessful or if the current file pointer is at the end of the file.

The asterisk in the format code means that the next integer argument (NAME_LEN) is taken as the field width of the string **s**. The minus sign left-justifies the string.

Updating a record

Updating information in our student record database involves finding the student to be updated, changing his mark, say, and rewriting the updated mark to the disk. In this context it's helpful to define the concept of a *record* as a convenient unit of information on the binary file. The obvious candidate for a record in this sense is the information relating to a particular student, i.e. a variable of type **studentType**, taking up 25 bytes (21 for **name** and four for **mark**). We will number the records from 1, so the total number of records is the same as the record number of the last record. This definition is purely for our own convenience. As far as the file is concerned it is simply a stream of bytes.

To update a student's record, we have to know which record it is, and we have to be able to find it.

The easiest way to find out which record we want is simply by displaying the file with **bshow.cpp** above and counting the records. In the program below, **item** is the record we want. To find the record we use **fseek()** to move the current file pointer to the correct byte. The variable **sizeItem** below is the number of bytes occupied by each record. Since the first record starts at byte 0, record number **item** will start at byte number (**item-1**) * **sizeItem**. The statement

```
fseek( fp, (item-1) * sizeItem, SEEK_SET );
```

moves the current file pointer this number of bytes from the beginning of the file. The record there is read into **student**, and **student.mark** is assigned the new value.

Now the modified record must be written back to the file. However, **fread()** has advanced the current file pointer by one record. So it first must be moved *back* one record, before writing. This can either be done by **fseek()**ing from the beginning again with **SEEK_SET**, or with the statement

```
fseek( fp, -sizeItem, SEEK_CUR );
```

which moves the current pointer *backwards* **sizeItem** bytes from the *current* position. The record is then rewritten with **fwrite()**. The update program is as follows:

```
// bupdate.cpp
// finds a particular record and updates it
#include <stdio.h>
#include <stdlib.h>
#include "student.h"
main()
```

```
    {
      int item;
      int sizeItem = sizeof( studentType );

      fp = fopen( "student.rec", "r+b" );      // opens for binary update
      if (!fp) {
        puts( "File not found" );
        return 1;
      }

      puts( "Which record ?" );
      gets( buffer );
      item = atoi( buffer );
      fseek( fp, (item-1) * sizeItem, SEEK_SET );    // find
      fread( &student, sizeItem, 1, fp );            // read
      printf( "%-*s  %5.0f\n", NAME_LEN, student.name, student.mark );
      puts( "Change mark to?" );
      gets( buffer );
      student.mark = atoi( buffer );
      fseek( fp, -sizeItem, SEEK_CUR );              // reposition
      fwrite( &student, sizeItem, 1, fp );           // rewrite

      fclose( fp );
    }
```

Try it out and use **bshow.cpp** to check that it worked!

The operations of entering, displaying and updating records have all been presented as separate programs, for the sake of clarity. With not too much work they could be combined as functions of a single menu-driven database program. Updating can be made more convenient and efficient by using the searching and sorting ideas discussed in Sections 12.5 and 12.6.

fseek()

The general form of `fseek()` is

```
    fseek( fp, offset, whence );
```

where *fp* is the pointer to FILE, *offset* is the number of bytes to move the current file pointer from the position indicated by *whence*. *whence* may have the values SEEK_SET (beginning of the file), SEEK_END (end), or SEEK_CUR (present position). If *whence* has the value SEEK_CUR, the current pointer is moved fowards or backwards according as the sign of *offset* is positive or negative.

When `fseek()` is used to find records, the access is said to be *random*, as opposed to *sequential*. A text file can only be accessed sequentially; a binary file may be accessed in either way.

You may of course access the bytes of a text file randomly by opening it as a binary file. You need to be fairly confident to do this!

12.5 A binary search

The program **update.cpp** in Section 12.4 is rather unwieldy to use if the database is large, since you must know the record number in order to find it. In order to search more efficiently, the records must first be sorted into alphabetical order. However, we will discuss searching first, assuming the records to be sorted.

An obvious (and easy) method of searching is to go through the (sorted) list of items one by one comparing them with the search item. The process stops either when the search item is found, or when the search has gone past the place where the item would normally be. This is called a *linear* search. Its disadvantage is that it can be very time consuming if the list is long. A much more cunning method is the *binary* search.

Suppose you want to find the page in a telephone directory that has a particular name on it. A linear search would examine each page in turn from page 1 to determine whether the name is on it. This could clearly take a long time. A binary search is as follows. Find the middle of the directory (by consulting the page numbers), and tear it in half. By looking at the last name in the left-hand half (or the first name in the right-hand half), determine which half the required name is in. Throw away the unwanted half, and repeat the process with the half that contains the name, by halving it again. After a surprisingly low number of halvings, you will be left with one page containing the required name. Although this can be a little heavy on telephone directories, it illustrates the principle of a binary search quite well.

The method is very efficient. For example, my local directory has 1 243 pages with subscribers' names and numbers. Since the method halves the number of pages each time, the number of halvings (or *bisections*) required to find a name will be the smallest power of 2 that exceeds 1 243, i.e. 11, since

$$2^{10} = 1\,024 < 1\,243 < 2^{11} = 2\,048.$$

The smart way to find the maximum number of bisections N required is to observe that N must be the smallest integer such that $2^N > 1\,243$, i.e. such that $N > \log_2 1\,243$. In the worst possible case, the required name would be the last one in the directory. A linear search would involve examining all 1 243 pages, whereas a binary search requires you to look at only 11 pages!

Suppose our student database file contains **numRecs** records altogether, sorted so that the names are in alphabetical order. We would like to search for a given student (e.g. in order to be able to view his marks, and change them if necessary). A binary search through the file must try to find the record number (mid) of the required student's name (find). The lower and upper bounds of the record numbers for the search are low and high respectively. mid is the average of these two values. Successive bisections change the value of either low or high, keeping the alphabetical position of find between these bounds each time. Each bisection will truncate the fractional part of mid; hence the starting value of high must be 1 more than the last record number, or the last student can never be found (as a quick experiment with small values of high and low soon demonstrates). The maximum number of bisections required, numBis, is found as described above. This requires computing a logarithm to the base 2 in terms of the natural logarithm. The formula for this is $\log_2 a = \log_e a / \log_e 2$.

The coding for the binary search is as follows:

```
// bsearch.cpp
// binary search through student records
#include <stdio.h>
#include <string.h>
#include <math.h>
#include "student.h"          // include after stdio.h
main()
{
  char find[NAME_LEN+1];
  unsigned int count;         // bisection counter
  unsigned int found;         // 0 false; 1 true
  unsigned int high;
  unsigned int low;
  unsigned int mid;
  unsigned int numRecs;       // number of records in file
  unsigned int numBis;        // number of bisections needed
  int posn;                   // result of strcmpi
  int sizeItem = sizeof( studentType );

  fp = fopen( "student.rec", "rb" );   // open binary file for read
  if (!fp) {
    puts( "File not found" );
    return 1;
  }

  fseek( fp, 0, SEEK_END );                 // find the end of the file
  numRecs = ftell( fp ) / sizeItem;         // no. of student records
  numBis = floor( log( numRecs ) / log(2) ) + 1;
  puts( "Enter name to search for (ctrl-z + ENTER to end):" );

  while (gets(buffer) != NULL) {            // input until ctrl-z
    strncpy( find, buffer, NAME_LEN );
```

```
        if (strlen( buffer ) >= NAME_LEN)
          find[NAME_LEN] = '';              // insert null terminator
        found = count = 0;                  // re-initialize for search
        low = 1;
        high = numRecs + 1;

        do {                                // start binary search
          mid = floor( (high + low) / 2);   // bisect
          fseek( fp, (mid-1) * sizeItem, SEEK_SET );  // rec 1 at 0 bytes
          fread( &student, sizeItem, 1, fp );         // read the record
          posn = strcmpi( find, student.name );       // compare with find
          if (posn == 0)
            found = 1;
          else if (posn < 0)
            high = mid;
          else
            low = mid;
          count++;
        } while (!found && count <= numBis);

        if (found)
          printf( "name found at record %d\n", mid );
        else
          puts( "name not found" );

        puts( "Enter name (ctrl-z + ENTER to end):" );
      }

      fclose( fp );    // tidy up
    }
```

Note the use of `ftell()` to find the number of records in the file.

Try the program out on a small database. Remember to enter the names in alphabetical order, or the chances of finding the right name are pretty slim!

12.6 Sorting student records

In Section 12.5 we pointed out that to search for items they must be sorted. To sort the records in our student database into alphabetical order we could perform a sort (e.g. a Bubble Sort for simplicity) directly on the file with `fseek()`, `fread()` and `fwrite()`. Using the notation of the Bubble Sort in Chapter 9 we could seek and read record $j-1$, seek and read record j, compare their **name** members, and swop them if necessary using `fseek()` and `fwrite()`. While this is fairly easy to program, it could be involve a horrendous amount of disk I/O if the records are large. Remember that not only must the name be swopped around, but also all the other information in the record!

A much neater solution is to use the concept of an array of pointers, introduced for string sorting in Chapter 10, to point to the records. The records themselves can be read once from disk into a dynamic array. In the program below, the array of pointers is also dynamic: this calls for fairly careful use of the indirection operator!

```cpp
// bsort.cpp
// display all student records
#include <stdio.h>
#include <string.h>
#include "student.h"
main()
{
  int sizeItem = sizeof ( studentType );
  int numRecs;
  int i, j, k, posn, sorted;
  studentType *recArray, *temp;      // pointer to dynamic array of sType
  studentType **index;  // pointer to dynamic array of pointers to sType

  fp = fopen( "student.rec", "rb" );      // for binary read only
  if (!fp) {
    puts( "File not found" );
    return 1; }
  fseek( fp, 0, SEEK_END );
  numRecs = ftell( fp ) / sizeItem;
  fseek( fp, 0, SEEK_SET );               // reposition at the beginning
  recArray = new studentType[numRecs];   // dynamic array of records
  *index = new (studentType*)[numRecs];  // dynamic array of pointers

  for (i = 0; i < numRecs; i++)
    fread( &recArray[i], sizeItem, 1, fp );

  for (i = 0; i < numRecs; i++)            // initialize (any order)
    index[i] = &recArray[i];

  k = 0;                                  // sort them
  do {
    k++;
    sorted = 1;
    for (j = 1; j <= numRecs - k; j++) {
      posn = strcmpi( index[j-1]->name, index[j]->name );
      if (posn > 0) {
        temp = index[j-1];
        index[j-1] = index[j];
        index[j] = temp;
        sorted = 0;
      }
```

```
    }
} while (!sorted);

for (i = 0; i < numRecs; i++)                 // display sorted names
    printf( "%s\n", index[i]->name );

fclose( fp );
}
```

The number of records in the student record file is found in the same way as before and stored in **numRecs**. A dynamic array **recArray** is created, and the student records are read into it from disk.

index is a *dynamic* array of pointers (to save space). Look carefully at how it is declared and created. Remember that an array of pointers is in fact a pointer to a pointer. It is this form we must use here because the size of the array is not known at compilation. Hence the declaration

```
studentType **index;
```

A **new** statement then creates an array of type **studentType***, i.e. an array of pointers to **studentType**. Note that the starting address of this array is assigned to ***index**, which means literally that the "value at" **index** is a pointer to **studentType**. The address of each record (**&recArray[i]**) is then assigned to each pointer in the array (**index[i]**).

In the sort that follows, the arrow operator is used to make **index[j]->name** an alias for the much more cumbersome **recArray[index[j]].name**, etc. The actual swopping is done on the pointers, and not on the records.

This could be written as a function and included in your student database package. You could write the pointer array **index** to disk, and read it back each time, like dBASE does.

You could incorporate **index** to display the database. You would only need to resort after adding new records.

You could adapt the binary search to use a pointer array as well. The coding

```
fseek( fp, (mid-1) * sizeItem, SEEK_SET );   // rec 1 at 0 bytes
fread( &student, sizeItem, 1, fp );          // read the record
posn = strcmpi( find, student.name );        // compare with find
```

from **bsearch.cpp** of Section 12.5 may simply be replaced by

```
posn = strcmpi( find, index[mid-1]->name );
```

as long as the same alias relationship is set up between **index** and the records.

Summary

- A file is a physical device such as a disk file or a printer.
- A stream is an abstract connection between a program and a file. Streams are often loosely referred to as files.
- There are five standard file streams: stdin, stdout, stdaux, stderr, and stdprn. They can be passed to any function which takes a FILE* argument. stdin and stdout may be redirected by DOS.
- Except for the standard file streams, all files must be opened with fopen(), which returns a file pointer of type FILE*. FILE is a predefined structure with details of the file being opened.
- fopen() returns NULL if a file cannot be opened. You should always check whether a file is actually open before attempting any I/O.
- It is a good idea to close all files explicitly with fclose().
- A text file is an ASCII file of printable characters.
- Text files may be read or written a line or a character at a time. Formatted file I/O may be done with fprintf() and fscanf().
- Text file I/O can only take place at the beginning or end (append) of the file.
- Binary files are streams of bytes which may be accessed sequentially or randomly.
- Binary file I/O is performed with fread() and fwrite().
- The current file pointer marks the position in a binary file where I/O is taking place. The current file pointer may be moved with fseek().
- Random access binary files are ideally suited for constructing data-bases.

Exercises

12.1 Write a program which converts all the characters in a text file to uppercase. The filename should be entered on the DOS command line. The program should make a backup of the original file first. Use the time of day (hours, minutes, seconds) to construct a name for the scratch file: it is unlikely to be duplicated.

12.2 Write a program to join two text files into one larger file.

Chapter 13

Graphics

13.1 Some basics
- Autodetection of graphics hardware • Overriding autodetection
- Toggling between graphics and text mode • Bars and pies
- Current position and functions relating to it • Line style
- Text on the graphics screen • Viewports • Clearing the screen • Colour
- Plotting points • Animation • Saving a graphics image to disk

13.2 myworld: a world coordinate graphics module
- **myworld** declarations and implementations • **myworld** explained

13.3 Examples
- Fourier square wave approximation • Fractal trees with Turtle graphics
- Lissajous boxes

13.4 The Julia set

13.5 The Mandelbrot set

13.6 Other graphics goodies

Summary

Exercises

A picture, as we said earlier, is worth a thousand words. If you are into scientific and engineering programming, you will doubtless want to draw graphs. In this chapter we look at the basics of C++ graphics, and introduce a useful module for drawing "mathematical" graphs with a minimum of fuss.

13.1 Some basics

Without further ado, you should enter and run the following program, which draws a rectangle with diagonals, covering the screen.

```
#include <graphics.h>
#include <conio.h>
```

231

```
#include <stdlib.h>
#include <stdio.h>
main()
{
   int grDriver = DETECT, grMode, grErr;
   unsigned xMax, yMax;

   initgraph( &grDriver, &grMode, "c:\\borlandc\\bgi" );
   grErr = graphresult();
   if (grErr != grOk) {
     printf( "BGI error: %s\n", grapherrormsg( grErr ) );
     exit( grErr );
   }

   xMax = getmaxx();
   yMax = getmaxy();
   rectangle( 0, 0, xMax, yMax );    // draw rectangle
   line( 0, 0, xMax, yMax );         // draw diagonals
   line( 0, yMax, xMax, 0 );
   getch();
   closegraph();                     // shut down BGI graphics
   return 0;
}
```

The third argument of **initgraph()** must be a string giving the path to the Borland **.bgi** files, which are needed to run Borland/Turbo C++ graphics. Remember that the backslash must be repeated in a string, since a single backslash indicates an escape sequence. This example assumes the **.bgi** files are stored in the subdirectory **c:\borlandc\bgi**.

The graphics functions are prototyped in **graphics.h**.

Autodetection of graphics hardware

initgraph() initializes graphics, by actually calling another function **detectgraph()**, which in turn detects which of the many types of graphics hardware cards (if any) is installed on your computer. Calling **initgraph()** with **grDriver** set to the predefined constant DETECT, as above, means we are requesting *autodetection*. This means that the arguments **grDriver** and **grMode** are set (by the invisible call to **detectgraph()**) to the *driver code* and *mode code* of the graphics device detected. These codes may be found in **graphics.h**. Since the first two arguments of **initgraph()** must be modified they must be passed by reference — hence the ampersands.

For example, if you have a VGA card installed, the value of **grDriver** returned will be the value of the predefined constant VGA (9), and the value returned for **grMode** will be VGAHI (2). This allows for a resolution of 640 pixels horizontally by 480 pixels vertically. A *pixel* (picture element) is the smallest point addressable on the graphics screen with a particular graphics card.

By the way, since `initgraph()` expects an address as its first argument you cannot pass `DETECT` directly as that argument. You must first assign it to a variable, the address of which can then be passed. Terrible things may happen if you call `initgraph()` with the first argument uninitialized.

Having detected your graphics card, the compiler will then attempt to find and load the appropriate *graphics driver*—a file with a **.bgi** extension. BGI stands for Borland Graphics Interface. As the name implies, a graphics driver handles the details of the interface between your C++ graphics program and the hardware device.

If a graphics driver can't be loaded, well and good, because `initgraph()` doesn't attempt to do any graphics; it simply tries to load the driver. However, attempting to do any graphics if the driver is not loaded could cause a disaster. Therefore you should always use `graphresult()` to return the error code. If it is zero (`grOk`) you may proceed. Otherwise you should exit after calling `grapherrormsg()` to interpret the error code. *All graphics programs should have this error trapping code!*

Having got through all that, we can now draw some pictures. Pixels are numbered from the top down, and to the right. So the top left corner of the screen is (0, 0) (PC graphics was not designed by mathematicians!). `getmaxx()` returns the maximum horizontal (x) coordinate. This will be 639 in `VGAHI` mode, since the leftmost coordinate is 0. `getmaxy()` similarly returns 479. The point at the bottom right of the screen will therefore be (639, 479).

```
rectangle( x1, y1, x2, y2 );
```

draws a rectangle with top left corner at (`x1, y1`), and bottom right corner at (`x2, y2`). (Arguments representing pixels are integers.)

```
line( x1, y1, x2, y2 );
```

draws a straight line from (`x1, y1`) to (`x2, y2`).

You must call `closegraph()` when you have finished graphics, since DOS doesn't take kindly to being left hanging in graphics mode.

Overriding autodetection

Some graphics cards cannot be autodetected (in which case graphics is done in default CGA mode), or you may specifically want to override auto-detection. You do this by passing a particular driver and mode code to initgraph(), e.g.

```
grDriver = ATT400;     // ATT card not autodetected
grMode = ATT400HI;
initgraph( &grDriver, &grMode, "c:\\borlandc\\bgi" );
```

It is probably safer, however, to call detectgraph() directly with

```
detectgraph( &grDriver, &grMode );
```

to ascertain the recommended ideal values for these parameters, and then to program a call to initgraph() accordingly. Note that detectgraph() does not initialize graphics; a call to initgraph() is still necessary.

Toggling between graphics and text mode

The function restorecrtmode() restores the screen to its original state before initgraph() was called. Similarly, setgraphmode(grMode) restores the graphics screen after a call to restorecrtmode(). You can therefore use these two functions to toggle back and forth between text and graphics (e.g. to prompt for data) without having to call initgraph() and closegraph() each time:

```
#include <graphics.h>
#include <conio.h>
main()
{
   int grDriver = DETECT, grMode, grErr;

   initgraph( &grDriver, &grMode, "c:\\borlandc\\bgi" );
   outtext( "In graphics mode" );
   getch();
   restorecrtmode();
   cputs( "In text mode" );
   getch();
   setgraphmode( grMode );
   outtext( "Back in graphics" );
   getch();
   closegraph();
   return 0;
}
```

Bars and pies

The following code draws boxes in different coloured *fill patterns* at random:

```
int graphdriver, graphmode;
int x1, y1, x2, y2, style, colour;
graphdriver = DETECT;
initgraph( &graphdriver, &graphmode, "c:\\borlandc\\bgi" );

randomize();
do {
  x1 = random( getmaxx() );
  x2 = random( getmaxx() );
  y1 = random( getmaxy() );
  y2 = random( getmaxy() );
  style = random( 12 );
  colour = random( 15 ) + 1;
  setfillstyle( style, colour );
  bar3d( x1, y1, x2, y2, 0, 0 );
  delay( 10 );
} while ( !kbhit() );

closegraph();
```

The function

```
setfillstyle( style, colour );
```

sets the fill pattern and colour to `style` (0–11) and `colour` (0–15). Possible styles are given in the `setfillstyle()` entry in Appendix D. See below for typical colours.

```
bar3d( x1, y1, x2, y2, depth, topflag );
```

draws a 3-D box with opposite corners at (x1, y1) and (x2, y2) filled with the current fill pattern and colour. `depth` is the depth in pixels (0 if you want a 2-D bar). If `topflag` is true (non-zero) a 3-D lid is drawn on top of the bar.
    There is also a 2-D version:

```
bar( x1, y1, x2, y2 );
```

It is filled with the current fill pattern and colour. The difference between `rectangle()` and `bar()` is that `rectangle()` is not filled with the current fill pattern.
    To fill other shapes like a rectangle use

```
floodfill( x, y, border );
```

to flood an enclosed area. (x, y) is a seed point within the enclosed area to be filled. The area bounded by the colour `border` is flooded with the current fill pattern and fill colour. If the seed point is inside an enclosed area, the inside will be filled. If the seed is outside the area, the exterior will be filled.

The function

```
pieslice( x, y, startangle, endangle, radius );
```

draws a pie slice centred at (x, y) with radius `radius`. The angles are in degrees, and are measured counter-clockwise from $0°$ at 3 o'clock.

Current position and functions relating to it

The *current position* (CP) is the graphics equivalent of the cursor position on the text screen: it is the point on the graphics screen where the next output will go (if appropriate). Functions like `rectangle()` and `line()` don't update the CP. Others, however, do.

```
lineto( x, y );
```

draws a line from the CP to the point (x, y) updating the CP.

```
linerel( dx, dy );
```

draws a line *relative* to the CP, updating the CP. That is, if the CP is (x, y), `linerel(dx, dy)` draws a line from the CP to (x+dx, y+dy).

```
moveto( x, y );
```

moves the CP to (x, y), without drawing on the way.

```
moverel( dx, dy );
```

moves the CP `dx` pixels horizontally and `dy` pixels vertically, again without drawing on the way. `getx()` and `gety()` return the x- and y-coordinates of the CP respectively.

Line style

```
setlinestyle( style, 0, thickness );
```

enables you to change the style and thickness of all subsequent lines drawn, e.g. by `rectangle()`, `line()`, etc. The possible values for `style` and `thickness` are in Appendix D.

Text on the graphics screen

The function

```
outtextxy( x, y, str );
```

displays the text in the string **str** in such a way that the smallest box containing the text will have its top left corner at the position (**x**, **y**). **outtextxy**() does not update the CP.

A related function,

```
outtext( str );
```

outputs **str** at the CP, updating the CP at the same time.

The style, orientation and magnification of text on the graphics screen is controlled by **settextstyle**(), e.g.

```
settextstyle( SANS_SERIF_FONT, HORIZ_DIR, 8 );
outtextxy( 1, 100, "C++ is for me!" );
```

The first argument specifies the *font* (details in Appendix D), the second the orientation (horizontal or vertical), and the third the magnification, on a scale of 1–10.

To output numeric data on the graphics screen, first use **sprintf**() to write the number to a string, and then use **outtext**() to write the string, e.g.

```
char buffer[80];
...

sprintf( buffer, "%9.2f", number );
outtext( "The answer is: " );
outtext( buffer );
```

Viewports

A *viewport* is a "window" on the graphics screen set up with the function

```
setviewport( left, top, right, bottom, clip );
```

The opposite corners of the viewport are (**left**, **top**) and (**bottom**, **right**). If **clip** is true, drawing is clipped off at the viewport boundary. All subsequent graphics coordinates are *relative to this viewport*, the point (0, 0) will be plotted at the top left corner of the viewport. The exceptions to this rule are **getmaxx**() and **getmaxy**() which always return *absolute* coordinates (otherwise you could never enlarge a viewport).

If `clip` is false, points with negative coordinates may be plotted. When you change viewports, the original viewport is not cleared. You can clear a viewport with `clearviewport()`.

Clearing the screen

The whole graphics screen (as opposed to the current viewport) is cleared with

```
cleardevice();
```

Note that `clrscr()` clears the *text* screen. If you attempt to `clrscr()` the graphics screen you will get garbage on the screen.

Colour

Colour is an intriguing and complicated subject. 16 colour constants are defined in a **graphics.h** enumeration for the VGA card:

```
enum COLORS {
    BLACK, BLUE, GREEN, CYAN, RED, MAGENTA, BROWN, LIGHTGRAY,
    DARKGRAY, LIGHTBLUE, LIGHTGREEN, LIGHTCYAN, LIGHTRED,
    LIGHTMAGENTA, YELLOW, WHITE
};
```

These are numbered from 0 to 15, so integers in this range may be used for these colours.

The current drawing colour is set with

```
setcolor( colour );
```

(note the American spelling in the function name) where `colour` may be one of the predefined constants (if that colour is available for the graphics card in the current mode) or an integer in the range 0 to `getmaxcolor()`. E.g. the two statements

```
setcolor( MAGENTA );
setcolor( 5 );
```

have the same effect.

The background colour is set with

```
setbkcolor( colour );
```

These remarks apply to the default *palette* on a VGA card. A palette controls which of the many colours you can choose from when drawing. On

a VGA card this runs into a few hundred thousand (defined with
`setrgbpalette()`, which allows you to set the monitor's red, green and blue
electron "guns"). The Borland/Turbo manuals explain how to use palettes.

Plotting points

An individual pixel may be drawn with

```
putpixel( x, y, colour );
```

Animation

Animation is achieved by repeatedly drawing and moving an image. There are
very sophisticated ways of doing this. The following code demonstrates the
easiest (and crudest) form of animation. An image of PacMan is drawn, and is
moved sedately across the screen:

```
int picSize, x, y, dx;
char *pic;

int graphDriver, graphMode;
graphDriver = DETECT;
initgraph( &graphDriver, &graphMode, "c:\\borlandc\\bgi" );

picSize = imagesize( 0, 0, 40, 40 );
if (picSize == -1) {
  outtext( "Image size exceeds 64K" );
  exit(1);
}
pic = new char[picSize];
pieslice( 20, 20, 30, 330, 20 );
getimage( 0, 0, 40, 40, pic );
x = 0;
y = 0;
dx = 10;
getch();                        // hit any key to animate
cleardevice();

do {
  putimage( x, y, pic, XOR_PUT );   // draw image
  delay( 100 );                     // pause so we can see it
  putimage( x, y, pic, XOR_PUT );   // rub it out
  x = x + dx;                       // advance x
} while (!kbhit());

getch();
closegraph();
delete pic;
```

`imagesize()` returns the number of bytes required to save a copy of the graphics image in the given rectangular area, i.e. bound by the points (0, 0) and (40, 40) in this case. Since not more than one 64K segment of dynamic memory can be addressed by default, `imagesize()` returns −1 if this is the case.

A dynamic array of `char` is allocated to save the image. This is simply a means of addressing a chunk of `picSize` bytes with the pointer `pic`.

`pieslice()` draws PacMan, and `getimage()` copies the part of the graphics screen specified (called a *bitmap image*) into the memory addressed by `pic`.

The `do-while` loop then uses `putimage()` to copy the saved bitmap image addressed by `pic` to the screen. The coordinates specify where the top left corner of the image must be drawn. The effect of `XOR_PUT` is to draw a pixel if there isn't one there already, and to rub one out if there is one there already. So after a short delay, the image is rubbed out by XORing it in the same place. The position is then updated, before the loop XORs it in a new place.

Saving a graphics image to disk

A bitmap image can be written to disk, and read back again, as the following example shows. An image of PacMan is written to disk, and read back to demonstrate that it got there and back safely:

```
int picSize, x, y, dx;
char *pic;
FILE *fp;

int graphDriver, graphMode;
graphDriver = DETECT;
initgraph( &graphDriver, &graphMode, "c:\\borlandc\\bgi" );

picSize = imagesize( 0, 0, 40, 40 );
if (picSize == -1) {
  outtext( "Image size exceeds 64K" );
  exit(1);
}

pic = new char[picSize];
pieslice( 20, 20, 30, 330, 20 );      // draw PacMan
getimage( 0, 0, 40, 40, pic );        // save bitmap image
getch();
fp = fopen( "pacman", "w+b" );         // open for binary read/write
if (!fp) {
  puts( "Can't open file" );
  exit(1);
}
```

```
fwrite( pic, picSize, 1, fp );     // write image to disk as 1 item
cleardevice();
getch();

delete pic;                // destroy bitmap image to make sure!
pic = new char[picSize];   // get some new memory
fseek( fp, 0, SEEK_SET );  // current file pointer to beginning
fread( pic, picSize, 1, fp );  // read image from disk

putimage( 100, 100, pic, XOR_PUT );    // put it somewhere else

getch();
closegraph();
delete pic;
fclose( fp );
```

13.2 myworld: a world coordinate graphics module

Having struggled with a few graphics programs you will readily appreciate that drawing even fairly simple mathematical functions poses a non-trivial challenge. E.g. try to draw the graph of

$$y(t) = e^{-0.1t} \sin t \tag{13.1}$$

for t from 0 to 8π, in steps of $\pi/20$. Also draw in the y- and t-axes (where t is the horizontal coordinate usually represented by x).

The main problem is that a point with problem or *world* coordinates (t, y) must be transformed into a plottable pixel somewhere on the screen. An additional slight irritation is that you might get your graph upside down, because the vertical pixels increase downwards, whereas conventional mathematical coordinates increase upwards.

What we need is a set of functions which will transform our more natural world coordinates into absolute screen coordinates. This is achieved by the module **myworld**, the listing of which appears immediately below. An example and explanation follows.

myworld declarations and implementations

The header file for the module is:

```
// myworld.h: header file for myworld
void wbar(double x1, double y1, double x2, double y2);
void wbar3d(double x1, double y1, double x2, double y2,
            int depth, int top);
```

```
void wline(double x1, double y1, double x2, double y2);
void wlineto(double x, double y);
void wmoveto(double x, double y);
void wouttextxy( double x, double y, char *string );
void wputpoint(double x, double y, int colour);
void wrectangle(double x1, double y1, double x2, double y2);
void setwindow(double xmin, double xmax, double ymin, double ymax);
int h( double x );
int v( double y);
int xrange( void );
int yrange( void );
double grRead( void );
```

In what follows the header file is called **myworld.h**.

The implementations of the functions are as follows:

```
// myworld.cpp: implementation of myworld
#include "myworld.h"
#include <graphics.h>
#include <conio.h>
#include <stdlib.h>
#include <string.h>
viewporttype viewport;
double xleft, xright, yup, ydown;    // globals set by setwindow
void wbar(double x1, double y1, double x2, double y2)
// world coordinate analogue of bar
{
  bar( h( x1 ), v( y1 ), h( x2 ), v( y2 ) );
}
void wbar3d(double x1, double y1, double x2, double y2,
            int depth, int top)
// world coordinate analogue of bar3d
{
  bar3d( h( x1 ), v( y1 ), h( x2 ), v( y2 ), depth, top );
}
void wline(double x1, double y1, double x2, double y2)
// world coordinate analogue of line
{
  line( h( x1 ), v( y1 ), h( x2 ), v( y2 ) );
}
void wlineto(double x, double y)
// world coordinate analogue of lineto
{
  lineto( h( x ), v( y ) );
}
void wmoveto(double x, double y)
// world coordinate analogue of moveto
{
  moveto( h( x ), v( y ) );
}
```

```
void wouttextxy( double x, double y, char *string )
// world coordinate analogue of outtextxy
{
  outtextxy( h(x), v(y), string );
}
void wputpoint(double x, double y, int colour)
// world coordinate analogue of putpixel
{
  putpixel( h( x ), v( y ), colour );
}
void wrectangle(double x1, double y1, double x2, double y2)
// world coordinate analogue of rectangle
{
  rectangle( h( x1 ), v( y1 ), h( x2 ), v( y2 ) );
}
void setwindow(double xmin, double xmax, double ymin, double ymax)
// passes world coordinates from calling program ...
// sets them globally
{
  xleft    = xmin;              // smallest world X-coordinate
  xright   = xmax;              // largest world X-coordinate
  ydown    = ymin;              // smallest world Y-coordinate
  yup      = ymax;              // largest world Y-coordinate
}
int h( double x )
{
// scales world x-coordinate into absolute coordinate h
  return xrange() * (x - xleft) / (xright - xleft);
}
int v( double y )
// scales world y-coordinate into absolute coordinate v
// vertical axis is inverted
{
  return yrange() * (y - yup) / (ydown - yup);
}
int xrange( void )
// calculates xrange for use in function h
{
  getviewsettings( &viewport );
  return viewport.right - viewport.left;
}
int yrange( void )
// calculates yrange for use in function v
{
  getviewsettings( &viewport );
  return viewport.bottom - viewport.top;
}
double grRead( void )
// reads numeric input from graphics screen with echo and basic check
{
```

```
char numSet[] = "0123456789.+-eE";    // numeric character set
char c, cStr[2] = " ";                // cStr needed for outtext
char numStr[80];                      // the number as a string
double num;                           // the number itself
int i = 0;

do {
  c = getch();
  if (c != 13) {                      // code for newline is 13
    if (strchr( numSet, c )) {        // c is legal for a number
      numStr[i] = c;                  // insert c
      i++;
      outtext( strnset( cStr, c, 1 ) );  // display c as a string
    }
    else {
      putch( 7 );                     // ring the alarm
      putch( 7 );
    }
  }
}
while (c != 13);                      // newline signals end of number

numStr[i] = '\n';                     // insert null terminator
return atof( numStr );
}
```

This could be saved in a file, e.g. **myworld.cpp**, compiled separately, and
linked into projects which need it, as described in Chapter 8.

myworld explained

A program which uses **myworld** to draw the attenuated sine graph of
Equation (13.1) is as follows. Note that the header file **myworld.h** must be
included, as well as **graphics.h**:

```
#include <conio.h>
#include <graphics.h>
#include "myworld.h"
#include <math.h>
main()
{
  const double pi = 3.1415927;
  double t, y;
  int graphdriver, graphmode;
  graphdriver = DETECT;

  initgraph( &graphdriver, &graphmode, "c:\\borlandc\\bgi" );
  setwindow( 0, 8 * pi, -1, 1 );              // set the scale
```

```
    wline( 0, -2, 0, 2 );                    // y axis
    wline( 0, 0, 8 * pi, 0 );                // t axis
    wmoveto( 0, 0 );                         // move to origin

    for (t = 0; t <= 8.01 * pi; t += pi / 20) { // remember rounding error
        y = exp( - 0.1 * t ) * sin( t );
        wlineto( t, y );
    }

    getch();
    closegraph();
    return 0;
}
```

As suggested, you will need to link this example program to **myworld.cpp** in a project.

First, let's just see what the program does, before looking into the messy details of **myworld**.

The fundamental function in **myworld** is

```
    setwindow( left, right, bottom, top );
```

This sets up a world coordinate system running from **left** to **right** in the x-direction (t-direction here) across the whole screen, and from **bottom** to **top** in the y-direction. So this particular call to **setwindow()** sets up horizontal world coordinates from 0 to 8π, and vertical world coordinates from -1 to 1.

wline() is the **myworld** counterpart of the library function **line()** (generally, **myworld** functions simply prefix the corresponding library function with a **w**). So

```
    wline( x1, y1, x2, y2 );
```

draws a line between world points (all world coordinates are **double** type) (x1, y1) and (x2, y2). The two **wline()** calls draw the axes. You could add your own axis-drawing functions to **myworld**—why not add tic marks as well?

wmoveto() sets the current position at the world origin, ready for drawing.

wlineto() draws incremental lines from the current position to the specified world point.

Note that **myworld** does not initialize or close graphics. You must still do this.

Now we need to look at **myworld** in a little detail. As already mentioned, **setwindow()** is the crucial function that holds it all together. It sets four global variables, xleft, xright, ydown and yup (declared in the implementation **myworld.cpp**, outside any functions) to its arguments received from the calling program. These variables are used in the subsequent scaling, so they must be global.

Two other fundamental functions are h() and v(). They respectively transform x and y world coordinates into absolute horizontal and vertical screen coordinates. v() also inverts the vertical axis.

Let's take a closer look at h(), for example:

```
int h( double x )
{
// scales world x-coordinate into absolute coordinate h
   return xrange() * (x - xleft) / (xright - xleft);
}
```

It makes use of the globals xleft and xright, as expected, and invokes a further function xrange() which also warrants closer examination:

```
int xrange( void )
// calculates xrange for use in function h
{
   getviewsettings( &viewport );
   return viewport.right - viewport.left;
}
```

It calls a library function getviewsettings() with the address of an argument viewport, declared in **myworld.cpp** of type viewporttype. This is a structure defined in **graphics.h**, with members left, top, right, bottom. Passing a structure variable of this type to getviewsettings() gets it filled with the current viewport settings. What is returned therefore by xrange() is the width of the current viewport in absolute terms, and this is used in turn by h() to scale correctly.

The effect of this is that world coordinate graphs may be drawn in several viewports, *because* setwindow() *works in the current viewport*. If you have different world coordinate limits in different viewports, you will have to remember to call setwindow() after each call to setviewport().

After that, the remaining functions are pretty straightforward. Look at wline() for example:

```
void wline(double x1, double y1, double x2, double y2)
// world coordinate analogue of line
{
   line( h( x1 ), v( y1 ), h( x2 ), v( y2 ) );
}
```

Its arguments are world coordinates. Each argument (e.g. x1) is converted into the appropriate absolute screen coordinate (e.g. h(x1)), and these absolute coordinates are passed to the library function line() to do the actual drawing.

You can make your own world coordinate counterpart of any of the other library functions in a similar way, simply by transforming the world coordinates first with h() and v().

Finally, the **myworld** function grRead() needs a mention. Its purpose is to echo numeric input to the graphics screen, to avoid having to change back to text mode. It has a rather crude syntax checker in that only legal characters for numeric constants are accepted. The legal character set is in the string numSet:

```
char numSet[ ] = "0123456789.+-eE";
```

The **string.h** function strchr() is used to check whether the input character is in this set. It doesn't parse the input to check whether it is a legal number; it only checks that the current character is legal. It also doesn't allow you to correct an entry. You may like to pretty it up a bit.

13.3 Examples

All the examples in this section use the **myworld** module.

Fourier square wave approximation

A square wave of period T may be defined by the function $f(t)$ which is 1 for $0 < t < T$ and -1 for $-T < t < 0$. The Fourier series for $f(t)$ is given by

$$\frac{4}{\pi} \sum_{k=0}^{\infty} \frac{1}{2k+1} \sin\left[\frac{(2k+1)\pi t}{T}\right].$$

It is of interest to know how many terms are needed for a good approximation to this infinte sum. The following program takes $T = 1$, and displays the sum to n terms of the series for t from -1 to 1 in steps of 0.1. The program stops when a non-positive value for n is entered. There are one or two places where you might like to tidy it up. Try some different values of n, between 1 and 30, say.

```
#include <graphics.h>
#include "myworld.h"
```

```
#include <math.h>
#include <conio.h>
float frsqu( int n, float t );
main()
{
    int n;
    float t;
    int graphdriver, graphmode;

    graphdriver = DETECT;
    initgraph( &graphdriver, &graphmode, "c:\\borlandc\\bgi" );
    setwindow( -2, 2, -2, 2 );

    do {
        t = -1;
        moveto( 0, 0 );                   // for input prompt
        outtext( "Value of N (<= 0 to end): " );
        n = grRead();
        wmoveto( t, frsqu( n, t ) );

        while (t <= 1) {
            wlineto( t, frsqu( n, t ) );
            t = t + 0.05;
        }

        getch();
        setviewport( 0, 0, getmaxx(), 15, 0 );   // clear input prompt
        clearviewport();
        setviewport( 0, 0, getmaxx(), getmaxy(), 0 );  // reset viewport!
    } while (n);

    closegraph();
    return 0;
}
float frsqu( int n, float t )
{
    int k;
    float sum = 0;
    float const pi = 3.1415927;

    for (k = 0; k <= n; k++)
        sum = sum + sin( (2 * k + 1) * pi * t ) / (2 * k + 1);
    return (sum * 4 / pi);
}
```

Fractal trees with Turtle graphics

The next program simulates LOGO Turtle graphics. The turtle (which is not
shown, although its path can be drawn) can turn left or right a specified

number of degrees, and can move forward or back a specified distance. It uses world coordinates.

The program uses turtle graphics to draw a tree using a recursively defined shape, which is an example of a *fractal*. (A fractal can be thought of as an object with fractional dimensions, e.g. 1.2, and which is characterized by infinite structure, often with self-replicating features.) The program draws a tree with a vertical stem of height **leng**, which branches symmetrically, so that **ang** is half the angle between the branches. Each branch is made a fraction **frac** of the stem, and branches in the same way as the stem. New branches are always a fraction **frac** of their "parent" branches. This pattern is repeated while the branches remain longer than two units. With a little thought you should be able to see how the recursive procedure **tree** does this. Values of 50, 0.6 and 20 for **leng**, **frac** and **ang** respectively give a fairly common or garden tree, while values of 60, 0.7 and 90, for example, give a slightly less usual looking tree.

```c
#include <graphics.h>
#include "myworld.h"
#include <conio.h>
#include <math.h>
void back( float d );
void clearscreen();
void forward( float d );
void left( float dangle );
void right( float dangle );
void tree( float leng, float frac, float ang );
float angle, x, y;  // angle, position
main()
{
    int graphdriver, graphmode, oldcolour;
    graphdriver = DETECT;
    initgraph( &graphdriver, &graphmode, "c:\\borlandc\\bgi" );
    setwindow( -140, 140, -120, 120 );
    clearscreen();
    oldcolour = getcolor();
    setcolor( getbkcolor() );
    back( 120 );
    setcolor( oldcolour );
    tree( 50, 0.6, 20 );
    getch();
    closegraph();
    return 0;
}
void tree( float leng, float frac, float ang )
{
    if (leng < 2)
        return;
```

```
        forward( leng );
        left( ang );
        tree( frac * leng, frac, ang );
        right( 2 * ang );
        tree( frac * leng, frac, ang );
        left( ang );
        back( leng );
}
void back( float d )
{
        forward( -d );
}
void clearscreen()
{
        clearviewport();
        x = y = 0;
        angle = 90;
}
void forward( float d )
{
        float dx, dy, newx, newy;
        dx = d * cos( angle * M_PI / 180 );
        dy = d * sin( angle * M_PI / 180 );
        newx = x + dx;
        newy = y + dy;
        wline( x, y, newx, newy );
        x = newx;
        y = newy;
}
void left( float dangle )
{
        angle = angle + dangle;
}
void right( float dangle )
{
        left( -dangle );
}
```

Lissajous boxes

This program, which is also purely for fun, draws a series of coloured boxes
based on Lissajous figures:

```
#include "myworld.h"
#include <graphics.h>
#include <conio.h>
#include <math.h>
#include <stdlib.h>
int nx, ny, outlined;
```

```
void reset( void );
main()
{
  int color, clock, style;
  int grdriver, grmode, maxx, maxy;
  int ix, iy;
  float i, x, y;

  outlined = 1;
  grdriver = DETECT;
  initgraph( &grdriver, &grmode, "c:\\borlandc\\bgi" );
  randomize();
  setwindow( -1.3, 1.55, -1.3, 1.55 );
  color = 15;
  clock = 0;
  i = 0;
  nx = 1;
  ny = 3;

  do {
    if (clock % 970 == 0) {
      cleardevice(); reset();
    }
    x = sin( nx * i );
    y = cos( ny * i );
    i = i + 0.01;
    clock = clock + 1;
    style = clock % 15;
    color = clock % 15;
    setcolor( color );
    setfillstyle( style, color );
    wbar3d( x, y, x + 0.22, y + 0.22, 0, 0 );
    if (outlined) {
      setcolor( color );
      rectangle( x, y, x + 0.22, y + 0.22 );
    };
  } while (!kbhit());
  return 0;
}
void reset( void )
{
  nx = 7 * rand()/RAND_MAX + 1;
  ny = 9 * rand()/RAND_MAX + 1;
  if (nx == 1)
    nx = 3;
  if (ny == 1)
    ny = 3;
  if (nx == ny)
    nx = nx + 1;
  if (rand()/RAND_MAX < 0.3)
```

```
        outlined = 1;
    else
        outlined = 0;
}
```

13.4   The Julia set

The discovery of fractals in the past few years has led to a wealth of coffee table books with the most beautiful and fascinating pictures. One such fractal is the *Julia set*. In this section we give a simple program for drawing the Julia set of the complex polynomial

$$z^2 - \mu, \qquad\qquad (13.2)$$

where z is a complex variable, $z = x + iy$, and μ is a complex constant (parameter), $\mu = a + ib$.

A working definition of the Julia set of this family of polynomials is as follows. Take a region of the complex plane. For *every point* z_0 in this region calculate the *iterated function sequence* (IFS) of the polynomial (13.2):

$$z_1 = z_0^2 - \mu,$$
$$z_2 = z_1^2 - \mu,$$
$$\dots$$
$$z_n = z_{n-1}^2 - \mu$$

If an n can be found such that $z_n^2 > R$, where R is the radius of a (large) disk in the complex plane, z_0 is said to have *escaped*. The set of all points z_0 in the region of interest which do *not* escape is the Julia set of the polynomial.

One way to compute the IFS requires the real and imaginary parts of the polynomial $z^2 - \mu$, which are $x^2 - y^2 - a$, and $2xy - b$ respectively.

The code below draws the Julia set of $z^2 - 1.1$, so $a = 1.1$ and $b = 0$. Ideally R should be as large as possible, but we will take it as 4, since this gives quite a reasonable picture. You can experiment with larger values if you have the time! If z_0 has not escaped by the time n has reached the value of `maxIts` (40), we will assume that it will never escape. The program checks each pixel in the world coordinate range $-2 \le x \le 2$, $-2 \le y \le 2$, to see if it escapes (applying the reverse of the transformation used in **myworld** to change world coordinates to absolute coordinates). If the pixel escapes it is lit up. The Julia set is then the set of pixels shaded in the background colour. (Strictly speaking, the Julia set is the *boundary* of the region in the background colour, and the region itself is the *filled* Julia set.) Note that the code does not use the **myworld** module:

```
int maxIts = 40;                   // maximum no. of iterations
double r  = 4;                     // infinity
double a, b;                       // real and imaginary parts of mu
double xmin, xmax, ymin, ymax;     // range of world coordinates
double x, y, x0, y0, newx, newy;   // world coordinates
int colour, grDriver, grMode, grErr;   // graphics variables
int n;                             // counter
int xp, yp;                        // absolute coordinates
int maxxPix, maxyPix;

xmin = -2;
xmax = 2;
ymin = -2;
ymax = 2;
a = 1.1;
b = 0;
grDriver = DETECT;
initgraph( &grDriver, &grMode, "o:\\ama\\borlandc\\bgi" );
grErr = graphresult();
if (grErr != grOk) {
  printf( "BGI error: %s\n", grapherrormsg( grErr ) );
  exit( grErr );
}
maxxPix = getmaxx();
maxyPix = getmaxy();

for (xp = 0; xp <= maxxPix; xp++)
  for (yp = 0; yp <= maxyPix; yp++) {
    x0 = (xmax - xmin) * xp / maxxPix + xmin;
    y0 = (ymin - ymax) * yp / maxyPix + ymax;
    x = x0;
    y = y0;
    n = 0;

    while (n < maxIts && x * x + y * y <= r) {
      n = n + 1;
      newx = x * x - y * y - a;
      newy = 2 * x * y - b;
      x = newx;
      y = newy;
    }

    if (x * x + y * y > r)
       putpixel( xp, yp, 1 );  // see below for colour effects
  }
```

```
getch();              // you do want to admire it after all that!
closegraph();
```

You can approximate some of the beautiful colour pictures you may have seen of the Julia set by drawing an escaped pixel in a different colour, depending on how quickly it escapes:

```
if (x * x + y * y > r) {
    n = (n + 1) % 15;      // colour shows how quickly it escaped
    putpixel( xp, yp, n );
}
```

(n + 1) % 15 is just a matter of taste. n % 15 will give a different colouring.
    Finally, you can speed up the drawing of this particular picture by a factor of four by observing that it has symmetry about both the x- and y-axes:

```
for (xp = 0; xp <= maxxPix / 2; xp++)
    for (yp = 0; yp <= maxyPix / 2; yp++) {
        ...
    if (x * x + y * y > r) {
        n = (n + 1) % 15;      // colour shows how quickly it escaped
        putpixel( xp, yp, n );
        putpixel( maxxPix - xp, yp, n );
        putpixel( xp, maxyPix - yp, n );
        putpixel( maxxPix - xp, maxyPix - yp, n );
    }
}
```

The boundary of the filled Julia set has the self-replicating property characteristic of fractals. Change the program (by adjusting xmin, xmax, etc.) to "zoom" in on one of the "spires" sticking out of the main body of the set. A little patience will be richly rewarded.

13.5   The Mandelbrot set

The *Mandelbrot set* was discovered by Benoit Mandelbrot, and has been described as the most complicated object known to man (?). It is related to the Julia set, and is drawn in much the same way, although it is more difficult to think about.
    The Julia set above is for the polynomial $z^2 - \mu$, with $\mu = 1.1$. If you run the program for a different value of the parameter μ, the set will look different. The Mandelbrot set is concerned with μ, and is drawn in the *parameter* space of the polynomial. The Mandelbrot set is in fact the set of all values of μ for which the *origin* does not escape.

Recall that $\mu = a + ib$. For all possible values of a and b now (as opposed to x and y for the Julia set) we compute the IFS of $z^2 - \mu$, starting at $z = 0$ each time. If z_n (the nth iterate) for a particular μ does not escape it belongs to the Mandelbrot set. The program is very similar to the one for the Julia set. Only the relevant lines are shown here:

```
...
    int maxIts = 20;                // maximum no. of iterations
    double r   = 10;                // infinity
    ...
    xmin = -0.5;
    xmax = 1.5;
    ymin = -1;
    ymax = 1;
    ...

    for (xp = 0; xp <= maxxPix; xp++)
        for (yp = 0; yp <= maxyPix / 2; yp++) {
            a = (xmax - xmin) * xp / maxxPix + xmin;
            b = (ymin - ymax) * yp / maxyPix + ymax;
            x = 0;
            y = 0;
            ...

            if (x * x + y * y > r) {
                n = (n + 1) % 15;       // colour shows how quickly it escaped
                putpixel( xp, yp, n );
                putpixel( xp, maxyPix - yp, n );
            }
```

The Mandelbrot set of this particular function has symmetry about the a axis; this is exploited to speed up the program.

The Mandelbrot set is a "fuzzy" fractal. If you enlarge one of the little "snowmen" on its boundary (coastline) you will see a figure which is similar but not *identical* (zooming on the Julia set coastline reveals identical replicas of the Julia set). In fact the structures on the boundaries of the Mandelbrot set resemble Julia sets. It is as if the coastline of the Mandelbrot set is made by stitching together microscopic copies of the Julia sets which it represents.

Zooming in on the "sea" outside the Mandelbrot set may be rewarding too. You may find islands there that no-one else has ever seen.

13.6 Other graphics goodies

A number of other graphics library functions, e.g. `arc()`, `circle()`, `drawpoly()`, `ellipse()`, `getaspectratio()`, etc., are described in Appendix D.

Summary

- The Borland Graphics Interface (BGI) can automatically detect most graphics devices with `initgraph()`.
- Error trapping with `graphresult()` should always be practised when calling `initgraph()`.
- Absolute coordinates are the coordinates of a pixel on the screen.
- The module **myworld** developed in this chapter is useful for transforming world (problem) coordinates into absolute screen coordinates.
- One way to write numeric data on the graphics screen is to convert it to a string first with `sprintf()` and then to `outtext()` it.
- Different viewports may be opened in different parts of the screen. Text and graphics output may be sent to the viewports.
- Pixel coordinates in the current viewport are relative to the top left corner of the viewport.
- Bitmap images of the graphics screen may be stored in dynamic memory.
- A graphics image may be saved in a disk file, to be read and viewed again later.

Exercises

Most of the exercises are much easier if you use the **myworld** module developed in this chapter.

13.1 Write a program to set up world coordinates from −1 to 1 horizontally, and from −1 to 1 vertically. Draw a border around the perimeter of the screen, and draw the x- and y-axes.

Now draw the graph of your favourite function.

13.2 Rework Exercise 6.6 with graphics output.

13.3 Draw a graph of the population of the USA from 1790 to 2000, using the model

$$P(t) = \frac{197\,273\,000}{1 + e^{-0.03134(t-1913.25)}}$$

where t is the date in years.

Actual data (in 1000s) for the years 1790 to 1950 are as follows: 3 929, 5 308, 7 240, 9 638, 12 866, 17 069, 23 192, 31 443, 38 558, 50 156, 62 948,

75 995, 91 972, 105 711, 122 775, 131 669, 150 697. Superimpose this data on the graph of $P(t)$. Plot the data either as single characters, or as little rectangles.

13.4 The Spiral of Archimedes may be represented in polar coordinates by the equation

$$r = at,$$

where r is the distance along a ray from the origin making an angle t radians with the x-axis, and a is some constant. (The shells of a class of animals called nummulites grow in this way.) Write a program to draw the spiral for some values of a. (If a point has polar coordinates (r, θ), its cartesian coordinates are $x = r \cos \theta$, $y = r \sin \theta$.)

13.5 Another type of spiral is the logarithmic spiral, which describes the growth of shells of animals like the periwinkle and the nautilis. Its equation is

$$r = aq^t,$$

where r and t are as in Exercise 13.4 and $a > 0$, $q > 1$. Write a program to draw this spiral.

13.6 The arrangement of seeds in a sunflower head (and other flowers, like daisies) follows a fixed mathematical pattern. The nth seed is at position

$$r = \sqrt{n},$$

with angular coordinate $\pi dn/180$ radians, where d is the constant angle of divergence (in degrees) between any two successive seeds, i.e. between the nth and $(n+1)$th seeds. A perfect sunflower head is generated by $d = 137.51°$. Write a program to plot the seeds (either use a point for each seed, or construct a symbol to represent each seed). A remarkable feature of this is that the angle d must be exact to get proper sunflowers. Experiment with some different values, e.g. 137.45° (spokes, fairly far out), 137.65° (spokes all the way), 137.92° (Catherine wheels).

13.7 The equation of an ellipse in polar co-ordinates is given by

$$r = a(1 - e^2)/(1 - e \cos \theta),$$

where a is the semi-major axis and e is the eccentricity, if one focus is at the origin, and the semi-major axis lies on the x-axis. Halley's Comet, which visited us recently, moves in an elliptical orbit about the sun (at one focus) with a semi-major axis of 17.9 A.U. (A.U. stands for Astronomical Unit, which is the mean distance of the Earth from the Sun: 149.6 million km.) The eccentricity of the orbit is 0.967276. Write a program which draws the orbit of Halley's Comet and the Earth (assume the Earth is circular).

13.8 A rather beautiful fractal picture can be drawn by plotting the points (x_k, y_k) generated by the following difference equations

$$x_{k+1} = y_k(1 + \sin 0.7x_k) - 1.2\sqrt{|x_k|},$$
$$y_{k+1} = 0.21 - x_k,$$

starting with $x_0 = y_0 = 0$. Write a program to draw the picture (plot individual points; do not join them).

13.9 Have a look at the Julia sets of $z^2 - \mu$, for $\mu = 1.25$, and $\mu = -0.27334 + 0.007421i$. You may need to use a slightly smaller region than the one in the program above for the best effect.

13.10 Zoom in on some parts of the coastline of the Mandelbrot set, e.g. the region $0.04 \le a \le 0.06$, $0.98 \le b \le 1$, where $\mu = a + ib$.

Chapter 14

Objects: a touch of class

14.1 Encapsulation
  - Data members • Member functions • `this` is the way
  - Classes and multiple modules • Inline member functions
  - Overloaded member functions • Default member function parameters
14.2 Constructors and destructors
  - Constructors • Destructors • Local class objects • Pointers to objects
  - Reference objects • Parameter objects • Copy constructors
  - Copying pointer data members • Object return types
  - Type conversion constructors • Arrays of class objects
14.3 Inheritance
  - Single inheritance • Protected members • Qualifying access selectively
  - Replacement member functions • Multiple inheritance • Class types
14.4 Polymorphism
  - Virtual member functions • Virtual destructors
Summary
Exercises

> You'd have to be living face down in a moon crater not to have heard about object-oriented programming. *Tom Swan*
>
> Object-oriented programming is an exceptionally bad idea which could only have originated in California. *Edsger Dijkstra*

Object-oriented program (OOP) seems to be taking over as the fundamental model of software programming in the 90s. It is a vast subject, which cannot be comprehensively covered in one book, let alone an introductory text of this nature. It is necessary to cut through a lot of the hype to get to the really important aspects that affect scientific programming. One of these is the concept of *operator overloading*; we will see in Chapter 17 how to make good use of this in matrix manipulation. Another is the concept of *inheritance*,

259

which enables one to "adapt" previously compiled code without access to the source code. The C++ `iostream` class provides a good example of this. However, fundamental to OOP is the idea of *encapsulation*, and we begin with this.

14.1   Encapsulation

To start with something fairly basic, suppose we want a simple database of citizens. The absolute minimum information needed for each citizen is a name and an identity number (strictly the ID number is enough, but we include the name for illustration). The obvious way to represent a citizen is with a structure:

```
struct citizen {
   int id;
   char name[80];
} you, me, theRestOfUs;
```

In addition we will need some functions, e.g. to assign values to the structure members, and to display them. We can distinguish quite clearly between two entirely separate entities here:

- the data of each citizen, represented by a structure;
- functions which perform operations on the data.

In a nutshell, the object-oriented programming model says that the data and the functions are indissolubly bound up in a single entity, or object: a citizen. You as a citizen have a name and an ID. You acquired these at some stage of your existence (you could even change them); you can "display" them in some way, e.g. by telling the rest of us. Exactly how you display your name and ID may change from time to time. But the data and functions are intimately joined together in a warm body: you, the citizen.

This concept of joining together data and functions is called encapsulation. It is implemented in C ++ by a derived type, the *class*, which looks remarkably like a structure with the keyword **struct** replaced by **class**. We could define a class for our citizen as follows:

```
class TCitizen {
private:
   int id;
   char name[80];
public:
   void Display( void );
   void Set( int idn, char *n );
};
```

The initial T is to remind you that TCitizen is a new data type. What will immediately strike you is that two of the members, Display() and Set(), appear to be function prototypes. Well they are, and they are called *member functions* to be precise.

Data members

The other two more conventional looking members, id and name, are now called *data members* (or *instance variables*). The private access modifier specifies that the data members *are not available outside the class definition*. Their scope extends only through the class definition. They will not conflict with other variables of the same name declared outside the class. We will see soon that this feature is an extremely powerful one: it means you can change the details of the class implementation without reference to any code which may use the class. Class data members are actually private by default. You can declare them public instead if you want to.

Member functions

It has been said that the key to understanding C++ classes is understanding how member functions work. You should therefore be careful not to proceed past any new feature of member functions until you understand it thoroughly (by testing it with sample code).

The member functions must be defined further down in the code. Set() could be defined like this:

```
void TCitizen::Set( int idn, char *n )
{
  id = idn;
  strcpy( name, n );
}
```

The member function name must be prefaced by the class name and a scope resolution operator (::) to show that it belongs to the class TCitizen. Otherwise it looks very similar to an ordinary function. It will expect two parameters which it will assign to the class' two data members, id and name. Note an absolutely fundamental feature of a class: its *member functions have direct access to its data members*.

Display() could be defined like this:

```
void TCitizen::Display( void )
{
  printf( "ID %04d: ", id );
```

```
    puts( name );
}
```

It too has unhindered access to **TCitizen**'s data members.

We can use our class in a small **main()** function as follows. For completeness, the entire program is given:

```
// Citizen class
#include <stdio.h>
#include <string.h>
class TCitizen {
private:
    int id;
    char name[80];
public:
    void Display( void );
    void Set( int idn, char *n );
};
main()
{
    TCitizen me;
    me.Set( 12345, "Smith JR" );
    me.Display();
    return 0;
}
void TCitizen::Set( int idn, char *n )
{
    id = idn;
    strcpy( name, n );
}
void TCitizen::Display( void )
{
    printf( "ID %04d: ", id );
    puts( name );
}
```

The declaration **TCitizen me** declares **me** an *object* of that class type, i.e. class "variables" are called objects. They are also called *instances* of the class type.

Note that a member function is referenced rather like a **struct** member, except that any arguments must be supplied. The reference to **me.Set()** assigns values to both data members; these values can then be output with **me.Display()**. References to the object **me** do not refer explicitly to its (**private**) members: the class definition can be changed without reference to the code using it.

Note also that we are in a sense letting the object **me** decide what to output, by calling the **Display()** member function through **me**. We have shifted the orientation of the program to the object me. That is, we have made the program *object oriented*.

You can arrange to have indirect access to the data members through a member function. We can write a member function GetData() to do this:

```
void TCitizen::GetData( int &idn, char *n )
{
  idn = id;
  strcpy( n, name );
}
```

Don't forget the class name and scope resolution operator, especially in the definition. Adding the following declarations

```
int pubId;
char pubName[80];
```

to main() we can then access the data members with

```
me.GetData( pubId, pubName );
```

Note that GetData() must have a reference parameter &idn so that the argument pubId passed to it can be modified.

Although the member functions in this example are all public, they may also be private.

this is the way

It is worth mentioning in passing that a member function has a special hidden argument, this, which always points to its associated object. So inside Display() the expression

```
this->name
```

is an alias for me.name when me.Display() is referenced. Quite literally, this is how member functions refer to the class objects for which they are called. It is the glue that makes encapsulation work. We will see a lot of this when we look at operator overloading later.

Classes and multiple modules

Class declarations and definitions can get rather large. It is a good idea to declare classes in header files, with the member function definitions (the implementation) in separate modules, which can be precompiled. You can then link them to programs using a project.

We will illustrate this process with our **TCitizen** class. First declare the class in a header file **citizen.h**:

```
// citizen.h: TCitizen class declaration

#ifndef __CITIZEN_H
#define __CITIZEN_H 1 // prevents multiple #includes

class TCitizen {
private:
  int id;
  char name[80];
public:
  void Display( void );
  void Set( int idn, char *n );
  void GetData( int &idn, char *n );
};

#endif /* __CITIZEN_H */
```

Note the device to prevent multiple includes. This becomes important when the classes get more involved.

Next, implement the **TCitizen** class member functions in a separate module **citizen.cpp**:

```
// citizen.cpp: TCitizen class implementation

#include <stdio.h>
#include <string.h>
#include "citizen.h"

// Assign
void TCitizen::Set( int idn, char *n )
{
  id = idn;
  strcpy( name, n );
}

// Display id and name
void TCitizen::Display( void )
{
  printf( "ID %04d: ", id );
  puts( name );
}

// return id and data to caller
```

```
void TCitizen::GetData( int &idn, char *n )
{
  idn = id;
  strcpy( n, name );
}
```

Note that it includes **citizen.h**. This arrangement of classes into headers and implementation files is typical. Declare one or more classes in a header file *name*.**h**, and implement (define) the class member functions in a separate file *name*.**cpp**.

Finally, we use the class in a program **testctzn.cpp**:

```
//testctzn.cpp: include citizen.h and link citizen.cpp
#include "citizen.h"
main()
{
  TCitizen me;
  int pubId;
  char pubName[80];
  me.Set( 12345, "Smith JR" );
  me.Display();
  me.GetData( pubId, pubName );
  ...
  return 0;
}
```

From the Turbo C++ IDE the easiest way to compile **testctzn.cpp** is to use **P**roject/**O**pen to create a new project named **testctzn.prj**. Use the **P**roject/**A**dd command to add **testctzn.cpp** and **citizen.cpp** to the project. Then press **F9** to compile and link the program.

Inline member functions

Strictly speaking, calling a member function such as **Set()** to access class data members may not be the most efficient way of doing things. Fortunately, this doesn't usually impact on the performance of a program. However, there may be times when every millisecond counts. C++ does therefore allow you to declare *inline* member functions. As mentioned earlier, this means that its statements are inserted directly into the compiled code at each point of call.

To declare **Set()** as an inline member function all we have to do is move the function definition from the implementation section to the declaration section. Our class **TCitizen** declaration then looks like this:

```
class TCitizen {
private:
  int id;
  char name[80];
```

```
public:
  void Display( void );
  void Set( int idn, char *n )   // inline declaration now
  {
    id = idn;
    strcpy( name, n );
  }
  void GetData( int &idn, char *n );
};
```

Overloaded member functions

We saw in Chapter 8 that functions with the same name could be overloaded as long as they differed in at least one parameter. Class member functions can be overloaded in the same way. At the moment `Set()` assigns values to both data members `id` and `name`. It may be convenient to change only one of them. Change the class declaration to:

```
#include <stdio.h>
class TCitizen {
private:
  int id;
  char name[80];
public:
  void Display( void );
  void Set( int idn, char *n );
  void Set( int idn );
  void Set( char *n );
  void GetData( int &idn, char *n );
};
```

Then add the following definitions to the implementation:

```
void TCitizen::Set( int idn )
{
  id = idn;
}
void TCitizen::Set( char *n )
{
  strcpy( name, n );
}
```

The statement

```
me.Set( 007 );
```

will then change only `me.id`, while

```
me.Set( "Bond J" );
```

will change only **name**. For that matter you could also overload a version with no parameters which sets the data members to some default value.

Default member function parameters

Member functions may also have default parameters; these are sometimes more convenient than overloading. Suppose we want to build a class **TVector** with three data members **x**, **y** and **z**, to represent a vector with three components. We want a member function, which we may as well call **Set()** again, to set values of these data members. We could implement it as

```
void TVector::Set( double xi, double yi, double zi )
{
  x = xi;
  y = yi;
  z = zi;
}
```

We can use default parameters to allow **Set()** to be called with from zero to three parameters as follows:

```
#define DEFAULT -911
class TVector {
private:
  double x;
  double y;
  double z;
public:
  void Set( double xi = DEFAULT, double yi = DEFAULT,
            double zi = DEFAULT );
};
main()
{
  TVector a;
  a.Set( 1, 2, 3 );
  a.Set( 4, 5 );
  a.Set( 6 );
  a.Set();
  return 0;
}
void TVector::Set( double xi, double yi, double zi )
{
  if (xi != DEFAULT)
    x = xi;
  if (yi != DEFAULT)
    y = yi;
  if (zi != DEFAULT)
```

```
        z = zi;
    if (xi == DEFAULT && yi == DEFAULT && zi == DEFAULT)
        x = y = z = 0;
}
```

Each parameter of Set() is given a default value in its declaration. (This is not a fantastic example, because the default value should really be one that the parameter would not normally take; however, it illustrates the point!) If Set() is called with fewer than its full complement of parameters, the unspecified parameters are given the default value. Appropriate action is then taken inside Set(). If a parameter has the default value the corresponding data member is left unchanged, unless all three parameters have the default value, in which case all data members are set to zero.

Step through the program with a in the Watch window to check that it works.

Note that the default values are listed only in the member function prototype. If the function has any non-default parameters, they must precede all the default parameters.

A neater solution may of course be to define separate member functions to set each data member, e.g.

```
void TVector::i( double xi )
{
    x = xi;
}
```

The x component of a can then be set to 17, for example, with a.i(17). You can similarly define further member functions j() and k() to assign values to data members y and z respectively.

We will have to wait a bit for the ultimate solution, using operator overloading, when we will be able to assign the three components quite naturally as

```
a(1) = 17;
a(2) = 13;
a(3) = 0;
```

14.2   Constructors and destructors

Class objects of type TCitizen in our example of Section 14.1 remain uninitialized until data members are assigned values by the member function Set().

Accidental use of uninitialized data can cause major problems, so class objects may be initialized on declaration in the same way as **struct** variables, but there are a number of restrictive conditions:

- The object can't have private members (so that rules out **TCitizen**).
- The object can't have constructors (see below).
- The object can't have virtual functions (see later).
- The object can't be from a derived class (see later).

More generally, however, a class may define a special member function called a *constructor* to initialize a class object automatically when it is created. Another special member function called a *destructor* may be used for mopping up operations on an object before a programs ends, or when an object goes out of scope.

The C++ compiler automatically inserts constructors and destructors into code that has none.

As an example, run the following program which implements a simplified version of our **TCitizen** type. Put the objects **you** and **me** in the Watch window and step through the program with **F8**. The new features are discussed below.

```
#include <string.h>
class TCitizen {
private:
    int id;
    char *name;
    int nameLen;
public:
    TCitizen( void );                    // default constructor
    TCitizen( int idn, char *n );        // constructor
    ~TCitizen( void );                   // destructor
};
main()
{
    TCitizen me, you( 12345, "Smith JR" );
    return 0;
}
TCitizen::TCitizen( void )               // default constructor
{
    name = NULL;                         // no name yet
    id = 0;                              // no id
    nameLen = 0;                         // no name
}
TCitizen::TCitizen( int idn, char *n )   // constructor
{
    id = idn;
    name = strdup( n );                  // creates dynamic memory
```

```
            nameLen = strlen( name );
        }
        TCitizen::~TCitizen( void )          // destructor
        {
            delete name;                     // delete object's name
        }
```

Note that the data member **name** is now a pointer to **char**, just to be a little different, and that there is a third data member, **nameLen**.

Constructors

A constructor is a special member function of a class. It must have the same name as the class, and may not have a return type (not even **void**). Constructors may be overloaded in the same way as member functions. Constructors are called automatically when a class object is declared. Although they may be called explicitly, this is very rarely done.

The **TCitizen** constructor with **void** arguments initializes the pointer **name** to NULL, and sets **id** and **nameLen** (the length of the object's name) to zero. The declaration of **me** with no arguments automatically calls this (default) constructor. One advantage of this constructor is immediately apparent: all class objects declared like this have their **name** pointers initialized to NULL.

The two-argument form of the constructor is automatically called when

```
    you( 12345, "Smith JR" );
```

is declared. It is similar to the member function **Set()** of Section 14.1, except that **name** is a dynamic string, created with **strdup()**, and the extra data member **nameLen** is assigned the length of **name** (in case the object needs this at any stage).

We could also overload constructors with only one argument if we wished.

Constructors may also have default arguments, and may be coded inline.

Note that a *default* constructor is one with *no* arguments. It is not the same as a constructor with *default* arguments. Default constructors are useful in declaring arrays of objects, as we shall see later.

An object's constructor is actually called when its declaration is encountered. If the object is *global*, the constructor is called just before **main()** is entered. However, if your program consists of multiple files, there is no way of knowing in what order the constructors of any global objects are called. You should therefore avoid having one global object constructor use objects created by another global constructor.

If you have a class with a non-default constructor (i.e. with parameters), then to declare an object *without* initializing it you *must* provide a default constructor. Otherwise you will get the error message

```
Could not find match for arguments
```

Destructors

Whereas a class may have many constructors, it may have only one destructor. Destructors are usually declared in the class' `public` section, although they don't have to be. The destructor's name must be the same as the constructor name, preceded by a tilde (~). This symbol is used in mathematics to denote negation or antitheses. This is precisely what a destructor is: the antithesis of a constructor.

The only work our destructor needs to do is to delete its object's `name`. We don't need to test whether `name` is NULL because `delete` ignores NULL arguments. Destructors are mainly used to deallocate any dynamic memory being used by an object.

A destructor is called whenever an object leaves its scope. You can see this very clearly if you step through a program in debugging mode with **F7** (which goes into functions).

A destructor may not have any arguments, and like constructors can't have a return type.

Destructors are almost always public. If a destructor is private, the entire class becomes a *private class*. This means that only member functions or friend functions (see later) of the class can use objects from the class.

Local class objects

The constructor of an automatic class object which is declared locally to a function is called when the function is entered. The destructor is called when the function returns.

If a program ends with a call to `exit()`, global class object destructors are called, but destructors for any existing automatic local variables (including those local to `main()`) are *not* called.

Pointers to objects

You can declare a pointer to a class object. Initializing it with **new** automatically calls the constructor, e.g.

```
TCitizen *pNewBaby;
pNewBaby = new TCitizen;
```

In this case the default constructor is called. You can dereference pointers to objects with the arrow operator. So the value of

```
pNewBaby->id
```

is zero. Any of the constructors may be called, e.g.

```
TCitizen *pAlien;
pAlien = new TCitizen( 001, "ET" );
```

Member functions of a dynamic variable may also be dereferenced with the arrow operator.

Remember that objects addressed by pointers have global scope and must be deleted explicitly, even if the pointer is declared locally in a function.

If `delete` has a class object operand it automatically calls the object's destructor.

Reference objects

A reference to an object may be declared:

```
TCitizen me( 12345, "Soap J" );
TCitizen &alias = me;    // reference to me
```

`alias` is literally an alias for `me`, and may be used in its (my?) place. Neither a class constructor nor the destructor is called when a reference object is declared, because the reference refers to an existing object.

Reference objects are used mainly as function parameters.

Parameter objects

A reference to a class object may be passed to a function, e.g.

```
void BeamUp( TCitizen &spacePerson )
{
  ...
}
```

It is passed in the normal way:

```
BeamUp( me );
```

Since a reference to `me` is passed, `BeamUp` does not create a new class object, so a constructor is not called. (`BeamUp()` is not a class member, so it is not prefaced with the class name.)

A pointer to a class object may also be passed.

A class object may be passed by value. This is not generally recommended, since it involves creating a new class object (a copy). This could be inefficient if the object passed is large and complicated. There is another implication: a constructor must be called when the new object is created. The question is, which constructor? Well, C++ allows you to set up a special *copy* constructor for other purposes (see below), but which is automatically called when an object is passed by value. The problem is that if you haven't provided a copy constructor, the compiler will make up its own one, and this could be potentially disastrous. It is better to avoid passing class objects by value.

Copy constructors

It is convenient sometimes to declare a class object, and at the same time to initialize it with another object of the same class, i.e. we would like to be able to say something like

```
TCitizen me( 12345, "Smith JR" );
TCitizen clone = me;
```

In order to do this, a special constructor called a *copy* constructor is needed. Like any constructor, it must be named with the class name. However, its first argument *must* be a reference parameter of the class type. So amongst the public member of the class you could have the declaration

```
TCitizen( TCitizen &copy );   // copy constructor
```

The implementation could be like this:

```
TCitizen::TCitizen( TCitizen &copy )
{
    id = copy.id;
    if (copy.name)
        name = strdup( copy.name );
    else
        name = NULL;
    nameLen = copy.nameLen;
}
```

The declaration

```
TCitizen clone = me;
```

then automatically causes me to be passed by reference to the copy constructor (so &copy is an alias for me. The data members id, etc., refer to the data members of the object being created (clone).

If a copy constructor has more than one parameter, the first one must be a reference parameter of the class type, and all the subsequent ones must be default parameters.

Copying pointer data members

There is a potential danger involved when pointer data members are copied from one class object to another. This could cause duplicate pointers to address the same location in memory. Deleting one of these pointers (when the object's destructor is called) might cause others to address freed memory. Even worse, deleting the same space more than once, when other destructors are called, might corrupt the heap. So you have been warned!

The way the names are copied in the example is a "safe" copy; it prevents this disaster from happening.

Please note carefully that the (safe) copy constructor is called to initialize a class object on declaration, *not* if when a normal assignment of objects is made. C++ allows you to assign one object to another:

```
me = you;
```

However, the copy constructor is *not* called for an ordinary assignment. By default, what happens is that *memberwise* assignment takes places, i.e. values of data members are copied from the source object to the target object. It is precisely here that the danger of multiple pointers addressing the same space could occur, because during memberwise assignment of pointer data members, the *addresses* are copied, not the values at the addresses.

We will see later how to prevent this by overloading the assignment operator, so that a safe assignment can be made.

If you attempt to initialize a class object on declaration where the class has no copy constructor, a *memberwise* copy will take place. This is effectively the same as memberwise assignment, and again raises the spectre of multiply addressed heap space.

As mentioned above, when a class object is passed to a function by value, the copy constructor is called. If there is none, a default constructor is used.

The copy constructor is also called when a function returns a class object directly.

The moral is: make sure you have written a safe copy constructor if you use pointer members!

Object return types

A function (member or non-member) may return a class object directly, in which case the local object returned is initialized with the class copy constructor. There is not much point in doing this.

More common is the situation where a function returns a pointer to a class object, e.g.

```
TCitizen *newOne( void )
{
  TCitizen *p = new TCitizen;
  return p;
}
```

Although the pointer **p** exists only inside the function, the object addressed by it has global scope, so its address may be returned, e.g.

```
TCitizen *tp = newOne();
```

In this case the default constructor is called, as you can verify with the debugger (use **F7** in debug mode to step into functions). This will take you into the constructor being called.

Finally a function may return a reference to a class object. This looks rather artificial but it can be useful. If, for example, **me** is a global object you could define a reference function to refer to it:

```
TCitizen &alias( void )
{
  return me;
}
```

You can declare a **TCitizen** reference and assign **alias()**'s result to it:

```
TCitizen &ref = alias();
```

Reference **ref** is now an alias for **me**, and can be used in a statement:

```
ref.Display();
```

The reference function itself can also be used directly:

```
alias().Display();
```

This could be helpful if **alias()** also performs some sort of search operation, returning a reference to one of several global **TCitizen** class objects.

Type conversion constructors

A *type conversion constructor* is a constructor whose first parameter is of a different type from the class type, and whose subsequent arguments (if any) are all default arguments. This is used rather like a typecast. E.g. we can have the following type conversion constructor for our `TCitizen` class:

```
TCitizen( char *n, int idn = 0 ) { name = strdup(n); id = idn; }
```

We can then declare a class object, and effectively typecast a string to it:

```
TCitizen you;
you = TCitizen( "Jones XY" );    // calls type conversion constructor
```

The second statement creates a `TCitizen` object from the string `"Jones XY"` and initializes you with it.

Arrays of class objects

You can declare arrays of class objects (why ever not?). There is one paramount rule about such arrays:

Class objects stored in arrays must have default constructors.

When an array of objects is declared, the class default constructor is called once for each object in the array. Here's an example:

```
TCitizen firstClass[10];
int i;
for (i = 0; i < 10; i++)
  firstClass[i].Display();
```

If you want to call a different constructor you have to initialize each array element explicitly, e.g.

```
TCitizen firstClass[3] = {
  { TCitizen() },
  { TCitizen( 001, "Clinton B" ) },
  { TCitizen() }
};
```

The default constructor is called for elements 0 and 2. The arrayed objects are initialized with nested braces in the same that you would initialize an array of `struct` elements.

Dynamic arrays of class objects may also be created:

```
TCitizen *hamlet;
hamlet = new TCitizen[5];    //allocate dynamic memory
```

To delete an dynamic array of objects you *must* add empty brackets to delete:

```
delete[ ] hamlet;
```

Since C++ can't distinguish between arrays and pointers, if you omit the brackets (as suggested in Chapter 9) the compiler doesn't realise it's freeing up a whole array. Normally this doesn't matter. But in the case of a dynamic array of objects, the brackets are needed to force the class destructor to be called for each object in the array.

14.3 Inheritance

In the previous sections we have seen how classes can encapsulate data and functions into packages. In this section we look at how new classes can be built from existing ones using the technique of *inheritance*. This is a powerful facility which enables you, among other things, to re-use precompiled code, adapting it to your own purposes without recompiling it, or without even knowing its inner details. Re-usable code is every programmer's dream, and code written as a C++ class is eminently re-usable.

Single inheritance

Single inheritance is the process where classes are derived from a single *base* class. Some times the base class is called the *ancestor*, while the derived classes are naturally called *descendants*.

Suppose we want to design a database for university students. We could start from scratch, but before long we will realise that students are citizens (well, let's pretend they are), and that we may need some of their citizen properties. It would be nice to have a new class **TStudent**, which inherits all the properties of the class **TCitizen** described earlier in the chapter. At the same time, we will add a new property (only one to keep things simple) which only students have: a (student) registration number. So our derived class **TStudent** will have an ID number, a name, and a registration number. We could begin declaring our derived class like this:

```
class TStudent: public TCitizen {
private:
   int reg;
public:
   TStudent(): TCitizen() { reg = 0; }      // default constructor
   ...
};
```

You need to be particularly careful of the syntax. The colon after the class name TStudent means it is going to be derived. The colon must be followed by the keyword public, private or protected, followed by the base class name, and an opening brace as usual.

public TCitizen means that all the public members of TCitizen remain public in the derived class. Any private members of the base class remain private to the original declaring class, and may not be accessed explicitly in the derived class.

If the base class is declared private,

```
class TStudent: private TCitizen {
```

then all public members in TCitizen become private in TStudent. Any subsequent descendants of TStudent may then not access any member in TCitizen.

TStudent has one private member of its own, reg, which is declared int instead of the more cumbersome unsigned long for convenience.

The derived class' (default) constructor has the following form:

```
TStudent(): TCitizen() { reg = 0; }        // default constructor
```

It invokes the base class default constructor using the notation :TCitizen() (it doesn't matter how many spaces, if any, you have around the colon). *If a derived class has a constructor, its constructor must call the base class constructor, if there is one.* However, if the base class has a *default* constructor, it is not necessary to call it; the compiler will do so automatically. If you do need to call a base class constructor, it must be called before the body of the derived class constructor, to ensure that the base portion of an object is properly initialized before the derived portion is.

In addition, the TStudent constructor sets the new member reg to zero. The constructor is written inline purely for ease of reference.

You can now declare a derived object as

```
TStudent him;
```

If you put him in the watch window, only one member will be shown: reg (0). However, you can insert the inherited members him.id and him.name into the Watch, although the program code can't access them directly.

Let's extend our TStudent class by adding a constructor which uses the two-argument base class constructor and also initializes reg to a value specified on declaration:

```
TStudent( int idn, char *n, int regi ): TCitizen( idn, n )
    { reg = regi; }
```

We are intending to initialize **TStudent** objects with three parameters: ID number, name and registration number. So these three parameters are declared, followed by a call to the base constructor **TCitizen** with two *arguments* (so declarations are not appropriate). The body of the **TStudent** constructor then initializes **reg**. Note again that the base constructor is called before the body of the **TStudent** constructor is executed. We could then declare an object as

```
TStudent him( 001, "Smith JR", 999 );
```

Student Smith's ID number is 001, while his registration number is 999.

In case the inline code for the constructors is bothering you, here is how you could declare the derived class and implement the constructor without inline code:

```
class TStudent: public TCitizen {
private:
  int reg;
public:
  TStudent(): TCitizen() { reg = 0; }       // default constructor
  TStudent( int idn, char *n, int regi );   // derived constructor
  ...                                        // member functions
};
```

The implementation of the non-default constructor is

```
TStudent::TStudent( int idn, char *n, int regi ) // constructor header
  : TCitizen( idn, n )      // call base constructor
{
  reg = regi;               // derived constructor body
}
```

Let's now define a derived class member function **SDisplay()** which uses the function **Display()** inherited from **TCitizen** to display all the student's particulars. Insert into the **TStudent** class declaration the member function declaration with an inline body:

```
void SDisplay( void ) { printf( "Reg: %04d ", reg ); Display(); }
```

Now the statement

```
him.SDisplay();
```

will display ID, name and registration number, while the statement

```
him.Display();
```

will display only the inherited `TCiziten` data: ID and name. Note that the inherited function is accessible to the derived class because it is public.

Protected members

In addition to the `private` and `public` access specifiers, a class member may be declared with the `protected` access specifier. A protected class member is a cross between a private and a public member. Like private members, protected members are inaccessible outside their class. However, like public members, they are accessible to member functions in any derived classes.

It may help to summarize the properties of the three access specifiers.

- A private member is accessible only to members of its own class.
- A protected member is accessible only to members of its own class and to any members in any derived class.
- A public member is accessible anywhere.

E.g.

```
class TAnyOne {
private:
   int a;          // only for this class
protected:
   int b;          // only for this class and all descendants
public:
   int c;          // for all members, descendants and users
};
main()
{
   return 0;
}
```

The access specifiers `private`, `public` or `protected` may also be used as base class specifiers in a derived class declaration, e.g.

```
class TDerived: protected TAdam {
```

If no base class specifier is used, members of the inherited class default to private status.

The base class specifier affects the status of *inherited* members. In a derived class,

- a public base class' members retain their original status;
- a protected base class' public members become protected in the derived class, while protected and private members retain their original status;

- a private base class' members all become private in the derived class, regardless of their original status.

Qualifying access selectively

Consider the following (rather trivial) base class:

```
class TDad {
public:
  int a;
  int b;
  TDad() { a = 0; }      // default constructor
};
```

Class **TSon** (even more trivial) can inherit **TDad** as a private base class:

```
class TSon: private TDad {
  public:
  TSon(): TDad() { }     // default constructor
};
```

Because **TDad** is private to **TSon**, all of **TDad**'s formerly public members become private to **TSon**. This means that any subsequent descendants of **TSon** have no access to them, and neither do any statements outside **TSon**. So if **me** is a class **TSon** object the statement

```
me.a = 23;
```

will not compile.

However, if you want only some inherited members of a private base class to remain private in the derived class, you can exempt one or more members from this restriction by *selectively qualifying* them. Suppose you want **TDad**'s **a** member to be accessible outside **TSon** (while **b** remains inaccessible). You can do this by altering the class declaration of **TSon** to the following:

```
class TSon: private TDad {
public:
  TDad::a;                         // selectively qualify a
  TSon(): TDad() { }               // default constructor
};
```

The qualification **TDad::a;** instructs the compiler to retain the public status of this inherited member while leaving other inherited members private. **me.a** can then be referenced.

Replacement member functions

At the beginning of this section we defined the class TStudent as a derived class of the base class TCitizen. One of the derived class' member functions was SDisplay(), which used the base class member Display() to output the inherited data members as well as its own data member. We could however have *replaced* the inherited function with a new one of the same name:

```
void Display( void )
    { printf( "Reg: %04d ", reg ); TCitizen::Display(); }
```

If him is a TStudent object as before, the statement

```
him.Display();
```

will then invoke the derived class member function. Incidentally, if you omit the base class name and scope resolution operator TCitizen:: from the new version you will make Display() a recursive function.

You can still reference the base class version of Display() with

```
him.TCitizen::Display();
```

Multiple inheritance

Multiple inheritance is when a single class inherits properties from more than one base class. E.g. if A, B and C are classes, a new class D could inherit all of them as follows:

```
class D: public A, private B, protected C {
    ...
};
```

Note that base class specifiers may be mixed.

A derived class may need to call multiple base class constructors. E.g. if A, B and C have default constructors, D can call them like this:

```
class D: public A, public B, public C {
public:
  D(): A(), B(), C() { ... }        // default constructor
    ...
};
```

The C++ iostream library (Chapter 16) makes heavy use of multiple inheritance, which is mercifully hidden from the user.

Class types

In C++ structures and unions are also classes, so they may also have member *functions*. They may also be inherited or derived. Classes, structures and unions are collectively known as *class types*.

14.4 Polymorphism

Polymorphism is a biological term describing related organisms that can take on a variety of forms. In C++ it means the ability of class objects addressed by pointers to change form at runtime. It is an advanced topic, a full study of which is beyond the scope of this book. However, we touch on it here for completeness.

C++ makes polymorphism possible with the following golden rule, which should be inscribed in tablets of stone above your computer:

A base class pointer may address an object of that class or an object of any class derived from that base class.

The converse is *not* true, in other words,

A pointer to a derived class object may not address an object of the base class.

From our extended example with base class TCitizen and derived class TStudent we have seen that if him is a TStudent object, him.Display() will output a registration number, ID and name (using the replacement function defined for the derived class at the end of Section 14.3). If, on the other hand, me is a TCitizen object, me.Display() will output only an ID and a name.

Let's see what happens now if we address our base and derived classes with pointers. Consider first the declaration

```
TCitizen *cp = new TCitizen( 001, "Soap J" );
```

The statement

```
cp->Display();
```

will display only the base class data members (obviously). Now declare

```
TStudent *sp = new TStudent( 002, "Doe J", 911 );
```

In this case the statement

```
sp->Display();
```

will naturally invoke the derived class' version of Display().

Now let's try invoking the C++ golden (or concrete) rule about base class pointers addressing derived classes, and declare a pointer to the base class:

```
TCitizen *basep;
```

To test the rule assign the address of a derived object to this pointer:

```
basep = new TStudent( 002, "Doe J", 911 );
```

This compiles because of the golden rule. What do you think the output of the following statement will be?

```
basep->Display();
```

It does not produce the expected result: we only see the base class data displayed, in other words the base class member `Display()` is invoked, although `basep` addresses the derived class. A bit of thought will reveal that this is only right and proper, for was not `basep` declared a pointer to the base class? C++ therefore expects to call the base class member.

Virtual member functions

This problem is solved simply by declaring `Display()` as a *virtual* member function in both the base and derived classes. This device works because calls to virtual member functions are only linked at runtime (*late binding*). Normally, calls to common-or-garden member functions are linked at compile time (*early binding*). The main characteristic of polymorphism is this feature, which makes it possible for class objects to determine their behaviour at runtime.

The following complete program declares `Display()` as `virtual` in the base and derived classes. The classes have been slightly abbreviated for the sake of clarity, and all member functions are implemented inline:

```
#include <stdio.h>
#include <string.h>

class TCitizen {
private:
  int id;
  char *name;
public:
  TCitizen( void ) {  name = NULL; id = 0; }        // default constructor
  TCitizen( int idn, char *n ) { id = idn; name = strdup( n ); }
  ~TCitizen( void ) { delete name; }                // destructor
```

```
    virtual void Display( void )
      { printf( "ID: %04d ", id ); puts( name ); }
};
class TStudent: public TCitizen {
private:
  int reg;
public:
  TStudent(): TCitizen() { reg = 0; }               // default constructor
  TStudent( int idn, char *n, int regi ): TCitizen( idn, n )
    { reg = regi; }
  virtual void Display( void ) { printf( "Reg: %04d ", reg );
                                TCitizen::Display(); }
};
main()
{
  TCitizen *basep;
  basep = new TCitizen( 001, "Soap J" );
  basep->Display();              // displays Citizen info only
  delete basep;
  basep = new TStudent( 002, "Doe J", 911 );
  basep->Display();              // displays Student info
  delete basep;
  return 0;
}
```

Because both versions of `Display()` are now virtual, the first reference to it invokes the base class version, whereas the second reference now invokes the derived class version, as intended, since `basep` addresses the derived class in this case.

Technically, the addresses of virtual function members are stored in an internal table. When virtual functions are called C++ looks up the correct address from this table at runtime. This does take a little time, so you should be aware that virtual member functions might degrade a program's performance somewhat. If this becomes a problem you may have to revise your code.

Virtual destructors

Destructors (but never constructors) may also be virtual.

Consider a case where both a base class and a derived class have pointer members, say to address strings. Clearly both classes must have destructors. (`TStudent` above doesn't need a destructor since it has no pointer members of its own.) Suppose a pointer to the base class is made to address an object of the derived class. When the derived class object is deleted, C++ correctly calls the *base* class destructor (if the destructors are not virtual), which deletes only the string member of the base class object. The derived class string member is left on the heap, which could cause a serious bug. If both classes have virtual destructors, however, late binding will ensure that the derived class destructor is called *as well*, in this case, ensuring that both derived and base string members are deleted.

Summary

- Object-oriented programming is a way of reducing program complexity and re-using existing code.
- A class is similar to a structure, except that it may also have member functions.
- The collection of data and function members in a class is called encapsulation.
- Class members are private by default. This means they cannot be accessed outside the class. Public members may be accessed outside. Members may also be protected.
- Variables declared of class type are called objects.
- Class member functions must include the class name and the scope resolution operator in their headers.
- Class member functions have a hidden argument `this` which points to their associated object.
- Constructors are special member functions with the same name as the class. They are called when class objects are declared in order to initialize them. A class may have more than one constructor. The default constructor has no arguments.
- Destructors are called when class objects go out of scope (or are deleted). A class may have only one destructor.
- A copy constructor is a constructor where the first argument must be a reference parameter of the class type. It is called when a class object is initialized with another class object on declaration.
- If one class object is assigned to another, memberwise assignment takes place. If one or more of the members are pointers, this means that both objects will have pointer members addressing the same area of memory. This could cause disaster. Assignment of class objects to each other should be done with overloading of the assignment operator (see later).
- Class objects stored in arrays must have default constructors.
- Single inheritance is where classes are derived from a single base class. In multiple inheritance, a class may be derived from more than more base class.

- Class members may be private, public or protected. A base class may have these specifiers. A base class specifier affects the status of inherited members.
- Access to inherited members may be qualified selectively.
- A derived class member replaces an inherited member with the same name. The original member may be referenced with the class name and the scope resolution operator.
- Polymorphism is the ability of objects addressed by pointers to change form at runtime.
- The golden rule of polymorphism is that a pointer to a base class may address a derived class, and not vice versa.
- Polymorphism is made possible by virtual class members, which are only linked at runtime. This is called late binding, as opposed to early binding.
- Destructors (as opposed to constructors) may be virtual. Virtual destructors are needed in cases where a pointer of a base class addresses an object of a derived class, and the classes themselves have pointers addressing dynamic memory.

Exercises

14.1 Add a few more members (e.g. address) of your own to the `TCitizen` class introduced early in the chapter, and experiment a bit with objects of the enlarged class.

14.2 Also add more members to the derived `TStudent` class, such as term address, etc.

Chapter 15

Operator overloading for a complex class

15.1 Constructors for our complex class
15.2 Basics of operator overloading
   • Member operator functions • Operator function syntax
   • Restrictions on operator functions
15.3 Overloading the + operator
15.4 Overloading the assignment operator
   • Assignment and initialization • Assignments involving dynamic memory
15.5 Friends
15.6 Overloading complex multiplication and division
15.7 TComplex class declaration and implementation
15.8 Complex roots by Newton's method
15.9 A complex transfer function
15.10 Overloading the [ ] (subscript) operator
Summary
Exercises

From the point of view of scientific and engineering programming, one of the most interesting features of C++ is that it makes *operator overloading* possible. The concept of operator overloading seems to be surrounded by an aura of mysticism. It is, however, fairly straightforward, once you cut through all the fat to the bone.

As we have seen, C++ has a complex class for handling various aspects of complex arithmetic. It is however very instructive (and satisfying) to build our own complex class from first principles, and this we proceed to do.

15.1   Constructors for our complex class

The first thing is to define the class data members and constructors. Well, everybody knows that complex numbers have a real and imaginary part, so there's not a large prize for guessing what the data members should be. We need a default constructor to be able to make declarations, and at least one other constructor to initialize real and imaginary parts. Since the data members should be private, to avoid accidental tampering, we also need two member functions to return the real and imaginary parts.

So we will start with the following, using inline implementations to save space:

```
// TComplex class
class TComplex {
private:
    double re;                              // real part
    double im;                              // imaginary part
public:
    TComplex() { re = im = 0; }             // default constructor
    TComplex(double r, double i) { re = r; im = i; }  // constructor
    double Imag( void ) { return im; };     // return imaginary part
    double Real( void ) { return re; };     // return real part
};
main()
{
    TComplex a(1, 1 );
    TComplex b;
```

The default constructor sets real and imaginary parts to zero. The other constructor initializes real and imaginary parts at declaration. The member functions `Imag()` and `Real()` return the appropriate data members.

Run this program and use the Watch window to verify that the complex numbers **a** and **b** are correctly initialized.

15.2   Basics of operator overloading

To illustrate some fundamental ideas we are going to look at one way of overloading the `+=` operator for our `TComplex` class. It won't be the neatest way of doing it, but it is probably the easiest to understand. We will develop a more elegant form shortly. (Recall that x `+=` a is the same as x = x + a; the left operand is updated by the value of the right operand.) Mathematically, complex addition is defined naturally: the real (imaginary) part of the sum is the sum of the real (imaginary) parts of the operands.

First of all, let's define two further public member functions, `SetReal()` and `SetImag()`, to change the real and imaginary parts of our class objects:

```
void SetImag( double i ) { im = i; }
void SetReal( double r ) { re = r; }
```

The point about these is that they can be used outside the class to change the class data members (we will be able to do away with them eventually).

Now, without knowing anything about operator overloading, you could write a perfectly ordinary (non-member) function, `PlusEquals()`, to do the job:

```
void PlusEquals( TComplex &left, TComplex &right )
{
  left.SetReal( left.Real() + right.Real() );
  left.SetImag( left.Imag() + right.Imag() );
}
```

Two `TComplex` arguments are passed by reference (passing by value incurs additional overheads as we have seen). The left operand's real part is set to the sum of the real parts of both operands. Its imaginary part is similarly dealt with. Since `PlusEquals()` is not a member function of the class, it must use the class' public member functions to access and change class data members. You would invoke the function with

```
PlusEquals( a, b );
```

All of which looks rather involved and inelegant. What we would really like is to be able to write this as simply

```
a += b;
```

Well, to make our coding more expressive of what we are actually doing, C++ has a collection of special *operator* functions which are available for operator redefinition and overloading. They have the general form

```
operator Op ()
```

where *Op* is the operator to be redefined. To use an operator function to redefine `+=` simply replace the header for `PlusEqual()` with the header

```
void operator+=( TComplex &left, TComplex &right );
```

The function implementation remains the same. This allows you to code the operation in a much more natural way (operator syntax):

```
a += b;
```

If you insist, you can still use the more conventional notation (function syntax),

```
operator+=( a, b );
```

but this defeats the purpose of operator redefinition. Both forms generate identical code when compiled.

The terms operator overloading and operator redefinition tend to be used interchangably. Strictly speaking, we have just *redefined* the += operator. We would be *overloading* the redefinition if we define a similar operator function with a **double** second argument, to update only the real part, say, of the first argument.

You should add SetImag(), SetReal() and operator+=() to your TComplex class, and try them out.

Member operator functions

We needed to introduce member functions SetReal() and SetImag() specifically in order to be able to change the data members from outside the class. This need falls away if we rewrite our operator+=() as a class *member* function. It then looks rather different, and much tidier:

```
void TComplex::operator+=( TComplex &right )
{
  re = re + right.re;
  im = im + right.im;
}
```

Note that now the left operand comes from the hidden **this** argument, so that **re** and **im** are the data members of the left operand. The right operand is passed by reference as before. The operator syntax is still the same,

```
a += b;
```

but the equivalent function syntax is different now, because the operator function is a class member:

```
a.operator+=( b );
```

It can no longer be referenced without its class object.

If you are worried that reference parameters might be accidentally changed, you can preface them with the `const` modifier.

As already mentioned, the operator function itself can be further over-loaded. If you want to be able to update only the real part of a `TComplex` class object with statements such as

```
a += 2;
```

then simply overload `operator+=()` with another (member) function:

```
void TComplex::operator+=( double right ) { re = re + right; }
```

Operator function syntax

Almost all the operators may be redefined (including some things you probably didn't realise were operators, such as ( ) and [ ]). The syntax is governed by three issues:

- Is the operator unary or binary?
- If the operator is unary, is it prefix or postfix?
- Is the operator function to be a class member or not?

If the operator is binary, non-member operator functions have two arguments, corresponding to the left and right operands respectively. In the case of member functions, however, the hidden `this` argument refers to the left operand, so there is only one visible argument, corresponding to the right operand.

If the operator is prefix unary (e.g. `++a`), non-member functions have one argument, while member functions have none.

If the operator is postfix unary, an extra "dummy argument" (just the type name) must be added to enable the compiler to distinguish between the prefix and postfix case. E.g.

```
class TComplex {
    ...
    void operator++( void );    // prefix
    void operator++( double );  // postfix
    ...
```

In general, therefore, member operator functions take one less argument than non-members because the left operand comes from the hidden `this` argument in the case of member functions. The order of the operands must the same as the order of the arguments.

Restrictions on operator functions

- You can't invent new operators, since operator functions *re*define existing operators. So you can't invent an operator @, for example.
- You can't change the "arity" (whether it is unary or binary) or precedence of an operator. So the division operator / cannot be redefined as a unary operator.
- At least one argument of an operator function must be a class object; otherwise the operator function must be a class member. This is deliberately intended to prevent you from redefining the way operators work with built-in types. So it is impossible to redefine the addition operator + for integers, say. (You would have to define a class with one integer data member if you really wanted to.)
- Operators can't be combined to form new operators.
- The operator functions redefining =, [ ], ( ), and -> must be *non-static member* functions. (Static data and function members have their declarations prefaced with the keyword **static**, and may be referenced with or without associated objects. Static member functions have no hidden **this** argument.)
- Five operators may not be overloaded:

        .   .*   ::   ?:   sizeof

15.3   Overloading the + operator

The other assignment operators are overloaded in exactly the same way as the += operator. We now consider overloading the + operator, which must be handled slightly differently. The remaining binary arithmetic operators (-, *, /) can be handled similarly. The implementation of the **operator+()** function is as follows:

```
TComplex TComplex::operator+( TComplex &right )
{
  TComplex temp(*this);      // temp object initialized to left operand
  temp.re = temp.re + right.re;  // add right operand to it
  temp.im = temp.im + right.im;
  return temp;                   // return it
}
```

We are also going to define a copy constructor (inline):

```
TComplex( TComplex &copy )
    { re = copy.re; im = copy.im; }              // copy constructor
```

There are three important points to note concerning the `operator+()` function:

- It returns a `TComplex` class object, as opposed to our `operator+=()` function, which had a `void` return type. The reason is that we want to be able to chain additions together in the same expression, e.g. `a + b + c`. To do this, the result of any two additions must also be a class object of the same type as the operands. (Our `operator+=()` could also have returned a class object, but it wasn't necessary, as we don't want to chain the assignment operators, do we?)

- Unlike `operator+=()`, the `operator+()` function must not *update* the left operand (represented by `this` since it is a member function). Therefore a temporary copy `temp` of the left operand must be made with

    ```
    TComplex temp(*this);
    ```

    and `temp` must be updated before being returned.

- The declaration of `temp` invokes the copy constructor (you can verify this by stepping through the program with **F7**. Since `this` is a pointer it must be dereferenced to match the argument type required by the copy constructor.

    In order to return a class object, the function actually returns a copy of `temp`, which again necessitates calling the copy constructor.

    If there is no copy constructor, a memberwise copy takes place. In this case that isn't a problem (as you can verify by omitting an explicit copy constructor). However, if the class has pointer members, you could be in for a shock as we pointed out in Chapter 14. It is therefore best to get into the habit of writing explicit (safe) copy constructors.

Having seen how to overload + we now need to look at how to assign the result of the addition.

15.4 Overloading the assignment operator

C++ allows you to assign class objects to each other by default, performing a memberwise copy from the right operand to the left. (Default assignment is not allowed if the class has constant members, reference members, or members that have private `operator=()` functions of their own.)

In most cases this will work perfectly, but there will be problems if the class has pointer members, and there may also be other subtle problems. The safest solution to overload the assignment operator.

The easiest way to do this is the obvious way,

```
void TComplex::operator=( TComplex &right )
{
  re = right.re;
  im = right.im;
}
```

and this certainly works as you can easily verify.

However, if you want to chain assignments, like

```
a = b = c;
```

this form won't work. Remember that this multiple assignment is interpreted as

```
a = (b = c);
```

If we use our **operator+=()** as defined above, it will return **void** when doing the first assignment. This **void** result becomes the right operand for the second assignment, but since our operator function expects a reference to **TComplex** as the right operand, there will be a type mismatch. The solution looks a little strange at first, but you should warm to it. Since the operator function expects a reference to the right operand, it should *return* a reference to a class object, in order to be chained, right? Do it like this:

```
TComplex &TComplex::operator=( TComplex &right )
{
  re = right.re;
  im = right.im;
  return *this;          // return reference to left operand
}
```

The tricky part is the **return** statement. Think of how you would declare a reference variable:

```
TComplex &ref = object;
```

Before the operator function returns, a temporary reference **&ref** is made. Since the class object itself must be "assigned" to this temporary reference, **this** must be dereferenced, i.e. the object, not its address, must be returned.

You might be wondering why we didn't design our **operator+()** function in Section 15.3 to return a reference also. The technical explanation is as follows. In the **operator+()** function we are compelled to create a temporary object, to avoid updating the left operand. This temporary object is created on the stack, and you should at all costs avoid returning a reference to a local object created on the stack. The function will return a reference to this stack location. However, the stack might be used for something else before the operation is completed, possibly resulting in a program crash.

You can of course further overload the assignment to cater for mixed type assignments, e.g. of a real number to a complex number:

```
z = 1;
```

The imaginary part of the left operand must be set to zero. This is left as an exercise.

Assignment and initialization

When overloading the assignment operator, it's very important to distinguish between assignment and initialization. The statement

```
TComplex a = b;
```

is an initialization, so the copy constructor is called. If there isn't one, a default memberwise copy takes place.

However, in the code

```
TComplex a(1, 1), b;
b = a;
```

the second statement is an assignment, and since the class has a `operator=()` function, that function is called. Otherwise, a default memberwise assignment takes place.

The key to remember is that an initialization *declares* the type of the object being initialized.

Assignments involving dynamic memory

If you want to overload assignment for a class with a pointer member, dynamic memory (if any) allocated to the left operand should always be deleted before new space is allocated for the area addressed by the right operand's pointer member. For example, we could overload assigment for our `TCitizen` class of Chapter 14 as follows:

```
void operator=( TCitizen &right )
{ delete name;                    // free up old space
```

```
        name = strdup( right.name );   // allocate new space and copy
        id = right.id;
        ...
    }
```

More generally, you can use the function

```
memcpy( void *dest, void *source, size_t n );
```

prototyped in **mem.h** to copy an array of n bytes from **source** to **dest**.

15.5   Friends

It would be useful to be able to mix types in complex arithmetic, e.g. to be able to write

```
    a = 2 + b;
```

where **a** and **b** are **TComplex**. This example needs an **operator+()** function with a real (**double**) left operand, and a complex right operand. However, we can't use our present **operator+()** function for this, because being a member function the left operand must always be a class object, pointed to by **this**. So we have to declare another **operator+()** function which is not a member. However, it still needs access to the private data members of the right operand. The solution is to make it a *friend* function of the class. This is done by including the following header in the class declaration of **TComplex**:

```
    friend TComplex operator+( double left, TComplex &right );
```

(the return type is still **TComplex**). A class may declare any non-member function to be friend. This means that the friend function has access to the private members of the declaring class (friendship is a privilege conferred by the declaring class), while not being a member itself. An entire class may also be declared as a friend. Our friend function is then implemented as an ordinary function:

```
    TComplex operator+( double left, TComplex &right )
    {
      TComplex temp(right);        // temp initialized to right operand now
      temp.re = temp.re + left;    // only real part is affected
      return temp;
    }
```

Note that the **temp** object is now initialized with a copy of the *right* operand.

To allow addition of a complex left operand to a real right operand you will need to overload yet again, but this time the operator function could be a member (since the left operand is a class object) or not. The choice is entirely up to you.

15.6 Overloading complex multiplication and division

To make our complex class really useful it must be able to handle complex multiplication and division. This involves some careful coding, but no further new C++ concepts.

Suppose we have two complex numbers z_1 and z_2,

$$z_1 = x_1 + iy_1,$$

$$z_2 = z_2 + iy_2,$$

where x_1, x_2 and y_1, y_2 are their real and imaginary parts respectively. The product $z_1 z_2$ is defined so that the real part of the product is $x_1 x_2 - y_1 y_2$, while the imaginary part of the product is $y_1 x_2 + x_1 y_2$. We can code this as a member **operator*()** function to handle two complex operands as follows:

```
TComplex TComplex::operator*( TComplex &right )
{
    TComplex product;              // temp object for product
    product.re = this->re * right.re - this->im * right.im;
    product.im = this->im * right.re + this->re * right.im;
    return product;
}
```

Remember that **this->** is an alias for the left operand.

It is also convenient to be able to multiply a real number (left operand, say) by a complex number. We need another friend function for this:

```
TComplex operator*( double left, TComplex &right )
// friend of TComplex
{
    TComplex temp(right);
    temp.re = left * temp.re;
    temp.im = left * temp.im;
    return temp;
}
```

The quotient z_1/z_2 of our two complex numbers has a real part of $(x_1x_2 + y_1y_2)/(x_2^2 + y_2^2)$ and an imaginary part of $(y_1x_2 - x_1y_2)/(x_2^2 + y_2^2)$. We code this as a member **operator/()** function with two complex operands as follows:

```
TComplex TComplex::operator/( TComplex &right )
{
  TComplex quotient;
  double den;          // denominator
  den = right.re * right.re + right.im * right.im;
  quotient.re = (this->re * right.re + this->im * right.im) / den;
  quotient.im = (this->im * right.re - this->re * right.im) / den;
  return quotient;
}
```

15.7   TComplex class declaration and implementation

The complete declaration of the **TComplex** class is as follows:

```
class TComplex {
private:
  double re;                                    // imaginary part
  double im;                                    // real part
public:
  TComplex() { re = im = 0; }                   // default constructor
  TComplex( double r, double i ) { re = r; im = i; }  // constructor
  TComplex( TComplex &copy )
    { re = copy.re; im = copy.im; }             // copy constructor
  double Imag( void ) { return im; };           // return imaginary part
  double Real( void ) { return re; };           // return real part
  void SetImag( double i ) { im = i; }
  void SetReal( double r ) { re = r; }
  void operator+=( TComplex &right );           // complex update
  void operator+=( double right ) { re = re + right; }  // real update
  TComplex operator+( TComplex &right );
  TComplex operator-( TComplex &right );
  TComplex &operator=( TComplex &right );
  TComplex operator*( TComplex &right );
  TComplex operator/( TComplex &right );
  friend TComplex operator*( double left, TComplex &right );
  friend TComplex operator+( double left, TComplex &right );
};
```

An **operator-()** member function has been included to handle an example using Newton's method below. Note that some of the implementations are inline.

The complete implementation of **TComplex** is:

```
void TComplex::operator+=( TComplex &right )
{
  re = re + right.re;
  im = im + right.im;
}
TComplex TComplex::operator+( TComplex &right )
{
  TComplex temp(*this);    // temp object initialized to left operand
  temp.re = temp.re + right.re;  // add right operand to it
  temp.im = temp.im + right.im;
  return temp;                    // return it
}
TComplex TComplex::operator-( TComplex &right )
{
  TComplex temp(*this);    // temp object initialized to left operand
  temp.re = temp.re - right.re;  // subtract right operand from it
  temp.im = temp.im - right.im;
  return temp;                    // return it
}
TComplex &TComplex::operator=( TComplex &right )
{
  re = right.re;
  im = right.im;
  return *this;         // return reference to left operand
}
TComplex TComplex::operator*( TComplex &right )
{
  TComplex product;            // temp object for product
  product.re = this->re * right.re - this->im * right.im;
  product.im = this->im * right.re + this->re * right.im;
  return product;
}
TComplex TComplex::operator/( TComplex &right )
{
  TComplex quotient;
  double den;          // denominator
  den = right.re * right.re + right.im * right.im;
  quotient.re = (this->re * right.re + this->im * right.im) / den;
  quotient.im = (this->im * right.re - this->re * right.im) / den;
  return quotient;
}
```

The two friends' implementations are:

```
TComplex operator*( double left, TComplex &right )
{
  TComplex temp(right);
  temp.re = left * temp.re;
```

```
    temp.im = left * temp.im;
    return temp;
}
TComplex operator+( double left, TComplex &right )
{
    TComplex temp(right);      // temp initialized to right operand now
    temp.re = temp.re + left;  // only real part is affected
    return temp;
}
```

15.8   Complex roots by Newton's method

Newton's method is perhaps the easiest numerical method to implement for finding roots of equations of the form $f(x) = 0$. It is an *iterative* method, meaning that it repeatedly attempts to improve an estimate of the root: if x_k is an approximation to the root, the next approximation x_{k+1} is given by

$$x_{k+1} = x_k - \frac{f(x_k)}{f'(x_k)}$$

where $f'(x)$ is df/dx.

A structure plan to implement Newton's method is:

1. Read in the starting value x_0 and required accuracy e
2. While $|f(x_k)| \geq e$ repeat up to $k = 20$, say:
   $x_{k+1} = x_k - f(x_k)/f'(x_k)$
   Print x_{k+1} and $f(x_{k+1})$
3. Stop.

It is necessary to limit step 2 since the process may not converge.

Newton's method can also find complex roots, but only if the starting guess is complex. The following program finds a complex root of $x^2 + x + 1 = 0$, starting with $(0, 2)$, i.e. $x = 2\sqrt{-1}$:

```
TComplex F( TComplex &x );
TComplex dF( TComplex &x );
double Cabs( TComplex &x );
#include <stdio.h>
#include <math.h>
main()
{
    TComplex x;
    int i;

    x = TComplex( 0, 2 );
    printf( "   Re(x)    Im(x)\n\n" );
```

```
    i = 1;
    while (Cabs( F(x) ) >= 1e-6 && i < 20) {
        x = x - F( x ) / dF( x );
        printf( "%9.4f%9.4f\n", x.Real(), x.Imag() );
        i++;
    }

    return 0;
}
TComplex F( TComplex &x )
{
    return 1 + x * x + x;
}
TComplex dF( TComplex &x )
{
    return 1 + 2 * x;
}
double Cabs( TComplex &x )
{
    return sqrt( x.Real() * x.Real() + x.Imag() * x.Imag() );
}
```

The declaration and implementation of class `TComplex` is not included. You should set up a header file for the declaration and a separate module for the implementation.

We need two `TComplex` functions, `F()` and `dF()` for $f(x)$ and its derivative, and we also need a function `Cabs()` to return the absolute value of a `TComplex` class object.

The statement

```
    x = TComplex( 0, 2 );
```

creates a complex constant and *assigns* it to `x` (`x` is not initialized; the constant is).

The output is:

```
    Re(x)    Im(x)

    -0.2941  1.1765
    -0.4512  0.8975
    -0.4983  0.8653
    -0.5000  0.8660
    -0.5000  0.8660
```

Since complex roots occur in pairs, the other root is $(-0.5, -0.866)$.

15.9   A complex transfer function

The response (output) of a linear system, which may be thought of as a "black box", is characterized in electrical engineering by its transfer function. An input signal with a given angular frequency (ω radians/s) is applied at one end of the box. The output from the other end is then given by the input multiplied by the absolute value of the transfer function, with its phase shifted by the phase angle of the transfer function.

Suppose a servomechanism is characterized by the complex transfer function

$$T(i\omega) = \frac{K(1 + 0.4i\omega)(1 + 0.2i\omega)}{i\omega(1 + 2.5i\omega)(1 + 1.43i\omega)(1 + 0.02i\omega)^2}$$

where K is an amplification factor. If the real and imaginary parts of $T(i\omega)$ are a and b respectively then its phase angle ϕ is given by $\arctan b/a$. If the `atan2()` library function is used, the angle returned will be in the range $-\pi$ to π, so that the correct quadrant is given (which is not the case for `atan()`).

The program below shows how the servomechanism responds to different input frequencies ω. This information is necessary in the design of stable feedback control devices. The initial input frequency is 0.02 radians/sec. This is multiplied by a factor (`fact`) of 1.25 each time for a given number of steps. The amplification factor K is 900. The phase shift ϕ of the output is given in degrees. The `main()` function for the program, which uses our `TComplex` class, is as follows:

```
int n;                  // counter
double fact = 1.25;     // scaling factor
double k = 900;         // amplification
double phase;           // phase angle
double omega = 0.02;    // angular frequency
TComplex i (0, 1);      // sqrt(-1)
TComplex iom;           // for i * omega
TComplex t;             // transfer function

printf( "  %-7s %-12s %-12s %-12s %-9s\n\n", "omega", "Re t", "Im t",
        "Abs t",  "phase" );
for (n = 0; n<= 10; n++)
{
  iom = omega * i;
  t = k * (1 + 0.4 * iom) * (1 + 0.2 * iom) /
      (iom * (1 + 2.5 * iom) * (1 + 1.43 * iom) * (1 + 0.02 * iom ) *
      (1 + 0.02 * iom));
```

```
    phase = atan2( t.Imag(), t.Real() ) * 180 / M_PI;
    printf( "%7.3f %12.4e %12.4e %12.4e %9.3f\n",
            omega, t.Real(), t.Imag(),
            sqrt(t.Real() * t.Real() + t.Imag() * t.Imag()), phase );
    omega = omega * fact;
  }
  return 0;
```

Sample output:

omega	Re t	Im t	Abs t	phase
0.020	-3.0236e+03	-4.4825e+04	4.4927e+04	-93.859
0.025	-3.0183e+03	-3.5782e+04	3.5909e+04	-94.822
0.031	-3.0101e+03	-2.8528e+04	2.8687e+04	-96.023
...				
120.371	-1.6514e-02	1.8296e-02	2.4647e-02	132.069
150.463	-7.5115e-03	1.1000e-02	1.3320e-02	124.327

If you run the program you will see how the input signal is amplified at first, but is then attenuated. The phase shift starts at about $-90°$ and moves gradually to about $-180°$, after which it swings backwards and forwards across the real axis as the input frequency gets larger.

You may like to implement a graphical solution.

15.10 Overloading the [ ] (subscript) operator

This section has nothing to do with our TComplex class, but it is the most appropriate place to put it.

You may not have realized that the subscript operator [ ] was an operator at all. In fact it is a binary operator, but instead of sitting between its two operands, it encloses its right operand. In the expression num[23], num is the left operand, and 23 is the right operand.

Like the operator=() function, the operator[ ]() function must be a member function. The first operand is the class object itself, and the second argument (the subscript) is the single visible argument of the function.

Overloading the subscript operator makes it possible to deal very neatly with two major gripes with old-fashioned C: the lack of array bounds checking, and array elements being numbered from 0. The following example shows how to achieve this. Declaring x(10) a class object of type TSafeIntArr makes it an array of integers with subscripts numbered 1 to 10, in the more usual non-C way, and causes the program to stop with an error message if these subscripts are violated in either direction:

```
class TSafeIntArr {
private:
  int *elements;
  int mySize;
public:
  TSafeIntArr( int sz )
  { elements = new int[ sz ]; mySize = sz; }
  ~TSafeIntArr( void ) { delete[ ] elements; }
  int &operator[ ] (unsigned i);              // overload subscript
};
#include <stdio.h>
#include <stdlib.h>
main()
{
  TSafeIntArr x(10);           // "subscripts" now range from 1 to 10
  x[1] = 3;
  x[8] = x[1];
  ...
  return 0;
}
int &TSafeIntArr::operator[ ] (unsigned i)
{
  if (i > mySize || i < 1) {
    puts( "Subscript out of bounds" );
    exit(1);
  }
  return elements[i-1];               // normal human subscripting!
}
```

The actual array elements are a dynamic array addressed by the class pointer member **elements**, set up by the constructor. The constructor's single argument is the number of elements you want, with subscripts starting from 1. This is passed to the other data member **mySize**. We can't of course use the normal subscript notation in declaring x because it has been over-loaded.

The **operator[ ]** () function with argument i returns a *reference* to **elements[i-1]**. Illegal subscript values are screened out.

A reference is returned so that we can use our overloaded subscripts on both sides of an assignment. Recall that if a function returns a reference, the function name may appear on the left-hand side of an assignment (and the full function name is x.**operator[ ]**(i)). We can therefore have statements like

```
x[8] = x[1];
```

You might think that the statement

```
return elements[i-1];
```

inside the **operator[ ]()** function is a recursive call. It isn't, because fortunately the compiler is smart enough to know that a normal subscripting operation is to be performed here.

You may decide to develop **TSafeIntArr** into a full blown array handling class, with overloaded assignment, so that you can assign arrays directly to each other. In that case remember to make provision for safe copying of the dynamic memory.

We will see in Chapter 17 how to overload the function call operator ().

Summary

- Special operator functions may be used to overload operators. Operator overloading makes for more natural syntax. At least one of the operands must be a class object.
- If the operator function is a class member, the hidden **this** argument points to the left operand in the case of a binary operator, or to the only operand in the case of a unary operator.
- Friends of a class are granted access to that class' private and protected members. Functions or whole classes may be declared friends.
- If the left operand of a binary operator is not a class object, the operator function must be a friend function.
- It is important to distinguish between initialization (which declares a class object and invokes a constructor) and assignment (which may be default or overloaded). Default assignment involves memberwise copy of members. If one of the members is a pointer this will cause problems.
- When overloading the assignment operator care must be taken to copy dynamic memory correctly.
- Making the **operator[ ]()** function return a reference means that overloaded subscripts may be used on the left-hand side of an assignment.

Exercises

15.1 Make the **TComplex** class more general by allowing for more mixtures of type between left and right operands in overloaded operators, e.g.

division of complex numbers by reals, and vice versa, assignment of reals to complex variables, etc.

Put the class declaration into a header file **tcomplex.h**, and the implementation into a separate file **tcomplex.cpp**, and use a project to compile a sample program which uses the class.

15.2 Develop the `TSafeIntArr` class to allow "safe" assignment of arrays. Overload addition and subtraction. Design some I/O member functions.

Chapter 16

The C++ iostream library

16.1 The ios class
16.2 Output
  • Formatting with manipulators • Defining your own manipulators
  • Character-level output
16.3 Input
  • Testing the state of the stream • Character-level input
16.4 Stream I/O with files
16.5 Overloading the stream operators
Summary
Exercises

C++ input/output streams are usually simply referred to as *iostreams*. They provide all the facilities available in the C **stdio** library. However, many programmers prefer to use a mixture of the old and the new. For example, you may prefer to continue using `printf()` for most output (simply because **stdio.h** includes much faster than **iostream.h**) and `cin` for input (it beats `scanf()` hands down any day). For binary file I/O the C functions `fread()` and `fwrite()` are sufficient for most standard applications.

16.1 The `ios` class

In this chapter we give a brief outline of some of the vast collection of iostream facilities. Details are in the Borland/Turbo C++ manuals.

The iostream library has two parallel families of classes (in the C++ sense): those derived from the class `ios`, and those derived from the class `streambuf`. We will consider only the `ios` family. Any object created from `ios` or any of its derived classes is generically referred to as a *stream object*.

The `ios` hierarchy manages all the I/O operations. The part of the family tree relevant to our discussion is shown in Figure 16.1. `istream` handles input, `ostream` handles output, and since the `iostream` class is derived from both these classes it can handle both input and output.

16.2   Output

The `iostream` class predefines a stream object called `cout`, which we have seen from time to time. It corresponds to the **stdio** standard output stream. Most of the prototypes required are in **iostream.h**.

The standard left shift operator `<<` is overloaded to provide the *insertion* (or *put to*) operator. Its left operand is a stream object of type `ostream` (e.g. `cout`), and its right operand is any type for which stream output has been defined, i.e. any of the fundamental data types, and any derived types you have overloaded for it (see below).

The `<<` (insertion) operator returns a reference to the `ostream` object for which it is invoked. This allows several insertions to be *cascaded* together (like chaining overloaded assignments), e.g.

```
cout << "The answer is: " << x;
```

where `x` is of fundamental type.

The `<<` operator has default format codes, e.g. `cout`ing an `int` is like `printf()`ing it with the `"%d"` format code. A float is output according to the code `"%.g"`, etc.

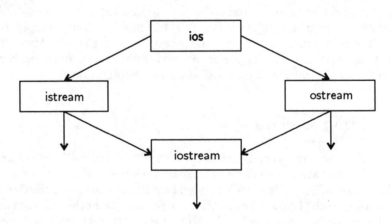

Figure 16.1: The `ios` hierarchy

Formatting with manipulators

You can control iostream formatting with special **ios** class functions called
manipulators. These can be embedded in a chain of insertions (or extractions,
for input) to alter the stream state. They do not actually perform insertions/
extractions themselves. E.g. the **hex** manipulator converts all subsequent
output to hexadecimal, until changed by the **dec** or **oct** manipulators:

```
cout << hex;
for (i = 1; i <= 20; i++)
   cout << i << endl;
```

Most of the manipulators are shown in Table 16.1. Note that some may be
used for input also/only. E.g.

```
#include <iomanip.h>
   ...
   cout << setfill( '*' );
   cout << setw(6) << 13 << endl;
```

gives the output

```
****13
```

If you use one of the manipulators that takes an argument you must include
iomanip.h (you don't need to include **iostream.h** as well in that case).

Manipulator	*Direction*	*Action*
dec	in/out	set base to decimal
hex	in/out	set base to hexadecimal
oct	in/out	set base to octal
ws	in	extract whitespace characters
endl	out	insert newline and flush stream
ends	out	insert null terminator in string
tt flush	out	flush stream
setfill(int c)	out	set fill character to c
setprecision(int n)	out	set precision to n digits after the decimal point
setw(int w)	in/out	set total field width to n

Table 16.1: Some I/O manipulators

The `setw()` manipulator only affects the current output statement. The field width is reset to zero after every output (meaning the minimum width is used to output the value).

In addition `cout` (and any other stream objects) inherit a whole host of member functions from the granddaddy `ios`, such as `eof()`, which returns non-zero (true) on end-of-file. E.g. `cin.eof()` will be true only when you enter **Ctrl-z** at the keyboard (DOS end-of-file). The complete list of `ios` (and other) member functions appears in the user manuals.

Defining your own manipulators

You can easily define your own manipulators. This example shows how to define a manipulator `bell` for an output stream:

```
ostream &bell( ostream &outstrm )
{
   return outstrm << '\a';        // escape code for bell
}
```

To ring the bell then all you need is

```
cout << bell;
```

The `ostream` parameter is a stream object, so the insertion operator `<<` may be used on it. The function returns a reference to an `ostream` object allowing it to be cascaded in the same way as the standard manipulators.

Character-level output

The `ostream` class has one character-level output member function `put()`. It is inherited by all stream objects. E.g. the expression `cout.put(c)` inserts the character `c` into the standard output stream, returning a reference to the output stream.

16.3   Input

Stream input uses the overloaded right shift operator `>>`, known as the *extraction (get from)* operator. It takes as its left operand an `istream` object, like `cin` (which corresponds to the **stdio** standard input stream). It provides a much more convenient means of input than `scanf()` .

The right operand of `>>` may be any of the fundamental types, and it may also be cascaded.

By default, >> skips whitespace (blanks, newlines, horizontal tabs) and reads up to the last character of the type being input. *Trailing whitespace is neither extracted nor ignored.* The **ws** manipulator may be used to extract whitespace characters. This is useful if you want to get past a newline character, for example.

For inputting strings, the extraction operator considers a string to consist of any non-whitespace characters. If you want to input whitespace as part of a string, you must use one of the character-level functions (see below).

Note that some of the I/O manipulators listed in Table 16.1 may be used to format input.

Testing the state of the stream

Hidden away in the **ios** class is a special overloaded function that converts a stream object into a **void** pointer, of all things. This is to enable us to test easily for the state of the stream, since the only time a null pointer is returned is when the stream has failed, e.g. on end-of-file. So we can use code like the following to read a list of integers from the keyboard and sum them, until **Ctrl-Z** is entered:

```
int i;
int sum = 0;
while (cin >> i)        // returns null only when input stream fails
    sum += i;
```

Character-level input

The **ios** class has a number of member functions dealing with character-level input. Among them are overloaded forms of **get**. For example, you can copy the standard input file to the standard output file with

```
char c;
while ((c = cin.get()) != EOF)
    cout.put( c );
```

or

```
while (cin.get( c ))
    cout.put( c );
```

The first form of **get**() returns an **int**, whereas the second returns a reference to the input stream.

Some of the character-level member functions are as follows:

`int eof( void )` returns non-zero on end of file.

`int get( void )` extracts and returns the next character, or `EOF`.

`istream &get( char &c )` extracts the next character.

`istream &get( char *str, int n, char t = '\n' )` extracts characters
into `str` until the delimiter character `t` (last and optional parameter) is
found, or until $n - 1$ bytes have been read. A null terminator is always
placed in `str`; the delimiter never is. The delimiter remains in the stream.

`istream &getline( char *str, int n, char t = '\n' )` behaves like
`get()` except that the delimiter is also extracted. The delimiter is not
copied to `str`.

`istream &ignore( int n, int t = EOF )` causes up to n characters in the
input stream to be skipped, stopping if the delimiter if found.

`int peek( void )` returns the next character from the input stream without
extracting it. `EOF` is returned on end-of-file.

Note that many of them return (references to) the input stream.

16.4   Stream I/O with files

`cin` and `cout` are predefined stream objects. You can easily create your own
stream objects and attach them to files, as we have seen.

There is a complex hierarchy of classes for handling stream-oriented I/O.
The main ones you need to be concerned about are `ifstream` (input only),
`ofstream` (output only) and `fstream` (input and output). We will restrict our
discussion to `fstream` since it is more general.

There are two different ways opening and closing `fstream` files. You can
either create an `fstream` object, and open and close it explicity with the
`open()` and `close()` member functions. Or you can create the object with an
`fstream` constructor, which automatically opens the file. The file is then
automatically closed with the `fstream` destructor.

The second way is the one we have used so far. The following example
shows how to read some lines from a text file **data** of unknown length. Each
line consists of a 10-character string (which may include whitespace), followed

by two **int** marks. The data are written on standard output:

```
#include <fstream.h>
#include <iomanip.h>
#define STR_LEN 11
main()
{
  char name[STR_LEN];
  int mark1, mark2;
  int i = 0;
  fstream myin( "data", ios::in );    // call constructor

  if (!myin) {
    cout << "File not found" << endl;
  }

  while (myin) {
    myin.get( name, STR_LEN );
    myin >> mark1 >> mark2 >> ws;
    cout << setw( STR_LEN) << name;
    cout << setw( 5 ) << mark1;
    cout << setw( 5 ) << mark2 << endl;
  }
  return 0;
}
```

The statement

```
fstream myin( "data", ios::in );
```

calls the **fstream** constructor to create your stream object **myin**, and to attach it to the file **data**. The first parameter is the file name. The second parameter is the access mode. Some possible values of the access mode are **in** (open for read), **out** (open for write), and **app** (open in append mode). These values actually come from an enumerated type defined in the **ios** class, so they must be preceded with an **ios** qualifier. They are defined so that several modes can be ORed together. E.g. you can open for both input and output with

```
fstream myin( "data", ios::in | ios::out );
```

The **fstream** constructor has an optional third parameter, the protection mode, which we do not need to be concerned about.

Note that the **ws** manipulator is used to extract the newline character at the end of each line.

The **fstream.h** header file includes the **iostream.h** header.

fstream objects inherit all the facilities available to stream objects.

To open and close the file explicitly use the following alternative code:

```
#include <fstream.h>
fstream myin;                     // create unopened stream object

myin.open( "data", ios::in );  // open file for input
...

myin.close();                     // close the file
```

16.5   Overloading the stream operators

It is easy to overload the stream insertion and extraction operators to handle I/O of your own class objects.

For example, we can overload the insertion << operator for our **TComplex** class of Chapter 15 as follows:

```
ostream &operator<<( ostream &outstrm, TComplex object )
For ouput of TComplex objects
{
  outstrm << setw(6) << object.re;
  outstrm << setw(6) << object.im << endl;
  return outstrm;
}
```

(include **iomanip.h** before the class declaration). The first argument must be a reference to a stream object. The function must return a reference to this object if you want to cascade the operator. The second argument must be the class object you wish to I/O (it must be passed by reference for input).

Since the operator function requires access to the private members of the class, and since the first argument cannot be the class object itself, the operator function should be a friend function of the class. **TComplex** must declare it a friend:

```
friend ostream &operator<<( ostream &outstrm, TComplex object );
```

Now to output both the real and imaginary parts of the **TComplex** object **x** simply use **cout**:

```
cout << x;
```

We can overload the extraction >> operator to input a **TComplex** class object as follows:

```
istream &operator>>( istream &instrm, TComplex &z )
```

```
    {
        instrm >> z.re >> z.im;
        return instrm;
    }
```

Note that for input the class object must be passed by reference, so that it can be modified.

Summary

- C++ input/output streams are called iostreams.
- All C++ I/O operations are handled by the **ios** class hierarchy, using multiple inheritance.
- Any object created from the **ios** class or any of its descendants is called a stream object.
- The **iostream** class library is the C++ counterpart of the C **stdio** library, and handles standard stream I/O.
- The **iostream** (input/output) class is derived from the **istream** (input only) and **ostream** (output only) classes (among others).
- **cin** and **cout** are the predefined **iostream** stream objects corresponding to the **stdio** streams **stdin** and **stdout**.
- Stream objects inherit all the member functions of their ancestors.
- The << operator is overloaded as the insertion (put to) output operator for **ostream** stream objects. It returns a reference to an **ostream** object, which means that it can be cascaded.
- Formatting may be achieved with the help of special I/O manipulators.
- Standard I/O declarations appear in **iostream.h**, except that manipulators requiring an argument are prototyped in **iomanip.h** (which automatically includes **iostream.h**).
- You can define your own manipulators as functions returning references to **ostream** objects (which allows a manipulator to be cascaded).
- The >> operator is overloaded as the extraction (get from) input operator for **istream** objects.
- A stream object returns a null pointer when it fails. This can be used as an easy end-of-file test, for example.
- Character-level I/O is handled by **ios** member functions inherited by stream objects.
- File I/O may be handled with **fstream** class objects.

- Creating an `fstream` class object with a constructor automatically attaches a file. The destructor is automatically called to close the file.
- `fstream` objects may also be attached explicitly to files with the `open()` member function, and closed explicitly with `fclose()`.
- The stream operators `<<` and `>>` may be overloaded as friend functions of a class in order to use `cout` and `cin` to handle class object I/O. The overloaded function must return a reference to the relevant stream if it is to be cascaded.

Exercises

16.1 Design an overloaded function for the insertion operator `<<` for the `TMatrix` class of Chapter 17, to output a matrix neatly by rows, and a vector in a single row.

Chapter 17

Matrices with class

17.1 Developing a matrix class
- Data members and constructors • Overloading the () (function call) operator
- Matrix assignment • Matrix addition • Matrix multiplication • Matrix input

17.2 Reachability of spies

17.3 Leslie matrices: population growth

17.4 Markov chains
- A random walk • Simulating the random walk

17.5 Solution of linear equations
- Gauss reduction • Matrix inversion by Gauss reduction

17.6 Binary file matrix I/O

17.7 The finite element method

17.8 TMatrix class declaration and implementation

Summary

Exercises

In this chapter we will see how to use encapsulation and operator overloading to develop a powerful C++ class for handling matrix arithmetic. We will consider examples from such areas as networks, populations dynamics and linear algebra.

17.1 Developing a matrix class

A *matrix* is a two-dimensional array which may be used in a wide variety of representations. For example, a distance array representing the lengths of direct connections in a network is a matrix. We will deal mainly with *square* matrices in this chapter (i.e. matrices having the same number of rows as columns), although in principle a matrix can have any number of rows or columns. A matrix with only one column is also called a *vector*.

A matrix is usually denoted by a bold capital letter, e.g. **A**. Each entry, or element, of the matrix is denoted by the small letter of the same name followed by two subscripts, the first indicating the row of the element, and the second indicating the column. So a general element of the matrix **A** is called a_{ij}, meaning it may be found in row i and column j. If **A** has three rows and columns—(3 × 3) for short—it will look like this in general:

$$\begin{bmatrix} a_{11} & a_{12} & a_{13} \\ a_{21} & a_{22} & a_{23} \\ a_{31} & a_{32} & a_{33} \end{bmatrix}.$$

A special matrix which we will come across later is the *identity* matrix. This has ones on the *main diagonal*, and zeros everywhere else. E.g. the (3 × 3) identity matrix is

$$\begin{bmatrix} 1 & 0 & 0 \\ 0 & 1 & 0 \\ 0 & 0 & 1 \end{bmatrix}.$$

A matrix may be represented by a two-dimensional array in C, e.g.

```
double a[2][3];
```

which could stand for a (2 × 3) matrix. However, the element numbering is hideous, since both subscripts start at 0, and not at 1 as is conventional with matrices. Passing such arrays to functions is a non-trivial problem, especially if you want to allow for variable dimensions.

C++ encapsulation and operator overloading provide an ideal solution to these and other problems encountered with conventional array handling.

Data members and constructors

In trying to design a new class, we need to think in object-oriented terms. If a matrix is going to be an object, what must it know about itself? Any self-respecting matrix will tell you that if you are a matrix, you need to know your shape, and the values of your elements. It turns out that it is best to store the actual elements in dynamic memory, so all we need for data members are the row and columns sizes, and a pointer to the elements:

```
class TMatrix{
private:
    int row, col;
```

```
    double *elements;
    ...
```

How should we declare such a beast? Well, the natural way to declare, say a (2×3) matrix, is

```
    TMatrix a(2,3);
```

So the general constructor could be declared as

```
    TMatrix( int r, int c );
```

with the implemention

```
    TMatrix::TMatrix( int r, int c )
    {
        elements = new double[r * c + 1];
                            // start at elt 1 like normal humans
        memset( elements, '', (r * c + 1) * sizeof( double ) );
        row = r; col = c;
    }
```

This sets the number of rows and columns as specified, and allocates dynamic memory. Notice how we are representing the matrix: as a one-dimensional array, strung out row by row. To overcome C++'s confounded array indexing convention, we add one extra element, which we will never use. This tiny waste of space is a small price to pay for being able to use normal human subscripting. So for our matrix a(2,3), we will have *seven* elements. The first one, elements[0], will never be used, and the remaining six must represent the two rows of a, the first row by elements[1], elements[2] and elements[3], and the second row by elements[4], elements[5] and elements[6]. It will be the job of TMatrix member functions to allocate and handle element values correctly. (We could of course make use of elements[0] by means of a suitable transformation, but this makes the coding that much more subtle.)

memset() sets all the bytes in the memory addressed by its first argument to the value of its second argument (zero). The number of bytes to be so set is given by its third argument.

While we are about it, it would be convenient to represent vectors with our TMatrix class as well. The natural way to declare a vector with three components, say, would be

```
    TMatrix v(3);
```

So we also need a constructor with only one argument, declared as

```
    TMatrix( int r );
```

and implemented as

```
TMatrix::TMatrix( int r )
{
  elements = new double[ r + 1];
  memset( elements, '', (r + 1) * sizeof( double ) );
  row = r;
  col = 1;      // vectors only have one column, don't they?
}
```

Again, `elements[0]` is never used.

While we are about it, we should design a copy constructor to be on the safe side:

```
TMatrix::TMatrix( TMatrix &copy )
{
  row = copy.row;
  col = copy.col;
  elements = new double[ row * col + 1];
  memcpy(elements, copy.elements, (row * col + 1) * sizeof(double));
}
```

Note how the number of bytes to be copied by `memcpy()` is calculated.

If you think you may need a default constructor you should write one.

If we ever need access to the size of a matrix outside the class we can write member functions to return the number of rows and columns.

The destructor is easy (implemented inline):

```
~TMatrix( void ) { delete elements; }
```

Overloading the () (function call) operator

It would be convenient to refer to particular elements of our matrix a in the normal way, so that a(2,1), for example, refers to the element in row 2 and column 1, i.e. a_{21} in matrix notation. What this really means is that a(2,1) should *return* the appropriate element, which in turn means we want an operator function to overload the () function call operator. Like the curious subscript operator, the function call operator is a binary operator. Its left operand is the name (a), and its right operand is the list of arguments enclosed in parentheses. We can have as many of these as we like. This is how it's done:

```
double &TMatrix::operator()( int r, int c )
{
  return elements[ (r-1) * col + c ];
}
```

Note two things. Firstly, how the correct element is found. r and c are the row and column of the required element. col is the total number of columns of the matrix. So a(2,1), for example, returns elements[4], if a is (2×3).

Secondly, note that a *reference* to the element is returned. This enables us to use the overloaded () on *either* side of an assignment, so we can write statements like

```
a(2,1) = 38;
a(1,3) = a(2,1);
```

You should of course add a check that r and c are not out of bounds.

We can also overload () separately for vectors, since they only require one argument:

```
double &TMatrix::operator()( int r )
{
  return elements[ r ];
}
```

We need a member function to output a matrix neatly:

```
void TMatrix::Print( void )
{
  int i, j;
  for (i = 1; i <= row; i++) {
    for (j = 1; j <= col; j++)
      printf( "%4.0f", (*this)(i,j) ); printf( "\n" );
  }
}
```

To sum up, we so far have the following declaration for **TMatrix** (including necessary headers):

```
#include <stdio.h>
#include <mem.h>
class TMatrix{
private:
  int row, col;
  double *elements;
public:
  TMatrix( int r, int c );              // proper matrix
  TMatrix( int r );                     // vector
  TMatrix( TMatrix &copy );             // copy constructor
  ~TMatrix( void ) { delete elements; }
  TMatrix operator+( TMatrix &right );
  TMatrix operator*( TMatrix &right );
  TMatrix &operator=( TMatrix &right );
```

```
        double &operator()( int r, int c );      // proper matrix
        double &operator()( int r );             // vector
        void Print( void );
};
```

Try the class out with the following `main()` function (remember to insert the implementations):

```
main()
{
  TMatrix a(2,2), d(2);
  a(1,1) = 1; a(1,2) = 2;         // assign elements
  a(2,1) = 3; a(2,2) = 4;
  d(1) = 2; d(2) = 3;
  a.Print();
  d.Print();
  return 0;
}
```

Matrix assignment

We can overload the assignment operator to handle the assignment of one matrix to another as follows:

```
TMatrix &TMatrix::operator=( TMatrix &right )
// should check that left is same shape as right
{
  delete elements;                            // free up old space
  elements = new double[ row * col + 1];      // allocate new space
  memcpy( elements, right.elements, (row * col + 1) * sizeof( double) );
                                              // copy the data
  return *this;
}
```

You should build in code to check whether the two matrices have the same number of rows and columns.

Note that the elements of the target matrix (left operand) must be deleted and new space allocate before the elements of the source matrix are copied.

As before, the function returns a reference so that assignments may be chained.

Matrix addition

Matrix addition is defined in the obvious way. Each element c_{ij} of the matrix sum

$$C = A + B$$

is given by $c_{ij} = a_{ij} + b_{ij}$, i.e. the sum of the corresponding elements of **A** and **B**. We overload the addition operator as follows:

```
TMatrix TMatrix::operator+( TMatrix &right )
{
  TMatrix temp (*this);              // copy of left operand
  int i;
  for (i = 1; i <= row * col; i++) {
    temp.elements[i] = temp.elements[i] + right.elements[i];
  }
  return temp;
}
```

Matrix multiplication

Probably the most important matrix operation is matrix *multiplication*. It is used widely in such areas as network theory, solution of linear systems of equations, transformation of coordinate systems, and population modelling, just to quote a few.

When two matrices **A** and **B** are multiplied together, their product is a third matrix **C**. The operation is written as

$$C = AB,$$

and the general element c_{ij} of **C** is formed by taking the *scalar product* of the *i*th row of **A** with the *j*th column of **B**. (The scalar product of two *vectors* **x** and **y** is $x_1y_1 + x_2y_2 + \ldots$, where x_i and y_i are the components of the vectors.)

It follows that **A** and **B** can only be successfully multiplied (in that order) if the number of columns in **A** is the same as the number of rows in **B**.

The general definition of matrix multiplication is as follows: If **A** is an $(n \times m)$ matrix and **B** is an $(m \times p)$ matrix, their product **C** will be an $(n \times p)$ matrix such that the general element c_{ij} of **C** is given by

$$c_{ij} = \sum_{k=1}^{m} a_{ik}b_{kj}.$$

Note that in general **AB** is not equal to **BA** (matrix multiplication is not *commutative*). Example:

$$\begin{bmatrix} 1 & 2 \\ 3 & 4 \end{bmatrix} \times \begin{bmatrix} 5 & 6 \\ 0 & -1 \end{bmatrix} = \begin{bmatrix} 5 & 4 \\ 15 & 14 \end{bmatrix}.$$

If you are serious about scientific and engineering programming it's part of your education to code a matrix multiplication on your own. Try to code it directly in a **main()** function like the one above before looking at the code for the overloaded * operator. Use the **TMatrix** class so that you can make use of the overloaded () operators to reference elements like **a(i,k)** and **b(k,j)** directly.

This is how to overload matrix multiplication:

```
TMatrix TMatrix::operator*( TMatrix &right )
{
  TMatrix prod(row, right.col);
  int i, j, k;
  for (i = 1; i <= row; i++) {
    for (j = 1; j <= right.col; j++) {
      prod(i,j) = 0;
      for (k = 1; k <= col; k++)
        prod(i,j) = prod(i,j) + (*this)(i,k) * right(k,j);
    };
  };
  return prod;
}
```

(*this) is the left operand, **right** is the right operand, and **prod** is the product, which will have the same number of rows (**row**) as the left operand and the same number of columns (**right.col**) as the right operand.

To make the function foolproof you should check that the left operand has the same number of *columns* as the right operand has *rows*.

Try it out on the example given above.

Since a vector is simply a one-dimensional matrix, our overloaded **operator*()** function also multiplies a matrix by a vector of the right size, e.g.

$$\begin{bmatrix} 1 & 2 \\ 3 & 4 \end{bmatrix} \times \begin{bmatrix} 2 \\ 3 \end{bmatrix} = \begin{bmatrix} 8 \\ 18 \end{bmatrix}.$$

Try it out on this example too.

It's worth pointing out how well our **TMatrix** class demonstrates the principles of encapsulation. The way matrices are represented and manipulated is completely hidden from the user, who cannot tamper with those sort of details. In fact the class design and implementation could be completely changed (e.g. a matrix could be represented by a linked list) without affecting any code that uses it.

Matrix input

Assigning a matrix element by element as in the example above is not very smart. We can overload the input stream operator **>>** to enable **cin** to input a whole matrix from the keyboard. The overloading function must be declared a friend by `TMatrix`:

```
friend istream &operator>>( istream &instrm, TMatrix &m );
```

The implementation is

```
istream &operator>>( istream &instrm, TMatrix &m )
{
  int i, j;
  for (i = 1; i <= m.row; i++) {
    for (j = 1; j <= m.col; j++)
      instrm >> m(i,j);
  }
  return instrm;
}
```

It works for vectors as well.

Input is now a lot neater:

```
TMatrix a(2,2), d(2);
cout << "Enter matrix:" << endl;
cin >> a;
a.Print();
cout << "Enter vector:" << endl;
cin >> d;
d.Print();
```

This class `TMatrix` that we have developed may of course be used for general array handling. You can start all your arrays at 1 instead of zero, and you can build in subscript range checking. You could even think about having subscripts which don't necessarily start at 1.

17.2 Reachability of spies

In this section we see how to use our `TMatrix` class to calculate a *reachability* matrix.

Suppose five spies in an espionage ring have the code names Alex, Boris, Cyril, Denisov and Eric (whom we can label A, B, C, D and E respectively). The hallmark of a good spy network is that no agent is able to contact all the others. The arrangement for this particular group is:

- Alex can contact only Cyril;
- Boris can contact only Alex or Eric;

- Denisov can contact only Cyril;
- Eric can contact only Cyril or Denisov.

(Cyril can't contact anyone in the ring: he takes information out of the ring to the spymaster. Similarly, Boris brings information in from the spymaster: no-one in the ring can contact him.) The need for good spies to know a bit of matrix theory becomes apparent when we spot that the possible paths of communication between the spies can be represented by a (5×5) matrix, with the rows and columns representing the transmitting and receiving agents respectively, thus:

	A	B	C	D	E
A	0	0	1	0	0
B	1	0	0	0	1
C	0	0	0	0	0
D	0	0	1	0	0
E	0	0	1	1	0

We will call this matrix $\mathbf{A}$. It represents a *directed network* with the spies at the *nodes*, and with *arcs* all of length 1, where a network is a collection of points called nodes. The nodes are joined by lines called arcs. In a directed network, movement (e.g. of information) is only possible along the arcs in one direction (see Figure 17.1).

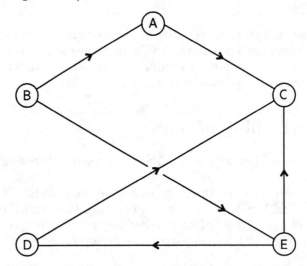

Figure 17.1: The network represented by the matrix $\mathbf{A}$

The matrix $\mathbf{A}$ is known as an *adjacency* matrix, with a 1 in row i and column j if there is an arc from node i to node j, or a 0 in that position if there is no arc between those two nodes. The diagonal elements of $\mathbf{A}$ (i.e. a_{11}, a_{22}, etc.) are all zero because good spies do not talk to themselves (since they might then talk in their sleep and give themselves away). Each 1 in $\mathbf{A}$ therefore represents a single path of length 1 arc in the network.

If we multiply the adjacency matrix $\mathbf{A}$ by itself, we get $\mathbf{A}^2$. The rules of matrix multiplication enable us to interpret the entry in row i and column j of $\mathbf{A}^2$ as representing the number of paths of length 2 between nodes i and j (on the clear understanding that all arcs in the network are of length 1).

In general the element in row i and column j of the kth power of an adjacency matrix is equal to the number of paths consisting of k arcs linking nodes i and j.

The *reachability* matrix $\mathbf{R}$ of an $(n \times n)$ network may be defined as the sum of the first $(n-1)$ powers of its associated adjacency matrix $\mathbf{A}$. You may be wondering why we can stop at the $(n-1)$th power of $\mathbf{A}$. The elements of $\mathbf{A}^{(n-1)}$ will be the number of paths that have $(n-1)$ arcs, i.e. that connect n nodes (since each arc connects two nodes). Since there are no further nodes that can be reached, it is not necessary to raise $\mathbf{A}$ to the nth power (assuming that the network has no cycles).

In our example, the reachability matrix is

$$\mathbf{R} = \mathbf{A} + \mathbf{A}^2 + \mathbf{A}^3 + \mathbf{A}^4.$$

The elements of $\mathbf{R}$ give the total number of paths of communication between the agents. Carrying out the calculations by hand gives

$$\mathbf{R} = \begin{bmatrix} 0 & 0 & 1 & 0 & 0 \\ 1 & 0 & 3 & 1 & 1 \\ 0 & 0 & 0 & 0 & 0 \\ 0 & 0 & 1 & 0 & 0 \\ 0 & 0 & 2 & 1 & 0 \end{bmatrix}.$$

So we can read off from the reachability matrix $\mathbf{R}$ the fact that there are, for example, three different paths between Boris and Cyril, but only two between Eric and Cyril (the actual lengths of these paths will have been calculated in finding the powers of $\mathbf{A}$). The name "reachability" is used because the non-zero elements of $\mathbf{R}$ indicate who may contact whom, directly or indirectly, or for a general distance network, which nodes can be reached from each node.

The code below uses the `TMatrix` class to compute the reachability matrix $\mathbf{R}$ for any network given the adjacency matrix $\mathbf{A}$. It uses the array `b` to store the intermediate powers of the array a, adding them to r each time.

```
int i, n;
cout << "How many nodes? ";
cin >> n;
TMatrix a(n,n), b(n,n), r(n,n);          // matrices
cout << endl << "Enter the adjacency matrix:" << endl;
cin >> a;
r = b = a;                               // set r and b to a

for (i = 1; i <= n-2; i++) {
  b = b * a;
  r = r + b;
}

cout << endl << "The reachability matrix is:" << endl;
r.Print();
```

Note that the matrices may be declared with a variable size n at runtime.

It may help to go through the code by hand for $n = 5$ to see how it works. Keep track of the contents of b and r in terms of the adjacency matrix a.

17.3   Leslie matrices: population growth

Another very interesting and useful application of matrices is in population dynamics.

Suppose we want to model a population of rabbits, in the sense that given their number at some moment, we would like to estimate the size of the population in a few years' time. One approach is to divide the rabbit population up into a number of age classes, where the members of each age class are one time unit older than the members of the previous class, the time unit being whatever is convenient for the population being studied (days, months, etc.).

If X_i is the size of the ith age class, we define a *survival factor* P_i as the proportion of the ith class that survive to the $(i + 1)$th age class, i.e. the proportion that "graduate". F_i is defined as the *mean fertility* of the ith class. This is the mean number of newborn individuals expected to be produced during one time interval by each member of the ith class at the beginning of the interval (only females count in biological modelling, since there are always enough males to go round!).

Suppose for our rabbit model we have three age classes, with x_1, x_2 and x_3 members respectively. We will call them young, middle-aged and old-aged for convenience. We will take our time unit as one month, so x_1 are the number that were born during the current month, and which will be considered as youngsters at the end of the month. x_2 are the number of middle-aged rabbits at the end of the month, and x_3 the number of oldsters. Suppose the youngsters cannot reproduce, so that $F_1 = 0$. Suppose the fertility rate for middle-aged rabbits is 9, so $F_2 = 9$, while for oldsters $F_3 = 12$. The probability of survival from youth to middle-age is one third, so $P_1 = 1/3$, while no less than half the middle-aged rabbits live to become oldsters, so $P_2 = 0.5$ (we are assuming for the sake of illustration that all old-aged rabbits die at the end of the month — this can be corrected easily). With this information we can quite easily compute the changing population structure month by month, as long as we have the population breakdown to start with.

If we now denote the current month by t, and next month by $(t + 1)$, we can refer to this month's youngsters as $x_1(t)$, and to next month's as $x_1(t + 1)$, with similar notation for the other two age classes. We can then write a scheme for updating the population from month t to month $(t + 1)$ as follows:

$$x_1(t + 1) = F_2 x_2(t) + F_3 x_3(t),$$

$$x_2(t + 1) = P_1 x_1(t),$$

$$x_3(t + 1) = P_2 x_2(t).$$

We now define a population vector $\mathbf{x}(t)$, with three components, $x_1(t)$, $x_2(t)$, and $x_3(t)$, representing the three age classes of the rabbit population in month t. The above three equations can then be rewritten as

$$\begin{bmatrix} x_1 \\ x_2 \\ x_3 \end{bmatrix}_{(t+1)} = \begin{bmatrix} 0 & F_2 & F_3 \\ P_1 & 0 & 0 \\ 0 & P_2 & 0 \end{bmatrix} \times \begin{bmatrix} x_1 \\ x_2 \\ x_3 \end{bmatrix}_t$$

where the subscript at the bottom of the vectors indicates the month. We can write this even more concisely as the matrix equation

$$\mathbf{x}(t + 1) = \mathbf{L}\mathbf{x}(t), \tag{17.1}$$

where $\mathbf{L}$ is the matrix

$$\begin{bmatrix} 0 & 9 & 12 \\ 1/3 & 0 & 0 \\ 0 & 1/2 & 0 \end{bmatrix}$$

in this particular case. **L** is called a *Leslie matrix*. A population model can always be written in the form of Equation (17.1) if the concepts of age classes, fertility, and survival factors, as outlined above, are used.

Now that we have established a matrix representation for our model, we can easily write a program using matrix multiplication and repeated application of Equation (17.1):

$$\mathbf{x}(t+2) = \mathbf{L}\mathbf{x}(t+1),$$

$$\mathbf{x}(t+3) = \mathbf{L}\mathbf{x}(t+2), \text{etc.}$$

However, we only need a single vector **x** in the program, because repeated matrix multiplication by the matrix L will continually update it:

```
x = L * x;
```

We will assume to start with, that we have one old (female) rabbit, and no others, so $x_1 = x_2 = 0$, and $x_3 = 1$.

The relevant part of the program is then simply:

```
TMatrix L(3,3);              // Leslie matrix
TMatrix x(3);                // population vector
int i, t;

L(1,2) = 9;                  L(1,3) = 12;
L(2,1) = 1.0 / 3;            L(3,2) = 0.5;
x(3) = 1;

printf( "%5s%15s%15s%15s%15s\n\n",
        "Month", "Young", "Middle", "Old", "Total" );

for (t = 1; t <= 24; t++) {
  x = L * x;
  printf( "%5d", t );

  for (i = 1; i <= 3; i++)
    printf( "%15.0f", x(i) );

  printf( "%15.0f", x.Sum() );
  printf( "\n" );
}
```

We have written another member function for the class, Sum(), to return the sum of the elements of a class object:

```
double TMatrix::Sum( void )
```

```
{
    int i, j;
    double temp = 0;
    for (i = 1; i <= row; i++)
        for (j = 1; j <= col; j++)
            temp += (*this)(i,j);
    return temp;
}
```

Since only about half the Leslie matrix entries are non-zero, it is convenient to assign them directly.

It is also more convenient to print the vector components x(i) directly than to use the member function Print().

The output of the program, over a period of 24 months, is:

Month	Young	Middle	Old	Total
1	12	0	0	12
2	0	4	0	4
3	36	0	2	38
4	24	12	0	36
5	108	8	6	122
6	144	36	4	184
...				
22	11184720	1864164	466020	13514904
23	22369716	3728240	932082	27030038
24	44739144	7456572	1864120	54059836

It so happens that there are no "fractional" rabbits in this example (you can check by changing the format code). If there are any, they should be kept, and not rounded (and certainly not truncated). They occur because the fertility rates and survival probabilities are averages.

If you look carefully at the output you may spot that after some months the total population doubles every month. This factor is called the *growth factor*, and is a property of the particular Leslie matrix being used (for those who know about such things, it's the *dominant eigenvalue* of the matrix). The growth factor is 2 in this example, but if the values in the Leslie matrix are changed, the long-term growth factor changes too (try it and see).

You probably didn't spot that the numbers in the three age classes tend to a limiting ratio of 24:4:1. This can be demonstrated very clearly if you run the model with an initial population structure having this limiting ratio. This limiting ratio is called the *stable age distribution* of the population, and again it is a property of the Leslie matrix (in fact, it is the *eigenvector* belonging to the dominant eigenvalue of the matrix). Different population matrices lead to different stable age distributions.

The interesting point about this is that a given Leslie matrix always eventually gets a population into the *same* stable age distribution, which increases eventually by the *same* growth factor each month, *no matter what the initial population breakdown is*. For example, if you run the above model with any other initial population, it will always eventually get into a stable age distribution of 24:4:1 with a growth factor of 2 (try it and see).

17.4   Markov chains

Often a process that we wish to model may be represented by a number of possible *discrete* (i.e. discontinuous) states that describe the outcome of the process. For example, if we are spinning a coin, then the outcome is adequately represented by the two states "heads" and "tails" (and nothing in between). If the process is random, as it is with spinning coins, there is a certain probability of being in any of the states at a given moment, and also a probability of changing from one state to another. If the probability of moving from one state to another depends on the present state only, and not on any previous state, the process is called a *Markov chain*. Markov chains are used widely in such diverse fields as biology and business decision making, to name just two.

A random walk

Suppose a street in a university suburb has six intersections. An inebriated student wanders down the street. His home is at intersection 1, and his favourite bar at intersection 6. At each intersection other than his home or the bar he moves in the direction of the bar with probability 2/3, and in the direction of his home with probability 1/3. He never wanders down a side street. If he reaches his home or the bar, he disappears into them, never to reappear (when he disappears we say in Markov jargon that he has been *absorbed*).

We would like to know: what are the chances of our student ending up at home or in the bar, if he starts at a given corner (other than home or the bar, obviously)? He can clearly be in one of six states, with respect to his random walk, which can be labelled by the intersection number, where state 1 means *Home* and state 6 means *Bar*. We can represent the probabilities of being in these states by a six-component *state vector* $\mathbf{x}(t)$, where $x_i(t)$ is the probability of him being at intersection i at moment t. The components of $\mathbf{x}(t)$ must sum to 1, since he has to be in one of these states.

We can express this Markov process by the following *transition probability matrix*, $\mathbf{P}$, where the rows represent the next state (i.e. corner), and the columns represent the present state:

	Home	2	3	4	5	Bar
Home	1	1/3	0	0	0	0
2	0	0	1/3	0	0	0
3	0	2/3	0	1/3	0	0
4	0	0	2/3	0	1/3	0
5	0	0	0	2/3	0	0
Bar	0	0	0	0	2/3	1

The entries for *Home-Home* and *Bar-Bar* are both 1 because he stays put there with certainty.

Using the probability matrix **P** we can work out his chances of being, say, at intersection 3 at moment $(t+1)$ as

$$x_3(t+1) = \frac{2}{3}x_2(t) + \frac{1}{3}x_4(t).$$

To get to 3, he must have been at either 2 or 4, and his chances of moving from there are 2/3 and 1/3 respectively.

Mathematically, this is identical to the Leslie matrix problem. We can therefore form the new state vector from the old one each time with a matrix equation:

$$\mathbf{x}(t+1) = \mathbf{P}\mathbf{x}(t).$$

If we suppose the student starts at intersection 2, the initial probabilities will be $(0; 1; 0; 0; 0; 0)$. The Leslie matrix program may be adapted with very few changes to generate future states:

```
TMatrix P(6,6);              // probability transition matrix
TMatrix x(6);                // state vector
int i, t;

for (i = 3; i <= 6; i++) {   // construct P
  P(i,i-1) = 2.0 / 3;
  P(i-2,i-1) = 1.0 / 3;
}

P(1,1) = P(6,6) = 1;
x(2) = 1;

printf( "%4s%9s%9s%9s%9s%9s%9s\n\n",
        "Time", "Home", "2", "3", "4", "5", "Bar" );
```

```
for (t = 1; t <= 50; t++) {
  x = P * x;
  printf( "%4d", t );

  for (i = 1; i <= 6; i++)
    printf( "%9.4f", x(i) );

  printf( "\n" );
}
```

Note that because of the symmetries in the probability matrix we can construct it with a **for** loop. If necessary, the individual non-zero entries can be input, and the matrix constructed from them. The same applies to Leslie matrices.

Output is as follows:

Time	Home	2	3	4	5	Bar
1	0.3333	0.0000	0.6667	0.0000	0.0000	0.0000
2	0.3333	0.2222	0.0000	0.4444	0.0000	0.0000
3	0.4074	0.0000	0.2963	0.0000	0.2963	0.0000
4	0.4074	0.0988	0.0000	0.2963	0.0000	0.1975
5	0.4403	0.0000	0.1646	0.0000	0.1975	0.1975
6	0.4403	0.0549	0.0000	0.1756	0.0000	0.3292
7	0.4586	0.0000	0.0951	0.0000	0.1171	0.3292
8	0.4586	0.0317	0.0000	0.1024	0.0000	0.4073
9	0.4692	0.0000	0.0553	0.0000	0.0683	0.4073
10	0.4692	0.0184	0.0000	0.0596	0.0000	0.4528
...						
40	0.4839	0.0000	0.0000	0.0000	0.0000	0.5161
...						
50	0.4839	0.0000	0.0000	0.0000	0.0000	0.5161

By running the program for long enough, we soon find the limiting probabilities: he ends up at home about 48% of the time, and at the bar about 52% of the time. Perhaps this is a little surprising; from the transition probabilities, we might have expected him to get to the bar rather more easily. It just goes to show that you should never trust your intuition when it comes to statistics!

Simulating the random walk

While on the subject of random walks, it is fun to write a program to *simulate* the student's progress along the street (this has nothing to do with matrices).

Suppose the integer x represents his present intersection. Let's start him at intersection 2. We generate a random number (a decimal fraction in the range 0–1) to decide whether he moves toward the bar or home. Since the

random number is equally likely to have any value in its range, the probability
that it is less than 2/3 is precisely 2/3. So if it comes up less than 2/3 we move
him toward the bar (by incrementing **x**), otherwise we decrement **x**. We go on
repeating this until he either reaches home or the bar, and we record which he
reaches. That was one random walk. We repeat the whole process a large
number of times, say 1000. We then estimate his probability of reaching the
bar as the number of random walks that ended up there, divided by the total
number of simulations.

Obviously, the more walks we simulate, the more accurate the results. If
we use **randomize()** to reseed the random number generate each time, we can
expect slightly different results each time the program is run.

The simulation program is as follows:

```
#include <stdlib.h>
#include <stdio.h>
main()
{
  int count, x, walk;
  int gotToBar = 0;
  int nSims = 1000;
  double pBar, rnd;
  randomize();

  for (walk = 1; walk <= nSims; walk++) {
    x = 2;                          // start at 2 each time
    count = 0;                      // freshen up

    while (x > 1 && x < 6 && count < 10000) {
      count++;
      rnd = double( rand() ) / RAND_MAX;
      if (rnd < 2.0 / 3)
        x++;                        // barwards
      else
        x--;                        // homewards
    }

    if (x == 6)                     // where did he end up?
      gotToBar++;
  }

  pBar = double( gotToBar ) / nSims;
  printf( "After %d simulations chances of getting\
to the bar are: %6.3f\n", nSims, pBar );
  return 0;
}
```

Note that it is theoretically possible for the hapless student to wander up and
down the street for ever on a particular random walk. So to be on the safe side

the walk should stop if he hasn't reached either destination after, say, 10000 intersections!

`rand()` generates a random integer in the range 0 to `RAND_MAX`, so dividing it by `RAND_MAX` gives a fraction. Remember to convert `rand()` to `double` before dividing.

Some sample runs:

```
After 1000 simulations chances of getting to the bar are:  0.502
After 1000 simulations chances of getting to the bar are:  0.508
After 1000 simulations chances of getting to the bar are:  0.508
After 1000 simulations chances of getting to the bar are:  0.522
After 1000 simulations chances of getting to the bar are:  0.522
```

Note that the earlier Markov chain approach is *not* a simulation: we get the *theoretical* probabilities each time (it can all be done mathematically, without a computer). But it is interesting to confirm the limiting probabilities by simulating the student's progress, as we have just done.

17.5   Solution of linear equations

A problem that often arises in scientific applications is the solution of a system of linear equations, e.g.

$$2x - y + z = 4 \qquad (17.2)$$

$$x + y + z = 3 \qquad (17.3)$$

$$3x - y - z = 1. \qquad (17.4)$$

One method of solution is by *Gauss reduction*, which we discuss now.

Gauss reduction

Write the coefficients of the left-hand sides of the equations as a matrix, with the right-hand side constants as a vector to the right of the matrix, separated by a vertical line, thus:

$$\begin{bmatrix} 2 & -1 & 1 & | & 4 \\ 1 & 1 & 1 & | & 3 \\ 3 & -1 & -1 & | & 1 \end{bmatrix}.$$

This is simply shorthand for the original set, and is sometimes called the *augmented matrix* of the system. As long as we perform only *row* operations on the numbers, we can omit the symbols x, y, and z each time. We will refer to the augmented matrix as **A**.

We start with the first row (R_1), and call it the *pivot row*. We call the element $a_{11}(=2)$ the *pivot element*. Divide the whole pivot row by the pivot element, so the augmented array now looks like this:

$$\begin{bmatrix} 1 & -1/2 & 1/2 & 2 \\ 1 & 1 & 1 & 3 \\ 3 & -1 & -1 & 1 \end{bmatrix}.$$

Rows R_2 and R_3 are now called *target rows*. The object is to get zeros in all the target rows below (and above, if necessary) the pivot element. Take the target row R_2. Replace each element in the row by itself minus the corresponding element in the pivot row. The array now looks like this:

$$\begin{bmatrix} 1 & -1/2 & 1/2 & 2 \\ 0 & 3/2 & 1/2 & 1 \\ 3 & -1 & -1 & 1 \end{bmatrix}.$$

Now take the target row R_3. To reduce a_{31} to zero with an operation involving the pivot row requires replacing the target row by itself minus the pivot row multiplied by a_{31} (bearing in mind for the subsequent programming that this operation can change the value of a_{31} itself!):

$$\begin{bmatrix} 1 & -1/2 & 1/2 & 2 \\ 0 & 3/2 & 1/2 & 1 \\ 0 & 1/2 & -5/2 & -5 \end{bmatrix}.$$

We now designate R_2 as the pivot row, and the new a_{22} as the pivot element. The whole procedure is repeated, except that the target rows are now R_1 and R_3, and the object is to get zeros in these two rows above and below the pivot element. The result is:

$$\begin{bmatrix} 1 & 0 & 2/3 & 7/3 \\ 0 & 1 & 1/3 & 2/3 \\ 0 & 0 & -8/3 & -16/3 \end{bmatrix}.$$

Now take R_3 as the pivot row, with the new a_{33} as the pivot element, and R_1 and R_2 as target rows. After repeating similar operations on them, the array finally looks like this:

$$\left[\begin{array}{ccc|c} 1 & 0 & 0 & 1 \\ 0 & 1 & 0 & 0 \\ 0 & 0 & 1 & 2 \end{array}\right].$$

Since we have retained the mathematical integrity of the system of equations by performing operations on the rows only, this is equivalent to

$$x + 0y + 0z = 1$$

$$0x + y + 0z = 0$$

$$0x + 0y + z = 2.$$

The solution may therefore be read off as $x = 1$, $y = 0$, $z = 2$.

Unfortunately, things can go wrong:

1. The pivot element could be zero. This happens quite easily when the coefficients are all integers. However, rows of the array can be interchanged without changing the system of equations. So a non-zero pivot element can often be found in this way (but see the next two cases).

2. A row of zeros could appear right across the array, in which case a non-zero pivot element cannot be found. In this case the system of equations is indeterminate and the solution can only be determined down to as many arbitrary constants as there are rows of zeros.

3. A row of the array could be filled with zeros, except for the extreme right-hand element. In this case the equations are inconsistent, which means there are no solutions.

It is a nice little exercise to program a Gauss reduction using our TMatrix class as it presently stands. However, a little further investigation will yield an addition to the class which provides a much neater solution (which addresses the problem of a zero pivot).

Matrix inversion by Gauss reduction

Consider a different system of equations, just for a change:

$$2x + 2y + 2z = 0$$

$$3x + 2y + 2z = 1$$

$$3x + 2y + 3z = 1.$$

If we define the matrix **A** as

$$\mathbf{A} = \begin{bmatrix} 2 & 2 & 2 \\ 3 & 2 & 2 \\ 3 & 2 & 3 \end{bmatrix},$$

and the vectors **x** and **b** as

$$\mathbf{x} = \begin{bmatrix} x \\ y \\ z \end{bmatrix}, \qquad \mathbf{b} = \begin{bmatrix} 0 \\ 1 \\ 1 \end{bmatrix},$$

we can write the above system of three equations in matrix form as

$$\begin{bmatrix} 2 & 2 & 2 \\ 3 & 2 & 2 \\ 3 & 2 & 3 \end{bmatrix} \begin{bmatrix} x \\ y \\ z \end{bmatrix} = \begin{bmatrix} 0 \\ 1 \\ 1 \end{bmatrix},$$

or even more concisely as the single matrix equation

$$\mathbf{Ax} = \mathbf{b}.$$

The solution may then be written as

$$\mathbf{x} = \mathbf{A}^{-1}\mathbf{b}, \tag{17.5}$$

where $\mathbf{A}^{-1}$ is the *matrix inverse* of **A** (i.e. the matrix which when multiplied by **A** gives the identity matrix).

This provides a slightly different route to the solution. Gauss reduction can also be used to invert a matrix. To invert the matrix **A**, construct the augmented matrix **A** | **I**, where **I** is the identity matrix:

$$\left[\begin{array}{ccc|ccc} 2 & 2 & 2 & 1 & 0 & 0 \\ 3 & 2 & 2 & 0 & 1 & 0 \\ 3 & 2 & 3 & 0 & 0 & 1 \end{array} \right].$$

Now perform a Gauss reduction until the identity matrix has appeared to the left of the vertical line, so that the augmented array finally looks as follows:

$$\left[\begin{array}{ccc|ccc} 1 & 0 & 0 & -1 & 1 & 0 \\ 0 & 1 & 0 & 3/2 & 0 & -1 \\ 0 & 0 & 1 & 0 & -1 & 1 \end{array} \right].$$

The matrix to the right of the line is the inverse of **A**. If **A** is not invertible, the process breaks down and a row of zeros appears. The solution may then be found directly from Equation (17.5): $x = 1$, $y = -1$, $z = 0$.

If we are going to code a Gauss reduction, we might as well overload an operator to perform a matrix inversion directly. The following member function overloads the ˜ operator to do this:

```
TMatrix TMatrix::operator~( void )
// returns inverse of class object by Gauss reduction
// searches for a non-zero pivot
{
    int i, j, k, n;
    int pivRow, tarRow;
    double pivElt, tarElt;
    n = row;                        // number of equations - easier to follow
    TMatrix aug(n, 2*col);
    TMatrix inverse(n, col);

    for (i = 1; i <= n; i++ )
      for (j = 1; j <= col; j++ )
        aug(i,j) = (*this)(i,j);

    // now augment aug with the identity matrix
    for (i = 1; i <= n; i++ )
      for (j = n+1; j <= aug.col; j++ )
        if (i == j-n)
          aug(i,j) = 1;

    for (pivRow = 1; pivRow <= n; pivRow++) {    // process every row
      pivElt = aug(pivRow,pivRow);    // choose pivot element

      if (pivElt == 0) {        // check for zero pivot
        k = pivRow + 1;         // run down rows to find non-zero pivot
        while (pivElt == 0 && k <= n) {
          pivElt = aug(k,pivRow);    // why not try next row?
          k++;                       // k will be too by 1
        }
        if (pivElt == 0) {
          puts( "Cant't find non-zero pivot" );
          exit(1);
        }
        else {    // non-zero pivot in row k so swop rows pivRow and k
          k--;    // adjust for overcount
          TMatrix dum(2*col);              // temporary vector for row swop
          for (i = 1; i <= 2*col; i++)
            dum(i) = aug(pivRow,i);        //make a copy
          for (i = 1; i <= 2*col; i++)
            aug(pivRow,i) = aug(k,i);      //swop
          for (i = 1; i <= 2*col; i++)
```

```
              aug(k,i) = dum(i);
        }
    }

    // now proceed with the non-zero pivot
    for (j = 1; j <= 2*col; j++)
      aug(pivRow,j) = aug(pivRow,j) / pivElt;

    for (tarRow = 1; tarRow <= n; tarRow++)
      if (tarRow != pivRow) {
        tarElt = aug(tarRow,pivRow);
        for (j = 1; j<= 2*col; j++)
          aug(tarRow,j) = aug(tarRow,j) - aug(pivRow,j) * tarElt;
      };
  };

  // now extract the inverse from the left
  for (i = 1; i <= n; i++ )
    for (j = n+1; j <= aug.col; j++ )
      inverse(i,j-n) = aug(i,j);

  return inverse;
}
```

Note the following features:

- The hidden argument **this** addresses the matrix to be inverted. **aug** is the augmented matrix; it must have twice as many columns as (***this**). (***this**) is assigned to the first n columns of **aug**; the identity matrix is assigned to the rightmost **col** columns.
- The function handles a zero pivot element, by looking down the column under the pivot, until it finds a non-zero element. If it cannot find a non-zero pivot, it returns with a message. If it finds a non-zero pivot in row k, it swops row k with the pivot row, **pivRow**. A temporary row, **dum**, is used for the swop.
- Finally, the rightmost **col** columns of **aug** are assigned to the temporary matrix **inverse** and returned.

We can then write the following code to invert a matrix most elegantly:

```
int n;
cout << "How many equations? ";
cin >> n;
TMatrix a(n,n), x(n), b(n);
cout << endl << "Enter the coefficient matrix by rows:" << endl;
cin >> a;
cout << endl << "Enter the right-hand side constants:" << endl;
cin >> b;
```

```
x = ~a * b;     // invert a and find solution!

cout << endl << "Solution:" << endl;
x.Print();
```

You can test the inversion function on Equations (17.2)–(17.4), if you like, with the coefficient of x in the first equation replaced by zero. This gives a non-zero pivot immediately. The solution is $x = 1$, $y = -1$, $z = 3$.

This method, which is fairly straightforward to code, is quite adequate for smallish systems (less than about 20 equations?). Larger systems will often have many zero elements, which makes the Gauss reduction inefficient, since most of the row operations will be on zeros. There are more efficient procedures for such systems.

17.6   Binary file matrix I/O

It may be convenient to store a large matrix on disk as a binary file, for reading back later. One way to do is with two member functions, BPut() and BGet() as follows:

```
void TMatrix::BPut( char *filename )
{
  FILE *fp;
  fp = fopen( filename, "wb" );
  if (!fp) {
    puts( "Can't open file" );
    exit(1);
  }
  fwrite( elements, (row * col + 1) * sizeof( double), 1, fp );
  fclose( fp );
}
void TMatrix::BGet( char *filename )
{
// will read garbage if row and col are not correct
  FILE *fp;
  fp = fopen( filename, "rb" );
  if (!fp) {
    puts( "Can't find file" );
    exit(1);
  }
  fread( elements, (row * col + 1) * sizeof( double), 1, fp );
  fclose( fp );
}
```

Of course if you read the data back into a different shaped matrix you will get some garbage.

Test them with code like

```
TMatrix a(2,2), b(2,2);
... assign elements to a
a.BPut( "matrix" );    // write a to disk
b.BGet( "matrix" );    // read it back into b
b.Print();             // check it
```

17.7   The finite element method

Object-oriented programming has been applied in recent years to the finite element method. J.S. Rodrigues, A. Filho and P.R.B. Devloo, in their paper "Object oriented programming in scientific computations: the beginning of a new era" (*Engineering Computations*, Vol. 8, 81–87, 1991), describe how a matrix class similar TMatrix may be used in finite element programming.

17.8   TMatrix class declaration and implementation

The complete declaration of the TMatrix class we have been using is as follows:

```
#include <stdio.h>
#include <mem.h>
#include <stdlib.h>
#include <iostream.h>
class TMatrix{
private:
  int row, col;
  double *elements;
public:
  TMatrix( int r, int c );                    // proper matrix
  TMatrix( int r );                           // vector
  TMatrix( TMatrix &copy );                   // copy constructor
  ~TMatrix( void ) { delete elements; }
  TMatrix operator+( TMatrix &right );
  TMatrix operator*( TMatrix &right );
  TMatrix &operator=( TMatrix &right );
  double &operator()( int r, int c );         // proper matrix
  double &operator()( int r );                // vector
  void Print( void );
  double Sum( void );
  TMatrix operator~( void );
  void BPut( char *filename );
  void BGet( char *filename );
  friend istream &operator>>( istream &instrm, TMatrix &m );
};
```

The complete implementation is:

```
TMatrix::TMatrix( int r, int c )
{
  elements = new double[r * c + 1];
            // start at elt 1 like normal humans
  memset( elements, '', (r * c + 1) * sizeof( double ) );
  row = r; col = c;
}
TMatrix::TMatrix( int r )
{
  elements = new double[ r + 1];
  memset( elements, '', (r + 1) * sizeof( double ) );
  row = r;
  col = 1;                    // vectors only have one column, don't they?
}
TMatrix::TMatrix( TMatrix &copy )
{
  row = copy.row;
  col = copy.col;
  elements = new double[ row * col + 1];
  memcpy( elements, copy.elements, (row * col + 1) * sizeof(double) );
}
TMatrix TMatrix::operator+( TMatrix &right )
{
  TMatrix temp (*this);              // copy of left operand
  int i;
  for (i = 1; i <= row * col; i++) {
    temp.elements[i] = temp.elements[i] + right.elements[i];
  }
  return temp;
}
TMatrix TMatrix::operator*( TMatrix &right )
{
  TMatrix prod(row, right.col);
  int i, j, k;
  for (i = 1; i <= row; i++) {
    for (j = 1; j <= right.col; j++) {
      prod(i,j) = 0;
      for (k = 1; k <= col; k++)
        prod(i,j) = prod(i,j) + (*this)(i,k) * right(k,j);
    };
  };
  return prod;
}
TMatrix &TMatrix::operator=( TMatrix &right )
// should check that left is same shape as right
{
  delete elements;                          // free up old space
  elements = new double[ row * col + 1];    // allocate new space
```

```
  memcpy( elements, right.elements, (row * col + 1) * sizeof(double) );
          // copy the data
  return *this;
}
double &TMatrix::operator()( int r, int c )
{
  return elements[ (r-1) * col + c ];
}
double &TMatrix::operator()( int r )
{
  return elements[ r ];
}
void TMatrix::Print( void )
{
  int i, j;
  for (i = 1; i <= row; i++) {
    for (j = 1; j <= col; j++)
      printf( "%4.0f", (*this)(i,j) ); printf( "\n" );
  }
}
double TMatrix::Sum( void )
{
  int i, j;
  double temp = 0;
  for (i = 1; i <= row; i++)
    for (j = 1; j <= col; j++)
      temp += (*this)(i,j);
  return temp;
}
TMatrix TMatrix::operator~( void )
// returns inverse of class object by Gauss reduction
// searches for a non-zero pivot
{
  int i, j, k, n;
  int pivRow, tarRow;
  double pivElt, tarElt;
  n = row;                        // number of equations - easier to follow
  TMatrix aug(n, 2*col);
  TMatrix inverse(n, col);

  for (i = 1; i <= n; i++ )
    for (j = 1; j <= col; j++ )
      aug(i,j) = (*this)(i,j);

  // now augment aug with the identity matrix
  for (i = 1; i <= n; i++ )
    for (j = n+1; j <= aug.col; j++ )
      if (i == j-n)
        aug(i,j) = 1;

  for (pivRow = 1; pivRow <= n; pivRow++) {   // process every row
```

```
      pivElt = aug(pivRow,pivRow);    // choose pivot element

  if (pivElt == 0) {      // check for zero pivot
    k = pivRow + 1;        // run down rows to find non-zero pivot
    while (pivElt == 0 && k <= n) {
      pivElt = aug(k,pivRow);    // why not try next row?
      k++;                       // k will be too by 1
    }
    if (pivElt == 0) {
      puts( "Cant't find non-zero pivot" );
      exit(1);
    }
    else {     // non-zero pivot in row k so swop rows pivRow and k
      k--;     // adjust for overcount
      TMatrix dum(2*col);            // temporary vector for row swop
      for (i = 1; i <= 2*col; i++)
        dum(i) = aug(pivRow,i);     //make a copy
      for (i = 1; i <= 2*col; i++)
        aug(pivRow,i) = aug(k,i);   //swop
      for (i = 1; i <= 2*col; i++)
        aug(k,i) = dum(i);
    }
  }

  // now proceed with the non-zero pivot
  for (j = 1; j <= 2*col; j++)
    aug(pivRow,j) = aug(pivRow,j) / pivElt;

  for (tarRow = 1; tarRow <= n; tarRow++)
    if (tarRow != pivRow) {
      tarElt = aug(tarRow,pivRow);
      for (j = 1; j<= 2*col; j++)
        aug(tarRow,j) = aug(tarRow,j) - aug(pivRow,j) * tarElt;
    };
};

// now extract the inverse from the left
for (i = 1; i <= n; i++ )
  for (j = n+1; j <= aug.col; j++ )
    inverse(i,j-n) = aug(i,j);

return inverse;
}
void TMatrix::BPut( char *filename )
{
  FILE *fp;
  fp = fopen( filename, "wb" );
  if (!fp) {
    puts( "Can't open file" );
    exit(1);
  }
```

```
      fwrite( elements, (row * col + 1) * sizeof( double), 1, fp );
      fclose( fp );
   }
   void TMatrix::BGet( char *filename )
   {
   // will read garbage if row and col are not correct
      FILE *fp;
      fp = fopen( filename, "rb" );
      if (!fp) {
        puts( "Can't find file" );
        exit(1);
      }
      fread( elements, (row * col + 1) * sizeof( double), 1, fp );
      fclose( fp );
   }
   istream &operator>>( istream &instrm, TMatrix &m )
   {
      int i, j;
      for (i = 1; i <= m.row; i++) {
        for (j = 1; j <= m.col; j++)
          instrm >> m(i,j);
      }
      return instrm;
   }
```

Summary

- The TMatrix class developed in this chapter demonstrates the principles of encapsulation very well. The class implementation (data representation and handling) is hidden from the user, and may be changed without affecting any code that uses it.
- Overloading the function call operator () provides a neat way of checking array subscript bounds and of implementing a more natural way of numbering subscripts.
- Matrix input can be easily handled by overloading the >> stream insertion operator.

Exercises

17.1 Write a member function for TMatrix which assigns the same constant to all the elements of a matrix. E.g. the code

```
        TMatrix a(5,5) = 1;
```

must set every element of a to 1.

17.2 Write a member function `Idn()` for `TMatrix` which will transform a class object into the identity matrix.

17.3 Write a friend function for `TMatrix` which will allow multiplication of a scalar by a matrix, e.g.

```
a = 2 * b;
```

where a and b are matrices of the same shape (every element of b must be multiplied by 2).

17.4 The *transpose* of an $(n \times m)$ matrix is the $(m \times n)$ matrix that results when the rows and columns of the original matrix are interchanged, i.e. a_{ij} is replaced by a_{ji}. Write a member function for `TMatrix` which returns the transpose of the class object.

17.5 Write a member function for `TMatrix` which interchanges rows i and j of a matrix. Incorporate it into the inversion function where rows are swopped to get a non-zero pivot element.

17.6 Write member functions for `TMatrix` to return row and column sums of a given row and column.

17.7 Write a member function for `TMatrix` to return the largest element in a matrix.

17.8 Compute the limiting probabilities for the student in Section 17.4 when he starts at each of the remaining intersections in turn, and confirm that the closer he starts to the bar, the more likely he is to end up there.

17.9 The following system, suggested by T.S. Wilson, illustrates nicely the problem of ill-conditioning mentioned in Exercise 7.3:

$$10x + 7y + 8z + 7w = 32$$
$$7x + 5y + 6z + 5w = 23$$
$$8x + 6y + 10z + 9w = 33$$
$$7x + 5y + 9z + 10w = 31$$

Use the `TMatrix` class to show that the solution is $x = y = z = w = 1$. Then change the right-hand side constants to 32.01, 22.99, 32.99 and 31.01 (a change of about 1 in 3000) and find the new solution. Finally, change the right-hand side constants to 32.1, 22.9, 32.9 and 31.1 and observe what effect this has on the "solution".

Chapter 18

Numerical methods

18.1 Equations
- The Bisection method - Passing functions as arguments

18.2 Integration
- The Trapezoidal Rule - Library functions as arguments • Simpson's Rule

18.3 First-order differential equations
- Euler's method for air resistance • Euler's method for bacteria growth
- A predictor-corrector method

18.4 Runge-Kutta methods
- Runge-Kutta fourth-order formulae
- Systems of differential equations: a predator-prey model

18.5 A differential equation modelling package
- driver.h • deqns.cpp • driver.cpp

18.6 Partial differential equations: a tridiagonal system
- Heat conduction

Summary

Exercises

A major scientific use of computers is in finding numerical solutions to mathematical problems which have no analytical solutions, i.e. solutions which may be written down in terms of polynomials and the known mathematical functions. In this chapter we look briefly at three areas where *numerical methods* have been highly developed: solving equations, evaluating integrals, and solving differential equations.

18.1 Equations

In this section we consider how to solve equations in one unknown numerically. The general way of expressing the problem is to say that we want to solve the equation $f(x) = 0$, i.e. we want to find its *root* (or roots) x. There is no general method for finding roots analytically for any given $f(x)$.

In Chapter 15 we discussed one method of solving such equations: Newton's method. Another useful method is the *Bisection method*.

The Bisection method

Let's consider the problem of solving the equation $f(x) = 0$, where

$$f(x) = x^3 + x - 3.$$

We attempt to find by inspection, or trial-and-error, two values of x, call them x_L and x_R, such that $f(x_L)$ and $f(x_R)$ have different signs, i.e. $f(x_L)f(x_R) < 0$. If we can find two such values, the root must lie somewhere in the interval between them, since $f(x)$ changes sign on this interval (see Figure 18.1). In this example, $x_L = 1$ and $x_R = 2$ will do, since $f(1) = -1$ and $f(2) = 7$. In the Bisection method, we estimate the root by x_M, where x_M is the midpoint of the interval $[x_L, x_R]$, i.e.

$$x_M = (x_L + x_R)/2. \qquad (18.1)$$

Then if $f(x_M)$ has the same sign as $f(x_L)$, as drawn in the figure, the root clearly lies betwen x_M and x_R. We must then redefine the left-hand end of the interval as having the value of x_M, i.e. we let the new value of x_L be x_M. Otherwise, if $f(x_M)$ and $f(x_L)$ have *different* signs, we let the new value of x_R be x_M, since the root must lie between x_L and x_M in that case. Having

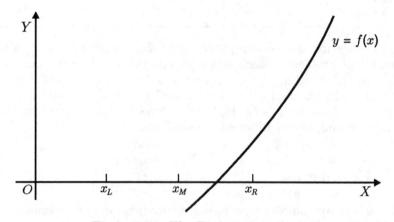

Figure 18.1: The Bisection method

redefined x_L or x_R, as the case may be, we bisect the new interval again according to Equation (18.1) and repeat the process until the distance between x_L and x_R is as small as we please.

The neat thing about this method is that we can calculate *before* starting how many bisections are needed to obtain a certain accuracy, given initial values of x_L and x_R. Suppose we start with $x_L = a$, and $x_R = b$. After the first bisection the worst possible error (E_1) in x_M is $E_1 = |a - b|/2$, since we are estimating the root as being at the midpoint of the interval $[a, b]$. The worst that can happen is that the root is actually at x_L or x_R, in which case the error is E_1. Carrying on like this, after n bisections the worst possible error E_n is given by $E_n = |a - b|/2^n$. If we want to be sure that this is less than some specified error E, we must see to it that n satisfies the inequality $|a - b|/2^n < E$, i.e.

$$n > \frac{\log(|a - b|/E)}{\log(2)} \tag{18.2}$$

Since n is the number of bisections, it must be an integer. The smallest integer n that *exceeds* the right-hand side of Inequality (18.2) will do as the maximum number of bisections required to guarantee the given accuracy E.

The following scheme may be used to program the Bisection method. It will work for any function $f(x)$ that changes sign (in either direction) between the two values a and b, which must be found beforehand by the user. The implementation follows below.

1. Read a, b and E
2. Initialize x_L and x_R
3. Compute maximum bisections n from Inequality (18.2)
4. Repeat n times:
   Compute x_M according to Equation (18.1)
   If $f(x_L)f(x_M) > 0$ then
   Let $x_L = x_M$
   otherwise
   Let $x_R = x_M$
5. Print root x_M
6. Stop.

We have assumed that the procedure will not find the root exactly; the chances of this happening with real variables are infinitesimal. The program is at the end of this section.

The main advantage of the Bisection method is that it is guaranteed to find a root if you can find two starting values for x_L and x_R between which the function changes sign. You can also compute in advance the number of bisections needed to attain a given accuracy. Compared to Newton's method it is inefficient. Successive bisections do not necessarily move closer to the root, as usually happens with Newton's method. In fact, it is interesting to compare the two methods on the same function to see how many more steps the Bisection method requires than Newton's method. For example, to solve the equation $x^3 + x - 3 = 0$, the Bisection method takes 21 steps to reach the same accuracy as Newton's in five steps.

Passing functions as arguments

You may want to write a general purpose numerical methods module containing among other procedures a function to carry out the Bisection method. In that case, it would be convenient to be able pass the function $f(x)$ as an *argument*. This cannot be done directly in C++; however, as you might have guessed, we can pass a *pointer* to the function.

Recall that the syntax

```
double *fn( void );
```

declares a function **fn()** which returns a pointer to a **double** value. However, if you enclose the indirection operator and the function name in parentheses, what you have is an entirely different animal: a *pointer to a function*:

```
double (*fnptr)( void );
```

fnptr is now a pointer to a function that returns a **double** value, instead of a function that returns a pointer to a **double** value. If the function thus addressed needs parameters, add them in the usual way, e.g.

```
double (* fnptr)( double x );
```

This declares **fnptr** as a pointer to any function that returns a **double** value, and takes one **double** argument. To call the function, declare it first in the usual way, and then assign the function address (i.e. its name) to **fnptr**. From then on, **(*fnptr)()** will reference the function, and what is more, it can be passed as an argument to another function. E.g. we can declare a function **F()** as

```
double F( double x )
{
   return x * x * x + x - 3;
}
```

If `fnptr` is declared as above, we can assign `F()` to it with

```
fnptr = F;
```

`(*fnptr)(x)` will then return `F(x)`.

The following complete program uses this technique to pass a pointer to `F(x)` to the function `Bisect()`, which uses the Bisection method to find a root of `F(x)`. Note that `Bisect()` could be precompiled in a separate module. The actual function to be passed to it is assigned to `fnptr` in `main()`. All the user needs to know is the return type and number and type of arguments of the function to be passed.

```c
#include <stdio.h>
#include <math.h>
double F( double x );
double Bisect( double a, double b, double e, int &n,
               double (*fpt)( double ) );
main()
{
  int n;
  double x;
  double (* fnptr)( double x );   // pointer to a function like F(x)

  fnptr = F;                      // point to F(x);
  x = Bisect( 1, 2, 1e-6, n, fnptr );   // pass F(x) to Bisect
  printf( "Number of bisections: %d\n", n );
  printf( "x and F(x): %8.4f %12.4e\n", x, F(x) );
  return 0;
}
double F( double x )
{
  return x * x * x + x - 3;
}
double Bisect( double a, double b, double e, int &n,
               double (*fpt)( double ) )
{
  double xl = a, xr = b, xm;
  int i;
  n = log( fabs(a - b) / e ) / log(2) + 1;
                          // n must exceed formula value
  for (i = 1; i <= n; i++)  {
    xm = (xl + xr) / 2;
    if ( (*fpt)(xl) * (*fpt)(xm) > 0 )
      xl = xm;
    else
      xr = xm;
  }
```

```
        return xl;
    }
```

Output from the program is:

```
    Number of bisections: 20
    x and F(x):    1.2134   -1.7962e-06
```

18.2   Integration

Although most "respectable" mathematical functions can be differentiated analytically, the same cannot unfortunately be said for integration. There are no general rules for integrating, as there are for differentiating. For example, the indefinite integral of a function as simple as

$$e^{-x^2}$$

cannot be found mathematically. We therefore need numerical method for evaluating integrals.

This is actually quite easy to do, and depends on the well-known fact that the definite integral of a function $f(x)$ between the limits $x = a$ and $x = b$ is equal to the area under $f(x)$ bounded by the x-axis and the two vertical lines $x = a$ and $x = b$. So all numerical methods for integrating simply involve more or less ingenious ways of estimating the area under $f(x)$.

The Trapezoidal Rule

One of the standard methods is the Trapezoidal (or Trapezium) Rule. The area under $f(x)$ is divided into vertical panels each of width h, called the *step-length*. If there are n such panels, then $nh = b - a$, i.e. $n = (b - a)/h$. If we join the points where successive panels cut $f(x)$, we can estimate the area under $f(x)$ as the sum of the area of the resulting trapezia. If we call this approximation to the integral S, then

$$S = \frac{h}{2}\left[f(a) + f(b) + 2\sum_{i=1}^{n-1} f(x_i) \right], \tag{18.3}$$

where $x_i = a + ih$. Equation (18.3) is the Trapezoidal Rule, and provides an estimate for the integral

$$\int_a^b f(x)\mathrm{d}x.$$

We can declare a function **Trap()** to evaluate an integral in this way, and again, we can pass it a pointer to the actual function to be integrated:

```
double Trap( double (*fpt)( double ), double a, double b, double h )
{
  double Sum = 0;
  int i, n;
  n = Round( (b - a) / h );

  for (i = 1; i <= n-1; i++)
    Sum = Sum + (*fpt)( a + i * h );

  Sum = h / 2 * ( (*fpt)( a ) + (*fpt)( b ) + 2 * Sum );
  return Sum;
}
int Round( double x )
// rounds to nearest integer
{
  double frac;
  frac = x - (int)( x );
  if (frac >= 0.5)
    return (int)(x) + 1;
  else
    return (int)( x );
}
```

Note that **Trap()** needs a function **Round()** to calculate the number of panels n correctly. In this way, 39.999 for example, will be rounded up to 40, whereas 40.001 will be rounded down to 40.

As an example, let's integrate $f(x) = x^3$ between the limits 0 and 4. All the declarations and the calling program are as follows:

```
double F( double x );
double Trap( double (*fpt)( double ), double a, double b, double h );
int Round( double x );
main()
{
  double ans;
  double (* fnptr)( double x );  // pointer to a function like F(x)
  fnptr = F;                      // point to F(x);
  ans = Trap( fnptr, 0, 4, 0.01 );  // pass F(x) to Trap
  ...
  return 0;
}
double F( double x )
{
  return x * x * x;
}
```

With $h = 0.01$, the estimate is 64.0004 (the exact integral is 64). You will find that as h gets smaller, the estimate gets more accurate.

This example assumes that $f(x)$ is a continuous function which may be evaluated at any x. In practice, the function could be defined at discrete points supplied as results of an experiment. For example, the speed of an object $v(t)$ might be measured every so many seconds, and one might want to estimate the distance travelled as the area under the speed-time graph. In this case, `Trap()` would have to be changed by replacing `(*fnptr)` with an array `values[n+1]`, say. References to `F(a)`, `F(a+i*h)` and `F(b)` would have to be changed to `values[0]`, `values[i]` and `values[n]` respectively.

Library functions as arguments

There is no reason why a pointer to a library function cannot be passed as an argument to `Trap()`. E.g. integrate $\sin x$ between 0 and π as follows:

```
fnptr = sin;
ans = Trap( fnptr, 0, M_PI, 0.01 );
```

Remember to include **math.h**.

Simpson's Rule

Simpson's rule is a method of numerical integration which is a good deal more accurate than the Trapezoidal Rule, and should always be used before you try anything fancier. It also divides the area under the function to be integrated, $f(x)$, into vertical strips, but instead of joining the points $f(x_i)$ with straight lines, every set of three such successive points are fitted with a parabola. To ensure that there are always an even number of panels, the step-length n is usually chosen so that there are $2n$ panels, i.e. $n = (b - a)/(2h)$.

Using the same notation as above, Simpson's rule estimates the integral as

$$S = \frac{h}{3} \left[f(a) + f(b) + 2 \sum_{i=1}^{n-1} f(x_{2i}) + 4 \sum_{i=1}^{n} f(x_{2i-1}) \right].$$

This rule can be coded as a function `Simp()` to join your growing stable of numerical utilities:

```
double Simp( double (*fpt)( double ), double a, double b, double h )
{
    double Sum = 0;
    int i, n;
    n = Round( (b - a) / (2 * h) );        // 2n panels now
```

```
        for (i = 1; i <= n-1; i++)      // use notation defined in text
          Sum = Sum + 2 * (*fpt)( a + 2 * i * h );

        for (i = 1; i <= n; i++)
          Sum = Sum + 4 * (*fpt)( a + (2 * i - 1) * h );

        Sum = h / 3 * ( (*fpt)( a ) + (*fpt)( b ) + Sum );
        return Sum;
      }
```

It also uses `Round()`. Note that n is half its previous size.

If you try Simpson's Rule out on $f(x) = x^3$ between any limits, you will find rather surprisingly, that it gives the same result as the exact mathematical solution. This is a nice extra benefit of the rule: it integrates cubic polynomials exactly (which can be proved).

18.3 First-order differential equations

The most interesting situations in real life that we may want to model, or represent quantitatively, are usually those in which the variables change in time (e.g. biological, electrical or mechanical systems). If the changes are continuous, the system can often be represented with equations involving the derivatives of the dependent variables. Such equations are called *differential equations*. The main aim of a lot of modelling is to be able to write down a set of differential equations that describe the system being studied as accurately as possible. Very few differential equations can be solved analytically, so once again, numerical methods are required. We will look at the simplest method of numerical solution in this section: Euler's method (Euler rhymes with boiler). We will also consider briefly how to improve it.

Euler's method for air resistance

To illustrate Euler's method, we will take an example from Newtonian dynamics, of motion under gravity against air resistance. Suppose a skydiver steps out of a hovering helicopter, but does not open his parachute for 24 seconds. We would like to find his velocity as a function of time during this period. Assuming air resistance cannot be neglected (ask any skydiver!), he falls subject to two opposing vertical forces: gravity acting downward, and air resistance acting upward. The air resistance force is assumed to be proportional to the square of his velocity (this is fairly accurate). Applying Newton's second law to the skydiver, we arrive at

$$\mathrm{d}v/\mathrm{d}t = g - kv^2, \tag{18.4}$$

where g is the acceleration due to gravity and v his velocity a time t after opening the parachute. Equation (18.4) is the differential equation describing the motion of the skydiver under gravity. The constant k varies with shape and mass, and may be found experimentally from the *terminal velocity* of the falling object. This terminal velocity (v_T) is reached when the object stops accelerating, and may be found by equating the right-hand side of Equation (18.4) to zero. Thus

$$v_T = \sqrt{g/k}.$$

For a man wearing an unopened parachute, k is found to be about 0.004 in MKS units. Before we proceed with the numerical solution of Equation (18.4) we should note that this particular differential equation can be solved analytically, since it is of the type called variable separable:

$$v(t) = \frac{a(C - e^{-2akt})}{C + e^{-2akt}}, \tag{18.5}$$

where $a = v_T$ and $C = [a + v(0)]/[a - v(0)]$.

Euler's method for solving Equation (18.4) numerically consists of approximating the derivative on the left-hand side with its Newton quotient. After a slight rearrangment of terms, we get

$$v(t + h) \approx v(t) + h[g - kv^2(t)]. \tag{18.6}$$

If we divide up the time period t into n intervals of h, then $t = nh$. If we define v_n as $v(t)$, then $v_{n+1} = v(t + h)$. We can therefore replace Equation (18.6) with the iterative scheme

$$v_{n+1} = v_n + h(g - kv_n^2). \tag{18.7}$$

Since we are given the initial condition $v_0 = 0$, Equation (18.7) provides a numerical scheme for finding the Euler approximation v_n to $v(t)$ in general.

It is very easy to program Euler's method. We can also test its accuracy by trying different values of h and comparing the results with the exact solution. The following program uses Euler's method as implemented in Equation (18.7) to estimate v for the first 24 seconds of the skydiver's motion. It also computes the exact solution for comparison.

```
#include <math.h>
#include <iostream.h>
#include <stdio.h>
```

```
#define G 9.8
double Vexact( double t, double v0, double k );
main()
{
  double k, h, t, t0, tend, v, v0;

  cout << "Enter k, h, t0, v(t0), tend: ";
  cin >> k >> h >> t0 >> v0 >> tend;
  v = v0;
  printf( "%10s%10s%10s\n\n", "Time", "Euler", "Exact" );

  for (t = t0; t <= tend + h/10; t += h) {
    printf( "%10.2f%10.2f%10.2f\n", t, v, Vexact( t, v0, k ) );
    v = v + h * (G - k * v * v);
  }

  return 0;
}
double Vexact( double t, double v0, double k )
{
  double a, c;
  a = sqrt( G / k );
  c = (a + v0) / (a - v0);
  return a * (c - exp(-2 * a * k * t)) / (c + exp(-2 * a * k * t));
}
```

Taking $h = 2$ and $k = 0.004$ we get:

Time	Euler	Exact
0.00	0.00	0.00
2.00	19.60	18.64
4.00	36.13	32.64
6.00	45.29	41.08
8.00	48.48	45.50
10.00	49.28	47.65
12.00	49.45	48.65
14.00	49.49	49.11
16.00	49.50	49.32
18.00	49.50	49.42
20.00	49.50	49.46
22.00	49.50	49.48
24.00	49.50	49.49

Euler's method gets more accurate if you reduce h, e.g. with $h = 0.5$ the worst error is only about 3%. Note that the errors get smaller as terminal velocity approaches.

In a real problem, we don't usually know the exact answer, or we wouldn't be using a numerical method in the first place. The only check is to use smaller and smaller values of h until it doesn't seem to make much difference, e.g. continue halving h until the results for a fixed t only change by an acceptably small amount.

Now let's see what happens when the skydiver opens his parachute. The air resistance term will be different now. For an open parachute, $k = 0.3$ is quite realistic. We can use the same program as before, although we need to supply a new starting value of 49.49 for v. Since $h = 0.5$ worked well before, we try the same value now. The results are rather surprising. Not only does Euler's solution show that the man flies upward, he does so with tremendous speed, and soon exceeds the speed of light! The results make nonsense physically. Fortunately, in this example our intuition tells us that something is wrong. The only remedy is to reduce h. Some experimenting will reveal that the results for $h = 0.01$ are much better.

Finally, note that Euler's method will be just as easy to compute if the air resistance term is not kv^2, but $kv^{1.8}$ (which is more realistic), although now an analytic solution cannot be found.

Euler's method for bacteria growth

Euler's method performs quite adequately in the skydiver problem once we have got the right value of the step-length h. In case you think that the numerical solution of all differential equations is just as easy, we will now consider an example where Euler's method doesn't do too well.

Suppose a colony of 1 000 bacteria are multiplying at the rate of $r = 0.8$ per hour per individual (i.e. an individual produces an average of 0.8 offspring every hour). How many bacteria are there after 10 hours? Assuming that the colony grows continuously and without restriction, we can model this growth with the differential equation

$$dN/dt = rN, \quad N(0) = 1\,000, \tag{18.8}$$

where $N(t)$ is the population size at time t. This process is called *exponential growth*. Equation (18.8) may be solved analytically to give the well-known formula for exponential growth, $N(t) = N(0)e^{rt}$. To solve Equation (18.8) numerically, we apply Euler's algorithm to it to get

$$N_{k+1} = N_k + rhN_k,$$

where $N_k = N(t)$, and $N_0 = 1\,000$. Taking $h = 0.5$ gives the results shown in Table 18.1, where the exact solution is also given.

This time the numerical solution (in the column headed *Euler*) is not too good. In fact, the error gets worse at each step, and after 10 hours of bacteria

Time	Euler	Predictor-Corrector	Exact
0.0	1 000	1 000	1 000
0.5	1 400	1 480	1 492
1.0	1 960	2 190	2 226
1.5	2 744	3 242	3 320
2.0	3 842	4 798	4 953
...			
5.0	28 925	50 422	54 598
...			
8.0	217 795	529 892	601 845
...			
10.0	836 683	2 542 344	2 980 958

Table 18.1: Bacteria growth

time it is about 72%. Of course, the numerical solution will improve if we take h smaller, but there will still always be some value of t where the error exceeds some acceptable limit.

We may ask why Euler's method works so well with the skydiver, but so badly with the bacteria. By using the Newton quotient each time in Euler's method, we are actually assuming that the derivative changes very little over the small interval h, i.e. that the *second* derivative is very small. Now in the case of the skydiver, by differentiating Equation (18.4) again with respect to time, we see that

$$d^2v/dt^2 = -(2kv)dv/dt,$$

which approaches zero as the falling object reaches its terminal velocity. In the bacteria case, the second derivative of $N(t)$ is found by differentiating Equation (18.8):

$$d^2N/dt^2 = rdN/dt = r^2N(t).$$

This is far from zero at $t = 10$. In fact, it is approaching three million! The Newton quotient approximation gets worse at each step in this case.

There are better numerical methods for overcoming these sorts of problems. Two of them are discussed below. More sophisticated methods may be found in most textbooks on numerical analysis. However, Euler's method may always be used as a first approximation as long as you realize where and why errors may arise.

A predictor-corrector method

One improvement on the solution of

$$dy/dx = f(x, y), \quad y(0) \text{ given},$$

is as follows. The Euler approximation, which we are going to denote by an asterisk, is given by

$$y_{k+1}^* = y_k + hf(x_k, y_k) \tag{18.9}$$

But this formula favours the old value of y in computing $f(x_k, y_k)$ on the right-hand side. Surely it would be better to say

$$y_{k+1}^* = y_k + h[f(x_{k+1}, y_{k+1}^*) + f(x_k, y_k)]/2, \tag{18.10}$$

where $x_{k+1} = x + h$, since this also involves the new value y_{k+1}^* in computing f on the right-hand side? The problem of course is that y_{k+1}^* is as yet unknown, so we can't use it on the right-hand side of Equation (18.10). But we could use Euler to estimate (predict) y_{k+1}^* from Equation (18.9) and then use Equation (18.10) to correct the prediction by computing a *better* version of y_{k+1}^*, which we will call y_{k+1}. So the full procedure is:

> Repeat as many times as required:
> Use Euler to predict: $y_{k+1}^* = y_k + hf(x_k, y_k)$
> Then correct y_{k+1}^* to: $y_{k+1} = y_k + h[f(x_{k+1}, y_{k+1}^*) + f(x_k, y_k)]/2$.

This is called a *predictor-corrector* method. The program above can easily be adapted to this problem. The relevant lines of code, which will generate all the entries in Table 18.1 at once, are:

```
for (t = 0; t <= 10 + h/10; t += h) {
    printf( "%5.1f%12.0f%12.0f%12.0f\n", t, ne, nc, n0 * exp(r * t) );
    ne = ne + r * h * ne;              // straight Euler
    np = nc + r * h * nc;              // predictor
    nc = nc + r * h * (np + nc) / 2;   // corrector
}
```

ne stands for the "straight" (uncorrected) Euler solution, np is the Euler predictor, and nc is the corrector. They must all be initialized to N_0. The worst error is now only 15%. This is much better than the uncorrected Euler solution, although there is still room for improvement.

18.4 Runge-Kutta methods

There are a variety of algorithms, under the general name of Runge-Kutta, which can be used to integrate ordinary differential equations. The *fourth-order* formula is given below, for reference. A derivation of this and the other Runge-Kutta formulae can be found in most books on numerical analysis.

Runge-Kutta fourth-order formulae

The general first-order differential equation is

$$dy/dx = f(x, y), \quad y(0) \text{ given.} \tag{18.11}$$

The fourth-order Runge-Kutta estimate y^* at $x + h$ is given by

$$y^* = y + (k_1 + 2k_2 + 2k_3 + k_4)/6,$$

where

$$k_1 = hf(x, y)$$
$$k_2 = hf(x + 0.5h, y + 0.5k_1)$$
$$k_3 = hf(x + 0.5h, y + 0.5k_2)$$
$$k_4 = hf(x + h, y + k_3).$$

Systems of differential equations: a predator-prey model

The Runge-Kutta formulae may be adapted to integrate *systems* of first-order differential equations. Here we adapt the fourth-order formulae to integrate the well-known Lotka-Volterra *predator-prey* model:

$$dx/dt = px - qxy \tag{18.12}$$

$$dy/dt = rxy - sy, \tag{18.13}$$

where $x(t)$ and $y(t)$ are the prey and predator population sizes at time t, and p, q, r and s are biologically determined parameters. We define $f(x, y)$ and

$g(x, y)$ as the right-hand sides of Equations (18.12) and (18.13) respectively. In this case, the Runge-Kutta estimates x^* and y^* at time $(t + h)$ may be found from x and y at time t with the formulae

$$x^* = x + (k_1 + 2k_2 + 2k_3 + k_4)/6$$
$$y^* = y + (m_1 + 2m_2 + 2m_3 + m_4)/6,$$

where

$$k_1 = hf(x, y)$$
$$m_1 = hg(x, y)$$
$$k_2 = hf(x + 0.5k_1, y + 0.5m_1)$$
$$m_2 = hg(x + 0.5k_1, y + 0.5m_1)$$
$$k_3 = hf(x + 0.5k_2, y + 0.5m_2)$$
$$m_3 = hg(x + 0.5k_2, y + 0.5m_2)$$
$$k_4 = hf(x + k_3, y + m_3)$$
$$m_4 = hg(x + k_3, y + m_3)$$

It should be noted that in this example x and y are the dependent variables, and t (which does *not* appear explicitly in the equations) is the independent variable. In Equation (18.11) y is the dependent variable, and x is the independent variable.

18.5　A differential equation modelling package

This section implements a skeleton *interactive modelling* program, **driver**. Its basis is a fourth-order Runge-Kutta procedure to integrate a time-based system (of any size) of first-order differential equations. It consists of three separate files, only one of which needs to be recompiled by users:

- a header file **driver.h** with class declarations for the model variables, and function prototypes;
- a file **deqns.cpp** containing a single function Deqns(), which defines the model differential equations—in principle, this is the only module which needs to be recompiled when the user sets up or changes a model;

- the basic package **driver.cpp**, including some utility functions, a Runge-Kutta procedure, and the `main()` function.

Each of these parts will be described in turn. To illustrate the package, it is set up here to run the predator-prey model of Section 18.4, with $x(0) = 105$, $y(0) = 8$, $p = 0.4$, $q = 0.04$, $r = 0.02$, and $s = 2$.

driver.h

The header file **driver.h** is:

```
// driver.h
class TVar {            // driver variables
public:
  char name[5];         // name
  double inVal;         // initial value (for I option)
  double val;           // current value (for C option)
};
class TPar {            // driver parameters
public:
  char name[5];         // name
  double val;           // value
};
void Deqns( double f[ ] );
void Headings( void );
void Initialize( void );
void Run( void );
void Runge( void );
void TidyUp( void );
```

Each model variable will be represented by an element of a dynamic array of type **TVar**, i.e. each model variable will be a class object, with a name, an initial value, and a current value. The current value is kept so that the user may run the model either from the initial values, or the current values. The model parameters will be represented by class objects of type **TPar**.

The remaining declarations are prototypes for **driver**'s utility functions, and include the prototype for **Deqns()**, where the user defines the model differential equations.

deqns.cpp

The only part of the package which the user writes and recompiles is the function **Deqns()**:

```
#include "driver.h"
extern double *x;
```

```
extern TPar *par;
void Deqns( double f[ ] )
// evaluates RHS of DEs
{
  // model equations are:
  // dx/dt = f[0] = px - qxy   (prey)
  // dy/dt = f[1] = rxy - sy   (pred)
  double &prey = x[0];      // aliases reduce chances of errors
  double &pred = x[1];
  double &p = par[0].val;
  double &q = par[1].val;
  double &r = par[2].val;
  double &s = par[3].val;
  f[0] = p * prey - q * prey * pred;
  f[1] = r * prey * pred - s * pred;
}
```

It is convenient to have a separate dynamic array addressed by x to hold the current values of the model variables. It is declared **extern** because it is a global variable declared in **driver.cpp** (below). **driver.cpp** allocates dynamic memory to it. The dynamic array **par** is similarly set up in **driver**, and so must also be declared **extern**. Its elements are class objects representing the model parameters.

Deqns() evaluates and returns the right-hand side of the ith differential equation in the $(i-1)$th element of the array f. To allow you to use more meaningful symbolic names for parameters and variables, reference variables are used to set up aliases between the symbolic names and the **driver** variables x and **par**. This is why the current values of the model variables must be held in the array x. The use of aliases makes it much easier to code large models.

driver.cpp

The main part of the package, **driver.cpp**, is as follows:

```
#include <conio.h>
#include <stdio.h>
#include <ctype.h>
#include <string.h>
#include "driver.h"
                          // global variables
int numVars;              // number of model variables
int numPars;              // number of model parameters
unsigned int runTime;     // number of time steps
double dt, t;             // step-length, model time
TVar *var;                // model variables
```

```
TPar *par;                // model parameters
double *x;                // current values of model variables

main()
{
  char choice;
  int i;
  Initialize();

  do {
    clrscr();
    printf( "Driver Demonstration\n\n" );
    printf( "C: Carry on\n" );
    printf( "I: Initial run\n" );
    printf( "Q: Quit\n\n" );
    printf( "Your choice: " );
    choice = toupper( getch() );

    if (choice == 'C') {        // carry on
      clrscr();
      for (i = 0; i < numVars; i++)
        x[i] = var[i].val;
      Run();
    }

    else if (choice == 'I') {  // initial run
      clrscr();
      for (i = 0; i < numVars; i++)
        x[i] = var[i].inVal;
      t = 0;                  // reset t
      Run();
    }

    else if (choice != 'Q')
      printf( "\a\a\a" );

  } while (choice != 'Q');

  TidyUp();
  return 0;
}
void Headings( void )
// output headings and current values of variables
{
  int i;
  printf( "%11s", "Time" );      // headings
  for (i = 0; i < numVars; i++)
    printf( "%11s", var[i].name );
  printf( "\n\n" );
  printf( "%11.2f", t );          // current values
```

```
      for (i = 0; i < numVars; i++)
        printf( "%11.2f", x[i] );
      printf( "\n" );
    }
    void Initialize( void )
    // all this info could be read from a disk file
    {
      int i;
      numVars = 2;
      numPars = 4;
      var = new TVar[ numVars ];
      par = new TPar[ numPars ];
      x = new double[ numVars ];
      var[0].inVal = 105;
      strcpy( var[0].name, "Prey" );
      var[1].inVal = 8;
      strcpy( var[1].name, "Pred" );
      par[0].val = 0.4;
      par[1].val = 0.04;
      par[2].val = 0.02;
      par[3].val = 2.0;
      dt = 1;
      t = 0;
      runTime = 10;
      for (i = 0; i < numVars; i++)  // set current values to 0 for safety
        var[i].val = 0;             // only for this demo
    }
    void Run( void )
    // actually runs the model
    {
      int i, j;
      Headings();
      for (i = 1; i <= runTime; i++)  {
        t += dt;
        Runge();
        printf( "%11.2f", t );
        for (j = 0; j < numVars; j++)
          printf( "%11.2f", x[j] );
        printf( "\n" );
      }
      getch();
      for (i = 0; i < numVars; i++)
        var[i].val = x[i];                    // current values
    }
    void Runge( void )
    // fourth-order Runge-Kutta
    {
      double *f = new double[ numVars ];
      double *a = new double[ numVars ];       // working space
      double *b = new double[ numVars ];
```

```
double *c = new double[ numVars ];
double *d = new double[ numVars ];
double *v = new double[ numVars ];
int i;

for (i = 0; i < numVars; i++)      // initialize for Runge-Kutta
  v[i] = x[i];
Deqns( f );
for (i = 0; i < numVars; i++)
  a[i] = dt * f[i];
for (i = 0; i < numVars; i++)
  x[i] = v[i] + a[i] / 2;
Deqns( f );
for (i = 0; i < numVars; i++)
  b[i] = dt * f[i];
for (i = 0; i < numVars; i++)
  x[i] = v[i] + b[i] / 2;
Deqns( f );
for (i = 0; i < numVars; i++)
  c[i] = dt * f[i];
for (i = 0; i < numVars; i++)
  x[i] = v[i] + c[i];
Deqns( f );
for (i = 0; i < numVars; i++)
  d[i] = dt * f[i];
for (i = 0; i < numVars; i++)
  x[i] = v[i] + (a[i] + 2 * b[i] + 2 * c[i] + d[i]) / 6;
                          // finally update x for return
delete[ numVars ] f;
delete[ numVars ] a;
delete[ numVars ] b;
delete[ numVars ] c;
delete[ numVars ] d;
delete[ numVars ] v;
}
void TidyUp( void )
// destroys dynamic memory, close files etc.
{
  delete[ numVars ] var;
  delete[ numPars ] par;
  delete[ numVars ] x;
}
```

Note the block of global variables, which are described in comments.

We will look at the functions roughly in the order in which they are executed.

`Initialize()` allocates dynamic storage, sets up model variable and parameter names and values, and also initializes other global variables. Note that all this information could be read from a disk file (which itself could be set up by another function), and written back to the file at the end of a session. In this way you can start a new session from where the previous one left off.

Suppose you choose the Initial run option from the main menu. The initial values of the model variables are copied to the array x, model time t is set to zero, and then Run() is called.

The function Run() actually runs the model. First, it calls Headings() to generate headings for the output from a run, including the starting values for that run (which will be initial values for an Initial run, but current values for a Carry on. Then it integrates the differential equations runTime times by calling Runge(). Finally Run() sets the final values of the class objects representing the variables to x.

Runge() integrates the differential equations over one step-length dt, calling Deqns() to supply their right-hand sides.

If you choose the Carry on option in the main menu, the *current* values of the model variables are copied into x before Run() is called, and model time t is left at its current value.

TidyUp() deletes dynamic storage, and would be the place to close files, etc.

A sample run using the data in this example is as follows:

```
Driver Demonstration

C: Carry on
I: Initial run
Q: Quit

Your choice: I
```

Time	Prey	Pred
0.00	105.00	8.00
1.00	110.88	9.47
2.00	108.32	11.65
3.00	98.83	12.57
4.00	91.12	11.26
5.00	90.30	9.24
6.00	95.81	7.98
7.00	104.30	7.99
8.00	110.45	9.34
9.00	108.61	11.48
10.00	99.58	12.52

. . .

Depending on your enthusiasm, you could extend this skeleton a great deal. For example, it doesn't make full use of the power of encapsulation, since for convenience the data members of TVar and TPar are public. You could make them private, to prevent unskilled users tampering with them accidentally in Deqns(). However, you would then have to write some member functions to access them. Some of the **driver** utility functions would then have to be friends of the classes.

You could also allow for parameter changes, and you could even write a procedure for setting up a new model, which asks the user for symbolic names of variables and parameters, and which *generates the aliasing code* for subsequent inclusion into Deqns. This is very useful for large models.

18.6 Partial differential equations: a tridiagonal system

The numerical solution of partial differential equations (PDEs) is a vast subject. Space only permits one example, which serves two important purposes. It demonstrates a powerful method of solving a class of PDEs called *parabolic*. It also illustrates a method of solving tridiagonal systems of linear equations.

Heat conduction

The conduction of heat along a thin uniform rod may be modelled by the partial differential equation

$$\frac{\partial U}{\partial t} = \frac{\partial^2 U}{\partial x^2},$$
(18.14)

where $U(x,t)$ is the temperature distribution a distance x from one end of the rod at time t. It is assumed that no heat is lost from the rod along its length.

Half the battle in solving PDEs is mastering the notation. We set up a rectangular grid, with step-lengths of h and k in the x and t directions respectively. A general point on the grid has co-ordinates $x_i = ih$, $y_j = jk$. A concise notation for $U(x,t)$ at x_i, y_j is then simply $U_{i,j}$.

Now $U_{i,j}$ is of course the exact solution of the PDE. Exact solutions can only be found in a few special cases; we want a general method for finding approximate solutions. This is done by using truncated Taylor series to replace the PDE by a *finite difference scheme*. We define $u_{i,j}$ as the solution of the finite difference scheme at the grid point x_i, y_j. We now attempt to find numerical solutions for $u_{i,j}$, which will therefore be our approximation to the exact solution $U_{i,j}$.

The left-hand side of Equation (18.14) is usually approximated by a *forward difference*:

$$\frac{\partial U}{\partial t} = \frac{u_{i,j+1} - u_{i,j}}{k}.$$

One way of approximating the right-hand side of Equation (18.14) is as follows:

$$\frac{\partial^2 U}{\partial x^2} = \frac{u_{i+1,j} - 2u_{i,j} + u_{i-1,j}}{h^2}. \tag{18.15}$$

This leads to a scheme, which although easy to compute, is only conditionally stable.

If however we replace the right-hand side of the scheme in Equation (18.15) by the mean of the finite difference approximation on the jth and $(j+1)$th time rows, we get the following scheme for Equation (18.14):

$$- ru_{i-1,j+1} + (2+2r)u_{i,j+1} - ru_{i+1,j+1} = ru_{i-1,j} + (2-2r)u_{i,j} + ru_{i+1,j}, \tag{18.16}$$

where $r = k/h^2$. This is known as the Crank-Nicolson *implicit* method, since it involves the solution of a system of simultaneous equations, as we shall see.

To illustrate the method numerically, let's suppose that the rod has a length of 1 unit, and that its ends are in contact with blocks of ice, i.e. the *boundary conditions* are $U(0, t) = U(1, t) = 0$. Suppose also that the initial temperature is given by the *initial condition*

$$U(x, 0) = \begin{cases} 2x, 0 \le x \le 1/2, \\ 2(1-x), 1/2 \le x \le 1. \end{cases}$$

This situation could come about by heating the centre of the rod for a long time, with the ends kept in contact with the ice, removing the heat source at time $t = 0$. This particular problem has symmetry about the line $x = 1/2$; we exploit this fact in finding the solution.

If we take $h = 0.1$ and $k = 0.01$, we will have $r = 1$, and Equation (18.16) becomes

$$- u_{i-1,j+1} + 4u_{i,j+1} - u_{i+1,j+1} = u_{i-1,j} + u_{i+1,j}.$$

Putting $j = 0$ then generates the following set of equations for the unknowns $u_{i,1}$ up to the midpoint of the rod, represented by $i = 5$, i.e. $x = ih = 0.5$.

Exact and approximate solutions coincide on the boundaries and at time $t = 0$. The subscript $j = 1$ has been dropped for clarity:

$$0 + 4u_1 - u_2 = 0 + 0.4$$

$$-u_1 + 4u_2 - u_3 = 0.2 + 0.6$$

$$-u_2 + 4u_3 - u_4 = 0.4 + 0.8$$

$$-u_3 + 4u_4 - u_5 = 0.6 + 1.0$$

$$-u_4 + 4u_5 - u_6 = 0.8 + 0.8.$$

Symmetry then allows us to replace u_6 in the last equation by u_4. This system can be written in matrix form as

$$
\begin{bmatrix}
4 & -1 & 0 & 0 & 0 \\
-1 & 4 & -1 & 0 & 0 \\
0 & -1 & 4 & -1 & 0 \\
0 & 0 & -1 & 4 & -1 \\
0 & 0 & 0 & -2 & 4
\end{bmatrix}
\begin{bmatrix}
u_1 \\
u_2 \\
u_3 \\
u_4 \\
u_5
\end{bmatrix}
=
\begin{bmatrix}
0.4 \\
0.8 \\
1.2 \\
1.6 \\
1.6
\end{bmatrix}.
\qquad (18.17)
$$

The matrix ($\mathbf{A}$) on the left of Equation (18.17) is known as a *tridiagonal* matrix. Such a matrix can be represented by three one-dimensional arrays: one for each diagonal. The system can then be solved very efficiently by Gauss *elimination*. This will not be explained here, but simply presented in a working program.

Care needs to be taken with the matrix representation. The following form is is often chosen:

$$
\mathbf{A} =
\begin{bmatrix}
b_1 & c_1 & & & & \\
a_2 & b_2 & c_2 & & & \\
 & a_3 & b_3 & c_3 & & \\
 & & & \ddots & & \\
 & & & a_{n-1} & b_{n-1} & c_{n-1} \\
 & & & & a_n & b_n
\end{bmatrix}.
$$

Take careful note of the subscripts!

The following program implements the Crank-Nicolson method to solve this particular problem over 10 time steps of $k = 0.01$. The step-length h is specified by N in the relationship $h = 1/(2N)$ because of the symmetry. r is therefore not restricted to the value 1, although it takes this value in the

program. To make life easier, natural subscripting is used, so most of the
arrays have some unused elements. For example, elements a[0] and a[1] are
never used, since the first subscript of *a* in the representation above is 2. As a
result of this some unnecessary assignments are made in the first for loop.
The alternative to wasting a few bytes is to get hopelessly tangled up in a
forest of subscripts!

```
#include <stdio.h>
void TriDiag( double a[ ], double b[ ], double c[ ],
              double x[ ], double g[ ], int n );
main()
{
   const int n = 5;
   int i, j;
   double h, k, r, t;
   double a[n+1], b[n+1], c[n+1], u[n+2], g[n+1], ux[n+1];
                     // most elements numbered 0 are unnecessary
   k = 0.01;
   h = 1.0 / (2 * n);     // symmetry assumed
   r = k / (h * h);

   // some elements at either end of arrays are assigned unnecessarily
   for (i = 1; i <= n; i++) {
     a[i] = -r;
     b[i] = 2 + 2 * r;
     c[i] = -r;
   }
   a[n] = -2 * r;               // from symmetry

   for (i = 0; i <= n; i++)     // initial conditions
     u[i] = 2 * i * h;
   u[n+1] = u[n-1];

   t = 0;
   printf( "%6s", "x =" );        // headings
   for (i = 1; i <= n; i++)
     printf( "%8.4f", i * h );
   printf( "\n  t\n" );
   printf( "%6.2f", t );
   for (i = 1; i <= n; i++)       // initial conditions
     printf( "%8.4f", u[i] );
   printf( "\n" );

   // solution will be in ux
   for (j = 1; j <= 10; j++) {
     t += 0.01;
     for (i = 1; i <= n; i++)
       g[i] = r * (u[i-1] + u[i+1]) + (2 - 2 * r) * u[i];
     TriDiag( a, b, c, ux, g, n );
```

```
      printf( "%6.2f", t );
      for (i = 1; i <= n; i++)
        printf( "%8.4f", ux[i] );
      printf( "\n" );

      for (i = 1; i <= n; i++)          // get ready for next round
        u[i] = ux[i];
      u[n+1] = u[n-1];
   }

   return 0;
}
void TriDiag( double a[ ], double b[ ], double c[ ],
              double x[ ], double g[ ], int n )
{
   int i, j;
   double d;
   double *w = new double[ n+1 ];    // working space

   for (i = 1; i <= n; i++)
     w[i] = b[i];

   for (i = 2; i <= n; i++) {
     d = a[i] / w[i-1];
     w[i] = w[i] - c[i-1] * d;
     g[i] = g[i] - g[i-1] * d;
   }

   x[n] = g[n] / w[n];               // start back substitution
   for (i = 1; i <= n-1; i++) {
     j = n-i;
     x[j] = (g[j] - c[j] * x[j+1]) / w[j];
   }

   // solution is in x
   delete[ n+1 ] w;
}
```

Output:

```
    x =   0.1000   0.2000   0.3000   0.4000   0.5000
    t
    0.00   0.2000   0.4000   0.6000   0.8000   1.0000
    0.01   0.1989   0.3956   0.5834   0.7381   0.7691
    0.02   0.1936   0.3789   0.5397   0.6461   0.6921
    ...
    0.10   0.0948   0.1803   0.2482   0.2918   0.3069
```

Note that the function **TriDiag()** can be used to solve any tridiagonal system, and could be made part of a general utility module.

You could redesign the program to use classes, so that the arrays a, b and c are represented as vectors, say.

Summary

- A numerical method is an approximate computer method for solving a mathematical problem which often has no analytical solution.
- A numerical method is subject to two distinct types of error: rounding error in the computer solution, and *truncation error*, where an infinite mathematical process, like taking a limit, is approximated by a finite process.
- A function can be "passed" as an argument to another function by declaring a pointer to the function.

Exercises

18.1 Use Newton's method in a program to solve some of the following (you may have to experiment a bit with the starting value):

(a) $x^4 - x = 10$ (two real and two complex roots)

(b) $e^{-x} = \sin x$ (infinitely many roots)

(c) $x^3 - 8x^2 + 17x - 10 = 0$ (three real roots)

(d) $\log x = \cos x$

(e) $x^4 - 5x^3 - 12x^2 + 76x - 79 = 0$ (two real roots near 2; find the complex roots as well)

18.2 Use the Bisection method to find the square root of 2, taking 1 and 2 as initial values of x_L and x_R. Continue bisecting until the maximum error is less than 0.05. Use Inequality (18.2) to determine how many bisections are needed.

18.3 Use the Trapezoidal to evaluate $\int_0^4 x^2 dx$, using a step-length of $h = 1$.

18.4 A human population of 1000 at time $t = 0$ grows at a rate given by

$$dN/dt = aN,$$

where $a = 0.025$ per person per year. Use Euler's method to project the population over the next 30 years, working in steps of (a) $h = 2$ years,

(b) $h = 1$ year and (c) $h = 0.5$ years. Compare your answers with the exact mathematical solution.

18.5 The basic equation for modelling radio-active decay is

$$\mathrm{d}x/\mathrm{d}t = -rx,$$

where x is the amount of the radio-active substance at time t, and r is the decay rate.

Some radio-active substances decay into other radio-active substances, which in turn also decay. For example, Strontium 92 ($r_1 = 0.256$ per hr) decays into Yttrium 92 ($r_2 = 0.127$ per hr), which in turn decays into Zirconium. Write down a pair of differential equations for Strontium and Yttrium to describe what is happening.

Starting at $t = 0$ with 5×10^{26} atoms of Strontium 92 and none of Yttrium, use the Runge-Kutta formulae to solve the equations up to $t = 8$ hours in steps of $1/3$ hours. Also use Euler's method for the same problem, and compare your results.

18.6 The impala population $x(t)$ in the Kruger National Park in South Africa may be modelled by the equation

$$\mathrm{d}x/\mathrm{d}t = (r - bx \sin at)x,$$

where r, b, and a are constants. Write a program which

- reads values for r, b, a and the step-length $h \leq 1$ (in months);
- reads the initial value of x;
- uses Euler's method to compute the impala population;
- prints the population at *monthly* intervals over a period of two years.

18.7 The luminous efficiency (ratio of the energy in the visible spectrum to the total energy) of a black body radiator may be expressed as a percentage by the formula

$$E = 64.77T^{-4} \int_{4\times10^{-5}}^{7\times10^{-5}} x^{-5}(e^{1.432/Tx} - 1)^{-1}\mathrm{d}x,$$

where T is the absolute temperature in degrees Kelvin, x is the wavelength in cm, and the range of integration is over the visible spectrum. Taking $T = 3500°$K, use Simpson's rule to compute E, firstly with 10 intervals ($n = 5$), and then with 20 intervals ($n = 10$), and compare your results.

18.8 Van der Pol's equation is a second-order non-linear differential equation which may be expressed as two first-order equations as follows:

$$\mathrm{d}x_1/\mathrm{d}t = x_2$$
$$\mathrm{d}x_2/\mathrm{d}t = \epsilon(1 - x_1^2)x_2 - b^2 x_1.$$

The solution of this equation has a stable limit cycle, which means that if you plot the phase trajectory of the solution (the plot of x_1 against x_2) starting at any point in the positive x_1-x_2 plane, it always moves continuously into the same closed loop. Use the Runge-Kutta method to solve this system numerically, with $h = 0.1$, $x_1(0) = 0$, and $x_2(0) = 1$. If you have access to graphics facilities, draw the phase trajectory for $b = 1$ and ϵ ranging between 0.01 and 1.0.

Epilogue

Programming style

Throughout this book the emphasis has been on writing clear, coherent programs to solve interesting problems. A program which is written any old how, although it may do what is required, is going to be difficult to understand when you go through it again after a month or two. This is especially so if you get into some of the bad habits that even the most dedicated C++ enthusiasts must admit it does allow.

Serious programmers therefore pay a fair amount of attention to what is called *programming style*, in order to make their programs clearer and more readable both to themselves, and to other potential users. You may find this irritating, if you are starting to program for the first time, because you will naturally be impatient to get on with the job. But a little extra attention to your program layout will pay enormous dividends in the long run, especially when it comes to debugging.

Some hints on how to improve your programming style are given below.

- You should make liberal use of comments, both at the beginning of a function, to describe briefly what it does and any special methods that may have been used, and also throughout the coding to introduce different logical sections. Any restrictions on the size and type of data that may be used as input should be stated clearly in the comments (e.g. maximum sizes of arrays).
- The meaning of each variable should be described briefly in a comment at its declaration. You should declare variables systematically, e.g. in alphabetical order by type.
- functions should be arranged in alphabetical order.
- Blank lines should be freely used to separate sections of coding (e.g. before and after loop structures).

- Coding inside structures (loops, decisions, etc) should be indented a few columns to make them stand out.
- Blanks should be used in statements to make them more readable, e.g. on either side of binary operators, and after commas in function prototypes. However, blanks may be omitted in places in complicated expressions, where this may make the logic clearer.
- The `goto` statement should **never be used**, under *any* circumstances.
- You should try wherever possible to avoid breaking out of structures in the middle, e.g. with `break`.

Appendix A

Keywords

The following Turbo C++ keywords are reserved and may not be used as identifiers:

_asm	_ds	int	_seg
asm	else	_interrupt	short
auto	enum	interrupt	signed
break	_es	_loadds	sizeof
case	extern	long	_ss
_cdecl	_far	_near	static
cdecl	far	near	struct
char	_fastcall	new	switch
class	float	operator	template
const	for	_pascal	this
continue	friend	pascal	typedef
_cs	goto	private	union
default	_huge	protected	unsigned
delete	huge	public	virtual
do	if	register	void
double	inline	return	volatile
		_saveregs	while

Appendix B

Operators

Operator precedence and evaluation order are set out in the following table.

Level	Operators	Evaluation order
1.	() [ ] -> :: .	left to right
2.	~ (bitwise flip) ++ -- + - & * *(typecast)* sizeof new delete ! (negation)	right to left
3.	.* ->* (pointer-to-member)	left to right
4.	* / % (modulus)	left to right
5.	+ -	left to right
6.	<< >> (left and right shifts)	left to right
7.	< <= > >=	left to right
8.	== (equals) != (not equals)	left to right
9.	& (bitwise AND)	left to right
10.	^ (bitwise exclusive OR)	left to right
11.	| (bitwise inclusive OR)	left to right
12.	&& (logical AND)	left to right
13.	|| (logical OR)	left to right
14.	? ... : (conditional expression)	right to left
15.	= += -= *= /= %= <<= >>= &= ^= |=	right to left
16.	,	left to right

Note that + and - at level 2 are unary, while at level 5 they are binary. The & at level 2 is the address-of operator. The * at level 2 is the pointer dereference (indirection) operator, while at level 4 it is the multiplication operator.

Parentheses always have the highest precedence.

Appendix C

Syntax quick reference

C.1 Pre-processor directives
C.2 Fundamental type declarations
C.3 Functions
C.4 Class declarations
C.5 Pointers *et al.*
C.6 General

C.1   Pre-processor directives

```
#include <cppheader.h>
#include "myheader.h"
#define MY_CONSTANT 123                    // macro
```

C.2   Fundamental type declarations

```
char c;                             // char or int -128 to 127

char msg[ ] = "Cannot open file\n";       // no need to count chars

char name[20];          /* string: array of characters; last element
                        ... for null terminator */

const float g = 9.8;          // can't be changed

double y;                     // 1.7e-308 to 1.7e308; 16 figures

extern int x;                 // x is declared global in another file

float x;                      // 3.4e-38 to 3.4e38; 11 figures
```

387

```
float y = 23.45;                    // initialize

float list[20];                     // array from list[0] to list[19]

float x[10] = {0, 1, 2, 3, 4, 5, 6, 7, 8, 9};  // initialize

float x[2][3];                      // two-dimensional array

int i, signed int j;                // -32768 to 32767

int &r = i;                         // reference (alias) to int i

long k, long int j;                 // -2147483648 to 2147483647

long double x;                      // 3.4e-4932 to 3.4e+4932; 19 figures

static float y;                     // retains value between function calls

unsigned char c;                    // ASCII char or int 0 to 255

unsigned int j;                     // 0 to 65535

unsigned long i;                    // 0 to 4294967295
```

C.3   Functions

```
double funcName( int i, double x );     // function prototype

double funcName( int *x );       /* simulate pass by reference;
                                    ... use & operator when calling */

float funcName( int &a, double &b );    /* reference parameters,
                                    ... no need to use & when calling */

void funcName( double const &a );       // constant reference

int funcName( void );                   // no arguments

return whatEver;             /* returns value from function; function
                                ... must have type of whatEver */

void funcName( double list[ ] );        // array argument

void funcName( TClass *ptr );           // pass ptr to class, struct

void funcName( void );                  // no return type or argument

void funcName( double x );              // no return type
```

C.4 Class declarations

```
class TClass {                      // structs and unions are also classes
// declarations
private:
  char name[80];
  int id;
public:
  TClass( void ) { inline declaration }   // default constructor
  ~TClass( void );                        // destructor
  void member1( void );
  TClass &operator=( TClass &right );     // overload = and return ref
  double member2( void );
  friend void member3( void );
  friend ostream &operator<<( ostream &out, TClass &object );
                    // overload insertion operator for use with cout
};
// implementations
TClass::~TClass( void ) ...
TClass &TClass::operator+( TClass &right ) ...
double TClass::member2( void ) ...
// TClass

class TSon: public TDad {           // TSon derived from TDad
  ...
public:
  TSon(): TDad( ... ) { ... }       // calls base constructor
};

struct TPerson {                    // struct declaration
  char name[20];
  int idNo;                         // members
};
TPerson me, you;                    // declare vars of struct type
TPerson jim = { "Bond J", 007 };    // initialize
TPerson village[200];               // array of struct
  village[i].name;                  // villager i's name
TPerson us[2] = { {"Me", 1}, {"You", 2} };
                                    // initialize array of struct

union ...                           /* like struct except all members
                                    ... start at same address */
```

C.5 Pointers *et al*.

```
char *name;                         // pointer to char (string)

char *names[MAX];                   // array of MAX pointers to char
```

```
char *name[ ]                    // pass array of pointers like this
char **name                      // ditto

char *message[ ] = { "One", "Two", "Three" };      // initialize

delete dp;                       // delete simple dynamic variable
delete[ ] array;                 // delete dynamic array
delete[ SIZE ] array;            // older form of delete for array

double *x;                       // pointer to double type

double *dp = new double;         // simple dynamic variable

double *dp;
dp = new double;                 // simple dynamic variable

double *array;
   array = new double[ SIZE ];   // dynamic array of SIZE elements

double (*ptr)( int a, double b );  // pointer to function
ptr = MyFunc;                      // assign pointer

FILE *fp;                        // file pointer

float *y;                        // pointer to a float

TClass *ptr;               // pointer to class, struct, union
   ptr->name;              // arrow operator to reference member

void *ptr;                 // void pointer to address chunk of heap
   p = malloc( numberOfBytes );
```

C.6   General

```
do {
   statement1;
   statement2;
   ...
} while ( !kbhit() )             // until you hit a key

enum days {                      // defines new type
   sun, mon, tue, wed, thu, fri, sat
};

double(i);                 // typecast to double

float(i) / j;              // typecast i to float before division

for (i = 1; i <= n; i++) {   // absolutely no semi-colon here!
```

```
  statement1;
  statement2;
  ...;
}

for (j = k; j >= m; j--)
  statement;

if (i == 1)                 // equals
  statement;

if (i != 2)                 // not equals
  statement;

if (i < 2 && j > 3) {       // AND
  statement1;
  statement2;
}

if (i < 1 || x == 3)        // OR
  statement;

if (x)                      // zero = false; anything else is true
  dothis;                   // semi-colon please
else
  dothat;

if (!x)                     // true only if x is zero (if NOT x)
  statement;

if (condition1) {           // if-else-if ladder
  statement1;
  statement2;
}
else if (condition2) {
  statement3;
  statement4;
}
...
else {
  statementi;
  statementj;
}

sizeof( x );                // number of bytes occupied by x

switch (choice) {
  case 'A':
    DoThis();
    break;
```

```
      case 'B':
        DoThat();
        break;
      case 'C':
        DoTheOther();
        break;
      default:
        DoNothing();
    }

    typedef declaration Alias;            /* Alias stands for a standard
                                             ... declaration */

    while (fscanf( fp, "%f", value )) {
      ... process values;                 // fscanf() false at EOF
    }

    while (condition) {
      statement1;
      statement2;
      ...
    }
```

Appendix D

Function quick reference

This appendix provides a quick reference to all functions used in this book (plus a few more). The header file on the right of each entry contains the function prototype. You can also get the function declaration and prototype from Borland/Turbo C++ by pressing **Ctrl-F1** with the cursor under any letter of the function name.

Many of the mathematical functions have complex versions prototyped in **complex.h**, as indicated.

Some prototypes refer to size_t. This is a convenient **typedef** for unsigned, declared in **stdlib.h**, **stdio.h**, etc.

Square brackets denote optional arguments.

In addition to declaring function prototypes, the header file **math.h** defines the following useful mathematical constants:

```
/* Constants rounded for 21 decimals. */
#define M_E          2.71828182845904523536   (e)
#define M_LOG2E      1.44269504088896340736   (log₂ e)
#define M_LOG10E     0.434294481903251827651  (log₁₀ e)
#define M_LN2        0.693147180559945309417  (ln 2)
#define M_LN10       2.30258509299404568402   (ln 10)
#define M_PI         3.14159265358979323846   (π)
#define M_PI_2       1.57079632679489661923   (π/2)
#define M_PI_4       0.785398163397448309616  (π/4)
#define M_1_PI       0.318309886183790671538  (1/π)
#define M_2_PI       0.636619772367581343076  (2/π)
#define M_1_SQRTPI   0.564189583547756286948  (1/√π)
#define M_2_SQRTPI   1.12837916709551257390   (2/√π)
#define M_SQRT2      1.41421356237309504880   (√2)
#define M_SQRT_2     0.707106781186547524401  (1/√2)
```

393

abs   Absolute value

```
int abs( int x );                                          math.h
double abs( complex x );                                   complex.h
```

Returns the absolute value of x. Note that `abs( int )` returns an integer. If you want to return a non-integer real value use `fabs()`.

acos   Arc cosine

```
double acos( double x );                                   math.h
complex acos( complex x );                                 complex.h
```

Returns the arc cosine (inverse cosine) of x, in radians.

arc   Draw arc

```
void arc( int x, int y, int stangle, int endangle, int radius );
                                                           graphics.h
```

Draws a circular arc centred at (x, y). The angles are in degrees measured from 3 o'clock.

arg   Complex argument

```
double arg( complex x );                                   complex.h
```

Returns the argument in radians of complex x, i.e. the angle x makes with the real axis in the complex plane.

asin   Arc sine

```
double asin( double x );                                   math.h
complex asin( complex x );                                 complex.h
```

Returns the arc sine (inverse sine) of x in radians.

atan   Arc tangent in range $-\pi/2$ to $\pi/2$

```
double atan( double x );                                   math.h
complex atan( complex x );                                 complex.h
```

Returns the arc tangent (inverse tangent) of x in the range $-\pi/2$ to $\pi/2$.

atan2   Arc tangent in range $-\pi$ to π

```
double atan2( double y, double x );                        math.h
```

Returns the arc tangent (inverse tangent) of y/x in the range $-\pi$ to π. It produces accurate results even when x is close to zero.

atof   ASCII to floating point

```
double atof( const char *strval );                           math.h
```

Converts the string representation `strval` of a floating point value to a `double` value. Returns ±`HUGE_VAL` if operation fails.

atoi   ASCII to integer

```
int atoi( const char *strval );                              stdlib.h
```

Converts the string representation `strval` of an integer to an `int` value. Returns zero if string cannot be converted.

atol   ASCII to long

```
int atol( const char *strval );                              stdlib.h
```

Converts the string representation `strval` of an integer to an `long` value. Returns zero if string cannot be converted.

bar   Draw bar

```
void bar( int left, int top, int right, int bottom );        graphics.h
```

Draws a rectangular bar filled with the current fill pattern and colour, between (`left`, `top`) and (`bottom`, `right`).

bar3d   Draw 3-D bar

```
void bar3d( int left, int top, int right, int bottom,
            int depth, int  top );                           graphics.h
```

Draws a 3-D bar, similar to `bar()`, but with a depth of `depth` pixels. If `top` is non-zero a lid is drawn on the bar.

calloc   Allocate and clear memory

```
void *calloc( size_t nitems, size_t size );                  stdlib.h
```

Allocates a block of memory on the heap for `nitems` items, of `size` bytes each, and sets every byte in the block to zero. Returns `NULL` if unsuccessful, otherwise returns the address of the first allocated byte.

ceil   Round up

```
double ceil( double x );                                     math.h
```

Returns the smallest integer which exceeds `x`, i.e. rounds up to the nearest integer. See also `floor()`. There is no function which rounds to the nearest integer in either direction.

chdir   Change directory

```
int chdir( const char *path );
```
dir.h

Changes current DOS directory to the specified **path** string. Use double backslashes to separate drive and subdirectory names, e.g. `"c:\\turboc\\include"`. Returns zero for success, and −1 for failure.

circle   Draw circle

```
void circle( int x, int y, int radius );
```
graphics.h

Draws a circle on the graphics screen. Use `setaspectratio()` if the circle does not appear round.

cleardevice   Clear graphics screen

```
void cleardevice( void );
```
graphics.h

Clears the graphics screen and moves the current position to (0, 0).

clearviewport   Clear current viewport

```
void clearviewport( void );
```
graphics.h

Clears the current viewport to the background colour, and sets the current position to relative coordinates (0, 0).

clock   Determine processor time

```
clock_t clock( void );
```
time.h

Returns the processor time elapsed since the program started running, in "clock ticks". To convert the time to seconds, divide the value returned by `clock()` by the **time.h** macro `CLK_TCK`. May not be 100% accurate, especially if you are running under Windows, for example.

The type `clock_t` is a **typedef** for an integer type.

closegraph   Shut down graphics

```
void closegraph( void );
```
graphics.h

Closes BGI graphics, and restores screen to mode that was in effect prior to calling `initgraph()`. Should always be used before returning to text mode. However, see also `restorecrtmode()`.

clreol   Clear to end of line

```
void clreol( void )
```
conio.h

Clears text display from cursor position to end of current line.

clrscr · Clear text screen

```
void clrscr( void );
```
conio.h

Clears the text screen to the background colour.

complex · Declare complex number

```
complex complex( double real, double imag );
```
complex.h

Invokes the C++ predefined `complex` class constructor to declare and initialize a complex number with real and imaginary parts as specified (which default to zero if not given). The class provides overloaded arithmetic operators, such as `+`, `-`, `*` and `/`, as well as assignment operators and the `==` and `!=` relational operators. See Chapter 4 for an example.

conj · Complex conjugate of complex number

```
complex conj( complex x );
```
complex.h

Returns the complex conjugate of `x`.

cos · Cosine

```
double cos( double x );
complex cos( complex x );
```
math.h
complex.h

Returns the cosine of `x`, where `x` is in radians.

cosh · Hyperbolic cosine

```
double cosh( double x );
complex cosh( complex x );
```
math.h
complex.h

Returns the hyperbolic cosine of `x`.

cprintf · Write formatted output to screen

```
int cprintf( const char *format [, arguments ... ] );
```
conio.h

Displays formatted output on the screen by means of direct-video routines. Similar to `printf()`, except that it does not translate the newline character `\n` into the `\n\r` newline/carriage-return pair as the `printf()` family does. Use `\n\r` to move the cursor to the beginning of a new line:

```
cprintf( "Hello, world\n\r" );
```

cputs   Write string to screen

```
int cputs( const char *str );
```
                                                        conio.h

Writes the string `str` directly to the screen. Does not start a new line. Returns last character displayed.

ctime   Convert date and time to string

```
char *ctime( const time_t *time );
```
                                                        time.h

Returns a string representation of the date and time stored in a variable addressed by the pointer `time`, and returned by a prior call to `time()`, for example. The return string has a newline character and a null terminator. Example:

```
time_t myTime;
time( &myTime );
puts( ctime( &myTime ) );
```

delay   Pause

```
void delay( unsigned millsecs );
```
                                                        dos.h

Suspends program operation for the specified number of milliseconds. Not always 100% accurate.

delline   Delete line

```
void delline( void );
```
                                                        conio.h

Deletes line containing cursor, moving following lines up.

detectgraph   Detect graphics capabilities

```
void detectgraph( int *graphdriver, int *graphmode );
```
                                                        graphics.h

Recommends values for `graphdriver` and `graphmode` that are best for the system's graphics card.

Request autodetection by setting `graphdriver` to zero, or to a specific value to select a particular driver.

Does not initialize graphics; this is done with a subsequent call to `initgraph()`.

div   Quotient and remainder of integer division

```
div_t div( int numer, int denom );
```
                                                        stdlib.h

Performs the integer division of `numer` by `denom` and returns the quotient and remainder as the `quot` and `rem` members respectively of a `div_t` structure. E.g.

```
div_t result;
result = div( 17, 5 );
cout << "Quotient: " << result.quot << "  Remainder: "
     << result.rem << endl;
```

drawpoly   Draw outline of polygon

```
void drawpoly( int numpoints, int *polypoints );          graphics.h
```

Draws a polygon of **numpoints** points. For a closed shape, the last point must be the same as the first.

polypoints is a pointer to a sequence of integers (e.g. an array) such that each pair of integers gives the *x*- and *y*-coordinates of a corner of the polygon. You can use the **graphics.h** structure **pointtype**, with **int** members **x** and **y**, to represent the corners of the polygon. The following code draws a triangle:

```
struct pointtype poly[4];
poly[0].x = 200;
poly[0].y = 200;
poly[1].x = 150;
poly[1].y = 150;
poly[2].x = 100;
poly[2].y = 200;
poly[3] = poly[0];    // close up
drawpoly( 4, (int *)poly );
```

drawpoly() expects a pointer to **int** as its second parameter. The **pointtype** variable **poly** must therefore be typecast.

ellipse   Draw an ellipse or arc

```
void ellipse( int x, int y, int stangle, int endangle,
              int xradius, int yradius);              graphics.h
```

Draws an elliptical arc with centre at (x, y) and horizontal and vertical axes **xradius** and **yradius** respectively. Angles are in degrees with $0°$ at 3 o'clock.

exit   Exit program

```
void exit( int status );                                  stdlib.h
```

Terminates program immediately, closing all open files and flushing any modified output buffers to disk. **status** is a parameter which may be passed back to a DOS batch file, for example.

exp   Exponential

```
double exp( double x );                                                    math.h
complex exp( complex x );                                                complex.h
```

Returns the exponential of x, i.e. e^x.

fabs   Floating point absolute value

```
double fabs( double x );                                                   math.h
```

Returns the floating point absolute value of x.

fclose   Close stream

```
int fclose( FILE *fp );                                                    stdio.h
```

Closes an open file stream, as returned by fopen(). Returns zero for success, EOF for failure.

fcloseall   Close all open streams

```
int fcloseall( void );                                                     stdio.h
```

Closes all open FILE * streams, except standard I/O files.

feof   End of file stream

```
int feof( FILE *fp );                                                      stdio.h
```

Returns non-zero (true) if an end-of-file marker was detected on the last input operation on the specified stream, or zero otherwise.

fflush   Flush stream

```
int fflush( FILE *fp );                                                    stdio.h
```

Writes any modified file buffers to disk for the specified stream. Does not close the file. Note the double f in the name.

fgetc   Get character from stream

```
int fgetc( FILE *fp );                                                     stdio.h
```

Reads one character from the specified stream. Returns character value if successful, EOF if unsuccessful or if the file's pointer is positioned beyond the end of the file.

fgetchar   Get character from stdin

```
int fgetchar( void );                                                      stdio.h
```

Reads one character from the standard input file stdin, i.e. equivalent to fgetc(stdin).

fgetpos   Get file pointer

```
int fgetpos( FILE *fp, fpos_t *pos );                    stdio.h
```

Copies the specified stream's current file pointer to the **fpos_t** variable addressed by **pos**. This value represents the offset in bytes from the beginning of the file to the position where the next I/O operation will take place. Returns zero for success and -1 for failure.

fgets   Get string from stream

```
char *fgets( char *str, int n, FILE *fp );               stdio.h
```

Reads characters from stream **fp** up to and including the next newline character, or at most $n-1$ characters, into string **str**. Appends a newline if read plus a null terminator. Returns the string for success, and null for failure. Eg.

```
FILE *fp;
char buffer[256];
    ...
while (fgets( buffer, 255, fp ) != NULL)   /* reads until EOF */
    ...
```

If you replace **fp** with **stdin** you can use **fgets()** to read a specified number of characters (including blanks) from the keyboard.

fillellipse   Draw filled ellipse

```
void fillellipse( int x, int y, int xradius, int yradius );   graphics.h
```

Draws a filled ellipse using the current filling colour and pattern.

fillpoly   Draw filled polygon

```
void fillpoly( int numpoints, int *polypoints );         graphics.h
```

Draws a filled polygon using the current filling colour and pattern. See **drawpoly()** for a description of the parameters and an example.

floodfill   Fill graphics area

```
void floodfill( int x, int y, int border );              graphics.h
```

Fills an area around the seed point (**x, y**). The area bounded by the colour **border** is flooded with the current fill pattern and fill colour. If the seed point is inside an enclosed area, the inside will be filled. If the seed is outside the area, the exterior will be filled.

floor   Round down

```
double floor( double x );
```
                                                                math.h

Returns the largest integer which does not exceed x, i.e. rounds down to the nearest integer. See also `ceil()`. There is no function which rounds to the nearest integer in either direction.

flushall   Flush all streams

```
int flushall( void );
```
                                                                stdio.h

Flushes all open streams, writing to disk any modified data held in memory. Leaves the streams open. Note that unlike `fflush()`, there is only one f in the name (just to keep you on your toes).

fmod   Floating point modulus

```
double fmod( double x, double y );
```
                                                                math.h

Returns x modulo y, the remainder after x is divided by y.

fopen   Open file stream

```
FILE *fopen( const char *filename, const char *mode);
```
                                                                stdio.h

Opens an existing file or creates a new one. If successful, returns a FILE pointer. If unsuccessful returns NULL. You should always test for a successful `fopen()` before attempting any I/O.

mode is the file access mode. Possible modes are listed in Table D.1. In addition a t or b may be appended to the string to specify a text or binary file (the default is governed by a global variable _fmode set in **stdio.h**). The t or b may also be inserted between the initial letter and the +. E.g. "rt+" is the same as "r+t". Example:

```
FILE *fp;

fp = fopen( "data", "r+" );
if (!fp) {
  puts( "Can't open file" );
  exit(1);
}

while (fscanf(fp, " %d", &i) != EOF)
  sum += i;
...
fclose( fp );
```

Mode string	Description
"r"	Read only.
"w"	Write only. Creates a new file or overwrites an existing one.
"a"	Append. Writes (only) at the end of an existing file, or creates a new file.
"r+"	Update. Reads/writes on an existing file.
"w+"	Update. Creates a new file for read/write or overwrites an existing one.
"a+"	Update. Appends (read or write) at the end of the file, or creates a new file.

Table D.1: File access modes

fprintf   Write formatted output to a stream

`int fprintf( FILE *fp, const char *format[, arguments ... ] );`   **stdio.h**

Identical to `printf()`, except that output is to a file stream opened for writing or appending in text mode.

fputc   Write character to a stream

`int fputc( int c, FILE *fp );`   **stdio.h**

Writes a single character to the specified stream. Returns the value of c for success, and EOF for failure.

fputchar   Write a character to stdout

`int fputchar( int c );`   **stdio.h**

Writes a single character to stdout, i.e. identical to fputc(c, stdout).

fputs   Write a string to a stream

`int fputs( const char *str, FILE *fp );`   **stdio.h**

Writes a null-terminated string str to the specified stream. Returns a non-negative value for success, and EOF for failure.

fread   Read from binary file stream

`size_t fread( void *ptr, size_t size, size_t n, FILE *fp );`   **stdio.h**

Reads a chunk of bytes from a file stream, starting at the position of the current file pointer. After reading data fread() leaves the current file pointer positioned after the last byte read (the pointer may be repositioned with `fseek()`). Returns the number of items read, or zero if unsuccessful or if the file pointer is at the end of the file. This means that reading and checking for EOF can take place in the same expression.

`ptr` is a pointer to the destination of the read. You must pass the address of the variable which is to receive the data. `size` is the number of bytes per item to be read. `n` is the number of such items to be read. `fp` is a pointer to the file stream to be read.

The following code writes an array of integers to a binary file, and reads them back one at a time:

```
int i, array[10] = {1, 2, 3, 4, 5, 6, 7, 8, 9, 10};
FILE *fp;

fp = fopen( "data", "w+b" );
if (!fp) {
  puts( "Can't open file" );
  exit(1);
}

fwrite( &array, sizeof( array ), 1, fp );
fseek( fp, 0, SEEK_SET );

while (fread( &i, sizeof( i ), 1, fp )) {
  printf( "%d ", i );
}
```

free   Free allocated memory

```
void free( void *ptr );
```
                                                                    alloc.h

Frees a block of memory addressed by `ptr` previously allocated by `malloc()`, etc.

freopen   Associate new file with stream

```
FILE *freopen( const char *filename, const char *mode,
               FILE *fp );
```
                                                                    stdio.h

Closes a currently open file and associates that stream (`fp`) with a new named file (`filename`). Used to redirect `stdin`, `stdout` and `stderr` streams. E.g.

```
FILE *ferr;
ferr = freopen( "errlog", "w", stderr );
...
```

Any error messages to `stderr` are redirected to the disk file **errlog**.

fscanf   Read formatted input from stream

```
int fscanf( FILE *fp, const char *format[, address, ... ] );        stdio.h
```

Reads text from a stream, according to the `format` string. See `scanf()` for examples. Returns `EOF` if it attempts to read at end-of-file, and 0 if it fails altogether. Example:

```
int i, sum = 0;
FILE *fp;

fp = fopen( "data", "r+" );
if (!fp) {
  puts( "Can't open file" );
  exit(1);
}

while (fscanf( fp, " %d", &i ) != EOF)
  sum += i;
```

fseek   Reposition file pointer

```
int fseek( FILE *fp, long offset, int whence );                    stdio.h
```

Repositions the file stream's current pointer. Returns zero for success and non-zero for failure.

`offset` is the number of bytes to move the current file pointer in the direction indicated by `whence`. It can be negative.

`whence` indicates the position from which the current file pointer must move `offset` bytes: `SEEK_SET` (from the beginning of the file), `SEEK_CUR` (from its current position), and `SEEK_END` (from the end of the file).

See `fread()` for an example.

fsetpos   Position file pointer

```
int fsetpos( FILE *fp, const fpos_t *pos );                        stdio.h
```

Restores a stream's current file pointer to the position returned by a preceding call to `fgetpos()`. Returns zero for success and non-zero for failure.

ftell   Get current file pointer

```
long int ftell( FILE *fp );                                        stdio.h
```

Returns a file stream's current (internal) file pointer, equal to the offset in bytes from the beginning of a binary file. This value can be passed to `fseek()` to position the file pointer relative to the current position.

fwrite   Write to binary file stream

stdio.h

```
size_t fwrite( const void *ptr, size_t size, size_t n, FILE *fp );
```

Writes to a file stream opened in binary mode. Returns the number of items written. `fwrite()` is the reverse of `fread()`. See `fread()` for a description of the parameters and an example.

getaspectratio   Graphics aspect ratio

```
void getaspectratio( int xasp, int yasp );                          graphics.h
```

The *aspect ratio* of a single graphics pixel is its width divided by its height. The monitor's aspect ratio may be found with `getaspectratio()`. The following example shows how to use it to draw a square that look square:

```
int xasp, yasp, xlen, ylen;
double ratio;
getaspectratio( &xasp, &yasp );
ratio = double( xasp ) / yasp;
xlen = 100 / ratio;
ylen = 100;
line( 0, 0, xlen, 0 );
line( xlen, 0, xlen, ylen );
line( xlen, ylen, 0, ylen );
line( 0, ylen, 0, 0 );
```

See also `setaspectratio()`, for changing the aspect ratio.

getbkcolor   Graphics background colour

```
int getbkcolor( void );                                             graphics.h
```

Returns the colour value of the graphics background, which may be modified with
`setbkcolor()`.

getc   Get character from stream

```
int getc( FILE *fp );                                                  stdio.h
```

Returns next character from the specified input stream. To read from **stdin**, **Enter** must be pressed after a character is typed. Returns EOF at end-of-file.

getch   Get character without echo

```
int getch( void );                                                     conio.h
```

Returns a character from the keyboard without echoing it.

getche   Get character and echo

```
int getche( void );
```
conio.h

Same as `getch()`, except that the returned character is displayed.

getcolor   Get drawing colour

```
int getcolor( void );
```
graphics.h

Returns the current graphics drawing colour, which may be modified
with `setcolor()`.

getdate   Get system date

```
void getdate( struct date *pDate );
```
dos.h

Sets the members `int da_year`, `char da_day` and `char da_mon` of a
`date` structure declared in **dos.h** to the current system date.

getdrivername   Get graphics driver name

```
char *getdrivername( void );
```
graphics.h

Returns a pointer to a string holding the name of the current graphics
driver.

getgraphmode   Current graphics mode

```
int getgraphmode( void );
```
graphics.h

Returns the current graphics mode as set by `initgraph()`.

getimage   Copy bit image to memory

```
void getimage( int left, int top, int right, int bottom, void *bitmap);
```
graphics.h

Copies the rectangular portion of the graphics screen defined by the four
`int` parameters into a buffer addressed by `bitmap`.

getmaxcolor   Maximum colour value

```
int getmaxcolor( void );
```
graphics.h

Returns the maximum graphics colour value.

getmaxx, getmaxy   Maximum graphics coordinates

```
int getmaxx( void );
int getmaxy( void );
```
graphics.h

Return the maximum horizontal and vertical graphics coordinates, starting at 0. E.g. if `getmaxx()` returns 639 there are 640 pixels available horizontally.

getpass   Read string without echo

```
char *getpass( const char *prompt );
```
conio.h

Displays the string `prompt` and returns a "password" string, which is not echoed to the screen.

getpixel   Pixel colour

```
unsigned getpixel( int x, int y );
```
graphics.h

Returns the colour value of the pixel at the specified point.

gets   Get string from stdin

```
char *gets( char *target );
```
stdio.h

Reads characters including whitespace from standard input into the `target` string, until reading a newline, which is replaced by a null terminator. Returns `target`, or null on end-of-file or any errors. You cannot specify how many characters to read. `target` should be large enough (e.g. char `target[128]`) to hold the expected input; otherwise expect data, or code, or worse to be overwritten.

gettext   Copy text to memory

```
int gettext( int left, int top, int right, int bottom, void *target );
```
conio.h

Copies text from the text screen to a buffer. The area bounded by the specified screen coordinates is copied, where $(1, 1)$ is the top left corner of the screen. Returns non-zero if operation succeeds, zero if it fails.

`target` addresses the buffer where the text is to be saved. Since each character requires two bytes of storage, the minimum required buffer size is $2hw$, where h is the height and w is the width in characters of the display rectangle to be copied.

gettime   Get system time

```
void gettime( struct time *mytime );
```
                                                                         dos.h

Fills in a predefined **dos.h** structure `time` with the current system time.
`time` is declared as

```
struct  time    {
     unsigned char   ti_min;     /* Minutes */
     unsigned char   ti_hour;    /* Hours */
     unsigned char   ti_hund;    /* Hundredths of seconds */
     unsigned char   ti_sec;     /* Seconds */
};
```

(yes, minutes come before hours).

The parameter `mytime` is a pointer to a `time` structure. So, for example,
after a call to `gettime()`, `mytime->ti_hour` will hold the hour of the
day.

getviewsettings   Current viewport

```
void getviewsettings( struct viewporttype viewport );
```
                                                                    graphics.h

Sets the members `left`, `top`, `right`, `bottom` and `clip` of a **graphics.h**
`viewporttype` structure with the current viewport settings.

getx, gety   Return graphics CP

```
int getx( void );
int gety( void );
```
                                                                    graphics.h

Return the horizontal and vertical coordinates of the current graphics
position (CP).

gotoxy   Position cursor

```
void gotoxy( int col, int row );
```
                                                                       (conio.h)

Moves the cursor to the specified column and row. E.g. `gotoxy(80, 25)`
moves the cursor to the bottom right corner of the screen.

grapherrormsg   Graphics error message

```
char *grapherrormsg( int errorcode );
```
                                                                    graphics.h

Returns a pointer to a string describing the specified error, as returned
by `graphresult()`.

graphresult   Graphics error code

```
int graphresult( void );
```
graphics.h

Returns the graphics error code after using a graphics function, such as
initgraph(). The return value should be saved for future reference
because calling graphresult() resets the error code to grOk (no error).
Result can be passed to grapherrormsg() for a text description of the
error. See initgraph() for example.

highvideo   Select high-intensity text

```
void highvideo( void );
```
conio.h

Selects high-intensity text characters for **conio.h** direct-video output
routines. See also lowvideo() and normvideo().

hypot   Hypotenuse of right-angle triangle

```
double hypot( double x, double y );
```
math.h

Returns the length of the hypotenuse of a right-angle triangle with sides
x and y.

imag   Imaginary part of complex number

```
double imag( complex x );
```
complex.h

Returns the imaginary part of a complex class object x.

imagesize   Bitmap size

```
unsigned imagesize( int left, int top, int right, int bottom );
```
graphics.h

Returns number of bytes needed to save a copy of the graphics image
outlined by the specified arguments. If more than 64K of storage is
required (the default maximum), −1 is returned.

initgraph   Initialize graphics

```
void initgraph( int *graphdriver, int *graphmode, char *path );
```
graphics.h

Initializes Borland Graphics Interface (BGI), and loads an appropriate
BGI driver, setting the current position to (0, 0). You should always test
whether initgraph() has succeeded. Example:

```
int grDriver = DETECT, grMode, grErr;
initgraph( &grDriver, &grMode, "c:\\borlandc\\bgi" );
grErr = graphresult();
  if (grErr != grOk) {
```

```
        printf( "BGI error: %s\n", grapherrormsg( grErr ) );
        exit( grErr );
    }
    ...
```

Don't forget the double backslash in the pathname.

insline   Insert blank line

```
void insline( void );                                    conio.h
```

Inserts a blank line in the text screen at the current cursor row. Any lines
below are shifted down.

is. . .   Character classification macros

```
int isalnum( int c );    // alphanumeric              ctype.h
int isalpha( int c );    // alphabetic
int isascii( int c );    // ASCII
int iscntrl( int c );    // ASCII contro code
int isdigit( int c );    // digit
int isgraph( int c );    // printable but non-space
int islower( int c );    // lowercase letter
int isprint( int c );    // printable or space
int ispunct( int c );    // punctuation symbol
int isspace( int c );    // whitespace
int isupper( int c );    // uppercase letter
int isxdigit( int c );   // hexadecimal digit
```

Return non-zero (true) if character c is a member of the specified set of
characters.

itoa   Convert integer to string

```
char *itoa( int value, char *str, int radix );           stdlib.h
```

Converts value to a null-terminated string str. A pointer to the string is
returned. radix is the base number, from 2 to 36, used for the
conversion. E.g. itoa(13, str, 2) returns "1101" in str .

kbhit   Check for keystroke

```
int kbhit( void );                                       conio.h
```

Returns true (non-zero) if a character is in the keyboard buffer waiting to
be read, i.e. if a key has been hit but not read yet. Returns false (zero) if
no character is waiting to be read. Useful at the end of a do-while loop
to end some operation with any keystroke.

labs   Long absolute value

```
long int labs( long int x );
```
math.h

Returns the absolute value of a long integer.

ldiv   Divide two longs

```
ldiv_t ldiv( long int numer, long int denom );
```
stdlib.h

The `long` version of `div()`.

line   Draw line

```
void line( int x1, int y1, int x2, int y2 );
```
graphics.h

Draws a line between (x1, y1) and x2, y2). Does not update the current position.

linerel   Draw relative line from CP

```
void linerel( int dx, int dy );
```
graphics.h

Draws a line from the current position (x, y) to the position (x + dx, y + dy). Updates the CP.

lineto   Draw line from CP

```
void lineto( int x, int y );
```
graphics.h

Draws a line from the current position (CP) to the specified point. Updates the CP.

log   Natural logarithm

```
double log( double x );
complex log( complex x );
```
math.h
complex.h

Returns the natural logarithm of x.

log10   Base 10 logarithm

```
double log10( double x );
complex log10( complex x );
```
math.h
complex.h

Returns the base 10 logarithm of x.

lowvideo   Select low-intensity text

```
void lowvideo( void );
```
conio.h

Selects low-intensity text characters. See also `highvideo()` and `normvideo()`.

_lrotl, _lrotr   Rotate left, right

```
unsigned long _lrotl( unsigned long val, int count );          stdlib.h
unsigned long _lrotr( unsigned long val, int count );
```

_lrotl (_lrotr) returns val rotated left (right) by count bits.

ltoa   Convert long to string

```
char *ltoa( long value, char *str, int radix );               stdlib.h
```

long version of itoa().

malloc   Allocate dynamic memory

```
void *malloc( size_t size );                          stdlib.h or alloc.h
```

Allocates a block of memory of size bytes from the heap. Returns a pointer to the allocated memory, or NULL if the requested number of bytes is not available. When you have finished with the memory, you should release it with free().

memcpy   Copy non-overlapping memory

```
void *memcpy( void *target, const void *source, size_t n );     mem.h
```

Copies an array of bytes from source to target. If any bytes overlap the results are not defined.

memset   Set memory

```
void *memset( void *target, int c, size_t n );                  mem.h
```

Sets n bytes of memory to the character c, starting at address target.

moverel   Move CP relatively

```
void moverel( int dx, int dy );                             graphics.h
```

Moves the current pointer (CP) from the current position (x, y) to $(x + dx, y + dy)$.

movetext   Move text rectangle

```
int movetext( int left, int top, int right, int bottom,
              int toleft, int totop );                        conio.h
```

Moves text within the specified rectangle to the location with top left corner given by (toleft, totop). Source and target rectangles may overlap. Returns non-zero for success, otherwise zero (e.g. if a coordinate falls outside the screen).

moveto   Move CP

```
void moveto( int x, int y );
```
graphics.h

Moves the graphics current pointer (CP) to the specified position.

norm   Square of absolute value

```
double norm( complex x );
```
complex.h

Returns the square of the absolute value of a complex number.

normvideo   Select normal intensity text

```
void normvideo( void );
```
conio.h

Selects normal intensity text characters. See also `highvideo()` and `lowvideo()`.

nosound   Turn off sound

```
void nosound( void );
```
dos.h

Switches off a tone started by `sound()`.

outtext   Display string on graphics screen

```
void outtext( char *string );
```
graphics.h

Similar to `outtextxy()`, except that text output is in relation to the current position (CP). Updates the CP.

outtextxy   Display string on graphics screen

```
void outtextxy( int x, int y, char *string );
```
graphics.h

Displays text `string` on graphics screen in the current font, size, etc. The top left corner of a box containing the text is at the specified position by default. See also `outtext()` and `settextjustify()` .

perror   Print system error message

```
void perror( const char *str );
```
stdio.h

Sends the system error message for the last library function that produced an error to `stderr`.

pieslice   Draw pie-slice

```
void pieslice( int x, int y, int stangle, int endangle, int radius );
```
graphics.h

Draws a pie-slice centred at (x, y) in the current fill pattern and colour. `stangle` and `endangle` specify the angles of the pie arms, in degrees measured from 3 o'clock.

polar   Convert magnitude and angle to complex

```
complex polar( double mag, double angle );
```
complex.h

Constructs a `complex` class object from a magnitude and angle (in radians) in the Argand plane. E.g. `polar(1, M_PI/2)` returns the unit imaginary number i.

poly   Evaluate polynomial

```
double poly( double x, int degree, double coeffs[ ] );
```
math.h

Evaluates a polynomial of specified degree in `x`, with coefficients stored in the array `coeffs`. The coefficients are stored in ascending powers of `x`, with the constant term in `coeff[0]`. E.g. the declaration

```
double coeff[3] = {1, 2, 3};
```

stores the coefficients of the polynomial $3x^2 + 2x + 1$.

pow   Raise to a power

```
double pow( double x, double y );
complex pow( complex x, complex y );
complex pow( complex x, double y );
complex pow( double x, complex y );
```
math.h
complex.h

Returns x^y.

pow10   Raise 10 to a power

```
double pow10( double y );
```
math.h

Returns 10^y.

printf   Write formatted output to stdout

```
int printf( const char *format [, arguments ... ] );
```
stdio.h

Values of the arguments are written to `stdout` according to the `format` string supplied as the first argument. Returns the number of characters written to `stdout`, in case you ever need to know!

Examples of the most common format codes follow, with the output in a comment (**b** stands for a blank).

```
printf( "%c", 65 );             /* character:              A              */
printf( "%8d", 32767 );         /* signed decimal (int):   bbb32767       */
printf( "%05d", -12 );          /* signed decimal (int):   -00012         */
printf( "%ld", -345678 );       /* signed decimal (long):  -345678        */
printf( "%10.4e", 12.3 );       /* double scientific:      1.2300e+01     */
printf( "%10.4E", .123 );       /* double scientific:      1.2300E-01     */
printf( "%5.1f", 1.23 );        /* double fixed point:     bb1.2          */
printf( "%g", 1.23 );           /* general                 1.23           */
printf( "%g", 123e10 );         /* general                 1.23e+12       */
printf( "%lu", 3234567890 );    /* unsigned long:          3234567890     */
printf( "%Le", 1.23e2001L );    /* long double scientific: 1.230000e+2001 */
printf( "\n" );                 /* newline                                */
printf( "%o", 13 );             /* unsigned octal:         15             */
printf( "%#o", 13 );            /* unsigned octal:         015            */
printf( "%p", 27 );             /* pointer (address):      001B           */
printf( "%s?", "Henry" );       /* string                  Henry?         */
printf( "%7s?", "Henry" );      /* string left-justified:  bbHenry?       */
printf( "%-7s?", "Henry" );     /* string right justified  Henrybb?       */
printf( "%.3s?", "Henry" );     /* string truncated        Hen?           */
printf( "%2u", 65535 );         /* unsigned int: b1        65535          */
printf( "%x", 30 );             /* unsigned hexadecimal:   1e             */
printf( "%X", 30 );             /* unsigned hexadecimal:   1E             */
printf( "%#x", 30 );            /* unsigned hexadecimal:   0x1e           */
printf( "%*.2f\n", ... );       /* asterisk means next int arg
                                   ... will be width                      */
```

The last character in the format string (e.g. **d**, **f**) is called the *conversion character*. It selects the data type when converting a value from binary to text for output. The *modifiers* (e.g. **1** and **L**) select between size-related characteristics (in this case between **long** and **long double** respectively).

e and **f** convert both **float** and **double** type.

If the field width (e.g. the 8 in **%8d**) is not specified, the minimum width required to output the value is used. This is useful if you don't know the magnitude of the output.

The escape codes listed in Table 2.5 may be used in the format string.

putc   Output character to stream

```
int putc( int c, FILE *fp );                                    stdio.h
```

Sends the character **c** to the specified stream. Returns **c** if successful, otherwise **EOF**.

putch   Display character

```
int putch( int c );
```
conio.h

Displays character `c` on the screen using direct-video routines. Returns `c` if successful, otherwise `EOF`.

putchar   Output character to `stdout`

```
int putchar( int c );
```
stdio.h

Outputs character `c` to standard output, i.e. equivalent to `putc(c, stdout)`. Returns `c` if successful, otherwise `EOF`.

putimage   Display bitmap

```
void putimage( int left, int top, void *bitmap, int op );
```
graphics.h

Copies a saved bitmap image from memory addressed by `bitmap` to the graphics screen. The top left corner of a rectangle containing the image will be at (`left`, `top`).

`op` can take the values `COPY_PUT`, `XOR_PUT`, `OR_PUT`, `AND_PUT`, or `NOT_PUT`, and determines how image bits combine with graphics already on the screen.

putpixel   Plot pixel

```
void putpixel( int x, int y, int colour );
```
graphics.h

Displays a single graphics pixel at the specified point in the given colour.

puts   Output string to `stdout`

```
int puts( const char *str );
```
stdio.h

Writes the string `str` plus a newline to standard output. `str` must be null-terminated. Returns non-negative value if operation succeeds, `EOF` if it fails.

puttext   Copy text to screen

```
int puttext( int left, int top, int right, int bottom, void *source );
```
conio.h

Copies text saved at address `source` by `gettext()` to the area of the screen specified by the parameters. Returns non-zero if operation succeeds, zero if it fails.

rand   Random integer

```
int rand( void );
```
                                                                              stdlib.h

Returns a random integer in the range zero to RAND_MAX (defined in stdlib.h). Use randomize() or srand() to seed it.

random   Random integer in range

```
int random( int num );
```
                                                                              stdlib.h

Returns a random integer in the range 0 to num − 1. Use randomize() or srand() to seed it.

randomize   Seed random number generator

```
void randomize( void );
```
                                                                              stdlib.h

Seeds the random number generator, causing it to begin a different random sequence. It calls time() to do this, so you should also include time.h. Use srand() to specify the seed.

real   Real part of complex number

```
double real( complex x );
```
                                                                              complex.h

Returns the real part of a complex class object.

realloc memory   Reallocate memory

```
void *realloc( void *block, size_t size );
```
                                                                              stdlib.h

Expands or shrinks an existing memory block to a new size, or creates a new block (if block is NULL). Copies existing block to a new location if necessary. Returns address of modified block.

If you use realloc() in conjunction with new, a typecast will be needed, e.g.

```
new block = (int *)realloc( block, size );
```

rectangle   Draw rectangle

```
void rectange( int left, int top, int right, int bottom );   graphics.h
```

Draws a rectangle using the current line style, thickness and colour between (top, left) and (right, bottom). The rectangle is not filled.

remove   Remove file

```
int remove( const char *filename );
```
                                       stdio.h

Deletes the named file (if it exists). Returns zero for success and −1 for failure.

rename   Rename file

```
int rename( const char *oldname, const char *newname );
```
                             stdio.h

Changes a filename. Can also move a file from one directory to another (on the same drive only).

restorecrtmode   Restore pre-graphics mode

```
void restorecrtmode( void );
```
                                        graphics.h

Restores screen mode in effect prior to calling initgraph(), *without* closing down graphics. Return to graphics again with setgraphmode(). Useful for toggling between graphics and text screen.

rewind   Reset file pointer

```
void rewind( FILE *fp );
```
                                           stdio.h

Resets a stream's current file pointer to the beginning of the file. See also fseek().

rmdir   Remove directory

```
int rmdir( const char *path );
```
                                         dir.h

Deletes the named directory, which must have no files, and cannot be the current directory, or a disk's root directory.

_rotl, _rotr   Rotate left, right

```
unsigned _rotl( unsigned value, int count );
unsigned _rotr( unsigned value, int count );
```
                          stdlib.h

Rotate bits in value left (_rotl()) or right (_rotr()). Return rotated value.

scanf   Get formatted input from stdin

```
int scanf( const char *format[, addresses, ...] );
```
                       stdio.h

Text input is read from stdin according to the format string. It works more-or-less like printf() in reverse (with the emphasis on less).

The C++ stream object `cout` is *much easier and safer* to use!

`scanf()` is very unforgiving of errors, the most common of which is to forget the address-of operator & when passing arguments (except in the case of arrays, and especially strings!). Between calls to `scanf()` you may need to call `fflush( stdin )` to reset the standard input file `stdin` after any input errors, and to flush any prompts, e.g. from `puts()` or `printf()`.

Whitespace characters (blanks, newlines or horizontal tabs) in the format control string cause `scanf()` to read and discard those characters in the input, up to the first non-whitespace character. So data can be separated by any number of blanks, for example, as long as the corresponding format codes are.

Non-whitespace characters in the control string causes `scanf()` to read and discard *matching* characters in the input.

Examples:

```
float a, b;
int i, j;
double x;
scanf( "%f %f", &a, &b );   /* input: 12    345 */
scanf( "%d,%d", &i, &j );   /* input: 12,345    */
scanf( "%2d%3d", &i, &j ); /* input: 12345    */
scanf( "%lf", &x );         /* input: 1.2345    */
```

Format codes are similar, but not identical, to those for `printf()`. For example, `f` reads only `float` values, not `double`. Use the `l` modifier to select both `long int` and `double` (as above). Use `L` to select `long double`.

`scanf()` returns the number of input fields successfully scanned, or `EOF` if attempting to read past the end-of-file. You can therefore read and test for `EOF` in the same statement. The following code reads and adds up integers entered at the keyboard until **Ctrl-Z/Enter** is pressed:

```
#include <stdio.h>
int i, sum = 0;

while (scanf(" %d", &i) != EOF)
    sum += i;
```

The leading blank in the format code is a precaution in case there is still some whitespace left in the keyboard buffer from a previous operation.

sector   Draw and fill elliptical wedge

```
void sector( int x, int y, int stangle, int endangle,
             int xradius, int yradius );              graphics.h
```

Similar to `ellipse()`, but fills the elliptical wedge with the current fill
pattern and colour. See `ellipse()` for explanation of parameters.

setaspectratio   Change graphics aspect ratio

```
void setaspectratio( int xasp, int yasp );            graphics.h
```

Changes the graphical aspect ratio to `double(xasp)/double(yasp)`.
The actual values of these parameters is unimportant, since it is their ratio
that matters. Helps to make circles round, etc. See `getaspectratio()`
for an explanation of the aspect ratio, and an example.

setbkcolor   Change graphics background colour

```
void setbkcolor( int color );                         graphics.h
```

Changes the graphic display's background colour. Possible colours are
shown in Table D.2.

setcolor   Change graphics drawing colour

```
void setcolor( int colour );                          graphics.h
```

Sets the current drawing colour, which can range from 0 to `getmax-`
`color()`. Drawing colours for the default EGA/VGA palette are shown
in Table D.2.

Value	Name	Value	Name
0	BLACK	8	DARKGRAY
1	BLUE	9	LIGHTBLUE
2	GREEN	10	LIGHTGREEN
3	CYAN	11	LIGHTCYAN
4	RED	12	LIGHTRED
5	MAGENTA	13	LIGHTMAGENTA
6	BROWN	14	YELLOW
7	LIGHTGRAY	15	WHITE

Table D.2: EGA/VGA drawing colours

_setcursortype   Change cursor shape

```
void _setcursortype( int cursor );
```
conio.h

Sets the cursor shape. `cursor` can have the value `_NOCURSOR` (turn it off), `_SOLIDCURSOR` (change it to block), or `_NORMALCURSOR` (normal underline).

setdate   Change system date

```
void setdate( struct date *pDate );
```
dos.h

Sets the system date according to the values (set by you) of members `int da_year`, `char da_day` and `char da_mon` of a `date` structure declared in **dos.h**.

setfillstyle   Set fill pattern and colour

```
void setfillstyle( int pattern, int colour );
```
graphics.h

Sets the fill pattern and colour. Predefined pattern names (and values) are shown in Table D.3.

setgraphmode   Switch to graphics mode

```
void setgraphmode( int graphmode );
```
graphics.h

Returns to graphics mode after a call to `restorecrtmode()`. Use the

Name	Value	Description
EMPTY_FILL	0	fill with back colour
SOLID_FILL	1	solid fill
LINE_FILL	2	fill with —
LTSLASH_FILL	3	fill with light slashes
BKSLASH_FILL	4	fill with heavy slashes
SLASH_FILL	5	fill with heavy backslashes
LTBKSLASH_FILL	6	fill with light backslashes
HATCH_FILL	7	light hatch fill
XHATCH_FILL	8	heavy cross-hatch fill
INTERLEAVE_FILL	9	interleaving line fill
WIDE_DOT_FILL	10	widely spaced dot fill
CLOSE_DOT_FILL	11	closely spaced dot fill

Table D.3: Fill patterns

value of `graphmode` returned by `initgraph()`. Can also be used to reset the graphics mode (e.g. to change resolution) while in graphics.

setlinestyle ## Set line width and style

```
void setlinestyle( int linestyle, unsigned upattern, int thickness );
```
graphics.h

Sets the style and thickness of lines drawn. Standard predefined names (and values) for `linestyle` are shown in Table D.4. `thickness` may be `NORM_WIDTH` (1 pixel) or `THICK_WIDTH` (3 pixels). The value of `upattern` is ignored for these standard styles.

setmem ## Fill memory

```
void setmem( void *target, unsigned length, char value );
```
mem.h

Fills a block of `length` bytes of memory addressed by `target` with the character `value`.

settextjustify ## Graphics text justification

```
void settextjustify( int horiz, int vert );
```
graphics.h

Justifies horizontal and vertical text output on the graphics screen around the current position (CP). `horiz` can take the value `LEFT_TEXT` (left-justify), `CENTER_TEXT` or `RIGHT_TEXT`. `vert` can take the value `BOTTOM_TEXT` (justify from the bottom), `CENTER_TEXT` or `TOP_TEXT`. Defaults are `LEFT_TEXT` and `TOP_TEXT`.

If `horiz` is `LEFT_TEXT` and the argument `direction` of `settextstyle()` is `HORIZ_DIR` the CP is advanced after a call to `outtext()` beyond the display string's last pixel.

Name	Value	Description
SOLID_LINE	0	solid line
DOTTED_LINE	1	dotted line
CENTER_LINE	2	centred line
DASHED_LINE	3	dashed line

Table D.4: Line styles

Parameter	TC Constant	Value	Description
Font	DEFAULT_FONT	0	8×8 bit-mapped font
Font	TRIPLEX_FONT	1	stroked triplex font
Font	SMALL_FONT	2	stroked smallfont
Font	SANS_SERIF_FONT	3	stroked sans-serif font
Font	GOTHIC_FONT	4	stroked gothic font
direction	HORIZ_DIR	0	left to right
direction	VERT_DIR	1	bottom to top
charsize	1..10	1–10	magnification

Table D.5: `settextstyle()` parameters

settextstyle   Set graphics text style

```
void settextstyle( int font, int direction, int charsize );    graphics.h
```

Sets text style for text output on the graphics screen from `outtext()` and `outtextxy()`. Standard values of the parameters and their meanings are shown in Table D.5. The default font is built-in. Stroked fonts are stored in **.chr** files, and kept in memory one at a time.

settime   Set system time

```
void settime( struct time *pTime );                              dos.h
```

Sets the system time according the values (set by you) of the members `ti_hour`, `ti_min`, `ti_sec` and `ti_hund` of a predefined **dos.h** structure time.

setusercharsize   Change graphics text size

```
void setusercharsize( int multx, int divx,
                      int multy, int divy );                  graphics.h
```

Adjusts the size of graphics text, *only* if `settextstyle()` has been previously called with a **charsize** of 0. The default character width is multiplied by **multx/divx**. The default height is multiplied by **multy/divy**. E.g.

```
settextstyle( TRIPLEX_FONT, HORIZ_DIR, 0 );
moveto( 10, 100 );
outtext( "hello" );
setusercharsize( 2, 1, 5, 1 );  // 2 times width, 5 times height
outtext( "hello again" );
```

setviewport   Change graphics viewport

```
void setviewport( int x1, int y1, int x2, int y2, int clip );        graphics.h
```

Sets a graphics viewport with top left corner at absolute position (x1, y1) and bottom right corner at absolute position (x2, y2). If clip is non-zero, drawing is clipped, i.e. any output outside the viewport is not shown.

setwritemode   How new pixels combine with old

```
void setwritemode( int mode );                                       graphics.h
```

Specifies how new pixels are combined with pixels already on display. Affects output of drawpoly(), line(), linerel(), lineto() and rectangle(). mode can take the value COPY_PUT (overwrite old pixels) or XOR_PUT (use exclusive OR logical to combine new with old).

sin   Sine

```
double sin( double x );                                                 math.h
complex sin( complex x );                                            complex.h
```

Returns the sine of x, where x is in radians.

sinh   Hyperbolic sine

```
double sinh( double x );                                                math.h
complex sinh( complex x );                                           complex.h
```

Returns the hyperbolic sine of x.

sleep   Suspend execution

```
void sleep( unsigned seconds );                                          dos.h
```

Suspends program execution for the specified number of seconds. Accuracy is about one hundredth of a second.

sound   Turn on tone

```
void sound( unsigned hertz );                                            dos.h
```

Begins sounding a tone at the given frequency. Call nosound() to stop it.

sprintf   Format output to string

```
int sprintf( char *buffer, const char *format[, arguments ... ] );
                                                                       stdio.h
```

Similar to printf(), except that output is written to the string buffer. Returns the number of bytes written to buffer, not including a null terminator. Useful for displaying numeric data on graphics screen, e.g.

```
char buffer[80];
int year;
...
sprintf( buffer, "%5d", year );
outtext( buffer );
```

sqrt   Square root

```
double sqrt( double x );                                      math.h
complex sqrt( complex x );                                  complex.h
```

Returns the square root of x.

srand   Seed random number generator

```
void srand( unsigned seed );                                  stdlib.h
```

Seeds the random number generator with seed. The sequence of random numbers produced by rand() and random() is then always the same. Useful for debugging programs that use random numbers. Use randomize() to seed randomly, or set seed to a rapidly changing value, such as the time of day.

strcat   Concatenate strings

```
char *strcat( char *target, const char *str );                string.h
```

Concatenates (joins) a string str to the end of an initialized string target, which is modified. Returns target. str and target are the addresses of the first characters in the strings. E.g.

```
char target[80] = "Tweedle";
puts( strcat( target, "Dum" ) );
```

modifies target to "TweedleDum" as well as displaying this string. Many of the string functions work like this, modifying a string argument, at the same time returning a pointer to the modified string.

strchr   Scan string for character

```
char *strchr( const char *str, int c );                       string.h
```

Searches string str from the front for the first occurrence of character c. Returns a pointer to the character if found, and NULL if not found. E.g.

```
char *p;
char filename[80] = "tweedle.dum";
```

```
p = strchr( filename, '.' );
printf( "Dot is at position %d\n", p - filename );
```

The difference in the addresses of the first character and the dot gives the position of the dot in the string (7). (The position of the first character is 0).

strcmp   Compare strings

```
int strcmp( const char *str1, const char *str2 );                  string.h
```

Compares two strings. Returns a negative value if $str1 < str2$ (i.e. if str1 is ahead of str2 alphabetically), zero if $str1 = str2$, or a positive value if $str1 > str2$. E.g.

```
i = strcmp( "TweedleDum", "TweedleDee" );
```

returns a positive value since the first string follows the second alphabetically.

strcmpi   Compare strings ignoring case

```
int strcmpi( const char *str1, const char *str2 );                 string.h
```

Similar to strcmp() except that differences between upper- and lower-case are ignored.

strcpy   Copy string to string

```
char *strcpy( char *target, const char *source );                  string.h
```

Copies source string and its null terminator to target string, over-writing any string in the target. Returns target. Example:

```
char name[80];
strcpy( name, "Soap, Joe" );  // name is now "Soap, Joe"
```

strcspn   Subset not in string

```
size_t strcspn( const char *str1, const char *sub );               string.h
```

Returns the number of characters in string str1 that are *not* also in string sub (the n in strcspn stands for "not"). Useful for finding the position in a string of a punctuation mark, e.g.

```
i = strcspn( string, "," );
```

returns the number of characters in string before the first comma, i.e. the comma is in element string[i].

strdup   Duplicate string

```
char *strdup( const char *str );                                        string.h
```

Allocates enough memory to store the string `str` and copies it to the
newly allocated memory. Returns a pointer to the duplicated string, or
null if not enough memory is available. The memory should be deallocated by passing the pointer to `free()`. Example:

```
char *dup;
dup = strdup( "TweedleDum" );
...
free( dup );
```

stricmp   Compare strings ignoring case

```
int stricmp( const char *str1, const char *str2 );                      string.h
```

Same as `strcmpi()`, which for compatiblity with other C compilers is
implemented as a macro that translates directly to `stricmp()`.

strlen   String length

```
size_t strlen( const char *str );                                       string.h
```

Returns the length of a string, i.e. the number of characters *preceeding*
the null terminator.

strlwr   String to lowercase

```
char *strlwr( char *str );                                              string.h
```

Converts uppercase letters in `str` to lowercase. Returns the converted
string.

strncat   Partial string concatenate

```
char *strncat( char *target, const char *source, size_t maxlen );   string.h
```

Concatenates at most `maxlen` characters of `source` to the end of `target`,
appending a null terminator. The `n` in this function name and in some of
the following `str`... family means the operation applies to a substring.
Returns `target`.

strncmp   Compare partial strings

```
int strncmp( char *str1, const char *str2, size_t maxlen );         string.h
```

Same as `strcmp()`, but compares at most `maxlen` characters in the two
strings.

strncmpi — Compare partial strings ignoring case

`int strncmpi( char *str1, const char *str2, size_t maxlen );`   string.h

Same as `strncmp()`, but ignores difference between upper- and lowercase letters.

strncpy — Copy partial strings

`char *strncpy( char *target, const char *source, size_t maxlen );` string.h

Copies at most `maxlen` characters from `source` to `target`, truncating or null-padding `target`. `target` might not be null-terminated if the length of `source` is `maxlen` or more. Beware of making `maxlen` greater than the number of characters that `target` can safely hold. Returns `target`.

strnicmp — Compare partial strings ignoring case

`int strnicmp( char *str1, const char *str2, size_t maxlen );`   string.h

Same as `strncmpi()`.

strnset — Set characters in string

`char *strnset( char *str, int c, size_t n );`   string.h

Sets up to a maximum of `n` characters of `str` to the characters `c`. Stops when either `n` characters have been set or the null terminator has been found. Returns `str`.

strpbrk — Scan string for characters

`char *strpbrk( const char *str, const char *sub );`   string.h

Scans string `str` for the first occurrence of any character in the subset `sub`. Returns a pointer to the first matching character in `str`, or `NULL` if no match found.

strrchr — Scan string in reverse

`char *strrchr( const char *str, int c );`   string.h

Same as `strchr()`, but searches for the last occurrence of the character `c` in the string. Returns a pointer to the character if found, or `NULL` if not found.

strrev — Reverse string

`char *strrev( char *str );`   string.h

Reverses the order of characters in `str` (except for the null-terminator). Returns `str`.

strset   Set characters in a string

```
char *strset( char *str, int c );
```

Sets all the characters in str to c, excluding the null terminator. Returns str.

strspn   Scan string for subset

```
size_t strspn( const char *str, const char *sub );          string.h
```

Returns the number of characters of string str which are also in the subset sub. Useful for verifying string data entry.

strstr   Scan string for substring

```
char *strstr( const char *str, const char *sub );          string.h
```

Returns address in str of the first occurrence of the substring sub (i.e. the address in str where sub begins), or NULL otherwise.

strtod   String to double

```
double strtod( const char *sval, char **endptr );          stdlib.h
```

Converts a floating point value in string form to a double or long double type. If the operation fails ±HUGE_VAL or ±LHUGE_VAL is returned.

sval is the string containing the value to be converted, either in fixed point form ("1.23") or scientific notation ("1.23e-5").

If not NULL, *endptr is set to the address of the character *after* the last character in sval that was used in the conversion. Useful for multiple parsing.

strupr   String to uppercase

```
char *strupr( char *str );                                 string.h
```

Converts lowercase letters in str to uppercase. Returns str.

strxfrm   Transform string to string

```
size_t strxfrm( char *str1, char *str2, size_t n );        string.h
```

Up to n characters (including the null-terminator) from str2 are effectively copied to str1. Returns the number of characters copied.

system   System command

```
int system( const char *command );                    stdlib.h
```

Gives a system command as though typed at a DOS prompt. Can be used to run DOS programs, issue DOS commmands, etc. E.g.

```
system( "dir *.cpp" );
```

tan   Tangent

```
double tan( double x );                               math.h
complex tan( complex x );                             complex.h
```

Returns the tangent of x, assumed to be in radians.

tanh   Hyperbolic tangent

```
double tanh( double x );                              math.h
complex tanh( complex x );                            complex.h
```

Returns the hyperbolic tangent of x.

textbackground   Set text background colour

```
void textbackground( int bkcolour );                  conio.h
```

Sets the background colour on the text screen for **conio.h** text output functions. The colour value may be in the range 0 to 7, corresponding to the colours in the first column of Table D.2.

textcolor   Set text foreground colour

```
void textcolor( int colour );                         conio.h
```

Sets the foreground colour (character colour) on the text screen for **conio.h** text output functions. The colour value may be in the range 0 to 15, corresponding to the colours in Table D.2. Logically OR a colour value with the constant BLINK to enable blinking characters.

textheight   String height in pixels

```
int textheight( char *textstring );                   graphics.h
```

Returns the height in pixels of a string to be displayed in graphics using the current font as selected by settextstyle().

textmode   Set text mode

```
void textmode( int mode );
```
                                               conio.h

Sets the text display mode. Not to be used with graphics (see rather `restorecrtmode()`). All modes are not available on all types of hardware.

`mode` can have the value `BW40`, `C40`, `BW80`, `C80`, `MONO`, `C4350` or `LASTMODE` (previously selected mode). `C` stands for colour, `BW` for black and white, and the numbers refer to the number of columns.

textwidth   String width in pixels

```
int textwidth( char *textstring );
```
                                               graphics.h

Returns the width in pixels of a string to be displayed in graphics using the current font as selected by `settextstyle()`.

time   Get system time

```
time_t time( time_t *theTime );
```
                                               time.h

Returns current date and time expressed as seconds elapsed since GMT midnight on 1 January 1970. The optional parameter (ignored if `NULL`) is a pointer to a variable in which the value returned by the function is stored.

toascii   Convert int to ASCII

```
int toascii( int c );
```
                                               ctype.h

Returns "pure" seven-bit ASCII value by forcing `int c` into the range 0–127.

tolower   Convert character to lowercase

```
int tolower( int c );
```
                                               ctype.h

Returns the lowercase of the ASCII character with value c. Affects only uppercase alphabetic characters. All other characters are returned unchanged, i.e. c is returned.

toupper   Convert character to uppercase

```
int toupper( int c );
```
                                               ctype.h

Returns the uppercase of the ASCII character with value c. Affects only lowercase alphabetic characters. All other characters are returned unchanged, i.e. c is returned.

ungetc   **Return character to input stream**

```
int ungetc( int c, FILE *fp );
```
                                                          stdio.h

Pushes one character pack to an input file stream, to be returned by the next input operation on that stream. Returns c for success, EOF for errors.

ungetch   **Return character to keyboard buffer**

```
int ungetch( int c );
```
                                                          conio.h

Similar to ungetc(), but pushes a character pack to the keyboard buffer for reading with **conio.h** input functions.

wherexy, wherey   **Get cursor position**

```
int wherex( void );
int wherey( void );
```
                                                          conio.h

Return the horizontal (wherex()) and vertical (wherey()) cursor position for text display modes.

window   **Text window**

```
void window( int left, int top, int right, int bottom );
```
                                                          conio.h

Limits **conio.h** text output to the portion of the text screen bounded by (left, top) (i.e. column, row) and (right, bottom).

Appendix E

ASCII character codes

The ASCII (American Standard Code for Information Interchange) collating sequence is as follows:

Dec	Hex	Char	Dec	Hex	Char	Dec	Hex	Char	Dec	Hex	Char
0	00	(null)	32	20	(blank)	64	40	@	96	60	`
1	01	☺	33	21	!	65	41	A	97	61	a
2	02	☻	34	22	"	66	42	B	98	62	b
3	03	♡	35	23	#	67	43	C	99	63	c
4	04	◇	36	24	$	68	44	D	100	64	d
5	05	♣	37	25	%	69	45	E	101	65	e
6	06	♠	38	26	&	70	46	F	102	66	f
7	07	•	39	27	'	71	47	G	103	67	g
8	08	◘	40	28	(	72	48	H	104	68	h
9	09	○	41	29	)	73	49	I	105	69	i
10	0A	◙	42	2A	*	74	4A	J	106	6A	j
11	0B	♂	43	2B	+	75	4B	K	107	6B	k
12	0C	♀	44	2C	,	76	4C	L	108	6C	l
13	0D	♪	45	2D	–	77	4D	M	109	6D	m
14	0E	♫	46	2E	.	78	4E	N	110	6E	n
15	0F	☼	47	2F	/	79	4F	O	111	6F	o
16	10	▶	48	30	0	80	50	P	112	70	p
17	11	◀	49	31	1	81	51	Q	113	71	q
18	12	↕	50	32	2	82	52	R	114	72	r
19	13	‼	51	33	3	83	53	S	115	73	s
20	14	¶	52	34	4	84	54	T	116	74	t
21	15	§	53	35	5	85	55	U	117	75	u
22	16	▬	54	36	6	86	56	V	118	76	v
23	17	↨	55	37	7	87	57	W	119	77	w
24	18	↑	56	38	8	88	58	X	120	78	x
25	19	↓	57	39	9	89	59	Y	121	79	y
26	1A	→	58	3A	:	90	5A	Z	122	7A	z
27	1B	←	59	3B	;	91	5B	[	123	7B	{
28	1C	∟	60	3C	<	92	5C	\	124	7C		
29	1D	↔	61	3D	=	93	5D	]	125	7D	}
30	1E	▲	62	3E	>	94	5E	^	126	7E	~
31	1F	▼	63	3F	?	95	5F	_	127	7F	Δ

Appendix F

Solutions to selected exercises

Chapter 1

```
1.1    #include <iostream.h>
       main()
       {
         float a, b;
         cin >> a >> b;
         cout << "Sum:        " << a + b << "\n";
         cout << "Difference: " << a - b << endl;
         cout << "Product:    " << a * b << endl;
         cout << "Quotient:   " << a / b << endl;
         return 0;
       }


1.2    #include <iostream.h>
       main()
       {
         float c, e, v
         cin >> c >> e >> v;
         e = c * v * v / 2;
         cout << "Stored energy: ", e << endl;
         return 0;
       }
```

Chapter 2

2.2 (a) comma should be replaced by decimal point
     (e) asterisk should be omitted
     (f) exponent must be integer
     (h) comma should be replaced by decimal point

2.3 (b) decimal point not allowed
    (c) first character must be a letter
    (d) quotes not allowed
    (h) blanks not allowed
    (i) decimal points not allowed
    (k) asterisk not allowed
    (l) reserved keyword

2.4 (a)   `cout << double(5 + 3) / (5 * 3) << endl;`
    (b)   `cout << pow( (2.3 * 4.5) , 1.0 / 3 ) << endl;`
    (c)   `cout << sqrt( 2 ) << endl;`
    (d)   `cout << pow( 2 * M_PI, 2 ) << endl;`
    (e)   `cout << 2 * pow( M_PI, 2 ) << endl;`
    (f)   `cout << 1000 * pow( 1 + 0.15/12, 60 ) << endl;`

2.5 (a)   `p + w / u;`
    (b)   `p + w / (u + v);`
    (c)   `(p + w / (u + v)) / (p + w / (u - v));`
    (d)   `pow( x, 0.5 );`
    (e)   `pow( y, y + z );`
    (f)   `y_ = pow( y, z );`
          `pow( x, y_ );`
    (g)   `x_ = pow(x, y );`
          `pow( x_, z );`
    (h)   `x - pow( x, 3 ) / 3 / 2 + pow( x, 5 ) / 5 / 4 / 3 / 2;`

2.6 (a)   `i++;`
    (b)   `i = pow( i, 3 ) + j;`
    (c)   `if (e > f)`
              `g = e;`
          `else`
              `g = f;`
    (d)   `if (d > 0)`
              `x = -b;`
    (e)   `x = (a + b) / (c * d);`

2.7   `double a, b, c, x;`
        `cin >> a >> b >> c;`
        `x = (-b + sqrt( b*b - 4*a*c )) / (2 * a);`
        `cout << "x = " << x << endl;`

2.8   `double g, p, l;`
        `cout << "Enter gallons and pints: ";`
        `cin >> g >> p;`
        `p = 8 * g + p;`   `// all pints`
        `l = p / 1.76;`   `// convert to liters`
        `cout << l << endl;`

2.9   `double km, l, km_l, l_100km;`
        `cin >> km >> l;`
        `km_l = km / l;`

```
      l_100km = 1 / (km / 100);
      printf( "%-15s%-15s%-15s%-15s\n\n", "Distance", "Litres used",
                                          "Km/L", "L/100Km" );
      printf( "%-15.2f%-15.2f%-15.2f%-15.2f\n", km, l, km_l, l_100km );
                                          // minus to left-justify
```

2.10
```
      t = a;
      a = b;
      b = t;
```

2.11
```
      a = a - b;
      b = b + a;
      a = b - a;
```

2.12b
```
      double f;
      int c;
      for (c = 20; c <= 30; c++) {      // C++!
        f = 9 * double( c ) / 5 + 32;
        printf( "%2d  %4.1f\n", c, f );
      }
```

2.15
```
      unsigned i, sum = 0;
      for (i = 1; i <= 100; i++)
        sum += 2 * i;
```

2.17
```
      #include <fstream.h>
      main()
      {
        int i, pass = 0;                  // initialize pass
        double avg, mark, sum = 0;        // initialize sum
        fstream fileIn( "marks", ios::in );
        for (i = 1; i <= 10; i++) {
          fileIn >> mark;
          sum += mark;
          if (mark >= 5)
            pass++;
        }
        avg = sum / 10;
        return 0;
      }
```

2.18
```
      unsigned i, less = 0, more = 0;
      randomize();
      for (i = 1; i <= 100; i++)
        if (rand() <= RAND_MAX/2)
          less++;
        else
          more++;
```

2.19 $a = 4$, $x = 1 + 1/2 + 1/3 + 1/4$.

2.20   ```
float x = 0;
int i;
for (i = 1; i <= 4; i++)
    x += 1.0 / i;   // why not 1 / i ?
```

2.21 The limit is $\pi$.

2.22    ```
#include <math.h>
...
double c, e, i, l, om, r, t;
c = 10; e = 2; l = 4; om = 2; r = 5;
t = 2 * M_PI * om * l - 1 / (2 * M_PI * om * c);
i = e / sqrt( r * r + t * t );
```

2.24   ```
double bal, dep, rate;
int mon;
bal = 0; dep = 50; rate = 0.01;
printf("%5s   %-17s\n\n", "MONTH", "MONTH-END BALANCE");
for (mon = 1; mon <= 12; mon++) {
    bal += dep;
    bal += rate * bal;
    printf("%3d%15.2f\n", mon, bal);
}
```

2.27    ```
double a, b, k, p;
int t;
k = 197273000;
a = 0.03134;
b = 1913.25;
for (t = 1790; t <= 2000; t += 10) {
    p = k / (1 + exp( -a * (t - b) ));
    printf( "%5d%15.0f\n", t, p );
}
```

2.28   ```
double p, r, t, l = 50000;
int n = 20;
r = 0.15;
t = pow(1 + r/12, 12*n);
p = r * l * t / (12 * (t - 1));
```

2.29    ```
double n, p, r, t, l = 50000;
r = 0.15;
p = 800;
t = log( p / (p - r * l / 12) );
n = t / 12 / log( 1 + r / 12 );
```

Chapter 3

3.1 You should get a picture of tangents to a curve.

3.2 (a) 4 (b) 2

(c) The algorithm (attributed to Euclid) finds the HCF (Highest Common Factor) of two numbers by using the fact that the HCF divides exactly into the difference between the two numbers, and that if the numbers are equal, they are equal to their HCF.

3.3
```
double c, f;
cin >> f;
c = (f - 32) * 5.0 / 9;
cout << c;
```

3.5
```
double a, b;
cin >> a >> b;
if (a > b)
  cout << a << " is greater" << endl;
else
  cout << b << " is greater" << endl;
```

3.6
```
double x, xMax = -HUGE_VAL;     // defined in math.h
unsigned i, maxPos;
fstream inFile( "data", ios::in );
if (inFile) {                   // check if file is there
  for (i = 1; i <= 10; i++) {
    inFile >> x;
    if (x > xMax) {
      xMax = x;
      maxPos = i;
    }
  }
}
```

3.7
```
double sum = 0;
int n;
for (n = 1; n <= 100; n++) {
  sum += 1 / double( n );      // avoid integer division
  if (n % 10 == 0)
    printf( "%9.5f\n", sum );
}
```

3.8
```
unsigned long hours, secs = 10000;
int mins;
hours = secs / 3600;
secs = secs % 3600;    // number of seconds left over
mins = secs / 60;
secs = secs % 60;
printf( "%lu:%02d:%02lu\n", hours, mins, secs );   // note lu format
```

Chapter 4

4.1
```
unsigned feet, yards;
```

```
double inches, metres = 3.51;
inches = 39.37 * metres;
yards = inches / 36;         // rounds down
inches = inches - 36 * yards;  // inches left
feet = inches / 12;
inches = inches - 12 * feet;   // inches left
```

4.2 (a) `c = sqrt(a * a + b * b);  // or use the library function hypot(a, b)`
    (b) `ang = ang * M_PI / 180;`
       `c = sqrt(a * a + b * b - 2 * a * b * cos( ang ));`

4.3 (a) `z = log(x + x * x + a * a);`
    (b) `z = (exp(3 * t) + t * t * sin(4 * t)) * pow( cos(3 * t), 2 );`
    (c) `z = 4 * atan( 1 );`
    (d) `z = pow( cos(x), -2 ) + 1 / atan( y );`
    (e) `z = atan( fabs(a / x) );`

Chapter 5

5.1
```
double a, b;
cin >> a >> b;
if (a > b)
   cout << a << " is larger";
else if (a < b)
   cout << b << " is larger";
else
   cout << "numbers are equal";
cout << endl;
```

5.2   1. Repeat 10 times:
                Read number
                If number < 0 then
                        increase negative counter
                otherwise if number $= 0$ then
                        increase zero counter
                otherwise
                        increase positive counter
       2. Print counters

5.5   1. Read a, b, c, d, e, f
       2. $u = ae - db, v = ec - bf$
       3. If $u = 0$ and $v = 0$ then
             Lines coincide
          Otherwise if $u = 0$ and $v \neq 0$ then
             Lines are parallel
          Otherwise
             $x = v/u, y = (af - dc)/u$
             Print x, y
       4. Stop.

```
    double a, b, c, d, e, f, u, v, x, y;
    cin >> a >> b >> c >> d >> e >> f;
    u = a * e - d * b;
    v = e * c - b * f;
    if (u == 0 && v == 0)
      cout << "Lines coincide";
    else if (u == 0 && v != 0)
      cout << "Lines parallel";
    else {
      x = v / u;
      y = (a * f - d * c) / u;
      cout << "x and y: " << x << "  " << y;
    }
    cout << endl;
```

5.6
```
    int i, j;
    i = j = 2 << 13;
    i--;
    i = i + j;    // i has the value 32767
```

Chapter 6

6.2
```
    double x;
    int ang;
    for (ang = 0; ang <= 90; ang += 15) {
      x = ang * M_PI / 180;
      printf( "%3d %7.4f %7.4f\n", ang, sin( x ), cos( x ) );
    }
```

6.3
```
    double bal, rate = 0.01;
    int mon, year;
    bal = 1000;
    for (year = 1; year <= 10; year++) {
      for (mon = 1; mon <= 12; mon++)
        bal *= (1 + rate);
    }
```

6.4 (a)
```
    double myPi = 1;
    unsigned k, n = 1000;
    float sign = 1;                 // +1 or -1
    for (k = 1; k <= n; k++) {
      sign = -sign;                 // change sign
      myPi += sign / (2 * k + 1);   // avoid integer division
    }
    myPi *= 4;
```

6.4 (b)
```
    double myPi = 0;
    unsigned k, n = 1000;
    for (k = 1; k <= n; k++)
      myPi += 1.0 / (4 * k - 3) / (4 * k - 1); // avoid integer division!
    myPi *= 8;
```

6.7
```
long double myE, x = 0.1;
int i;
for (i = 1; i <= 25; i++) {
  myE = pow( 1-x, -1/x );
  printf( "%20.15Lf\n", myE );
  x /= 10;
}
```

6.8
```
double fr, t, dt = 0.1;
int k, n = 10;
for (t = 0; t <= 1 + dt/2; t += dt) {   // make sure we hit t = 1
  fr = 0;
  for (k = 0; k <= n; k++)
    fr = fr + sin((2 * k + 1) * M_PI * t) / (2 * k + 1);
  fr *= 4 / M_PI;
  printf( "%4.1f %8.4f\n", t, fr );
}
```

6.10
```
unsigned ans, i, n, sum = 0;
i = 0;
while (sum < 100) {
  ans = sum;            // since sum will go over 100
  n = i;                // number of terms used
  i++;
  sum += i;
}
printf( "%u after %u terms\n", ans, n );
```

6.12
```
unsigned m, n;
m = 12; n = 30;        // or use Debug/Evaluate and Modify
while (m != n) {
  while (m > n)
    m -= n;
  while (n > m)
    n -= m;
}
```

6.14 The final payment is \$157.75 in the 54th month (don't forget the interest in the last
month).

Chapter 8

8.3
```
//#include <iostream.h>
double F( double x );
main()
{
  double h, nq, x = 1;
  int i;
  h = 1;
```

```
      for (i = 1; i <= 10; i++) {
        nq = (F(x + h) - F(x)) / h;
        printf( "%12.8f\n", nq );
        h /= 10;
      }
      return 0;
    }
    double F( double x )
    {
      return x * x * x;
    }
```

8.4
```
    void Half( double &a );        // prototype
    main()
      ...
      Half( x );                   // invocation
      ...
    void Half( double &a )         // implementation
    {
      a = a / 2;
    }
```

8.5
```
    void Half( double *p );        // prototype
    main()
      ...
      Half( &x );                  // invocation
      ...
    void Half( double *p )         // immplementation
    {
      (*p) = (*p) / 2;
    }
```

8.6
```
    void Swop( double *a, double *b );
    main()
      ...
      Swop( &x, &y );
      ...
    void Swop( double *a, double *b )
    {
      double temp;
      temp = (*a);
      (*a) = (*b);
      (*b) = temp;
    }
```

8.7
```
    double MyExp( double x )
    {
      double expo, term;
      int k = 1;
      expo = term = 1;
```

```
            while (fabs( term ) >= 1e-6) {
               term = term * x / k;
               expo = expo + term;
               k++;
            }
            return expo;
         }
```

8.10
```
double Norm( double x )
{
   double r, t;
   double a = 0.4361836;
   double b = -0.1201676;
   double c = 0.937298;
   r = exp( - x * x / 2 ) * M_SQRT_2 * M_1_SQRTPI;
   t = 1 / (1 + 0.3326 * x);
   return 0.5 - r * (a * t + b * t * t + c * t * t * t);
}
```

8.12
```
unsigned long F( int n )
{
   if (n == 0 || n == 1)
      return 1;
   else
      return F(n-1) + F(n-2);
}
```

Chapter 9

9.1
```
int num[100];
```
(a)
```
for (i = 0; i <= 99; i++)
      num[i] = i+1;
```
(b)
```
for (i = 0; i <= 49; i++)
      num[i] = 2 * (i+1);
```
(c)
```
for (i = 0; i <= 99; i++)
      num[i] = 100-i;
```

9.2
```
unsigned long f[47];
int n;
f[0] = f[1] = 1;
for (n = 2; n <= 46; n++) {
   f[n] = f[n-1] + f[n-2];
   printf( "%3d %10lu\n", n, f[n] );
}
```

9.4
```
int i, max, x, r;
int f[80];                          // frequencies
char string[80];
randomize();
clrscr();
_setcursortype( _NOCURSOR );
```

```
for (x = 0; x < 80; x++) {
  string[x] = ' ';              // initialize to blanks
  f[x] = 0;                     // initialize to zero
}

x = 40;                         // start at 40
max = 0;

do {
  r = random( 2 );              // r will be 0 or 1
  if (r)                        // 0 is false, 1 is true
    x++;
  else
    x--;
  if (x < 0 || x > 79)          // on the edge
    x = 40;
  f[x]++;                       // another time at x
  if (f[x] > max)
    max = f[x];
  for (i = 1; i <= x; i++)
    printf( " " );              // x blanks
  printf( "%c\n", 2 );          // followed by a smily
  delay( 100 );
}
while ( !kbhit() );

for (x = 29; x <= 51; x++) {    // display the frequencies
  printf( "%2d:", x );
  for (i = 1; i <= f[x] * 60.0 / max; i++ )  // largest will be 60 cols
    printf( "\x2");
  printf( "\n" );
}

getch();
_setcursortype( _NORMALCURSOR );
```

9.5
```
double d, furthest, mean, sum = 0;
double array[10] = {-4, 0, 5, -1, 10, 3, 4, 1, 2, 4};
int n;

for (n = 0; n < 10; n++)
  sum = sum + array[n];
mean = sum / 10;

d = fabs(array[0] - mean);      // it may be the first one
furthest = array[0];
for (n = 1; n < 10; n++) {
  if (fabs(array[n] - mean) > d) {
    furthest = array[n];        // should be 10
    d = fabs(array[n] - mean);
  }
}
```

9.6   1. Initialize: $N = 3, P_1 = 2, j = 1$ (prime counter)
2. While $N < 1000$ repeat:
$$i = 1$$
$R = \text{MOD}(\ N, P_i\ )$ (remainder)
While $R \neq 0$ and $P_i < \sqrt{N}$ repeat:
Increase i by 1
$R = \text{MOD}(\ N, P_i\ )$
If $R \neq 0$ then
Increase j by 1 (that's another prime)
$P_j = N$
Increase N by 2
3. Print all the P_j's
4. Stop.

Chapter 10

10.1
```
fstream inFile( "text", ios::in );
char ch;
int blanks = 0;

while (inFile.get( ch )) {        // get(ch) returns input stream
  if (ch == ' ')
    blanks++;
  else
    cout << ch;
}
```

10.2
```
char str[128];
int i, posDot;
gets( str );
posDot = strcspn( str, "." );
for (i = posDot-1; i >= 0; i--)
  printf( "%c", str[i] );
```

10.3
```
char *dayOfTheWeek[ ] = { "Sunday", "Monday", "Tuesday", "Wednesday",
                          "Thursday", "Friday", "Saturday" };
int cent, day, mon, year, f;
cout << "Enter day, month, year: ";
cin >> day >> mon >> year;
mon = mon - 2;
if (mon <= 0)
  mon = mon + 12;
if (mon >= 11)
  year--;
cent = year / 100;          // integer division
year = year % 100;          // remainder
f = int( 2.6 * mon - 0.2) + day + year + year / 4 + cent / 4 - 2 * cent;
f = f % 7;
cout << dayOfTheWeek[f] << endl;      // pointer to day
```

```
10.4   char str[128];
       gets( str );
       int n;
       unsigned long num, pow = 1;
       num = 0;

       for (n = strlen( str ); n >= 0; n--) {
         if (str[n-1] == '1')
           num = num + pow;
         pow = pow << 1;
       }


10.5   fstream inFile( "text", ios::in );
       char ch;

       while (inFile.get( ch ))
         cout << char( toupper( ch ) );   // toupper returns int, so convert
                                          // ... to char
       cout << endl;
```

Chapter 11

```
11.1   double Tis( void )
       {
         time t;
         double secs;
         gettime( &t );
         secs = double(3600) * t.ti_hour + 60 * t.ti_min + t.ti_sec
                + t.ti_hund / 100.0;  // double(3600) avoid int wrap around
         return secs;
       }


11.3   double react, start, end, wait;
       randomize();
       puts( "Press any key when you are ready ... " );
       getch();
       wait = 1 + random( 5 );   // wait up to 5 seconds
       sleep( wait );
       printf( "\a" );
       start = Tis();

       do {                      // do nothing
       } while (!kbhit());

       end = Tis();
       react = end - start;
       printf( "Reaction time: %5.2f\n", react );
```

Chapter 13

13.3   ```
       #include "myworld.h"
       ...
       double pop(float t);
       main()
       {
         int i, t, tmax;
         double p, pmax;
         fstream inFile("usa", ios::in);
         int graphdriver, graphmode;

         graphdriver = DETECT;
         initgraph(&graphdriver, &graphmode, "c:\\borlandc\\bgi");

         tmax = 2100;
         pmax = 200 * 1e6;
         setwindow(1780, tmax, 0, pmax);
         wline(1780, 0, tmax, 0);
         wline(1780, 0, 1780, pmax);

         t = 1790;
         wmoveto(t, pop(t));

         while (t <= tmax)
         for (t = 1790; t <= tmax; t += 10)
           wlineto(t, pop(t));

         for (t = 1790; t <= 1950; t += 10) {
           inFile >> p;
           wrectangle(t-1, 1000 * p + 1e6, t+1, 1000 * p - 1e6);
         }

         getch();
         closegraph();
         return 0;
       }
       double pop(float t)
       {
         const float K = 197273000, a = -0.03134;
         return K / (1 + exp(a * (t - 1913.25)));
       }
       ```

13.4   ```
       #include "myworld.h"
       ...
       main()
       {
         int graphdriver, graphmode;
         double a, r, t, x, y;
       ```

```
graphdriver = DETECT;
initgraph( &graphdriver, &graphmode, "c:\\borlandc\\bgi" );
setwindow( -10, 10, -10, 10 );
a = 0.1;
t = 0;
wmoveto( 0, 0 );

while (t <= 150) {
  r = a * t;
  x = r * cos( t );
  y = r * sin( t );
  wlineto( x, y );
  t += 0.1;
}

getch();
closegraph();
return 0;
}
```

Chapter 17

17.4   TMatrix TMatrix::Trans(void)

```
{
  TMatrix temp (col, row);    // transpose
  int i, j;
  for (i = 1; i <= col; i++)
    for (j = 1; j <= row; j++)
      temp(i,j) = (*this)(j,i);
  return temp;
}
```

Chapter 18

18.1 (a) Real roots at 1.856 and −1.697, complex roots at −0.0791 ± 1.780i.
      (b) 0.589, 3.096, 6.285, ...(roots get closer to multiples of π).
      (c) 1, 2, 5.
      (d) 1.303
      (e) Real roots at 1.768 and 2.241.

18.2 Successive bisections are: 1.5, 1.25, 1.375, 1.4375 and 1.40625. The exact answer is 1.414214..., so the last bisection is within the required error.

18.3 22 (exact answer is 21.3333).

18.4 After 30 years the exact answer is 2 117 ($1000e^{rt}$).

18.5 The differential equations to be solved are

$$dS/dt = -r_1 S,$$
$$dY/dt = r_1 S - r_2 Y.$$

The exact solution after 8 hours is $S = 6.450 \times 10^{25}$ and $Y = 2.312 \times 10^{26}$.

18.6
```
int i = 1;                              // counter for output
double a, b, h, r, t, x;
double outInt = 1;                      // output at monthly intervals
cin >> r >> b >> a >> x >> h;

for (t = 0; t <= 24 + h/10; t += h) {    // beware of rounding
  if ((i-1) % int( outInt/h + h/10 ) == 0)
    printf( "%8.2f %12.2f\n", t, x );
  i++;
  x = x + h * (r - b * x * sin(a * t)) * x;
}
```

18.7 With 10 intervals ($n = 5$), the luminous efficiency is 14.512725%. With 20 intervals it is 14.512667%. These results justify the use of 10 intervals in any further computations involving this problem. This is a standard way of testing the accuracy of a numerical method: halve the step-length and see how much the solution changes.

Index

abs() 61
access mode 216
acos() 61
adjacency matrix 329
air resistance 359
algorithm 53
alias 136, 141
ancestor 277
animation 239
argument 124
    default 150
    library function passed as 358
    pass by reference 136
    pass by value 124
array 157, 158
    base type 158
    constant 162
    deleting dynamic 168
    dynamic 166
    initialization 161
    multi-dimensional 162
    name is a pointer 164
    no subscript bounds checking 158
    of class objects 276
    of pointers 187
    of strings 183
    of strings, initialization 184
    parameter 165
    size 158
    sizeof() 162
arrow operator 202
ASCII code 185
asin() 61
aspect ratio 406
assignment 22
    multiple 23
    string 180
assignment operator 24
atan() 61
atan2() 61
atof() 61
atoi() 61
augmented matrix 339
autodetection of graphics card 232
    overriding 233

automatic variable 131

bacteria growth 362
bar chart 163
bar() 235
bar3d() 235
base class 277
base type of array 158
bending moment 67
.bgi file 104
binary digit 12
binary file 218
binary search 225
binary to decimal conversion 194
binomial coefficient 84
Bisection method 352
bit-field structure 201
bitmap image 240
bitwise operator 74
bit 12
block marker 9, 32
Boolean expression 38
break statement 98
Bubble Sort 169
bug 111
byte 13

camel caps 15
carriage-return 128
case sensitivity 15
ceil() 62
Cervantes 194
chaos 103
character constant 40
char 40
class 260
    base 277
    private 271
class type 283
cleardevice() 238
clearviewport() 238
clock() 62
clrscr() 62, 238
comma operator 24
command line arguments 189

comment 11
compilation error 111
complex class
    declaration 300
    implementation 301
complex division 299
complex multiplication 299
complex roots by Newton's method 302
complex transfer function 304
`complex()` 62
compound statement 32
conditional compilation 134
conditional expression 78
`conj()` 62
constant array 162
constant value 16
constant 16
constructor 270
    default 270
    copy 273, 295
    global object 270
    order of calling 270
    type conversion 275
`continue` statement 98
conversion character 416
conversion
    binary to decimal 194
    decimal to binary 75
copy constructor 273, 295
correlation coefficient 177
`cos()` 62
`cosh()` 62
counting words 189
`cprintf()` 102, 128
`cputs()` 128
Crank-Nicolson method 374
`ctime()` 62, 214
current file pointer 219
current position 236

data type 12
    alias 17
database, student records 220
debugger 114
debugging 111
`dec` manipulator 27
decile 163
decimal constant 14
decimal to binary conversion 75
decrement operator 20
default constructor 270
default parameter 150
    member function 267
`delay()` 63

`delete` operator 168
    dynamic array of objects 277
    dynamic array 168
dereferencing 140
derived type 197
descendant 277
destructor 271
    virtual 285
`detectgraph()` 232, 234
deterministic repetition 83
differential equation 359
    systems 365
direct-video 127
directed network 328
division operator 20
`do-while` statement 91
dot notation 198
doubling time of an investment 91
driver modelling package 366
dynamic array 166
dynamic object 271
dynamic string 187

early binding 284
eigenvalue 333
eigenvector 333
`else` statement 38, 67
encapsulation 260
end-of-file 99, 161
`endl` manipulator 27
EOF, **Ctrl-Z** from keyboard 213, 313, 420
error
    compilation 111
    interception 114
    logical 114
    rounding 114
    run-time 113
    syntax 111
escape code 41, 416
`exit()` 78
`exp()` 63
exponential growth 362
expression 19, 24
    logical 72
external variable 132
extraction operator 312

`fabs()` 63
factorial 84
far pointer 144
`fgetc()` 212
file pointer 211
file 209
    access mode 213, 216
    binary 218

check for existence 216
current pointer 219
open 211
finite difference scheme 373
floating point constant 14
floodfill() 235
floor() 63
flush() 213
flushall() 213
font 237
fopen() 211
for 31
   general form 83
   nested 89
   non-integer increments in 86
format code 28, 34
format, iostream 26
Fourier series 108
fprintf() 216
fputc() 213
fread() 220
free() 215
frequency distribution 163
friend class 298
friend function 298
fscanf() 218
fseek() 220, 224
fstream 314
ftell() 219
function
   argument 124
   array as parameter 165
   definition 123
   member of class 261
   modifier 133
   overloading 149
   parameter 124
   passing structure by reference 201
   pointer to 354
   prototype 122
   recursive 148
function call operator (), overloading 322
fundamental data type 12, 197

Gauss elimination 375
Gauss reduction 338
   matrix inversion 341
get(), iostream member function 191
getch() 63
getche() 63
getimage() 240
getmaxcolor() 238
getmaxx() 233
getmaxy() 104, 233
gets() 63

gettext() 129
gettime() 203
getx() 236
gety() 236
global variable 127, 131
   initialized to zero 131
gnu 99
goto statement 78
gotoxy() 63
grapherrormsg() 233
graphics
   autodetection 232
   autodetection override 233
   driver 233
   initialization check 232
   text on screen 237
guessing game 90

Hamlet 195
header file 124
heap 167
help in Turbo C++ 112
hex manipulator 27
hexadecimal 13
   constant 14
highvideo() 103
hot key 8

identifier 14
identity matrix 320
if 38
   general form 67
   if-else-if ladder 70
   nesting 71
#ifndef 147
ill-conditioning 117
illegal reference 138
imag() 63
imagesize() 240
#include, preventing multiple 147
incomplete struct declaration 207
increment operator 20
indirection operator 140
INF 114
inheritance 277
   single 277
   multiple 282
initgraph() 104, 232
initializing
   array 161
   array of objects 276
   string 162
inline function 134
inline member function 265
insertion operator 310

instance 262
instance variable 261
integer constant 14
interactive modelling 366
interception of errors 114
interpolation 177
inverse of a matrix 341
iostream 25, 309
    format 26
ios 309
itoa() 63

kbhit() 63
Knuth 95

label 78
late binding 284
least squares 176
Legendre polynomial 156
Leslie matrix 332
lexical collating sequence 185
librarian 146
library function, passed as argument 358
library 146
line() 233
linear equations, solution of 338
linear interpolation 177
linear search 225
linerel() 236
lineto() 236
linkage error 113
linked list 203
list, sorting 169, 171
literal constant 13
loan repayment 88
local variable 125, 130
    unpredictable value 131
log() 63
log10() 63
logical error 114
logical expression 72
logical operator 38
logistic model 109
loop, non-deterministic 89
lvalue 22

macro 17, 133
main function 10
    parameters 189
malloc() 215
Mandelbrot set 103
manipulator 26, 311
    user-defined 312
Markov chain 334
matching pair, search for 112

mathematical constants
    defined in **math.h** 393
matrix inversion 341
    by Gauss reduction 341
matrix 162, 319
    inversion 341
    multiplication 325
mean 159
member, of structure 198
member function 261
    default parameters 267
    inline 265
    overloading 266
    this hidden argument 263
    virtual 284
memberwise assignment 274
memberwise copy 274
memcpy() 298, 322
memory location 9
memset() 321
modelling a population of gnus 99
modifier 16, 416
module 146
modulus operator 20
moverel() 236
movetext() 129
moveto() 236
multi-dimensional array 162
multiple assignment 23
multiple files, programs of 144
multiple includes, preventing 147
multiple inheritance 282

nameless parameter 123
NAN 114
near pointer 144
nested **fors** 89
nested **ifs** 71
new operator 167
Newton quotient 154
Newton's method 33, 120
    complex roots 302
node 203
non-deterministic loop 33, 89
norm() 63
normvideo() 103
nosound() 63
NULL macro 43
null pointer 142
null terminator 42
numerical integration 356
numerical method 351
    bisection method 352
    differential equation 359
    integration 356

partial differential equation 373
predictor-corrector 364
Runge-Kutta method 365
Simpson's Rule 358
solution of equations 351
systems of differential equations 365
Trapezoidal Rule 356
numerical solution
    differential equation 359
    equation 351

object 262
    array of 276
    dynamic 271
    function return type 274
    initializing array of 276
    memberwise assignment 274
    memberwise copy 274
    parameter 272
    reference 272
object-oriented programming 259
oct manipulator 27
octal 13
    constant 14
operator 20
    arrow 202
    arithmetic 20
    assignment 22, 24
    bitwise 74
    comma 24
    decrement 20
    delete 168
    division 20
    function 291
    indirection 140
    increment 20
    logical 38
    modulus 20
    new 167
    overloading 289
    redefinition 291
    relational 38, 72
    sizeof() 162
    structure-member 198
    value-at 140
operator function 291
operator overloading 289
operator redefinition 291
output interval control 87
output to text file 191
outtext() 237
outtextxy() 237
overloading
    addition + operator 294
    assignment = operator 295

assignment += operator 292
function call () operator 322
member functions 266
stream operator 316
subscript [ ] operator 294

palette 238
palindrome 193
parameter 124
    array 165
    nameless 123
    object 272
    pass by reference 141
    pass by value 124
partial differential equation 373
passing by reference with pointer 141
passing a constant reference 202
π 106
pieslice() 236
pixel 104, 232
pointer 139
    array name is a pointer 164
    array of 187
    far 144
    near 144
    pass by reference 141
    string 180
    to function 354
    to object 271
    to pointer 188
    uninitialized, danger of 143
    void 144
polymorphism 283
pop-up window 128
pow() 63
pow10() 63
pre-processor directive 9
precedence
    arithmetic operators 20
    general table 385
    increment and decrement operators 21
precision specifier 34
predator-prey model 365
predictor-corrector method 364
prime number generation 176
prime number test 94
printf() 27
    format code 28
    precision specifier 34
    width specifier 28
private access specifier 277
private class 271
programming style 18
projectile motion 59
project 144

protected access specifier 280
prototype 122
pseudo-code 53
public access specifier 277
put(), iostream member function 191
putch() 128
putchar() 212
putpixel() 104, 239
puts() 64
puttext() 129

quadratic equation 55
    structure plan 55
Quick Sort 171

rand() 64, 338
RAND_MAX 338
random access memory 9
random access file 225
random number generator, seed 426
random walk 334
    simulation 336
random() 64
randomize() 32, 64
random() 32
reachability matrix 329
reading unknown amount of data 98, 161
real() 64
rectangle() 233
recursion 148
reference
    illegal 138, 297
    object 272
    parameter 136
    return by function 137, 296
    variable 136
register variable 132
relational operator 38, 72
remove() 214
rename() 214
return 123
rotation of coordinate axes 121
rounding error 87, 114
run-time error 113
Runge-Kutta method 365

saving graphics image to disk 240
scanf() 104
    reading double value 121
scientific notation 14
scope 130
scope resolution operator 131
search, binary 225
seeding random number generator 426
semantic error 113

sensitivity analysis 117
sentence length 189
series for π 106
setbkcolor() 238
setcolor() 238
_setcursortype() 128
setfill() manipulator 27, 151
setfillstyle() 235
setlinestyle() 236
setprecision() manipulator 27, 151
setrgbpalette() 239
setviewport() 237
setw() manipulator 27, 151, 312
Shakespeare 194
Simpson's Rule 358
simulation of switching circuit 74
simulation 336
    random walk 336
sin() 64
single inheritance 277
sinh() 64
sizeof() 76
    array 162
    array of pointers 189
    pointer 189
size_t 393
sort
    Bubble 169
    Quick 171
sound() 32, 64
spaghetti 79
sprintf() 218, 237
sqrt() 64
square root by Newton's method 33
stable age distribution 333
stack 131
standard deviation 159
standard input 210
standard output 210
standard stream 209
Starfield and Bleloch 99
statement 19
static data member 294
static member function 294
static variable 131
stderr 210
stdin 210
stdout 210
stdprn 210
storage class specifier 131
strcat() 192
strchr() 191
strcmp() 185
strcmpi() 185
strcpy() 181

strcpy() 64
strcspn() 192
strdup() 215
stream 209
stream object 309
stream operator, overloading 316
string 42, 179
    array of 183
    assignment 180
    dynamic 187
    initialization 162, 180
    literal 41
    literal, continuation of 180
    pointer 180
    variable 179
strlen() 187
strlwr() 192
strrev() 192
strset() 192
structure plan 53
    quadratic equation 55
structure 198
    array of 199
    array of, initialization 199
    bit-field 201
    incomplete declaration 207
    initialization 198
    member 198
    member operator 198
    pass by reference 201
structured programming 55
strupr() 192
stub 147
student record database 220
student.h 221
style 18
subscript
    no checking of range 158
    [ ] operator, overloading 305
switch statement 76
symbolic constant 16
syntax error 111
systems of differential equations 365

tag 200
tan() 64
tanh() 64
Taylor series
    exponential function 154
    sine 96
TComplex class
    declaration 300
    implementation 301

terminal velocity 360
text file, output to 191
text on graphics screen 237
this
    hidden argument 263
time of day 202
time() 64, 214
time_t 214
TMatrix class
    declaration and implementation 345
token 11
_tolower() 64
top down programming 55
transfer function 304
transpose of a matrix 350
Trapezoidal Rule 356
tridiagonal matrix 375
truncation error 378
type conversion constructor 275
typecast 25, 88
typed constant 16
typedef 17, 199

union 200
unknown amount of data, reading 98, 161
unsigned char 41

value-at operator 140
Van der Pol's equation 380
variable 9, 15
vertical motion, air resistance 359
viewport 237
virtual destructor 285
virtual member function 284
void function 122
void pointer 144
volatile variable 132

warning message 112
Watch window 136
while statement 93
whitespace 11, 313
width specifier 28
wildebees model 99
window 128
    pop-up 128
word count 189
ws manipulator 313

Zeller's congruence 193